Constructing Educational Achievement

International interest focuses on why pupils from East Asia tend to outperform pupils from the West and scholars have proposed a number of possible explanations to account for these international trends. Using Vygotsky's theory (1978) as a conceptual framework to 'construct' school achievement, this book puts forward culturally relevant contexts for understanding developmental aspects of children's school achievement and their implication for classroom practice and education progress. Converging the two important lines of inquiry – the child factor and the sociocultural factor – this book showcases evidence-based scholarly works from across the globe that shed light on causes of academic achievement in different contexts.

The book brings together eminent scholars from early childhood, primary, secondary and vocational education who expertly capture the vitality of development and processes of specific child factors and their interaction with their environment that explain their school achievement. Foregrounded in the five planes of cultural–historical, institutional, social, personal and mental, the research explains how children think, learn and form the will to perform amidst the changing social and family environment, and challenging school and educational environment.

Sivanes Phillipson is Senior Lecturer at the Faculty of Education, Monash University, Peninsula and formerly an Assistant Professor in the Department of Education Studies at the Hong Kong Baptist University. Sivanes is also an Adjunct Senior Lecturer with the Faculty of Education, University of Tasmania.

Kelly Y. L. Ku is Assistant Professor in the Department of Education Studies at the Hong Kong Baptist University. She attended Clark University (United States) for undergraduate studies and obtained her PhD from the University of Hong Kong.

Shane N. Phillipson is Associate Dean, Peninsula Campus and Associate Professor of the Faculty of Education (Monash University) and was previously at the Department of Special Education and Counselling at the Hong Kong Institute of Education. After working for many years as a mathematics and science teacher Shane obtained a PhD from Flinders University (Australia) with his thesis being awarded the International Award (1999–2000) for best PhD thesis by the National Association for Gifted Children (NAGC).

Constructing Educational Achievement

A sociocultural perspective

**Edited by
Sivanes Phillipson
Kelly Y. L. Ku
Shane N. Phillipson**

LONDON AND NEW YORK

First published 2013
by Routledge
2 Park Square, Milton Park, Abingdon, Oxon OX14 4RN

Simultaneously published in the USA and Canada
by Routledge
711 Third Avenue, New York, NY 10017

Routledge is an imprint of the Taylor & Francis Group, an informa business

© 2013 Sivanes Phillipson, Kelly Y. L. Ku and Shane N. Phillipson

The right of the editors to be identified as the authors of the editorial material, and of the authors for their individual chapters, has been asserted in accordance with sections 77 and 78 of the Copyright, Designs and Patents Act 1988.

All rights reserved. No part of this book may be reprinted or reproduced or utilised in any form or by any electronic, mechanical, or other means, now known or hereafter invented, including photocopying and recording, or in any information storage or retrieval system, without permission in writing from the publishers.

Trademark notice: Product or corporate names may be trademarks or registered trademarks, and are used only for identification and explanation without intent to infringe.

British Library Cataloguing in Publication Data
A catalogue record for this book is available from the British Library

Library of Congress Cataloging in Publication Data
Constructing educational achievement : a sociocultural perspective / edited by Sivanes Phillipson, Kelly Y. L. Ku and Shane N. Phillipson.
pages cm
Includes bibliographical references and index.
1. Academic achievement—Social aspects.
2. Vygotskii, L. S. (Lev Semenovich), 1896–1934.
I. Phillipson, Sivanes, editor of compilation.
II. Ku, Kelly Y. L., editor of compilation.
III. Phillipson, Shane N, editor of compilation.
LB1062.6.C66 2013
306.43—dc23
2012038344

ISBN: 978-0-415-51711-9 (hbk)
ISBN: 978-0-415-51712-6 (pbk)
ISBN: 978-0-203-55902-4 (ebk)

Typeset in Galliard
by Swales & Willis Ltd, Exeter, Devon

Printed and bound by CPI Group (UK) Ltd, Croydon, CR0 4YY

Contents

List of figures	viii
List of tables	ix
List of contributors	x
Preface	xiii

PART 1
Introduction   1

1 Constructing educational achievement within a sociocultural
   framework of planes   3
   SIVANES PHILLIPSON AND PETER D. RENSHAW

PART 2
Cultural–historical plane   11

2 Framing achievement when learning is unified: The concept of
   unity in Vygotsky's theory and methodology   13
   JENNIFER A. VADEBONCOEUR

3 Family capital, child's personal agency, and the academic
   achievement of Chinese migrant children   26
   QIAOBING WU

4 A psychometric view of sociocultural factors in test validity: The
   development of standardized test materials for Māori-medium
   schools in New Zealand/Aotearoa   42
   PETER J. KEEGAN, GAVIN T. L. BROWN AND JOHN A. C. HATTIE

vi *Contents*

PART 3
Institutional plane   55

5 Classroom chronotopes privileged by contemporary educational policy:
   Teaching and learning in testing times   57
   PETER D. RENSHAW

6 Teacher self-efficacy: Internalized understandings of competence   70
   JANET DRAPER

PART 4
Social plane   85

7 Parental expectations: The influence of the significant other on school
   achievement   87
   SIVANES PHILLIPSON

8 Examining the relations between a play motive and a learning motive
   for enhancing school achievement: Doing "school" at home   105
   MARILYN FLEER

9 Peer co-regulation of learning, emotion, and coping in small-group
   learning   118
   MARY McCASLIN AND RUBY INEZ VEGA

10 Teacher–student relationships and students' learning outcomes   136
   ATARA SIVAN AND DENNIS W. K. CHAN

11 Social learning, language, and instruction for adult learners where
   English is their second language   148
   IAN HAY, ROSEMARY CALLINGHAM AND FREDERICK WRIGHT

12 Two instead of one ZPD: Individual and joint construction in the
   ZPD   161
   ALEKSANDAR BAUCAL

PART 5
Personal plane   175

13 When Lev Vygotsky meets Francis Galton: On the nature and nurture
   of reading development   177
   SIMPSON W. L. WONG

Contents vii

14 Education for citizenship: An experiment in leadership development
of pupils making the transition from primary to secondary school   188
JIM O'BRIEN, EVGENIYA PLOTNIKOVA AND IAIN MILLS

15 How encouragement in everyday family practices facilitates
Hong Kong–Australian children's motive for learning   201
PUI LING WONG

PART 6
Mental plane   215

16 Cognitive style and achievement through a sociocultural lens: A new
way of thinking about style differences   217
ELIZABETH R. PETERSON AND KANE MEISSEL

17 The role of verbal reasoning in critical thinking   231
KELLY Y. L. KU

18 Cognitive perturbation with dynamic modelling: A reconceptualization
of conceptual change in science education   243
SANDY C. LI AND JACKY W. C. POW

PART 7
Conclusion   255

19 The role of culture in constructing educational achievement   257
SIVANES PHILLIPSON AND SHANE N. PHILLIPSON

Index   269

Figures

3.1	Hypothesized model of the effect of family social capital on the academic achievement of migrant children with children's personal agency as moderator	30
5.1	PISA mean scores for 15-year-old students in mathematics, reading, and science for Australian states and territories compared to QECD average and the highest country	67
5.2	Change in PISA mean scores for 15-year-old students from 2000 to 2009 for Australian states and territories	67
6.1	Model of four contrasting types of induction experience	77
6.2	Factors affecting the development of self-efficacy of beginning teachers and student achievement	78
10.1	The Model for Interpersonal Teacher Behavior	138
12.1	Research design	166
12.2	The number of items solved in EG and CG in different phases of the study	168
16.1	Example of stimuli used in the Norenzayan et al. (2002) study	223
18.1	Graph showing the total scores associated with different sub-groups' models at the different stages of model-building	248
18.2	Conceptual change is a non-linear process and students may regress to a lower level of understanding as their learning progresses	250
18.3	The zone of proximal development can be conceived metaphorically as an undulating terrain in which the local minimum points and the global minimum point represent, respectively, prevailing misconceptions and scientific conception	250

Tables

3.1	Descriptive statistics of sample characteristics	31
3.2	Zero-order correlations of major study variables	34
3.3	Standardized factor loadings of observed indicators on latent constructs	35
3.4	Standardized direct, indirect, and total effects of major predictor variables on children's academic achievements	36
7.1	List of cross-sectional studies completed at primary school levels	93
7.2	List of cross-sectional studies completed at secondary school levels	95
7.3	Overall effect of parental expectations on language, mathematics, and GPA outcomes at primary and secondary levels	98
7.4	Overall effect of types of parental expectations on achievement at primary and secondary school levels	99
9.1	The big picture: Variable descriptives	124
9.2	Intra-correlations within the expressed coping variable domain	128
9.3	Social/instructional context and expressed coping	130
9.4	Variable domain and achievement correlations	131
11.1	Blank's four levels of language complexity	149
14.1	Children who agree with the following statements	194
14.2	Distribution of pupils' choices for the group of pupils identified as leaders by teachers' evaluations	194
14.3	"I am able to lead group activities well"	195
14.4	"My ideas are usually supported by classmates"	196
14.5	Final results for training group and control group (based on comparison of the P7 and S1 rank order positions of the 32 pupils in the training and control groups)	196
14.6	Average rank order places, P7 and S1 (training and control group) where 1 is the highest placing	196
15.1	Particulars of the participant families	204
15.2	The social situation of learning and education for the participant children	207
15.3	Different forms of encouragement used by the participant families	211
17.1	Summary of essential skills to critical thinking proposed by various scholars	235
18.1	Number of explanatory statements at three different levels of explanation across the different stages of model-building for the four groups	247
18.2	The mean scores and standard deviations of the five classes	249

Contributors

Aleksandar Baucal
Department of Psychology
University of Belgrade
Čika Ljubina 18–20
11000 Belgrade
Serbia
Email: abaucal@f.bg.ac.rs

Gavin T. L. Brown
Faculty of Education
University of Auckland
74 Epsom Ave
Epsom, Auckland 1142
New Zealand
Email: gt.brown@auckland.ac.nz

Rosemary Callingham
Faculty of Education
The University of Tasmania
Locked Bag 1307
Launceston, Tasmania 7250
Australia
Email: Rosemary.Callingham@utas.edu.au

Dennis W. K. Chan
Department of Education Studies
Hong Kong Baptist University
Kowloon Tong
Hong Kong
Email: dennis@hkbu.edu.hk

Janet Draper
Department of Education Studies
Hong Kong Baptist University
Kowloon Tong
Hong Kong
Email: janetd888@gmail.com

Marilyn Fleer
Faculty of Education
Monash University, Peninsula Campus
Frankston, Victoria, 3199
Australia
Email: marilyn.fleer@monash.edu

John A. C. Hattie
Melbourne Graduate School of Education
The University of Melbourne
234 Queensberry Street
Melbourne 3010
Australia
Email: jhattie@unimelb.edu.au

Ian Hay
Faculty of Education
University of Tasmania
Locked Bag 1308
Launceston, Tasmania 7250
Australia
Email: I.Hay@utas.edu.au

Peter J. Keegan
Te Puna Wānanga
Faculty of Education
University of Auckland
74 Epsom Ave
Epsom, Auckland 1142
New Zealand
Email: p.keegan@auckland.ac.nz

Kelly Y. L. Ku
Department of Education Studies
Hong Kong Baptist University
Kowloon Tong

Hong Kong
Email: kellyku@hkbu.edu.hk

Sandy C. Li
Department of Education Studies
Hong Kong Baptist University
Kowloon Tong
Hong Kong
Email: sandyli@hkbu.edu.hk

Mary McCaslin
Department of Educational Psychology
Co-Director, Center for Research on
Classrooms
University of Arizona
Tucson, AZ 85721-0069
Email: mccaslin@u.arizona.edu

Kane Meissel
School of Curriculum and Pedagogy
Faculty of Education
University of Auckland
Private Bag 92019
Auckland, New Zealand
Email: k.meissel@auckland.ac.nz

Iain Mills
Moray House School of Education
The University of Edinburgh
Edinburgh, EH8 8AQ
United Kingdom
Email: Iain.Mills@inverclydeschools.org.uk

Jim O'Brien
Moray House School of Education
The University of Edinburgh
Edinburgh, EH8 8AQ
United Kingdom
Email: jim.obrien@ed.ac.uk

Elizabeth R. Peterson
School of Psychology
University of Auckland
Private Bag 92019
Auckland, New Zealand
Email: e.peterson@auckland.ac.nz

Shane N. Phillipson
Faculty of Education
Monash University, Peninsula Campus
McMahon Road
Frankston Victoria
Australia 3199
Email: shane.phillipson@monash.edu

Sivanes Phillipson
Faculty of Education
Monash University, Peninsula Campus
McMahon Road
Frankston Victoria
Australia 3199
Email: sivanes.phillipson@monash.edu

Evgeniya Plotnikova
Chrystal Macmillan Building
George Square
The University of Edinburgh
Edinburgh, EH8 8AQ
United Kingdom
Email: e.plotnikova@sms.ed.ac.uk

Jacky W. C. Pow
Department of Education Studies
Hong Kong Baptist University
Kowloon Tong
Hong Kong
Email: jackypow@hkbu.edu.hk

Peter D. Renshaw
School of Education
The University of Queensland
Brisbane 4072
Australia
Email: p.renshaw@uq.edu.au

Atara Sivan
Department of Education Studies
Hong Kong Baptist University
Kowloon Tong
Hong Kong
Email: atarasiv@hkbu.edu.hk

xii *Contributors*

Jennifer A. Vadeboncoeur
The University of British
 Columbia
Faculty of Education
2125 Main Mall
Vancouver, BC V6T-1Z4
Email: j.vadeboncoeur@ubc.ca

Ruby Inez Vega
Department of Educational
Psychology
University of Arizona
Tucson, AZ 85721-0069
Email: rvega@u.arizona.edu

Pui Ling Wong
24 Donbirn Way
Vermont South, Victoria 3133
Australia
Email: puiling.wong@hotmail.com

Simpson W. L. Wong
Department of Psychological Studies
The Hong Kong Institute of Education
10 Lo Ping Road
Tai Po
N.T., Hong Kong
Email: swlwong@ied.edu.hk

Frederick Wright
University of Tasmania/TAFE
Student Services, Waverley Campus
595 Glen Waverley Road
Glen Waverley
Victoria 3150
Australia
Email: fredwr@holmesglen.vic.edu.au

Qiaobing Wu
Department of Social Work
T. C. Cheng Building, United College
The Chinese University of Hong Kong
Shatin, N.T., Hong Kong
Email: qbwu@swk.cuhk.edu.hk

Preface

Educational achievement has always been a fascination throughout the world. Being educators, we find ourselves immersed in the idea of how our students perform and what they do to achieve. Most of all, having been educated and working as educators in different countries, all three of us are aware of the tensions of social and cultural equilibriums and nuances. We studied and achieved according to the social and cultural expectations in Asia, Australia, the United Kingdom and North America. With the experience that we gained from the different cultures, we teach and learn using our own social and cultural beliefs and principles. Whatever we do in the context of our teaching, we do it with our students in mind. Together, as teachers and students, we form the social and personal planes of teaching and learning that results in achievement.

This book began as a germ of an idea from the very thoughts of how our students achieve. As educators, we felt the need to dissect the components of educational achievement, and sociocultural perspectives were an obvious framework since students' performance seemed embedded in social and cultural activities. Hence this book – *Constructing Educational Achievement: A sociocultural perspective*!

The golden thread of this book is to unravel the crucial factors behind school achievement, arising from the child and its interaction with the environment. International interest focuses on the reasons why pupils from East Asia tend to outperform pupils from the West. Scholars have proposed a number of possible explanations to account for these international trends, such as differences in economics and systems of education. More than ever, however, scholars are realizing that the explanations are likely to be found in the complex interactions between the child and the environment and that the interactions vary with the cultural context.

Using Vygotsky's theory (1978) as a conceptual framework to "construct" school achievement, this book puts forward culturally relevant contexts for understanding developmental aspects of children's school achievement and their implication to classroom practice and education progress. Converging the two important lines of inquiry into the causes of school achievement, the child factor and the sociocultural factor, this book showcases evidence-based scholarly works from different continents and across the globe that shed light on causes of academic achievement in different contexts. The book brings together eminent scholars from early childhood, primary education, secondary and vocational education who expertly capture the vitality of development and processes of specific child factors and their interaction with their environment that explain their school achievement.

The 17 chapters (Chapters 2 to Chapter 18) in this book are foregrounded in five planes of cultural–historical, institutional, social, personal and mental to explain how children think, learn and form the will to perform amidst the changing social and family environment, and challenging school and educational environment. This discussion includes

xiv *Preface*

possible implications to classroom practice and educational movements. From the clarification of the thinking, learning and motivated child of the different interactive environment, the book reconstructs the empirical image of the achieving child in the face of educational reform, as discussed by Cole (2010). The conclusions that we draw from our analysis of the research in this book make a substantial contribution to our basic and applied knowledge, and to future research and practice in enhancing educational achievement in different socio-cultural contexts. Furthermore, we make a further leap by drawing a parallel between the sociocultural context of achievement and a systems approach in achievement to provide a continuum in the explanation of how students achieve and the possibility to empirically test Vygotsky's ideas of child development, making this book of interest to both undergraduate and postgraduate students, teachers, parents, education partners and policy makers.

This book transpired from a colloquium held on 7–8 December 2011 at The Hong Kong Baptist University (HKBU) and was supported by a generous grant from the Hong Kong Baptist University to the first and second editors. The colloquium was hosted by the Department of Education Studies and the Faculty of Social Sciences of Hong Kong Baptist University, in partnership with the International Society of Cultural Activity and Research (ISCAR), the International Research Association of Talent Development and Excellence (IRATDE), and Routledge Education. The colloquium was attended by delegates from East Asia, including Hong Kong, Singapore, the Philippines, Taiwan, and, more broadly, from New Zealand, Australia and Europe. The delegates included research students, parents, researchers and policy makers.

The success of the colloquium and, ultimately, this book is due to the work of several key persons. We would like to acknowledge the efforts of Mr. Jan Gube and his team of capable assistants, Miss Wing Chu and Miss Talia Wu, for organizing the colloquium and supporting the delegates. We also would like to thank Prof. Rick Wong, Vice President of Research and Development at Hong Kong Baptist University, and Prof. Adrian Bailey, Dean of the Faculty of Social Sciences, for their generous support in grant and kind. We also would like to thank the Faculty of Education Research Committee of Monash University for their support through a dissemination grant that saw this book through to its publication.

Finally, we acknowledge the contribution of the many international and eminent academics to the success of this book. They include Prof. Francesco Arcidiacono, Dr. Lynette Arnold, Ms Heather Butler, Prof. Arie Cohen, Prof. Ferdinand Gobet, Prof. Fernando González Rey, Assoc. Prof. Alex Kostogriz, Assoc. Prof. Anna Lau, Prof. John MacBeath, Prof. Bert van Oers, Prof. Steve Rayner, Prof. Jrène Rahm, Dr. Alysia Roehrig, Prof. Jeffrey Smith, Assoc. Prof. Raymond Wong and Dr. Gary Wooley, who voluntarily reviewed the chapters in this book and met very tight deadlines despite their busy schedules. To our families and friends, we are grateful for your patience and support during this past year of academic challenge and rigor.

Sivanes Phillipson, Kelly Y. L. Ku and Shane N. Phillipson
September 2012

References

Cole, M. (2010). What's culture got to do with it? Educational research as a necessarily interdisciplinary enterprise. *Educational Researcher*, 39(6), 461–470.

Vygotsky, L. S. (1978). *Mind in society: The development of higher mental process.* Cambridge, MA: Harvard University Press.

Part 1
Introduction

1 Constructing educational achievement within a sociocultural framework of planes

Sivanes Phillipson and Peter D. Renshaw

Introduction

The results from international achievement tests such as TIMSS, PISA and PIRLS continue to fascinate and preoccupy researchers, policy makers, and practitioners. As the results are published and examined, they generate significant debate on what types of schools, teaching practices, curriculum frameworks, sociocultural values, and conditions contribute to children's academic achievement. Of particular interest to researchers is how to explain the achievement of East Asian students, who continue to outperform their counterparts in North America, the UK, Australia, and other Western nations. Research has suggested that individual differences in academic achievement are determined by many interacting factors, including distinctive sociocultural experiences and values, personal characteristics of students, such as cognitive and motivational capabilities, and systemic differences in schooling structures, curriculum, and pedagogy.

Until the 1990s, when international testing programs became widespread and influential, Western educational researchers and practitioners were prone to criticize the approaches to teaching and learning adopted in Asian countries for their assumed deployment of rote and surface approaches (Biggs, 1994). Stevenson (Chen & Stevenson, 1995; Stevenson et al., 1990) and other researchers (Biggs, 1994; Hess & Azuma, 1991; Renshaw & Volet, 1995; Watkins & Biggs, 1996, 2001) critiqued these negative assumptions and began to document the distinctive and effective ways that Asian teachers and students engage in teaching and learning at school and university (Renshaw & Power, 2003). Such research has shown that students' academic achievement is related to a number of interacting factors, including the ways that schools are structured, how teaching is conducted, the support students receive from home and the surrounding society, and motivational and cognitive resources the students invest in their own learning and development.

Recent studies comparing the achievement of students from different national and ethnic groups within a country (e.g., Dandy & Nettelbeck, 2002; Phillipson, 2009) have highlighted the complexity of interacting factors required to account for different learning outcomes within each sociocultural situation. Accordingly, it is now understood that, amongst many factors, children need to deploy both *will* and *skill* to do well in school (Pintrich & Schunk, 2002). Studies have suggested that within the concepts of will and skill is the interplay of personal and social factors, such as the child's own capabilities, the supportive people who scaffold their learning and development, and their access to mediating tools and artifacts that contribute to academic achievement (Rogoff, 1984; Salili, Chiu, & Hong, 2001). Family and peers, in particular, are closer in proximity within this circle of social and cultural environment. Teachers and schools are also seen to be within this circle of children's school achievement (Stevenson & Stigler, 1992).

4 *Sivanes Phillipson and Peter D. Renshaw*

A sociocultural paradigm

To theorize these interacting factors at the personal and social planes, we draw upon Vygotsky's (1978) sociocultural theory. In a 1930 introduction to a monograph on development, Vygotsky and Luria (cited in Wertsch, 1985) suggested that:

> In child development, along with the processes of organic growth and maturation, a second line of development is clearly distinguished – the cultural growth of behavior. It is based on the mastery of devices and means of cultural behavior and thinking.
>
> (p. 23)

Vygotksy (1960, p. 118) proposed that "it is not nature, but society that above all else must be considered to be the determining factor in human behavior". Vygotsky (1978, p. 57) viewed children's cognitive development as existing on two planes: the social or *between the people* plane, and the personal or *inside the child* plane; and he proposed that these planes interact reciprocally across time. This classic distinction between the interpersonal plane and the intrapersonal plane has been extended and enriched by contemporary researchers, such as Rogoff (1995), who proposed three planes for analyzing the ways in which children learn, namely, the personal, the interpersonal, and the community plane. These are inseparable, mutually constituting planes but each plane can become the focus of separate analysis in particular studies if the whole system of interacting planes is not ignored. This approach moves beyond analytical schemes that separate the individual and the environment.

We build upon Rogoff's proposal by distinguishing five planes of analysis that might be foregrounded in different research studies in order to understand children's achievement and learning in educational contexts. These are the (i) cultural–historical plane, (ii) institutional plane, (iii) social plane, (iv) personal plane, and (v) mental plane.

Contributions in this book could be viewed from each of these planes and an overlap of the spaces in the planes. We provide an overview of each plane and how chapters in this book might place themselves under each plane. It is important to note though that the planes, whilst distinctive, remain intertwined and dynamic in nature; hence our placement of the chapters highlights the predominant analytical focus but does not imply that each plane can be considered isolated and independent of the others.

Cultural–historical plane

Presented first in this book is the cultural–historical plane. We begin with this plane because, as Vadeboncoeur shows in her chapter (Chapter 2) entitled "Framing achievement when learning is unified", we view educational achievement as deriving from a holistic process in the cultural–historical plane. In this plane, cultural–historical activity and change, where historic events such as mass migration within a nation or emigration across nations, create interactions between people of similar and different languages and cultures. Vadeboncoeur explores the Vygotskian notion of word meaning and emotional experience to demonstrate the importance of interactions between people and historical events as providing mediating tools in learning.

The historical events arise from changes in the economy, in technology, and in population densities that challenge people from different places to live, learn, and work together. In this book, Wu (Chapter 3) brings us back to historical events in China, and how societal changes impact upon the Chinese family's capacity to empower their child's personal agency

Constructing educational achievement 5

and their ability to achieve in their cultural setting. The cultural–historical plane also draws attention to the closeness and distance of differences and similarities between people over time. Taking this as the basis, Wu highlights the differences and similarities of Chinese families' social capital from the 1980s to the current day, to show the changes over time and how those changes impact on children's capacity to achieve.

Similarly, Keegan, Brown, and Hattie (Chapter 4) capture how historical events and culturally specific needs mandate culturally responsive and sensitive standardized assessment to cater for Māori children's educational achievement. They present a convincing argument regarding how a pluralist approach rather than an assimilationist practice of evaluating achievement could be effectively managed to fulfill the needs of different cultural groups with their own specific historical and cultural background within a multi-cultural setting. This approach, hence, has to take into account the different institutional demands in relation to the cultural needs.

Institutional plane

The second plane is the institutional plane. Educational tasks and processes are nested within institutions that have been designed, redesigned, adapted, and transformed over time. The institutional plane of analysis could include, for example, the analysis of schools and universities attended by students, as well as their homes and family arrangements, and the interaction and synchrony between these different institutional contexts. In such analysis, a researcher attempts to document the tools, interactive settings, speech genres, and other mediational means that are provided to students within these institutions and how such tools and mediational means function across settings.

Renshaw's chapter (Chapter 5) on classroom chronotopes foregrounds how this institutional plane interacts with the cultural–historical plane. His description of contrasting classroom chronotopes from different periods of the twentieth century shows what counts as effective learning and how achievement has changed across time. Renshaw proposes a relational learning time and space as opposed to the current testing orientation that narrows the objectives of education in current times.

Within this framework of relational learning, Draper (Chapter 6) focuses on the formation of teacher self-efficacy in the context of teaching and learning. She stresses the importance of teachers, as the core of any teaching institution, having a belief in their own competence because teachers' internalized competence impacts upon their ability to support learners. The role that teachers play in school affects learning in other institutions, such as the home. Where there is synchrony and compatibility across institutions, an apparent seamless space for learning can be created across contexts.

Social plane

Deriving from the cultural–historical and institutional plane is the social plane, which is an interactive space, created through communication (verbal, non-verbal; virtual or face to face) between two or more people. This is typically regarded as Vygotsky's interpersonal plane. In Chapter 7, Sivanes Phillipson provides an example of the communication of parental expectations as mediation for their children's educational achievement. Through a meta-analysis of past research on parental expectations and their impact on their children's achievement, Phillipson demonstrates how the parental expectations communicated to children within the family affect children's achievement at school. In her chapter on children's play and learning motives (Chapter 8), Fleer shows us how assisting a child in his homework can be integrated

6 *Sivanes Phillipson and Peter D. Renshaw*

within a family's everyday social events. Such a practice provides a platform for scaffolded tasks where dialogic speech is used to assist children to develop more independence in functions such as planning, convincing, deciding, judging, and choosing. In Fleer's study, the child was able to complete his homework tasks successfully and this provided further confidence in his learning capacity.

Four other chapters provide further examples of practices within the social plane, where structured dialogue is used to engage students in learning for specific outcomes. McCaslin and Vega (Chapter 9) draw upon their research on primary school students' co-regulation of learning in dynamic group work situations. They reveal how verbal dialogues and personal verbalization enable individual learning and coping within group dynamics. Sivan and Chan (Chapter 10) provide a contrasting cultural view by describing the Hong Kong classroom, where cooperative teacher–student interactions result in better learning outcomes for students, not only in their cognitive capacities but also in relation to heightened affective and moral values that facilitate holistic student development.

In a similar vein, Hay, Callingham, and Wright (Chapter 11) showcase their study on mature students of Asian backgrounds learning vocational subjects using English as a medium of instruction. Teachers engaged students in four levels of structured dialogues and interaction to facilitate their movement from lower order to higher order understanding of culturally challenging concepts. Teachers' own reflections and student–teacher interaction helped both teacher and students to improve upon their engagement in learning the subject matter whilst coping with language and cultural differences.

In Chapter 12, Baucal argues that the dynamic structure of learning within the zone of proximal development (ZPD) could be differentiated on a social and personal level. He characterizes the ZPD as joint collaboration necessarily followed by individual effort to construct knowledge. Baucal concludes that the individual construction of knowledge transcends that of the social paradigm. This conclusion shows that the nature of children's learning is socially constructed and yet individually culminated as a "uniquely cultural form of adaptation which involve[s] both an overlay on and a reorganization of more basic psychological functions" (Vygotsky, 1997, p. 107).

Personal plane

Embedded within the social plane is the personal plane, which involves a shift in focus to an individual engaged in a solo activity with the aid of cultural tools and mediational means. An observer can see the individual doing a cultural activity (reading, problem solving, planning, listening, or watching media) and the individual's activity can be described and compared to others or to changes in that individual's activity over time. In Chapter 13, Simpson Wong deploys twin studies to compare the reading capabilities of two children of similar genetic background. He concludes that, whilst genetic influences in children's ability to read are empirically proven, the environmental influences are also fundamental in shaping children's engagement in reading activities.

The personal plane is a point of departure for further analysis – for example, by observing a child solve a problem with and without the aid of a tool, or noting how a child's reflection on their own activity varies depending on whether they keep a journal. In some circumstances, self-evaluation of their engagement in problem solving or any other similar activities could be seen as personal space. O'Brien, Plotnikova, and Mills (Chapter 14) capture this notion of self-evaluation and reflection in their experimental study of student leadership development. Students who were exposed to a program of leadership training were able to engage in self-appraisal and gained confidence in many aspects of leadership and their own learning. This shows that activity at the personal plane creates the opportunity for further mental dialogue and possibly advancement in children's potential.

Similarly, Pui Ling Wong (Chapter 15) describes how, at the personal plane, encouragement of a child's learning in the home setting can motivate the child to achieve better. She shows how a child's personal plane of learning can be enhanced and result in higher achievement when it is driven by the child's motive to learn and achieve. Her case study illustrates that parental encouragement and rewards play an influential role in shaping the personal motive of a boy, Vincent, to practice and play his guitar on his own accord. Vincent's engagement in an individual activity ultimately is inspired by parental support and coaxing, which stimulates his mental engagement and his personal motive to learn.

Mental plane

Inseparable from the social and personal plane, but a distinct focus, is the mental plane. This internal plane is not static but an active dialogic space where thought itself retains its social origins. The mental plane is not like a reference library of knowledge, but a field of interacting functions (remembering, reasoning, imagining, associating, emoting) where change in the developmental trajectory of different functions is occurring unevenly and providing options for new ways of thinking. In this book, three chapters demonstrate how different cognitive exercises support developmental trajectory of learning and thinking. In Chapter 16, Peterson and Meissel provide an overview of research in cognitive style and educational achievement, and explore the existing research through the sociocultural approach of stimulating debate about the usefulness of such an approach. The authors conclude that aspects of cognitive style need to be taken into account to help students understand their mental space and assist in their own formulation of learning approaches in different contexts. Peterson and Meissel admit that such an approach cannot be done in isolation but rather by taking into account sociocultural elements that determine aspects of the tasks at hand.

Meanwhile, Ku (Chapter 17) argues that verbal reasoning ability is a skill that is important to promote critical thinking, and that encouragement from and facilitation by teachers in the contexts of classroom teaching ensures this development of critical thinking. Ku, however, stresses that cultural influences, such as Chinese culture, impact upon students' willingness to use their language skills to articulate their critical thinking.

When students are scaffolded by teachers using a computer-supported modeling environment, Li and Pow (Chapter 18) show that students are able to learn and produce scientifically sound conceptions that are relevant to their advancement in science education. They present two studies that demonstrate the usefulness of interactive social and cognitive environment between teacher facilitation and computer modeling to support students' learning of scientific concepts and rationale. Li and Pow argue that a dynamic modeling environment, consisting of teacher support, computer assistance, and peer interaction, allows for conceptual anchors at different points of student learning. These conceptual anchors in the teaching and learning process facilitate students' gradual understanding and their ability to articulate and reason their own thoughts in relation to discussions with their peers and teachers.

Constructing educational achievement and culture

In this introductory chapter, we presented five planes of analysis that allowed us to articulate different research studies in order to understand children's achievement and learning in

8 *Sivanes Phillipson and Peter D. Renshaw*

educational contexts. Indeed, we advocate that the planes construct a sociocultural framework in which we place our thesis on educational processes and achievement. The importance of approaching educational processes and achievement from a sociocultural framework is undeniable when each of these processes and children's learning outcomes are both a personal experience and socially situated and constructed, within cultural institutions and different times and spaces.

Cole (2010) suggested that culture has a fundamental role in shaping education and any educational reforms. He stressed that "assembly-line schooling" is not the ideal way to educate children. In response, the final chapter in this book tests Cole's thesis that culture and its components affect the success of educational reform against the existent literature and the contributions in this book. Sivanes Phillipson and Shane Phillipson provide a critical overview of Cole's argument that educational reform generally fails because of its inability to move beyond the architectural and instructional models that are rooted in antiquity. The chapter explores the conditions Cole considers are important for educational reform and draws on the contributions from this book for the evidence. Importantly, Phillipson and Phillipson argue that a child-centered instruction is not essential in cultures that expect and value academic achievement.

We conclude that, when the broader culture expects and values academic achievement, and promotes collaborative inquiry and learning, this greatly increases the likelihood of educational achievement – even when the educational processes seem to suggest the contrary. What seems to be important is the integration of the classroom culture with the general culture. The various contributions in this book describe the fundamental sociocultural processes of how children – through their interactions and relationships with families, peers, and teachers – think, learn, and achieve.

References

Biggs, J. (1994). What are effective schools? Lessons from east and west. *The Australian Educational Researcher, 21*, 19–39.

Chen, C.-S., & Stevenson, H. W. (1995). Motivation and mathematics achievement: A comparative study of Asian-American, Caucasian-American, and East Asian high school students. *Child Development, 66*, 1215–1234.

Cole, M. (2010). What's culture got to do with it? Educational research as a necessarily interdisciplinary enterprise. *Educational Researcher, 39*(6), 461–470.

Dandy, J., & Nettelbeck, T. (2002). Research note: A cross-cultural study of parents' academic standards and educational aspirations for their children. *Educational Psychology, 22*(5), 621–627.

Hess, R., & Azuma, H. (1991). Cultural support for schooling: Contrast between Japan and the United States. *Educational Researcher, 20*(2–8), 12.

Phillipson, S. (2009). Context of academic achievement: Lessons from Hong Kong. *Educational Psychology, 29*(4), 447–468.

Pintrich, P. R., & Schunk, D. (2002). *Motivation in education: Theory, research, and applications* (2nd ed.). Upper Saddle, NJ: Prentice-Hall.

Renshaw, P. D., & Power, C. (2003). Section editors: Learning and human development. In J. Keeves & R. Watanabe (Eds.), *The handbook of educational research in the Asia-Pacific region* (pp. 351–525). Dordrecht, the Netherlands: Kluwer Academic.

Renshaw, P. D., & Volet, S. (1995). South-east Asian students at Australian universities: A reappraisal of their tutorial participation and approaches to study. *The Australian Educational Researcher, 22*(2), 85–106.

Rogoff, B. (1984). Introduction: Thinking and learning in social context. In B. Rogoff & J. Lave (Eds.), *Everyday cognition: Its development in social context* (pp. 1–8). Cambridge: Harvard University Press.

Rogoff, B. (1995). Observing sociocultural activity on three planes: Participatory appropriation, guided participation and apprenticeship. In J. Wertsch, P. D. Rio, & A. Alvarez (Eds.), *Sociocultural studies of mind* (pp. 139–164). Cambridge: Cambridge University Press.

Salili, F., Chiu, C.-y., & Hong, Y.-y. (2001). The culture and context of learning. In F. Salili, C.-y. Chiu, & Y.-y. Hong (Eds.), *Student motivation: The culture and context of learning* (pp. 1–14). New York: Kluwer Academic/Plenum Publishers.

Stevenson, H. W., Lee, S.-y., Chen, C.-s., Stigler, J. W., Hsu, C.-c., & Kitamura, S. (1990). Contexts of achievement: A study of American, Chinese, and Japanese children. *Monographs of the Society for Research in Child Development, 55*(1–2), 1–107.

Stevenson, H. W., & Stigler, J. W. (1992). *The learning gap: Why our schools are failing and what we can learn from Japanese and Chinese education.* New York, NY: Summit Books.

Vygotsky, L. S. (1960). *Razvitie vysshikh psikhicheskikh funktsii [The development of higher mental functions].* Moscow: APN.

Vygotsky, L. S. (1978). *Mind in society: The development of higher mental process.* Cambridge, MA: Harvard University Press.

Vygotsky, L. S. (1997). *Problems of the theory and history of psychology* (Vol. 3). New York: Premium Press.

Watkins, D. A., & Biggs, J. B. (Eds.) (1996). *The Chinese learner: Cultural, psychological and contextual influences.* Hong Kong: Comparative Education Research Centre, The University of Hong Kong.

Watkins, D. A., & Biggs, J. B. (Eds.) (2001). *Teaching the Chinese learner: Psychological and pedagogical perspectives.* Hong Kong and Australia: Comparative Education Research Centre, The University of Hong Kong and ACER.

Wertsch, J. V. (1985). *Vygotsky and the social formation of mind.* Cambridge, MA: Harvard University Press.

Part 2
Cultural–historical plane

2 Framing achievement when learning is unified

The concept of unity in Vygotsky's theory and methodology

Jennifer A. Vadeboncoeur

Introduction

Framing educational achievement invariably raises questions regarding the definitions of learning and achievement, and how they are assessed. Additional questions also surface, including the kind of material to be learned and how it is learned, as well as the conditions under which it is learned and by whom. In the 1920s–1930s, Vygotsky proposed an approach to learning, development, pedagogy, and assessment that was different from the reductionism inherent in behaviorist approaches to learning and different, as well, from the "developmental readiness" required of Piagetian approaches to learning. At this historical moment, Vygotsky's theory and methodology remain significant to ongoing discussions regarding learning and the assessment of learning in light of the historical, political, and economic press of the latter to define the former (e.g., Cochran-Smith & Lytle, 2006; Darling-Hammond, 2007; Vygotsky, 1997a).

The aim of this chapter is to contribute to the framing of educational achievement from a Vygotskian perspective. In the first section, I introduce the concept of unity as central to Vygotsky's holistic theory of learning and development and describe two units of analysis: word meaning and emotional experience. In the second section, three educational implications are noted, when learning is conceptualized as unified, with consequences for educational achievement. The third section provides a brief summary.

The concept of unity and units of analysis

A central but lesser known concept in Vygotsky's theory is the concept of unity. Throughout his writings, the relationship among key concepts was grounded in a dialectic that united human beings, psychological functions, experiences, and the environment. As just a few examples, he noted the unity of consciousness and behavior (Vygotsky, 1925/1997), the unity of evolutionary, cultural, and developmental histories (Luria & Vygotsky, 1992), the unity of speech and thinking (Vygotsky, 1987), the unity of memory, imagination, and thinking (Vygotsky, 1998), the unity of student, teacher, and social environment (Vygotsky, 1997a), the unity of higher and lower psychological functions (Vygotsky & Luria, 1994), the unity of affective and intellectual processes (Vygotsky, 1987), the unity of the mental and the physical (Vygotsky, 1997a), and the unity of cognitive, social, and emotional experience (Vygotsky, 1994). Vygotsky's commitment to recognizing the dialectical relationship between these frequently atomized and decontextualized constituents provided a holistic lens for approaching problems in general psychology, development, and education, with methodological implications as well.

14   Jennifer A. Vadeboncoeur

Analysis by units

Regarding methodology, Vygotsky (1987, 1994) argued that science, typically conducted by reducing complex phenomena into constituent elements for analysis, should proceed instead through a unit of analysis: a unit that retains the properties that characterize the whole. To define this position, he noted that the study of psychological functions – for example, thinking and speech – can be conducted through two fundamentally different forms of analysis.

Using the first method of analysis requires the decomposition of a whole into its elements, and may or may not be followed by attempts to reintegrate the elements into the whole. Vygotsky (1987) compared this method to a chemical analysis of water in which water is reduced to its elements, hydrogen and oxygen, and cautioned:

> When one approaches the problem of thinking and speech by decomposing it into its elements, one adopts the strategy of the man who resorts to the decomposition of water into hydrogen and oxygen in his search for a scientific explanation of the characteristics of water, its capacity to extinguish fire or its conformity to Archimedes law for example. This man will discover, to his chagrin, that hydrogen burns and oxygen sustains combustion.
>
> (p. 45)

This form of analysis limited science to analyzing discrete elements, rather than processes. The outcome was a description, rather than a description and an explanation. In addition, while it enabled the investigation of a "fossilized behavior," a behavior that was automatized and required no further development, it did not allow for the study of behavioral change over time: the history of the development of behavior (see van der Veer, 2001). Most problematic, the reduction to elements changes the psychological phenomena studied; because the elements are of a "different nature," the relationships between the elements are lost, and reintegration is complicated and not guaranteed: "When the whole is analyzed into its elements, these characteristics evaporate. In his attempt to reconstruct these characteristics, the investigator is left with no alternative but to search for external, mechanical forms of interaction between the elements" (p. 45). The unity that is "characteristic of the whole" is lost and may become inaccessible.

As an alternative to the reduction of phenomena to the smallest elements, Vygotsky (1987) proposed a second form of analysis: This form "relies on the partitioning of the complex whole into *units*" (emphasis in original, p. 46). Unlike elements, units "possess *all the basic characteristics of the whole*" (emphasis in original, p. 46). This method retains the characteristics of the whole by using a "unit of analysis." Zinchenko (1985) offered several requirements for identifying units for the analysis of mind; four are noted here. A unit of analysis of the mind must: (i) be a unified whole; (ii) maintain the characteristics of the unified whole, including its heterogeneity, its internal contradictions; (iii) have the potential to develop, to transform; and (iv) be "a *living* part of the whole . . . a unified system that cannot be further decomposed" (emphasis in the original, p. 98). By conducting the second form of analysis, identifying and working with units of analysis, Vygotsky (1987) proposed that psychology may be able to address the complex problems of the discipline:

> As we suggested earlier, the problem of the relationships and connections among the various mental functions was inaccessible to traditional psychology. It is our contention that it is accessible to an investigator who is willing to apply the method of units.
>
> (p. 50)

Vygotsky's interest in units of analysis was similar to "a German, or rather European continental tradition of holistic thinking, a tradition that was antithetic to British associationism, American behaviorism, and so on" (van der Veer, 2001, p. 99).

An ongoing question for researchers, as noted by Luria (1987), is that Vygotsky did not leave behind a universally applicable formula for identifying units of analysis, nor did he identify a range of units suitable for use across the variety of psychological and educational phenomena that may be of interest to researchers.

> Indeed, this was hardly possible. He provided us with only a single very important index for identifying these units. He argued that these units must contain within themselves the *opposing* aspects of the dialectical unity. Of course, he did provide us with some important concrete examples of the search for these units. In particular, . . . Vygotsky arrived at fundamentally new results primarily because he sought a new unit of analysis where intellect and affect are fused in a unified whole.
>
> (emphasis in original, Luria, 1987, p. 373)

While a full discussion of dialectical logic is outside the scope of this chapter, it is worth mentioning that the move from formal to dialectical logic can be seen as a move that shifts thinking about entities in relation from either/or to both/and. Hegel's use of the verb *aufheben* has been translated as *sublation*: meaning *both* "to preserve" and "to cause to cease," *and* "to raise up" (Magee, 2010). These three meanings are often simultaneous, as when Hegel writes about the dialectic between subject and object. Although positioned as opposites, subject and object exist in relation; each requires the other and through the other becomes something more. In another example, Vygotsky (1997a) described one role of pedagogy as finding "those limits within which recall and forgetting could *work together and in harmony, like a pair of opposing, though collaborating functions*" (emphasis added, p. 145). The move from formal to dialectical logic both requires and enables the move from identifying two entities in a binary, *either* one *or* the other, to foregrounding the relationship between the two, *both* entities *and* the unity between them.

Two related units of analysis

Vygotsky identified at least two units of analysis: word meaning (1987) and emotional experience (1994).[1] Word meaning is a unit of analysis for the unity of speech and thinking in consciousness, but it also reflects "*a unity of generalization and social interaction, a unity of thinking and communication*" (emphasis in original, Vygotsky, 1987, p. 49). Emotional experience is a unit of analysis for the *social situation of development*, the unity of individual and environment, as well as the unity of cognition and emotion. Several commonalities exist between the two units of analysis. For example, both emphasize the unity of cognitive and emotional functions, social and individual, the role of meaning for an individual interlocutor or participant, and both units are dynamic, they develop and change over time.

Vygotsky introduced word meaning as the unit of analysis of speech and thinking in a larger discussion on his method of investigating the two psychological functions and the relation between them in consciousness. However, he noted that the psychological nature of word meaning needed to be defined; an associative or structural perspective of word meaning was not what he had in mind. For Vygotsky (1987), word meaning had at least three significant properties that enabled it to function as a unit of speech and thinking. First, words refer to an entire group or class of objects, rather than to a single object. Indeed,

16 *Jennifer A. Vadeboncoeur*

every word is a *generalization*; for this reason, it is a *"verbal act of thought"* (emphasis in original, p. 47). One way to think about this is to note that words can be used to categorize *super*ordinate groups, like "dogs," and *sub*ordinate groups, like a kind of dog, or "Siberian Husky." However, in addition, they can denote a *particular* Husky, a Husky with whom I have experience. Word meaning and the development of concepts occurs from both directions; from the particular to the general, and from the general to the particular. Meaning is inseparable from the word, the domain of thinking, but it is also inseparable from speech: "Is word meaning speech or is it thought? It is both at one and the same time; it is a *unit of verbal thinking*" (emphasis in original, p. 47), or thinking in words. Second, speech is a means of social interaction, a means of expressing ideas, feelings, and experiences, which is enabled by generalization and motivated by the necessity of participation in social practices. The role of speech is of primary significance in human relationships and social practices; it is a main difference between humans and primates and, as speech functions evolved from prehistoric to contemporary societies, psychological functions evolved as well (Luria & Vygotsky, 1992). Third, the ability to communicate through speech, to share different perspectives, to support and challenge claims, to offer reasons, to think together, enables a new form of social interaction. Words can represent lived experience, but they can also communicate something more or something that is yet to exist. Word meaning, from a Vygotskian perspective, includes these nuances, these relationships, which are central to the unity of speech and thinking.

As a second example of a unit of analysis, Vygotsky (1994) identified emotional experience, or *perezhivanie*, during a series of lectures regarding the *social situation of development*. At the time, he was concerned about the practice of separating the child and the environment in research as if they were two distinct entities that could be operationalized in isolation. This concern was concretely tied to the large numbers of disadvantaged and homeless children who had lost their parents during the civil war and World War I. How to manage and educate them was a significant concern for the government. Vygotsky's purpose was to shift attention from the "absolute" conditions of disadvantage, to the dynamic relationship between environmental conditions and how the child made sense of them, how the child understood them, or their "relative" meaning for the child.

> *An emotional experience* [*perezhivanie*] *is a unit where, on the one hand, in an indivisible state, the environment is represented, i.e.* that which is being experienced – an emotional experience [*perezhivanie*] is always related to something which is found outside the person – *and on the other hand, what is represented is how I, myself, am experiencing this,* i.e., all the personal characteristics and all the environmental characteristics are represented in an emotional experience [*perezhivanie*]; everything selected from the personality, all the features of its character, its constitutional elements, which are related to the event in question. So, *in an emotional experience* [*perezhivanie*] *we are always dealing with an indivisible unity of personal characteristics and situational characteristics, which are represented in the emotional experience* [*perezhivanie*].
>
> (emphasis in original, p. 342)

As a unit of analysis, emotional experience is a unity of environment and personal features; it unites cognitive and affective, social and individual, situational and personal, in one unit of analysis.

In emotional experience, Vygotsky (1994) united the social, the cognitive, and the emotional dimensions of experience. In addition, he defined the environment, the individual, and the relationship between them as dynamic, rather than static. The environment is continually changing over time. However, in addition, it is dynamic because the *meaning* of the environment changes for the child: "*One and the same event occurring at different ages of the child is reflected in his consciousness in a completely different manner and has an entirely different meaning for the child*" (emphasis in original, p. 344). This is an inherently unified, dialectical view of development: ". . . it is not just the child who changes, for the relationship between him and his environment also changes, and the same environment now begins to have a different influence on the child" (Vygotsky, 1994, p. 346). In *perezhivanie*, as in word meaning, the emphasis is on the unity of cognition and affect, the unity of social and individual, the *meaning* of the experience for a particular child or individual, the expectation of change over time, and the necessity of capturing this history.

Unifying child with cultural, historical, and social environment

Interestingly, Vygotsky (1994) brought together both units of analysis in a discussion of development that unified: (i) the role of the environment and (ii) the meaning of the environment for the child. He noted "that the development of thinking in children in itself, the *meaning of children's words*, is what determines the new relationship which can exist between the environment and the different developmental processes" (emphasis added, p. 346). This idea both enables and requires attention to features of the environment ". . . viewed in relation to the child" (p. 338). To elaborate on this relation, Vygotsky (1994) used examples that highlight how word meaning and emotional experience work together. He began by noting the common differences in the environment as children are born into cultural and social worlds and grow through them: from the time before birth, to the immediate environment after birth, then:

> gradually, a slightly wider range of the world around him begins to develop for the child . . . the room, the backyard nearby and the street where he lives. As he begins to walk about, his environment expands and ever new relationships are formed between the child and the people surrounding him.
>
> (p. 339)

Vygotsky was clear that the environment is not a container, it is not a setting, rather it is "the source of development" (p. 349).

As the source of development, Vygotsky (1994) highlighted the *general genetic law of cultural development*: the principle that the child's higher psychological functions originate as an *inter* psychological category in social practices with others, on the social plane first, and become an individual *intra* psychological category second. As children engage in collective behavior, everyday social practices, they internalize social interactions and speech, ultimately mastering them. The ideal or final form of development exists in a child's environment in the form of the social interactions and speech of adults and more experienced peers. This makes the developmental history of the child, or ontogenesis, considerably different from other developmental histories – for example, phylogenesis and sociocultural history. Adults, parents, teachers, and older and/or more experienced peers are continuous role models for younger and/or less experienced children. The environment contains people who provide examples of cultural ways of interacting, speaking, thinking, feeling, and learning that have meaning for the child and provide a potential influence.

To further elaborate the relation between child and environment, Vygotsky (1994) described the development of word meaning for a child: A child's word meaning is not

18   *Jennifer A. Vadeboncoeur*

the same as an adult's. Word meaning "at different ages has a different structure" (p. 344). Moving from concrete lived experience to abstract and back again, word meaning forms the foundation for the development of everyday and scientific concepts, as well as for integrating both kinds of concepts together. Everyday concepts are rich, deeply felt, contextual, and grounded in everyday social practices, while scientific concepts begin their development through schooling, through the process of using language to define systems of ideas that are abstract, potentially outside of one's experiences, and decontextualized. While the environment changes over time as the child explores and engages in more complicated activities, the child's word meaning changes over time, reflecting the child's evolving awareness, sense, interpretation, and understanding of the events and actions around her. Together, these units of analysis enable a nuanced understanding of the historical relationship between developing child and changing environment.

Both units of analysis, word meaning and *perezhivanie*, exemplify the richness of Vygotsky's theory and shed light on the complexity of his methodology. However, as noted by Luria (1987), the work of researchers and educators investigating learning and development, and developing pedagogical approaches and assessments that enable an understanding of the learning and development of students, is neither straightforward nor clear. Indeed, the richness of this holistic approach, the result of theoretical and methodological strength, can become a potential obstacle: the requirement to think through units of analysis appropriate to educational and psychological research, to use them in the conduct of this research, to ensure that the necessary knowledge translation occurs to engage educators in the development of theory/practice connections, and to muster the political will to address the economic requirements of the educational implications. Vygotsky (1997a) was not the first nor the last critical psychologist to argue for the power of psychology to make significant practical improvements for all members in society, citing Marx's adage, "it was enough for philosophers to have interpreted the world, now it's time to change it" (pp. 9–10). As he noted long ago, education and, more specifically, the process of schooling was one feature of society ready for change.

Educational implications: The question of educational achievement

With word meaning and emotional experience, Vygotsky (1987, 1994) advanced several claims about development that have important implications, in particular in relation to the dialogue around assessing learning and educational achievement. Three educational implications are addressed here, although there are most certainly more. The first implication, and perhaps the most obvious, is the necessity of defining learning and the purpose of learning as a step toward generating units of analysis for learning, as well as the necessity of grounding educational achievement in relation to learning. Two additional concepts are introduced in this section that are foundational to future chapters in this volume: *the zone of proximal development* and *dynamic assessment*. The second implication addresses the location of word meaning at the beginning, rather than the end, of concept development with consequences for assessing learning and educational achievement. The third implication foregrounds the significance of the educational environment for learning; disparities between environments are likely to have material effects on the learning, development, and achievement of children.

First, defining learning – what is to be learned, how it is learned, the conditions under which it is learned, and the purpose – is a necessary step toward identifying units for learning and educational achievement. As noted by a number of authors, learning, like other ubiquitous concepts, is frequently left undefined, although diverse, competing, and often mutually exclusive definitions exist depending on the theoretical locations of researchers (e.g., Säljö, 2009; Vadeboncoeur, 2006). From a Vygotskian perspective, learning and educational achievement are neither singular terms, nor universal ones; rather, they are both cultural and historical constructions that are defined by particular theoretical frames interpreted by human beings, again in cultural and historical context. Learning is a unified social, cognitive, and emotional process that is not reducible to any one of these constituents. Learning is a process of constructing concepts and knowledge, identity in social relationships and relations, as well as values related to the content of and participation in the process (e.g., Stetsenko, 2008; Vadeboncoeur, Vellos, & Goessling, 2011). Further, learning is always *learning of something* (Säljö, 2009) – for example, navigation (Hutchins, 1993) or literacy practices (Liu & Vadeboncoeur, 2010). As such, learning presupposes a purpose for the educational practices that are designed for the learner. Like learning, educational achievement must be defined: grounded in a particular definition of learning, what is to be learned, and the purpose, as well as in relation to a particular cultural, historical, and social environment. Unfortunately, learning and educational achievement are frequently defined by default: by how they are assessed. This was also a concern for Vygotsky (1997a), who noted in the 1920s that assessments were driving and narrowing instruction.

Vygotsky (1997b) radically redefined development as a cultural, historical, and social process, as well as a biological process and, in addition, he reversed the relationship between learning and development with the concept of the *zone of proximal development* (ZPD): the idea that informal or formal instruction aimed in advance of development facilitates *learning that leads development* (Vygotsky, 1978, 1987). Rather than assessing "developmental readiness" and aiming instruction at the actual level of development, or what a child can do independently, Vygotsky (1978, 1987) argued that, when teachers engaged students in tasks that were beyond their actual developmental level, and ensured the necessary cognitive and emotional supports for successful completion, learning had the potential to foster the "buds" of development. Good instruction enabled a child's evolving psychological functions to emerge through participation in shared or joint practices with a more experienced adult or peer. Both learning and development and the relationship between them are exemplified through the ZPD, along with the reciprocal way Vygotsky defined learning–teaching relationships. *Obuchenie*, translated as "learning and teaching," joined the two processes as inseparable (Cole, 2009).

The ZPD was also used by Vygotsky (2011) to advance the idea of *dynamic assessment*, or coupling assessment with instruction to differentiate between students' *readiness to learn*, and to predict gains in educational achievement resulting from enriched educational environments. Vygotsky (1978) compared two children of the same chronological and mental age and then asked: How will instruction influence how they deal with a specific problem-solving task? How will having the assistance of a more experienced adult shape their educational achievement? Experiments showed that, with assistance, one child could complete problems up to a 12-year-old's level, and the other a 9-year-old's level: "Now, are these two children mentally the same?" (p. 86). The emphasis here was on maximizing the benefits of instruction, on thinking about education *prospectively*: "The actual developmental level characterizes mental development retrospectively, while the zone of proximal development characterizes mental development prospectively" (p. 86–87). Vygotsky was interested in designing educational environments to enable learning experiences that ultimately fostered development, rather than assessing and teaching to what he considered to be an individual child's already "fossilized behaviors."

20 Jennifer A. Vadeboncoeur

Based on Vygotsky's theory, dynamic assessment has developed into a set of related approaches that embed assessment within the process of instruction. They can be used, for example, to understand individual differences (Lidz & Gindis, 2003), as a framework for integrating teaching and assessment (Lantolf & Poehner, 2010), and as a method of conceptualizing and measuring learning potential (Sternberg & Grigorenko, 2002). Although there are different emphases in these approaches, there are common commitments across them. For example, a commitment to learning as a dynamic process, rather than a static product; a commitment to linking insights gained from assessments to long-term instruction; a commitment to the learning–teaching relationship as the basis for understanding and promoting learning and, ultimately, development; and a commitment to developing culturally responsive methods of instruction and assessment that are not limited by socioeconomic, language, and educational differences. Approaches to dynamic assessment retain the unity of social and individual and provide in-depth and future-oriented understanding for the design of educational environments. However, in addition, they also establish and maintain learning–teaching relationships as students and teachers work jointly to construct scientific concepts, learn about themselves as learners and teachers, share responsibility for learning performances, and practice participation and engagement in culturally valued educational practices.

The purpose of education, for Vygotsky, was to promote the full and active life of intellectually, emotionally, and morally accomplished social beings (Bakhurst, 2007). He noted specifically that a goal of education was to facilitate the development of individuals who look beyond their own environment, who imagine possible futures and act to bring them into being, and citizens who can engage in an increasingly international, now global, world (Vygotsky, 1997a). Education should move between what is known and familiar to each child, from his or her interests, to authentic engagement with culturally and historically accumulated knowledge; this path enables the continuous interplay of everyday and scientific concepts. Students should be engaged in authentic tasks: Tasks that are meaningful and purposeful, as well as assessment that reflects educational experience, has a direct effect on future instruction, and honors both where the child is now and the future adult he or she may become.

Second, word meaning is located at the beginning of concept development; assessments of word meaning, recognition, and recall are not assessments of conceptual understanding. Although children often use the same words that adults do, their understanding of these words is often quite different. Uttering a word and using it in conversation is simply the beginning of a complex line of development that only becomes complete when children construct systems of relationships between concepts, and can operate with this system consciously and intentionally (Vygotsky, 1987). The development of word meaning into everyday and scientific concepts occurs through participation in social environments. Words as cultural tools are significant not simply as functional sign systems, but in addition, by virtue of the *meaning* they engender for the child in social practice. What this means is that children use words, and need to practice using words, before and sometimes long before they have a deep systematic understanding of the word: before the word becomes a scientific concept. Rather than a gradual replacement for everyday concepts, scientific and everyday concepts grow into and inform each other; scientific concepts grow "downward into the domain of the concrete, into the domain of personal experience," while everyday concepts begin "in the domain of the concrete and empirical" and move toward "conscious awareness and volition" (p. 220). Ideally, children and youths develop scientific concepts that are linked with concrete meanings, and everyday concepts that are linked with abstract systems; this depends, in large part, on instruction.

The problem of challenging and reconfiguring experientially based everyday concepts and restructuring them as scientific concepts was studied across child and adolescent development and into young adulthood by Howard Gardner and David Perkins, co-directors of *Project Zero,* from 1972 to 2000 (e.g., Boix Mansilla & Gardner, 2008; Gardner, 2011). A five-year project, *Teaching for Understanding* examined, in part, the discrepancy between favorable standardized multiple choice test scores – for example, in elementary, secondary, and university science courses – and an inability to answer even the most basic related science questions. This discrepancy reflects a lack of conceptual understanding: Students retain information presented long enough to complete assessments that require word recognition and recall, but they do not have an understanding of concepts or the relationships between concepts. From a Vygotskian (1987) perspective, they have not yet learned to think in systematic scientific concepts. Vygotsky used a geological metaphor to argue that, as layers in the earth's crust co-exist and include earlier and later geological strata, categories of thinking co-exist as historical layers. Development is not a simple mechanical process of moving from one type of concept or thinking to the next. Scientific concepts retain their beginnings in everyday concepts and are enriched by them, as well as potentially distorted by them, until a system of interrelated concepts is constructed.

In terms of assessing learning or educational achievement, this means that word recognition, and even word recall, are often not linked to conceptual knowledge or understanding. A student may be able to recognize a word, or even calculate a math problem through a series of memorized steps, without an understanding of the concepts or the relationships between concepts. Therefore, assessments of word recognition and recall should not be confused with assessments of conceptual understanding. As described earlier, assessment unified with instruction should be dynamic and formative; not individual, retrospective, but social and prospective. Assessing *for* learning, not assessment *of* learning, means that assessment should support the improvement of instruction and future learning opportunities for each particular child along the path toward conceptual development.

Third, educational environments matter; disparities between social environments have material effects on the learning, development, and achievement of children. Children grow into educational environments that are constituted by relationships with significant others, social practices, and cultural tools. As noted earlier, the environment is not a container for development, but its source. The significance of home and school environments cannot be overstated; both are implicated in what Vygotsky (1998) called the *social situation of development,* or the way in which the social environment changes as a result of both child development and changing social practices in which children participate within specific cultural locations. Infants and toddlers grow through home and alternative caretaking environments, to early childhood and preschool environments, to kindergarten and formal schooling environments. Many cultures have common trajectories of environments along which children travel, although there is significant variation in terms of availability, access, financial cost, as well as differences in federal, corporate, and local policies on maternity leave and support for parents with infants and young children. Many children experience combinations of these caretaking arrangements before they enter the formal school system, and for each of them the general genetic law of cultural development, noted earlier, highlights the role of the environment: Learning is social, *inter*psychological, then *intra*psychological, and mediated through social practices and cultural tools. When educational environments fail to provide for children the role models they need, exposure and participation in social practices, and opportunities to play with and practice using speech and other cultural tools, the consequences can be serious (Vygotsky, 1994).

A significant concern for Vygotsky (1997a) was the "class-based character" of schooling; the extent to which the interests of the dominant class shaped school culture and afforded limited opportunities to children from backgrounds different from the upper classes. He critiqued IQ testing and argued that most of the children who were assessed with a high IQ initially were not more intellectually gifted, but had grown up in more favorable conditions (Vygotsky, 2011). Further, that in most cases IQ was a symptom, or a sign, of privileged circumstances and, in a sense, an indicator of what is possible if these circumstances were made available to every child. The ZPD reminds us that the assessment of learning must be situated in relation to the social environment of the child. A case in point, in the United States, school and student funding is decidedly inequitable: In 27 of 49 states studied, "the highest-poverty school districts receive fewer resources than the lowest-poverty districts. . . . In 30 states, high minority districts receive less money for each child than low minority districts" (Education Trust, 2005, p. 2). Indeed, Ladson-Billings (2006) mapped the historical, economic, sociopolitical, and moral disparities in educational opportunities for minority and low-income communities and individuals and argued that the "achievement gap" is better defined as a historically accumulated "educational debt." The relationship between social class and educational achievement, as intersected by minority status, is a positive correlation that continues to persist both inside and outside of North America (OECD, 2004, 2005).

Concluding thoughts

As an alternative to what he saw as the traditional method of approaching scientific research, Vygotsky (1987, 1994) proposed a second method; all phenomena under study need to be viewed in terms of "a complex unity, a complex whole." Phenomena need to be understood in terms of "units" of the whole, rather than reduced to "elements," in order to ensure the relationships are maintained. Vygotsky identified two units of analysis, word meaning and emotional experience, and described how they work in concert to enable an understanding of learning and development. These units retain the relationships between social and individual, cognition and emotion, situational and personal, speech and thinking, and generalization and social interaction. Three educational implications were noted that draw attention to the dialectical relationship between child and cultural, historical, and social environments: (i) the necessity of defining learning and educational achievement and grounding our definitions in theory in order to generate units of analysis and design assessments that retain these units; (ii) the difference between word meaning, often the basis for word recognition and recall in standardized assessments, and systems of scientific concepts in assessing learning as understanding; and (iii) the significant role played by environments through which children grow, including both home and school, and the link between disparities in environments and disparities in learning, development, and educational achievement.

Educational achievement must be linked with the purpose of education, but it also recenters questions of educational equity. What sorts of learning environments do children have access to? Which children and under what conditions? What is the history of their participation? A focus on the social environment reminds us of the ways we are implicated in creating environments for our children and students; our responsibility for tending to and facilitating the learning and development of the least experienced and most vulnerable among us. Children with background experiences different from the dominant cultural group often need exposure to and experience with the taken-for-granted knowledge and curriculum that is culturally defined (see Kozulin, 1998). In addition, as a genre, standardized tests themselves, and the process of completing multiple choice questions, may not be culturally familiar (see Greenfield, 1997). Standardized assessments assume that equal educational opportunity exists across educational contexts and that the assessments themselves are not biased. In this regard, assessments of educational achievement may more accurately be read as assessments of social environments than as assessments of individuals, as assessing social indicators of disparity and inequality that need attention, or the ways in which the lives of children and families may be improved, and as a foundation for generating new opportunities for learning and development. This way, assessments of achievement could be used to improve instruction and educational environments for children: assessments *for* learning, rather than assessments *of* learning.

Like many early twentieth-century scholars, Vygotsky had confidence in the ability and commitment of human beings to invent cultural tools, artifacts, and practices that benefitted humanity, that reduced inequality and mediated biological learning differences, and that provided enabling conditions for the next generation. Like others, accumulated knowledge was a foundation for the improvement of society with direct material effects on the social environment to be shared with generations to come. Interestingly, Vygotsky was the first to admit that the discussions around education and the purposes of education were never final, but had to be revisited continually over the course of history as social, economic, and political structures changed. So while it is instructive to gain a sense of what Vygotsky thought about learning, teaching, and assessment, and the purpose of education, his ideas cannot replace the work we have to undertake to define and make explicit these concepts for ourselves. Rather than relying on the default definition for learning and educational achievement that results from allowing assessments to define these core concepts, we need to ask ourselves the following: What is a theoretically grounded unit of analysis for this view of learning? What is a theoretically grounded unit of analysis for educational achievement? How do we design methods of assessment that retain these units? And, what is the purpose: how ought the results of the assessment be used?

Note

1 The Russian word *perezhivanie* has been translated in at least two distinct ways: as lived experience and emotional experience. I make intentional use of emotional experience here, following van der Veer (2001), as it foregrounds emotion, the often forgotten component of the unity of cognition and emotion (see also Bozhovich, 2009, for a similar translation).

References

Bakhurst, D. (2007). Vygotsky's demons. In H. Daniels, M. Cole, & J. V. Wertsch (Eds.), *The Cambridge companion to Vygotsky* (pp. 50–76). New York: Cambridge University Press.

Boix Mansilla, V., & Gardner, H. (2008). Disciplining the mind. *Educational Leadership, 65*(5), 14–19.

Bozhovich, L. I. (2009). The social situation of child development. *Journal of Russian and East European Psychology, 47*(4), 59–86.

Cochran-Smith, M., & Lytle, S. L. (2006). Troubling images of teaching in No Child Left Behind. *Harvard Educational Review, 76,* 668–697.

Cole, M. (2009). The perils of translation: A first step in reconsidering Vygotsky's theory of development in relation to formal education. *Mind, Culture, and Activity, 16*(4), 291–295.

Darling-Hammond, L. (2007). Race, inequality and educational accountability: The irony of "No Child Left Behind." *Race, Ethnicity, and Education, 10*(3), 245–260.

Education Trust. (2005). *The funding gap 2005.* Washington, DC: Education Trust.

24   *Jennifer A. Vadeboncoeur*

Gardner, H. (2011). *The unschooled mind: How children think and how schools should teach* (2nd ed.). New York: Basic Books.

Greenfield, P. M. (1997). You can't take it with you: Why ability assessments don't cross cultures. *American Psychologist, 52*(10), 1115–1124.

Hutchins, E. (1993). Learning to navigate. In S. Chaiklin & J. Lave (Eds.), *Understanding practice: Perspectives on activity and context* (pp. 35–63). New York: Cambridge University Press.

Kozulin, A. (1998). *Psychological tools: A sociocultural approach to education.* Cambridge, MA: Harvard University Press.

Ladson-Billings, G. (2006). From the achievement gap to the education debt: Understanding achievement in U.S. schools. *Educational Researcher, 35*(7), 3–12.

Lantolf, J. P., & Poehner, M. E. (2010). Dynamic assessment in the classroom: Vygotskian praxis for second language development. *Language Teaching Research, 15*(1), 11–33.

Lidz, C. S., & Gindis, B. (2003). Dynamic assessment of the evolving cognitive functions of children. In A. Kozulin, B. Gindis, V. S. Ageyev, & S. M. Miller (Eds.), *Vygotsky's educational theory in cultural context* (pp. 99–116). New York: Cambridge University Press.

Liu, Y., & Vadeboncoeur, J. A. (2010). Bilingual intertextuality: The joint construction of bi-literacy practices between parent and child. *Mind, Culture, and Activity: An International Journal, 17(4)*, 1–15.

Luria, A. R. (1987). Afterword. In R. W. Rieber & A. S. Carton (Eds.), *The collected works of L. S. Vygotsky, Volume 1: Problems of general psychology, including the volume Thinking and speech* (pp. 359–373). New York: Plenum Press.

Luria, A. R., & Vygotsky, L. S. (1992). *Ape, primitive man, and child: Essays in the history of behavior* (E. Rossiter, Trans.). New York: Harvester/Wheatsheaf.

Magee, G. A. (2010). *The Hegel dictionary.* New York: Continuum.

Organisation for Economic Co-operation and Development. (2004). *Learning for tomorrow's world: First results from PISA 2003.* Paris: OECD.

Organisation for Economic Co-operation and Development. (2005). *School factors related to quality and equity: Results from PISA 2000.* Paris: OECD.

Säljö, R. (2009). Learning, theories of learning, and units of analysis in research. *Educational Psychologist, 44*(3), 202–208.

Sternberg, R. J., & Grigorenko, E. L. (2002). *Dynamic testing: The nature and measurement of learning potential.* New York: Cambridge University Press.

Stetsenko, A. (2008). From relational ontology to transformative activist stance on development and learning: Expanding Vygotsky's (CHAT) project. *Cultural Studies of Science Education, 3*, 471–491.

Vadeboncoeur, J. A. (2006). Engaging young people: Learning in informal contexts. *Review of Research in Education, 30*, 239–278.

Vadeboncoeur, J. A., Vellos, R. E., & Goessling, K. P. (2011). Learning as (one part) identity construction: Educational implications of a sociocultural perspective. In D. McInerney, R. A. Walker, & G. A. D. Liem (Eds.), *Sociocultural theories of learning and motivation: Looking back, looking forward* (Vol. 10, pp. 223–251). Greenwich, CT: Information Age.

van der Veer, R. (2001). The idea of units of analysis: Vygotsky's contribution. In S. Chaiklin (Ed.), *The theory and practice of cultural-historical psychology* (pp. 93–106). Aarhus, Denmark: Aarhus University Press.

Vygotsky, L. S. (1925/1997). Consciousness as a problem for the psychology of behavior. In R. W. Rieber & J. Wollock (Eds.), *The collected works of L. S. Vygotsky, Volume 3: Problems of the theory and history of psychology* (pp. 63–79). New York: Plenum.

Vygotsky, L. S. (1978). *Mind in society: The development of higher psychological processes* (M. Cole, V. John-Steiner, S. Scribner, & E. Souberman, Eds.). Cambridge, MA: Harvard University Press.

Vygotsky, L. S. (1987). *The collected works of L. S. Vygotsky, Volume 1: Problems of general psychology, including the volume Thinking and speech* (R. W. Rieber & A. S. Carton, Eds.). New York: Plenum Press.

Vygotsky, L. S. (1994). The problem of the environment. In R. van der Veer & J. Valsiner (Eds.), *The Vygotsky reader* (pp. 338–354). Cambridge, MA: Blackwell.

Vygotsky, L. S. (1997a). *Educational psychology* (R. Silverman, Trans.). Boca Raton, FL: St Lucie Press.

Vygotsky, L. S. (1997b). *The collected works of L. S. Vygotsky, Volume 4: The history of the development of higher mental functions* (R. Rieder, Ed.). New York: Plenum Press.

Vygotsky, L. S. (1998). *The collected works of L. S. Vygotsky, Volume 5: Child psychology* (R. W. Rieber, Ed.). New York: Plenum Press.

Vygotsky, L. S. (2011). The dynamics of the schoolchild's mental development in relation to teaching and learning (A. Kozulin, Trans.). *Journal of Cognitive Education and Psychology, 10*(2), 198–211.

Vygotsky, L. S., & Luria, A. R. (1994). Tool and symbol in child development. In R. van der Veer & J. Valsiner (Eds.), *The Vygotsky reader* (pp. 99–174). Cambridge, MA: Blackwell.

Zinchenko, V. P. (1985). Vygotsky's ideas about units for the analysis of mind. In J. V. Wertsch (Ed.), *Culture, communication, and cognition: Vygotskian perspectives* (pp. 94–118). New York: Cambridge University Press.

3 Family capital, child's personal agency, and the academic achievement of Chinese migrant children

Qiaobing Wu

Introduction

In the study of child development, Vygotsky's (1978) sociocultural theory and Coleman's (1990) social capital theory are two popular and influential frameworks that have been widely used to investigate a variety of developmental outcomes for children and youths. Sociocultural theory considers the learning and cognition of children as being molded by the collaboration between the child and her/his social environment. Family, as one most proximal context of the child's sociocultural system, provides the essential venue where interactions between children and their parents take place, which would shape the cognitive development of children, partly reflected by their academic achievement. On the other hand, social capital theory considers the development of children as being shaped by social resources inherent in various social relationships derived from a range of social contexts, such as the family, school, and neighborhood (Coleman, 1990), wherein family, again, as the most proximate social context, plays a paramount role in determining the child's development. However, in the theoretical tradition of social capital led by Coleman (1988), Bourdieu (1986), and Putnam (2000), children and young people are predominantly viewed as passive recipients of the influences of social capital, rather than active producers and consumers in their own right (Holland, Reynolds, & Weller, 2007). The bulk of social capital literature has generally failed to take into consideration the fact that children, as independent agents, may actively generate, draw on, or negotiate their own social capital, thus affecting the way that social capital works (Morrow, 1996, 1999). In other words, the role of children's personal agency in the functioning of social capital has been paid little attention. This has constrained our ability to fully exploit the potential of social capital for the adjustment and well-being of children, especially in terms of utilizing the potential of children themselves in motivating and mobilizing social capital for their better development.

Drawing on a sample of migrant children in mainland China, this study applies sociocultural theory and social capital theory to examine how children's personal agency – that is, their initiative and actual efforts in developing and mobilizing social capital embedded in the family – influences the way that family social capital operates on their academic achievement. The major research question addressed in the study is: Does the child's personal agency in generating and mobilizing social capital embedded in the family moderate the effect of family social capital on their academic achievement, and if so, how? It is hypothesized that migrant children who present higher degrees of personal agency in constructing social capital in the family will experience greater benefits of family social capital in the form of better academic achievement.

Education of migrant children in mainland China

Starting from the mid-1980s, rural–urban migration in mainland China has been characterized by a population flow from rural to urban areas in search of better job opportunities and living conditions. Given the huge size of the floating population, rural–urban migration is described as the largest peacetime population movement in world history (Roberts, 2002). The population growth has been especially drastic in recent years as the pattern of migration switches from personal migration to family resettlement, and from temporary inhabitation to permanent stay in the city (Li, 2006; Liang, 2007; Roberts, 2002). Along with the changing pattern of migration, increasing numbers of children have also migrated to cities with their parents. According to the 2000 census, there were a total of 121,070,000 migrants in China (National Bureau of Statistics, 2000). Of these, 19.37% were children under the age of 18 (National Working Committee on Children and Women, 2003). The number of migrants increased to 211 million by 2009, 20.8% of whom were children under the age of 14 (National Committee of Family Planning, 2010). In the city of Shanghai, there were 3.87 million migrants by the end of the year 2000, of which 320,000 were school-age children (Li, 2004). The number of migrants increased to 4.98 million and 5.81 million by 2003 and 2005, respectively, accounting for 24.6% of the city's entire population (China Business News, 2007). It is estimated that about 420,000 migrant children were receiving education in Shanghai by the end of 2009 (Xinhua News, 2009).

The continuously growing population of migrant children has evoked increasing attention from the government and society at large. However, under China's household registration system (*hukou*), which is usually assigned at birth and has been designed to control rural–urban mobility for economic and political purposes, migrant children are not granted equal access to education, medical care, and many other social services, due to urban residence requirements. Traditionally, the local government where a child's *hukou* is registered is solely responsible for providing her/him with an education. Large numbers of migrant children are thus denied entry into public schools in the city and are forced to enroll in the so-called "migrant children's schools", which are of significantly lower quality. Although recent policies have sought to address this problem and required public schools to accommodate migrant children, the delay in policy implementation has perpetuated a harsh situation. Therefore, to increase the opportunity of academic success of migrant children given their disadvantaged situation and restricted resources, it is important to examine what factors, be they individual, familial, or contextual, can exert positive influences on their academic achievement. Sociocultural theory and social capital theory provide two appropriate frameworks to understand the social determinants of children's academic achievement and the interactions between children and their social environments in shaping their cognitive development.

Family and child development: Theoretical frameworks

As a most immediate social context for children, family is considered a key determinant of children's educational development in both social capital theory and sociocultural theory.

According to Coleman (1988), one leading scholar in social capital, family is composed of three major components: human capital, financial capital, and social capital. Family human capital refers to the parents' cognitive skills and educational attainments, which are expected to influence the cognitive environment within a home (Coleman, 1988). Research has found human capital to be predictive of various developmental outcomes of children, such as their school achievement (Coleman & Hoffer, 1987; Teachman, Paasch, & Carver, 1997), success in obtaining employment (Furstenberg & Hughes, 1995), and decreased involvement in deviant behaviors (Putnam, 2000; Runyan et al., 1998). Family financial capital refers to the financial resources used for the household and the child, typically measured as the income and assets of the family. Like human capital, financial capital has also been consistently documented as exerting significant effects on various outcomes of child development (Coleman & Hoffer, 1987; Furstenberg & Hughes, 1995; Putnam, 2000; Runyan et al., 1998; Sampson, Morenoff, & Earls, 1999; Teachman et al., 1997). Family social capital, a third component of the family background, refers to the bonds between parents and children reflected in the time and attention spent interacting with children and monitoring their activities (Coleman, 1990). Following the general definition of social capital as "social resources inherent in social relationships that facilitate a social outcome" (Coleman, 1990, p. 302), family social capital involves purposeful investment of parents in their children, in the form of time, interests, or interactions, which would pass on their resources or family norms for the adjustment and well-being of children (Coleman, 1988). Derived from this conceptualization, the quality of parent–child interaction was typically used as a proxy measure to capture the stock of social capital in the family context (Coleman, 1988; Winter, 2000). Many empirical studies have suggested that family social capital is associated with a range of children's educational outcomes, including decreased likelihood of school dropout (Croninger & Lee, 2001), higher educational aspiration (McNeal, 1999), and better academic achievement (Hao & Bonstead-Bruns, 1998; Valenzuela & Dornbusch, 1994). These effects are mainly attributed to the intermediate function of family social capital in transmitting parental resources to children through interactions (Coleman, 1988).

On the other hand, the sociocultural approach to learning and development also emphasizes the importance of social environment on child development. According to Vygotsky (1960), society is the determining factor of human behavior. The learning and development of a child is thus shaped by the mediation process that takes place between the children's psychological self and the sociocultural environment (Robbins, 2001). Children tend to experience optimal learning when they work with a more knowledgeable other who can offer scaffolded support and guidance to help internalize the information and thinking tools provided to them (Rogoff, 1990). As one most proximal context of a child's sociocultural system, family provides the essential venue where interactions between children and their social environments take place, and parents, in this particular sociocultural setting, undoubtedly carry an important role to act as a human mediator for children's learning and development. Applying Vygotsky's sociocultural framework, studies have demonstrated how the scaffolded support within significant relationships facilitate optimal learning and achievement, such as academic performance (Phillipson & Phillipson, 2007), social and emotional development (Smith, 2010), quality of reasoning and collaborative activities (Mercer, Wegerif, & Dawes, 1999), and classroom participation and positive attitudes toward school (Gruman, Harachi, Abbott, Catalano, & Fleming, 2008).

Additionally, and importantly, one overarching focus of sociocultural theory is the dynamic interdependence of social and individual processes in the construction of knowledge (John-Steiner & Mahn, 1996). Vygotsky (1978) considers the development of children as the transformation of socially shared activities into internalized processes. Despite the influence of nature on man, he acknowledges that "man, in turn, affects nature and creates through his changes in nature new natural conditions for his existence" (Vygotsky, 1978, pp. 60–61). As Penuel and Wertsch (1995) also note, sociocultural processes and individual functioning exist in a dynamic and interactive manner, rather than being static and isolated. Nevertheless, the concept of interaction between children and the social environments in their learning and development in the sociocultural framework, especially from the child's perspective, is more of a theoretical conceptualization than empirical examination. It remains to be investigated by empirical data how the changed social conditions as a result of children's participation and intervention as active agents might function on the development and achievement of children. The present study attempts to supplement the theoretical construction with empirical evidence, using the academic achievement of migrant children in mainland China as an example.

The role of children's personal agency

In the extant literature, research has typically taken a top-down view of the effects of social environments on children and adolescents, considering children as passive recipients of social influences, with little recognition of their ability to generate and utilize social resources in their own right. For example, while examining the effect of family social capital, research focuses exclusively on how parents' abilities to invest in their parental practices and their degree of involvement determine the child's development and well-being (Coleman, 1988; Dorsey & Forehand, 2003; Putnam, 2000). This ignores the fact that children, as independent agents, may actively generate, draw on, or negotiate their own social capital (e.g., initiating interactions with parents, building closer relationships with parents, or providing support to parents), thus potentially modifying the way that social capital works (Becker, Aldridge, & Dearden, 1998; Morrow, 1996; Song, 1996). The role of the child's personal agency has been downplayed in the literature and requires further examination (Morrow, 1999), where the child's personal agency basically refers to the extent to which children are able to engage in communications and exert themselves as influential in the social environment (Corsaro, 1997).

Drawing on the sociology of childhood that considers children as active agents who shape the structures and processes around them (James & Prout, 1997) and manifest agency through interactions in multiple settings (Milkie, 1994), Morrow (1999) has firmly pinpointed that a more "active" approach in studying social capital is in great need to incorporate the examination of children's personal agency. Recent studies have started to explore the role that personal agency plays in shaping the life experiences of children and young people through a qualitative approach. Drawing on three studies from the Families and Social Capital ESRC Research Group Program, Holland, Reynolds, and Weller (2007) demonstrated a variety of ways that children and youths develop and use social capital to negotiate important life transitions and to construct their identities, leading to the conclusion that children and young people are active agents in the production and utilization of social capital. Leonard's (2005) exploration, based on two projects in Ireland, also demonstrated how children make use of parents' existing networks and develop their own social capital in order to gain access to employment opportunities. However, to my knowledge, to date there is a lack of systematic research to quantitatively examine the influences of personal agency in constructing social capital on the development of children and adolescents, especially in terms of how it modifies the effects of social capital.

To fill this gap in social capital literature and to better understand the interaction between children and their sociocultural environment, the present study employs a quantitative research design to investigate the role of children's personal agency in the functioning of family social capital on their academic achievement in the context of internal migration in mainland China. Conducted in 2008, this study is grounded on the assumption that social capital may differ among migrant children who are more or less active in constructing and utilizing resources embedded in their family sphere, with concomitant effects on their

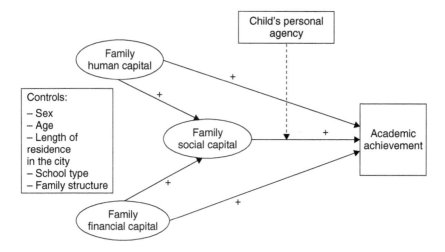

Figure 3.1 Hypothesized model of the effect of family social capital on the academic achievement of migrant children with children's personal agency as moderator

Note: The dashed line indicates moderating effect

academic achievement. The major hypothesis tested in this study is that, to the degree that migrant children actively generate and mobilize resources in their family spheres, the effect of family social capital on their academic achievement will be modified. The conceptual framework tested in the study is presented in Figure 3.1.

Methods

Participants and procedure

Participants of the study were 815 fourth-to-ninth grade migrant students from 14 schools located in four administrative districts of Shanghai. They were selected through a school-based multi-stage random sampling procedure. First, four administrative districts where migrants were most concentrated were selected. Three of the four districts provide education for migrant children in both public schools and migrant children's schools, while the fourth district has closed all the migrant children's schools and accommodated all migrant children in public schools. Second, a complete list of all public elementary and secondary schools that accommodate both native and migrant students in each of the four districts, as well as all migrant children's schools in the first three districts, were obtained from the Educational Bureau. In each district, one public elementary school and one public secondary school were randomly selected from the list of public schools. Likewise, in each of the first three districts, one elementary and one secondary school was randomly selected from the migrant children's schools. Therefore, a total of eight public schools and six migrant children's schools were selected into the study. Third, a complete list of migrant students in the fourth-to-ninth grades of the public elementary and secondary schools was obtained from school officials, and 60 migrant students were randomly selected from each school. Similarly, 60 migrant students were randomly selected from each of the migrant children's schools, based on a complete list of fourth-to-ninth grade students studying at those schools. By doing so,

Academic achievement of Chinese migrant children   31

a total of 840 migrant students from eight public schools and six migrant children's schools were recruited into the study, and 815 of them completed the student survey. One parent of each participating student, who considered himself/herself most knowledgeable regarding the student as well as their family and neighborhood environment, was also invited to participate in the study. A total of 772 parents completed the parent survey. Therefore, the final sample used for analysis included 772 pairs of migrant children and parents. Full descriptive statistics of the sample characteristics are presented in Table 3.1.

Table 3.1 Descriptive statistics of sample characteristics

	Frequency (n)	*Percent (%)*
Gender		
Male	400	53.2
Female	352	46.8
Age	Mean = 12.87 (SD = 1.932) (years)	
Length of residence in the city	Mean = 83.65 (SD = 49.56) (months)	
School type		
Public school	437	58.5
Migrant children school	310	41.5
Family structure		
Living with both parents	652	86.2
Living with one or neither parent	104	13.8
Education (father)		
Didn't attend or finish elementary school	84	11.3
Elementary school	177	23.8
Secondary school	350	47.0
High school (academic/professional/vocational)	117	15.7
Diploma	8	1.1
Bachelor or higher	8	1.1
Education (mother)		
Didn't attend or finish elementary school	182	24.8
Elementary school	223	30.3
Secondary school	231	31.4
High school (academic/professional/vocational)	82	11.2
Diploma	7	1.0
Bachelor or higher	10	1.4
Employment status (father)		
Full-time	391	51.8
Part-time	35	4.6
Unemployed	17	2.3
Self-owned business	312	41.3
Employment status (mother)		
Full-time	346	45.8
Part-time	46	6.1
Unemployed	155	20.5
Self-owned business	209	27.6
Monthly household income (RMB)		
999 or less	68	9.1
1000–1999	238	31.9
2000–2999	191	25.6
3000–3999	94	12.6
4000–4999	45	6.0
5000–5999	43	5.8
6000–6999	16	2.1
7000 or above	52	7.0

32 Qiaobing Wu

Measures

Academic achievement, the outcome variable of this study, was assessed by students' reports of their grades in the past academic semester. On a five-point scale, responses ranged from "Mostly F" (= 1) to "Mostly A" (= 5), with higher scores indicating better academic achievement.

Family human capital was assessed by parents' educational attainments, which were expected to influence the cognitive environment at home (Coleman, 1988). In this study, parents' educational levels were reported by children on seven categories ranging from "didn't go to or didn't graduate from primary school (1)" to "university graduate or higher (7)". This is a common operationalization of human capital from prior empirical studies (Coleman & Hoffer, 1987).

Family financial capital was assessed by three indicators: monthly household income, household equipment, and poverty index. Monthly household income, referring to income from all sources, was reported by parents on 12 categories ranging from "lower than 100 RMB" (about US$12.5) to "more than 10,000 RMB" (about US$1250). Household equipment was measured by asking parents to indicate the total number of electronic items (selected from a list of 10, including refrigerator, washing machine, computer, etc.) that their family possessed, which partly reflected the family's economic condition. The poverty index included three questions asking the parents how difficult it had been in the past year to purchase furniture or household equipment that needed to be replaced, to buy food for their children, and to obtain medical care for their children. Participants rated each question on a five-point scale ranging from "very difficult (1)" to "not difficult at all (5)", with higher scores indicating a lower poverty level. The standardized scores of the household income, household equipment, and poverty index were used as three observed indicators to form the latent construct of family financial capital.

Family social capital was assessed by the quality of parent–child interaction and parental monitoring. Parent–child interaction was measured by the Parent–Child Relationship Inventory (PCRI) (Dixon, Fair, & Bernies, 2004), which assessed the behavioral, affective, and cognitive components of the parent–child relationship from the child's perspective. The PCRI was composed of 40 items in four areas: things that parents are supposed to do for children (eight items), things that children are supposed to do for parents (nine items), things that parents and children are supposed to do together (eight items), and feelings that parents and children should have for each other and the ways they behave with each other (15 items). Participants rated each item on a five-point Likert scale ranging from "never (1)" to "always (5)", indicating how often these behaviors and feelings actually occurred. The Cronbach's α of the PCRI and of the four subscales were 0.938, 0.749, 0.740, 0.756, and 0.927, respectively. Parental monitoring was measured by two scales that incorporated items used in previous studies. One scale was composed of eight items asking about how often the parent was involved in the child's school activities, such as attending a school meeting, as well as how often he/she disciplined the child at home, such as limiting time for watching television. Each item was rated on a four-point scale ranging from "never (1)" to "often (4)". The other scale was composed of four items examining the parent's knowledge about the child's whereabouts after school, including location, companions, activities, and time they returned home. Each item was rated on a five-point Likert scale ranging from "never (1)" to "always (5)". The Cronbach's α of the two parental monitoring scales were 0.620 and 0.800, respectively. The standardized sum scores of the four PCRI subscales and the two parental monitoring scales were used as observed indicators to form the latent construct of family social capital.

Personal agency. There were no existing standard measures of child's personal agency. Questions were developed for use in this study, based on the conceptualization of personal agency in the literature (Corsaro, 1997; Morrow, 1996, 1999). Semi-structured interviews with migrant children conducted in the pilot study also helped elicit and refine appropriate items that assess children's personal agency. These measures tap into children's initiatives and actual efforts in generating and mobilizing social capital in the family. The child's personal agency in constructing family social capital was assessed by asking them how often they initiated interactions with or offered help to parents. Sample items included: "How often do you invite parents for activities together?"; "How often do you talk to parents about things on your mind", and so on. Each item was responded on a four-point scale ranging from "never" (1) to "often" (4). The Cronbach's α of the five-item Child's Personal Agency scale was 0.781. In data analysis, personal agency was tested as a moderator; that is, the effect of family social capital was hypothesized to be different when children's personal agency in constructing family social capital was at a higher or lower level (e.g., the effect of family social capital might be stronger when personal agency was higher). Therefore, the sum score of the five items assessing personal agency in constructing family social capital was median-split to create two subgroups characterized by high and low personal agency, respectively.

Socio-demographic variables. Socio-demographic variables included in the test of the hypothesized model included gender, age, length of residence in the city, family structure, and school type. Gender (1 = female, 0 = male), age (in years) and school type (1 = public school, 0 = migrant children's school) were self-explanatory. Family structure was examined by a binary variable (1 = living with both parents, 0 = other family arrangement) under the assumption that the physical presence of both parents would influence parental involvement (Coleman, 1988). Length of residence was measured by the number of months that the children had lived in the city.

Data analysis

Structural equation modeling (SEM) was conducted using Mplus 5.0 (Muthén & Muthén, 2007) to test the hypothesized model. SEM permits the use of latent constructs composed of multiple observed variables and allows for estimating the relationships among latent constructs while providing explicit estimates of measurement errors to increase the accuracy of analysis results (Byrne, 2001). Moreover, it offers a multiple-group approach that enables simultaneous model fitting for two (or more) samples at a time, which renders it an ideal method to test moderating effects. These features make SEM an especially well-suited technique for this study, given the hypothesized moderating effect of personal agency on the association between family social capital and the academic achievement of migrant children.

Results

Bivariate relationships

The zero-order correlations of major study variables are presented in Table 3.2. It provides an overview of the relationships among the family capital variables, child's personal agency, and academic achievement. As shown in the table, the two family human capital variables, father's and mother's educational levels, were significantly and positively related to children's academic achievements. They were also positively related to the six family social

Table 3.2 Zero-order correlations of major study variables

	1	2	3	4	5	6	7	8	9	10	11	12	13
1 Father education	—												
2 Mother education	0.560**	—											
3 Household income	0.305**	0.318**	—										
4 Family equipment	0.237**	0.257**	0.502**	—									
5 Poverty	−0.097**	−0.155**	−0.512**	−0.407**	—								
6 PCRI-1	0.175**	0.186**	−0.227**	−0.206**	0.170	—							
7 PCRI-2	0.157**	0.222**	−0.244**	−0.196**	0.221	0.625**	—						
8 PCRI-3	0.141**	0.209**	−0.212**	−0.158**	0.158**	0.543**	0.596**	—					
9 PCRI-4	0.152**	0.215**	−0.210**	−0.167**	0.174**	0.599**	0.656**	0.694**	—				
10 PM-1	0.124**	0.155**	−0.167**	−0.157**	0.036	0.391**	0.369**	0.336**	0.302**	—			
11 PM-2	0.088**	0.166**	−0.214**	−0.164**	0.170**	0.382**	0.362**	0.403**	0.403**	0.319**	—		
12 Personal agency	0.122**	0.195**	0.219**	0.168**	−0.094**	0.573**	0.473**	0.505**	0.554**	0.446**	0.474**	—	
13 Academic achievement	0.111**	0.128**	−0.130**	−0.084*	0.042	0.191**	0.235**	0.253**	0.233**	0.176**	0.212**	0.295**	—

Notes
PCRI refers to the Parent–Child Relationship Inventory; PCRI-1,2,3,4 are the four subscales of the PCRI.
PM refers to parental monitoring; PM-1 and PM-2 are the two parental monitoring scales.
* $p < 0.05$; ** $p < 0.01$; *** $p < 0.001$

capital variables. The three financial capital variables – namely, household income, family equipment, and poverty – were also significantly associated with their academic achievement and the family social capital variables, but in a negative direction. That is to say, higher levels of family financial capital were likely to be associated with lower levels of family social capital and poorer academic achievement of migrant children. The family social capital variables were all significantly and positively related to children's academic achievement, as expected. Lastly, the level of children's personal agency was strongly correlated with the family social capital variables as well as the academic achievement.

Test of measurement model

Invariance of factor structures of the latent constructs (i.e., family social capital, family human capital, and family financial capital) across the high and low personal agency groups were first evaluated before proceeding to test the hypothesized structural model. Multiple fit indices were used to assess the goodness of the model, including: (i) Chi-square (χ^2), the likelihood ratio test statistic, where a non-significant χ^2 represents a closer fit of the hypothesized model to the perfect fit; (ii) the Comparative Fit Index (CFI), where values above 0.90 denote a good model fit; and (iii) the Root Mean Square Error of Approximation (RMSEA), where values less than 0.05 indicate a "close fit" (Kline, 2005).

The multiple-group measurement model with factor loadings constrained to be equal across high and low personal agency groups provided good fits to the data with CFI greater than 0.90 and RMSEA smaller than 0.05 ($\chi^2 = 171.926$, df = 94, p < 0.001, CFI = 0.961, RMSEA = 0.048). All observed variables were significantly loaded on the corresponding latent constructs in the expected directions, suggesting that the selected indicators reasonably represented the underlying constructs in a statistically reliable manner, and the factor structures were the same for both groups. Standardized factor loadings of all observed variables on the latent constructs are reported in Table 3.3.

Table 3.3 Standardized factor loadings of observed indicators on latent constructs

Construct	*Indicator*	*Factor loading*	
		Agency low	*Agency high*
Family social capital (FSC)	Experience of things that parents are supposed to do for children (eight items)	0.736	0.688
	Experience of things that children are supposed to do for parents (nine items)	0.701	0.745
	Experience of things that parents and children are supposed to do together (eight items)	0.634	0.680
	Experience of feelings that parents and children should have for each other and the way they behave with each other (15 items)	0.669	0.743
	Parental monitoring of children's school activities and home discipline (eight items)	0.417	0.421
	Parents' knowledge of children's whereabouts (four items)	0.437	0.530
Family human capital (FHC)	Father education	0.632	0.749
	Mother education	0.767	0.820
Family financial capital (FFC)	Monthly household income	0.818	0.781
	Household equipment	0.565	0.687
	Poverty index	0.531	0.645

36   *Qiaobing Wu*

Test of structural model

The focus of this study was on whether the effects of family social capital on the academic achievement of migrant children varied while these children exerted differential levels of personal agency in generating and mobilizing social capital in the family sphere. Following the multiple-group approach in SEM, I first evaluated the fits of alternative structural models with various degrees of constraints, in order to identify the best fitting model and examine the invariance of path coefficients. The fully constrained model with all factor loadings and structural effects set to be equal across the high and low personal agency groups was tested first, and it provided a good fit to the data (χ^2 = 370.280, df = 209, p < 0.001, CFI = 0.930, RMSEA = 0.046). Based on the fully constrained model, the path linking family social capital to children's academic achievement was released in a second model, allowing free estimates of the path coefficient in each of the high and low personal agency groups, and this released model also provided a good fit to the data (χ^2 = 365.788, df = 208, p < 0.001, CFI = 0.930, RMSEA = 0.045). However, the significant decrease of χ^2 value from the fully constrained model to the released model ($\Delta\chi^2$ = 4.492, Δdf = 1, p < 0.05) suggested that allowing the path from family social capital to academic achievement to vary across groups would improve the overall fit of the multiple-group structural model. Therefore, the released model was selected as the best fitting structural model, which indicated that the effect of family social capital was significantly different across the two groups of migrant children with higher versus lower levels of personal agency. The standardized coefficients of all structural paths linking family capital and socio-demographic variables to children's academic achievement in both high and low personal agency groups are presented in Table 3.4.

As hypothesized, children's personal agency in generating and mobilizing social capital moderated the effects of family social capital on their academic achievement. Family social capital exhibited stronger positive effect on the academic achievement for children showing higher levels of personal agency in constructing social capital in their family spheres (β = 0.266, p < 0.001) than for those showing lower levels of personal agency (β = 0.181, p < 0.01). In other words, children who were more active in mobilizing resources in the family would receive greater benefits from those resources in the form of better educational outcomes. With regard to the other two family level variables, family human capital showed no significant direct effect on children's academic achievement in either high (β = 0.014,

Table 3.4 Standardized direct, indirect, and total effects of major predictor variables on children's academic achievements

Major predictor variables	Academic achievement					
	Low personal agency group			High personal agency group		
	Direct	Indirect	Total	Direct	Indirect	Total
Family social capital	0.181**	—	0.181	0.266***	—	0.266
Family human capital	0.017	0.023	0.040	0.014	0.028*	0.042
Family financial capital	−0.051	−0.040*	−0.091	−0.039	−0.048**	−0.087
Gender	−0.035	−0.014	−0.049	−0.032	−0.021	−0.053
Age	0.307***	0.005	0.312	0.305***	0.008	0.313
School type	0.132**	0.046**	0.178	0.132**	0.072***	0.204
Family structure	−0.051	−0.014	−0.065	−0.050	−0.021	−0.071
Length of residence in city	0.073	—	0.073	0.071	—	0.071

Note
* p < 0.05; ** p < 0.01; *** p < 0.001

p > 0.05) or low (β = 0.017, p > 0.05) personal agency group. However, for children with higher levels of personal agency, family human capital did influence their academic achievement indirectly through its significant positive effect on family social capital (β = 0.126, p < 0.05). That is, family social capital mediated the effect of family human capital on the academic achievement of children in the high personal agency group. Similarly, family financial capital exhibited no significant direct effect on children's academic achievement, but was influential through the mediating effect of family social capital, although in a negative direction opposite to the original expectation. Higher levels of family financial capital were significantly associated with lower levels of family social capital in both the high (β = –0.224, p < 0.001) and low (β = –0.180, p < 0.01) personal agency groups, which, in turn, led to inferior academic achievement. In other words, family financial capital exhibited a potential negative effect on children's academic achievement through its negative effect on family social capital, regardless of the degree of children's personal agency.

Of the socio-demographic variables, the type of school that the migrant children attended was a significant predictor of their academic achievement. Attending public schools instead of the migrant children's schools was associated with better academic achievement of children in both the high and the low personal agency groups (β = 0.132, p < 0.01). In addition, attending public school was also associated with higher levels of family social capital for both high (β = 0.272, p < 0.001) and low (β = 0.257, p < 0.001) personal agency children, which predicted their better academic achievement through an indirect pathway. Age was another significant predictor, with older children exhibiting better academic achievement no matter whether they showed higher (β = 0.305, p < 0.001) or lower (β = 0.307, p < 0.001) personal agency in constructing family social capital. Gender, family structure, and length of residence in the city appeared not to be predictive of children's academic achievement in either direct or indirect pathways. Overall, 18.4% and 15.6% of the variances in the academic achievement of migrant children were explained by the tested model, respectively, for children in the high and low personal agency groups.

Discussion

This study adopts the sociocultural framework and the social capital theory to investigate how the interactions between children and their sociocultural contexts shape their learning and development. Specifically, it examines how children's personal agency in generating and mobilizing social capital embedded in the family spheres modifies the effect of family social capital on the academic achievement of migrant children in mainland China. Major findings of the study are summarized as below, with further elaboration and interpretation of each.

Results of the study highlight the significance of children's personal agency in magnifying the positive effect of social capital in the family context. As suggested by the model, when migrant children present higher degrees of personal agency in developing social capital in the family, the effect of family social capital on their academic achievement is significantly stronger than it is for those who are less active in mobilizing resources inherent in the same context. This is possibly because children who actively develop or mobilize resources in the family spheres are those who consider family relationships important to them. While taking specific actions to strengthen the family relationship, they tend to be more conscious about social resources embedded in that relationship and tend to develop higher expectations of what those resources might bring to them, which generally increases the potential influences of social capital on their development. Moreover, this also echoes the proposition in Vygotsky's (1978) sociocultural theory that optimal learning occurs in the context of significant relationships. The increased quality interactions between children and parents, the human mediator in the family context, as a result of children's personal agency, may lead to increased scaffolded support and responsive instructions from parents. These supports would then largely facilitate the learning process of children and reduce the distance between the zone of actual development and the zone of potential development. Children's academic achievement is just one such learning outcome in which the benefit of scaffolding through significant relationships is manifested.

In addition, the increased stock of family social capital in the form of increased quality interactions with parents as a result of children's active agency also facilitates the transmission of resources from parents to children. This is another important pathway by which children's personal agency magnifies the effect of family capital on their academic achievements. The significant indirect effect of family human capital on children's academic achievements in the high personal agency group provides support to this interpretation. As presented in Table 3.4, for children who present higher personal agency in mobilizing family social capital, family human capital also significantly influences children's academic achievements through the mediating effect of family social capital. This is in line with Coleman's (1988) proposition that social capital plays an intermediate role that transmits parental resources to children through interactions.

An unexpected finding of this research that deserves special attention is the potential negative effect of family financial capital on children's academic achievement. This is against many research findings in the literature that typically delineate the wealth of a family as a protective factor for child development (Brooks-Gunn & Duncan 1997; McLoyd, 1998). However, this result is consistent with some earlier research on migrant children in China, which also demonstrates a negative effect of family financial capital on children's psychosocial adjustment through its association with poorer parent–child interactions (Wu, Palinkas, & He, 2011). The undesirable effect of family financial capital portrays a dilemma that is common among migrant families in China. On the one hand, migrant parents make great endeavors to improve the financial situation of the family in order to provide children with more opportunities for education and promote their development and well-being. On the other hand, the improvement of financial condition is usually accompanied by longer working hours of both parents outside the family, which largely reduces the time that parents could spend with children, thus decreasing the level of family social capital. As a consequence of the paradox, the increase of family financial capital and the decrease of family social capital become impediments to children's academic achievements.

In summary, the active investments of migrant children in their family relationships help create a favorable family context that benefits their academic achievements. With limited access to resources outside the family due to their marginalized status in the community and society, migrant children are largely dependent on their families for various aspects of development, which renders the family context an extremely important place for this group of children to exhibit their personal agency, which will pay off with the greatest benefits. As the study results suggest, children's interactions with their family context not only changes the sociocultural context by strengthening the stock of family social capital, but also magnifies the influences of the sociocultural context on their own learning and development.

Nevertheless, the results should be interpreted in light of two limitations of the study. First, with a cross-sectional study design, the study could not rigorously establish a causal relationship between family capital and the academic achievement of migrant children. Second, participants of the study are selected from elementary and junior high school students. This excludes migrant children who could not attend school in the city due to structural barriers or financial hardship. Therefore, the sample selection criteria employed in this study restricts the generalizability of research findings to the entire population of migrant children.

Despite the above limitations, findings of this research have several important implications for theory, practice, and future research. Theoretically, on the one hand, this study provides convincing empirical evidence to the theoretical conceptualization in the sociocultural framework that learning is interactive, contextual, and participatory (John-Steiner, Panofsky, & Smith, 1994; Rogoff, 1994). It is this interactive, dynamic process that shapes the cognitive development of children. On the other hand, this study fills a long-lasting gap in the social capital literature which downplays the role of children themselves as active agents in the interaction and negotiation with their sociocultural contexts. Rather than viewing children as passive recipients of the influences of the sociocultural context, the study results demonstrate the role that children's personal agency plays in recreating sociocultural contexts and modifying the contextual effects on their own learning and development. Practically, the salient effect of the child's personal agency in magnifying the function of social capital on their academic achievement has important implications for social services with migrant children. Given that children's personal agency magnifies the effects of family social capital, educational programs could consider employing empowerment strategies that encourage and enable migrant children to make investment in their family relationships, thus developing and mobilizing social resources that will work for their benefit. In essence, social capital is "the product of investment strategies, individual or collective, consciously or unconsciously aimed at establishing or reproducing social relationships that are directly useable in the short or long term" (Bourdieu, 1986, p. 251). It is something that must be continuously worked toward. This can be used as a general principle to guide the development of intervention programs in educational settings to promote the learning and development of children. Lastly, this study also points out a promising direction for future research. The examination of children's personal agency in modifying the function of family social capital on academic achievement can be applied to other developmental outcomes and in other sociocultural contexts. A further step in this field of research would be developing cross-cultural studies that explore how children's personal agency in negotiating with their social environment might reshape the contextual impact on their well-being in various sociocultural settings.

References

Becker, S., Aldridge, J., & Dearden, C. (1998). *Young carers and their families.* Oxford: Blackwell.

Bourdieu, P. (1986). The forms of capital. In J. G. Richardson (Ed.), *Handbook of theory and research for the sociology of education* (pp. 241–258). New York: Greenwood Press.

Brooks-Gunn, J., & Duncan, G. J. (1997). The effects of poverty on children. *The Future of Children, 7*(2), 55–71.

Byrne, B. M. (2001). *Structural equation modeling with AMOS: Basic concepts, applications, and programming.* Mahwah, NJ: Lawrence Erlbaum Associates, Inc.

China Business News. (2007). A picture of the migrant population in Shanghai. http://finance.sina.com.cn/g/20070329/02393450705.shtml. Retrieved September 19, 2008.

Coleman, J. S. (1988). Social capital in the creation of human capital. *American Sociological Review, 94,* s95–s120.

Coleman, J. S. (1990). *Foundations of social theory.* Cambridge, MA: The Belknap Press of Harvard University Press.

Coleman, J. S., & Hoffer, T. B. (1987). *Public and private schools: The impact of communities*. New York: Basic.

Corsaro, W. A. (1997). *The sociology of childhood*. Thousand Oaks, CA: Pine Forge Press.

Croninger, R. G., & Lee, V. E. (2001). Social capital and dropping out of high school: Benefits to at-risk students of teachers' support and guidance. *Teachers College Record, 103*(4), 548–581.

Dixon, M. D., Fair, S., & Bernies, E. (2004). An instrument to investigate the expectations of and experiences with the parent-child relationship: The parent-child relationship inventory. Paper presented at the National Communication Association Annual Convention, Chicago, IL.

Dorsey, S., & Forehand, R. (2003). The relation of social capital to child psychosocial adjustment difficulties: The role of positive parenting and neighborhood dangerousness. *Journal of Psychopathology and Behavioral Assessment, 25*(1), 11–23.

Furstenberg, F. F., & Hughes, M. E. (1995). Social capital and successful development among at-risk youth. *Journal of Marriage and the Family, 57*, 580–592.

Gruman, D. H., Harachi, T. W., Abbott, R. D., Catalano, R. F., & Fleming, C. B. (2008). Longitudinal effects of student mobility on three dimensions of elementary school engagement. *Child Development, 79*(6), 1833–1852.

Hao, L., & Bonstead-Bruns, M. (1998). Parent–child differences in educational expectations and the academic achievement of immigrant and native students. *Sociology of Education, 71*, 175–198.

Holland, J., Reynolds, T., & Weller, S. (2007). Transitions, networks and communities: The significance of social capital in the lives of children and young people. *Journal of Youth Studies, 10*(1), 97–116.

James, A., & Prout, A. (1997). *Constructing and reconstructing childhood*. London: Falmer Press.

John-Steiner, V., & Mahn, H. (1996). Sociocultural approaches to learning and development: A Vygotskian framework. *Educational Psychologist, 31*(3/4), 191–206.

John-Steiner, V., Panofsky, C. P., & Smith, L. W. (1994). *Sociocultural approaches to language and literacy: An interactionist perspective*. New York: Cambridge University Press.

Kline, R. B. (2005). *Principles and practice of structural equation modeling* (2nd ed.). New York: The Guilford Press.

Leonard, M. (2005). Children, childhood and social capital: Exploring the links. *Sociology, 39*(4), 605–622.

Li, B. (2004). The compulsory education of migrant children in Shanghai. *History Teaching and Research, 6*, 58–64.

Li, B. (2006). Floating population or urban citizens? Status, social provision and circumstances of rural–urban migrants in China. *Social Policy and Administration, 40*(2), 174–195.

Liang, Z. (2007). Internal migration in China in the reform era: Patterns, policies, and challenges. In Z. Zhao & F. Guo (Eds.), *Demography in China in the 21st century* (pp. 197–215). Oxford: Oxford University Press.

McLoyd, V. C. (1998). Socioeconomic disadvantage and child development. *American Psychologist, 53*, 185–204.

McNeal, R. (1999). Parental involvement as social capital: Differential effectiveness on science achievement, truancy, and dropping out. *Social Forces, 78*(1), 117–144.

Mercer, N., Wegerif, R., & Dawes, L. (1999). Children's talk and the development of reasoning in the classroom. *British Educational Research Journal, 25*(1), 95–111.

Milkie, M. (1994). Social world approach to culture studies. *Journal of Contemporary Ethnography, 23*, 354–380.

Morrow, V. (1996). Rethinking childhood dependency: Children's contribution to the domestic economy. *Sociological Review, 44*(1), 58–77.

Morrow, V. (1999). Conceptualizing social capital in relation to the well-being of children and young people: A critical review. *Sociological Review, 47*(4), 744–765.

Muthén, L. K., & Muthén, B. O. (1998–2007). *Mplus user's guide* (5th edn.). Los Angeles, CA: Muthén & Muthén.

National Bureau of Statistics. (2000). *China statistical yearbook 2000*. Beijing: National Bureau of Statistics of China.

National Committee on Family Planning. (2010). *Report on China's migrant population 2010*. Beijing: China Population Press.

National Working Committee on Children and Women. (2003). *Let's share the sunshine: Survey report on temporary migrant children in nine cities of China*. Department of National Affairs, Beijing, September.

Penuel, W. R., & Wertsch, J. V. (1995). Vygotsky and identity formation: A sociocultural approach. *Educational Psychologist, 30*, 83–92.

Phillipson, S., & Phillipson, S. N. (2007). Academic expectations, belief of ability, and involvement by parents as predictors of child achievement: A cross-cultural comparison. *Educational Psychology, 27*(3), 329–348.

Putnam, R. D. (2000). *Bowling alone: The collapse and revival of American community*. New York: Simon and Schuster.

Robbins, D. (2001). *Vygotsky's psychology-philosophy: A metaphor for language theory and learning*. New York: Kluwer Academic.

Roberts, K. D. (2002). Female labor migrants to Shanghai: Temporary 'floaters' or potential settlers? *International Migration Review, 36*(2), 492–519.

Rogoff, B. (1990). *Apprenticeship in thinking: Cognitive development in social context*. New York: Oxford University Press.

Rogoff, B. (1994). Developing understanding of the idea of communities of learners. *Mind, Cultural, and Activity, 1*, 209–229.

Runyan, D. K., Hunter, W. M., Socolar, R. S., Amaya-Jackson, L., English, D., Landsverk, J., . . . Mathew, R. M. (1998). Children who prosper in unfavorable environments: The relationship to social capital. *Pediatrics, 101*(1), 12–18.

Sampson, R. J., Morenoff, J. D., & Earls, F. (1999). Beyond social capital: Spatial dynamics of collective efficacy for children. *American Sociological Review, 64*, 633–660.

Smith, S. L. (2010). An exploration of the impact of contextual school factors on students' ways of thinking, speaking and acting. *Emotional and Behavioural Difficulties, 15*(3), 239–255.

Song, M. (1996). "Helping out": Children's labor participation in Chinese take-away businesses in Britain. In J. Brannern & M. O'Brien (Eds.), *Children in families: Research and policy* (pp. 101–113). London: Farmer Press.

Teachman, J. D., Paasch, K., & Carver, K. (1997). Social capital and the generation of human capital. *Social Forces, 75*(4), 1343–1359.

Valenzuela, A., & Dornbusch, S. M. (1994). Familism and social capital in the academic achievement of Mexican origin and Anglo adolescents. *Social Science Quarterly, 75*(1), 18–36.

Vygotsky, L. S. (1960). *Razvitie vysshikh psikhicheskikh funktsii [The development of higher mental functions]*. Moscow: APN.

Vygotsky, L. S. (1978). *Mind in society: The development of higher mental process*. Cambridge, MA: Harvard University Press.

Winter, I. (2000). *Towards a theorised understanding of social capital*. Working paper no. 21, Australian Institute of Family Studies.

Wu, Q., Palinkas, L. A., & He, X. (2011). Social capital in promoting the psychosocial adjustment of Chinese migrant children: Interaction across contexts. *Journal of Community Psychology, 39*(4), 421–442.

Xinhua News. (2009). Migrant children to receive compulsory education in Shanghai. http://news.xinhuanet.com/politics/2009-12/17/content_12663425.htm. Retrieved January 2, 2010.

4 A psychometric view of sociocultural factors in test validity

The development of standardized test materials for Māori-medium schools in New Zealand/Aotearoa

Peter J. Keegan, Gavin T. L. Brown and John A. C. Hattie

Introduction

Tests and assessments are implemented within societies and express the values, ideas, and attitudes of those same societies (Gipps, 1999; Padilla & Lindholm, 1995; Stobart, 2005). Where societies are constituted by a single cultural, historical, ethnic, or linguistic group (e.g., Iceland), there are generally few tensions about the sociocultural characteristics of assessments. However, most modern societies are, for historical reasons, multi-cultural. They generally have a dominant group, usually defined by language, race, ethnicity, and wealth, and one or more minority groups, who differ along at least one of those dimensions. For example, New Zealand's dominant sociocultural group is the white, English-speaking European or Pākehā, who constitute approximately 65% of the population. The most visible of the minority groups include the indigenous Māori people (approximately 14% of the population), Polynesian groups from a variety of Pacific Island nations and states currently referred to as "Pasifika" (8.6%), and Asian groups (6.6%).

Given large differences in language, history, culture, and ethnic identity, it is possible that educational assessments devised by the majority group may not lead to valid interpretations about the achievement, ability, or proficiency of children from different socioculturally defined groups. Poor performance on the tests may reflect non-membership in the majority group (a construct-irrelevant characteristic) rather than lack of competence in the skills, knowledge, or understandings being evaluated in the educational assessment. Inferences about minority group students based on assessments designed by or within another cultural group may be rendered invalid due to their not sharing the same values, beliefs, attitudes, knowledge, or experiences of the majority group. Hence, if educational assessments are to lead to valid actions and inferences about all students (Messick, 1989), it is crucial that sociocultural issues related to design, administration, and interpretation of assessments are taken into account.

In multi-cultural societies like New Zealand, there appear to be three possible responses to cultural diversity in how schooling processes (including assessment) are designed (Ferdman, 1991). *Assimilation* focuses on minority groups becoming members of the majority culture; such an approach to assessment would imply that all learners, regardless of background, do the same assessment and are judged as having had equal opportunity to acquire and value the constructs embedded in the assessment. *Amalgamation* focuses on all groups (minority and majority) creating a new common "melting pot" supra-culture; in terms of assessment, special care would be taken to ensure that assessments reflect the diversity of society, potentially including separate norms and standards for students, depending on their group membership. *Plurality* focuses on providing separate, group-controlled, but shared access to a state's resources; assessments in this situation would be aligned to the separate curriculum constructs, norms, and expectations of each group, independent of reference to the majority group. While many educational systems adopt assimilationist practices in their public examination system, some states do adopt a more plural approach in which different groups can be educationally evaluated in their own language; for example, South Africa provides education in 11 official languages and New Zealand provides for the majority English and the indigenous Māori languages in its assessment system.

In this chapter, we will focus on perspectives associated with different cultural groups as a way of examining sociocultural aspects of education assessment. Rather than focus on alternative perspectives within the dominant culture (e.g., neo-Marxist, neo-liberal, feminist, etc.), we will review critiques of assessment from the point of view of ethnic minority groups (especially those reported in New Zealand), before introducing the approaches taken within the psychometric tradition to address these concerns. To illustrate how a culturally appropriate educational assessment could be implemented, we describe a computerized school testing system developed in New Zealand for students in Māori-medium schools. Throughout, we make recommendations as to how educational assessments can be implemented in light of sociocultural diversities and psychometric principles.

Critiques of assessments from a sociocultural perspective

A number of concerns have been raised concerning the validity of educational assessments related to the language used in testing, cultural values, psychological responses of individuals within different cultural groups, and interactions between majority groups and minority groups.

Language

Vygotsky (1978, 1991) has argued that language-mediated communication is how children develop higher mental abilities, as well as personal, social, and cultural identity. Rogoff (1991) noted the importance of language in the social process of educating children and has identified (Rogoff, Gauvain, & Ellis, 1991) the significant effect schooling has on culture-specific cognitive and literacy activities. It has been argued (Chang & Wells, 1988, p. 106) that a prime function of schooling is to promote, through writing and speech, literate thinking (i.e., "the symbolic potential of language to enable the thought processes themselves to become the object of thought").

Success in the language of schooling is typically identified through performance on assessments, test, and/or examinations. Predominantly these assessments require competence in the written form of language. Thus, doing well on most assessments requires high levels of competence in the dominant language of a society and in the linguistic forms related to symbolic, decontextualized thought. Unsurprisingly, assessments are normally designed in, for, and by the main language group of any nation or state. This creates challenges for any student who has a different first or home language than that used in school and assessments.

A consensus formed more than 20 years ago stated that it took minority-language students four to seven years of schooling in addition to adult-like competence in their first language to reach national norms on standardized tests in subjects that require high levels of vocabulary or cognitive processing (e.g., reading, social studies, and science). However, less time was required in less language-dependent subjects (e.g., mathematics or grammar) (Collier, 1989). In the case of English-language learners, Cummins (1984) has argued that tests of academic knowledge and ability should not have serious consequences for new speakers of the language for the first five years of schooling. Consider the potential effect on minority-language students of assessment tasks that depend on English vocabulary using terminology borrowed from other languages (e.g., opera, ballet, bungalow), metaphoric idioms (e.g., blue-sky, feeling blue, yellow-bellied), or terminology unlikely to appear in normal conversational interactions (e.g., photovoltaic, erudite, aviatrix). Where the goal is not to test knowledge of vocabulary, but rather to use language communicatively, such usage in a test situation will potentially disadvantage children who do not have the sociocultural capital of schooling in their family habitus (Bourdieu & Passeron, 1977). Hence, a socioculturally sensitive educational assessment system would make appropriate accommodations before high-stakes consequences are implemented.

Cultural values

Groups with very different backgrounds tend to have different understandings of educational constructs. One important area is how intelligence is understood. For example, in the 1970s, Donna Awatere (1974), a Māori psychologist, vigorously rejected some of the picture vocabulary tests used to identify language deficiency by showing how the illustrations were racially skewed – the "pretty" woman was Pākehā (New Zealand European), while the "ugly" woman showed Māori racial characteristics. Māori children tended to pick the picture most like their grandmothers, whom they rightly deemed to be beautiful, even though this was not considered the correct choice by the Western test developers.

Criticisms of classroom and qualifications assessments were levelled at their being based on content and contexts not relevant to minority students. Even when presented in the language of the linguistic minority, the basis for item development or analysis is often the content, language, and performance of the majority group (Padilla & Lindholm, 1995; Rau, 2008). Another important aspect for consideration, insofar as standardized, norm-referenced tests are concerned, is that the performance norms for children are indexed to the performance of majority students, rather than to minority students themselves. Being compared to "unlike" students who may be more privileged is highly likely to show the minority students as being below average. This concern speaks to the importance of initiative or ownership by the minority group of the assessment system so that there is visible legitimacy in the system, accountability to the minority group, and benefit to the minority group (Bishop & Glynn, 1999).

Psychological differences between cultures

There are significant differences between and among cultural groups as to their beliefs, values, and attitudes concerning learning, studying, and achievement. These different psychological processes contribute to differential achievement and may require changes to pedagogical practices, if not assessments. If minority groups are more collectivist in their learning practices (Irvine & York, 1995; Sutton, 2001), then assessments that emphasize individual, academic activities or skills (as many societies tend to do in their examination practices) may disadvantage minority students not only for the mode of evaluation, but also for the lack of important group-oriented social and cultural knowledge and skills in the content of assessments.

Minority groups themselves may have different understandings of what academic achievement is and how it is attained. Jones (1991) showed that Pasifika (minority immigrant groups from Pacific Island nations) girls had conceptions and practices of learning for schooling that meant they did not succeed within the New Zealand qualifications system. The Pasifika girls believed that learning meant copying and repeating what the teachers said; while the European (cultural majority group) girls understood learning meant engaging the teacher with their own opinions. This study clearly showed that one contributor to low academic achievement was cultural difference in how learning and assessment were understood.

Another belief system in minority groups that can interfere with academic achievement is the "stereotype threat", which is a psychological pressure exerted on minority populations related to the presence of a robust negative stereotype that is inadvertently fulfilled so as to confirm those stereotypes. When explicitly reminded of the conventional underperformance of people like themselves (i.e., stereotype threat), African-American and female students performed considerably below their potential (as measured by their entrance to university scores) on tests of academic subject matter compared to how they performed when not reminded of the stereotype (Steele, 1988; Steele & Aronson, 1995). Hence, explicitly foregrounding the generally low performance of minority groups prior to an educational assessment appears to be a good way to falsely reduce performance.

It could be argued that minority students adopt negative stances towards school, perhaps through a deliberate resistance to assimilation into the majority culture (Fordham & Ogbu, 1986), and this leads to poor academic performance. However, 'Otunuku and Brown (2007) found that Pasifika (immigrants to New Zealand from Pacific Island nations) and Māori (indigenous group of New Zealand) students had generally positive attitudes (i.e., liking and self-confidence) towards school subjects, but those attitudes had very little or no systematic relationship to achievement. They argued that the zero relationship may reflect the lack of realistic feedback as to where the students really were relative to expected standards, perhaps because these students were not given challenging work, or not given explicit feedback as to their standing. This result seems consistent with the double handicap of low achievement (Dunning, Heath, & Suls, 2004); these students were low performers but were not aware of this.

Responses of majority groups to minority groups

In addition to any potential bias in favour of majority groups in assessments themselves, minority groups may also be disadvantaged by belief systems that place responsibility for academic outcomes on differences that are treated as deficits or inadequacies within the minority group (e.g., minority homes and families lack the financial, cultural, or educational resources that are required to succeed at school and that is their own fault). Treating difference as a deficit is considered a racist causal attribution. Māori academics have taken offence at deficit theories used to explain poor Māori performance (e.g., Māori homes and families are poor and, thus, Māori students cannot learn). For example, the *Te Kotahitanga Project*, a researched teacher professional development project aimed at helping non-Māori teachers improve their teaching of Māori students, clearly showed that deficit theories were still held by practising teachers (Bishop & Berryman, 2006). It is worth noting that concern about systemic racism is not unique to Māori – the same concerns are raised around the world among indigenous and migrant communities.

46 *Peter J. Keegan et al.*

Bishop et al. (2003, 2007) have argued that the issue is not a lack of academic ability on the part of indigenous Māori students, but rather the interaction of beliefs, perceptions, and actions between Māori students and mostly white teachers. Their research has shown that Māori students believed that their non-Māori teachers thought Māori students lacked ability and motivation, and were dumb. In other words, the students thought the teachers were racists and believed their resistance to schooling was legitimated. Not surprisingly, non-Māori teachers were shocked to be told that their students considered their pedagogical styles and practices racist; by changing their communicative style and relationships with Māori students, improved Māori student achievement has been documented (Bishop, Berryman, Cavanagh, & Teddy, 2007).

Rather than blame the victim for low performance, minority groups may legitimately consider that the assessments, their interpretations, and their uses are at fault. These studies show that, in addition to the explanatory power of poverty, linguistic or cultural diversity, or colonization/migration, there are psychological factors that impact on school achievement. How the students understand and go about learning, how teachers and students relate to each other, and how teachers challenge and guide learning are all powerful factors in academic performance. The research indicates ways that teachers can engage with minority students so as to mitigate the impact of structural obstacles. Nevertheless, there remains the potential problem that the assessments themselves are to blame for academic underperformance of minority students. It certainly would be inappropriate to base educational decisions on assessment results, if it can be shown that the assessments themselves are inappropriate or invalid. Clearly, differences in opportunities to learn the material that is included in the assessment system make assessments advantageous to the group with the high-quality opportunities; and where these opportunities are less prevalent among minority students, then inferences about student performance are contaminated by differential resources (Stobart, 2005).

Psychometric responses to sociocultural critiques of assessment

From the perspective of any minority (cultural or individual), there are two threats to the validity of assessments: bias and sensitivity. Further, depending on the type of diversity evident among students, certain accommodations may be permitted that vary normal assessment practices, even at the classroom level.

Bias

There is reasonably widespread acceptance of the cultural test bias hypothesis in education, health, and psychological circles (Reynolds, 2000). This hypothesis states that systematic differences in mean score by groups of students from different sociocultural backgrounds indicate that the tests are inherently biased against one or more sociocultural groups. In contrast, the assessment industry defines bias in terms of the probability of one group (perhaps identified by race/ethnicity, sex, or socio-economic status) consistently underperforming relative to another group after individuals are matched for overall ability in the domain (Zumbo, 1999). If the two groups are matched for overall mathematics ability, but one group consistently scores lower on certain items or tasks, then those items can be considered biased. That is, there is something about one group that helps them perform better on those items other than their overall ability. Since test items are designed to be positively correlated with the overall score, doing well on an item, above and beyond what can be attributed to general ability in the subject, is indicative that some construct-irrelevant factor is at play. Note that bias is not the same as each group receiving the same mean score on a test (a phenomenon highly unlikely when groups have unequal access to educational resources); rather it means the probability of getting it right is higher for students who are members of one group over the other group for reasons other than their total ability in the construct or subject being assessed. Systematic bias in an assessment is awarding scores or determining ability fundamentally on a construct-irrelevant basis. Assessment results are meant to measure the construct to which they are aligned rather than some characteristic of the test-takers. A good assessment does not give students of equal overall ability systematically different scores that correspond to the sex, race, ethnicity, or sociocultural characteristics of the student. The amount of differential item functioning bias in high-quality standardized tests has been determined to be relatively small (i.e., up to 5% of variance in scores) (Reynolds, 2000).

A second approach is to consider the differential validity impact of an assessment by examining the proportion of people from different demographic groups who gain an important social consequence, such as being hired or awarded a scholarship (Biddle, 2005). While there are no iron-clad standards, a common convention is to declare a differential impact if the ratio of the minority group to the majority group success rate is less than 80%. Hence, if a test results in 10% of white students being qualified for gifted-and-talented classes and only 5% of Māori students who take the same test ($10 - 5 / 10 = 50\%$), then evidence of differential validity is present.

The lack of bias does not mean groups will automatically get the same scores; an unbiased test may still generate results in which one group outperforms the other. What this means is that the systematic difference for the two different groups of students is not caused by bias in the items but rather by differing degrees of ability, skill, or knowledge in the two groups. The source of those differences may be a function of sociocultural bias in the provision of educational resources in the school system (Stobart, 2005) rather than deficiencies of the test. Nevertheless, mathematical bias identification is beyond the means of the classroom teacher. Teachers need to ask, when considering using a published test, whether the developers have eliminated bias as a source of differential scores.

Sensitivity

In contrast, the insensitivity of items is a more transparent aspect of assessment since this involves making a judgement as to whether there is something inherent in the item that may disadvantage or advantage one group over another. An item is insensitive if one group has a higher probability of getting it correct than others based on some attribute external to what the item is actually supposed to be measuring. In other words, differential access to assessed knowledge can make a perfectly good assessment task insensitive. Insensitivity can come about because the task assumes knowledge about the universe that is more readily available to one cultural group than others, or because the item portrays sociocultural groups in stereotypical fashion. In other words, the items may cause offence. This is such a complex judgement that large-scale test developers generally rely on panels of experts to consider whether items or tasks might advantage or disadvantage some groups of people required to take the assessment.

For example, the question *"How many US Presidents have been assassinated?"* may be insensitive on two counts: (1) talking about death and assassination of national leaders may be seen as being inappropriate given the age or nationality of respondents, and (2) certain

48 *Peter J. Keegan et al.*

people, by consequence of their upbringing, not the quality of their history teaching, are likely to know this information. Insensitivity comes when invalid assumptions about the community being assessed are made. Often these are inadvertently caused by the assessment writer not being fully aware of how their own cultural, social, or religious assumptions impact on their item writing. Each item writer is situated within certain sets of assumptions that the test-takers may not have had equal access to. Without feedback, the task writer may not be conscious of this aspect of their writing and this applies equally to classroom teachers creating their own tasks, as well as large-scale test writers.

In determining sensitivity, the focus must be on what knowledge, other than what is actually intended to be assessed, might certain populations have that would enable them to answer the question and, thus, artificially increase their score. Commonly, that construct-irrelevant knowledge is more available to students in higher socio-economic status groups. Thus, the validity of interpretations based on such items is jeopardized by their insensitivity to unequal access to knowledge that would assist in answering the items. Needless to say, the more culturally embedded items are, the more likely all members of that society are to get the item right because of their access to that cultural knowledge. Hence, a pluralist approach, in which items are written within, by, and for a cultural group would seem to overcome sensitivity issues.

The process of handling insensitivity is a judgement process where panelists of different groups are consulted to ensure that the whole assessment represents all participants equally and is equally accessible to all community groups. This does not mean rejecting items simply because they contain reference to marked cultural artefacts (e.g., those associated typically with one sex, ethnicity, or language), but rather seeking to minimize the impact of construct-irrelevant information on higher scores. Thus, the following questions may be useful in considering whether any assessment is sufficiently sensitive.

Sensitivity checklist

1   Is all the material in each item or task part of what I have been teaching?
2   Will some students be able to get the item right through use of material that I have not taught but which they have from their different home experiences?
3   Will the content of the item cause offence to any group?
4   Have I portrayed any group in a stereotypical or offensive way (e.g., girls as weak and dumb, active participants as male, etc.)?

(Brown, Irving, & Keegan, 2008, p. 92)

Accommodations

In addition to evaluating tests themselves for bias and sensitivity, it is possible to adjust the conditions under which assessments are administered (e.g., additional time, the assistance of a reader/writer, provision of technological helps) so as to compensate for differences among individuals and between sociocultural groups. Accommodations involve making changes to normal assessment practices.

In Hong Kong, for example, there are set criteria against which students are evaluated before determining whether they are valid candidates for the Territory-wide System Assessments or for how students with learning disabilities being educated in the mainstream can be assessed (Brown & Ngan, 2010). The fundamental principle is that ethical assessment that can inform education requires that students are not held back from their best performance by some assessment aspect irrelevant to the construct being evaluated. It is fair and appropriate to make adjustments in the language, customization, or support offered to some students because of exceptional circumstances that would otherwise prevent their real ability coming to the fore. Not all of these accommodations for children with exceptional circumstances (e.g., gifted, intellectually or physically challenged) are implemented just because the students belong to different sociocultural groups.

Translation

An interesting accommodation, practised in just a few systems, is the provision of equivalent assessments in the language of minority groups (Padilla & Lindholm, 1995). Translation means determining the degree of academic performance of a student in their dominant language. Translation is not without its fishhooks. A valid criticism is the tendency to centre the translation on the language of the majority group (Werner & Campbell, 1973). If back-translation procedures are used to validate the translation, this will often result in a translated test that does not use a natural idiomatic, age-appropriate version of the target language. In some cases, the translation process from the dominant language to minority languages can make the assessments more difficult in the translated language than they were in the source language. For example, assessments translated from English into the Māori language were deemed inappropriate for Māori-medium schools because the register used in the translated version was set at Māori as first-language, adult standard rather than a more appropriate Māori as second-language learner, child/adolescent standard (May & Hill, 2008).

A case study in sociocultural assessment

The New Zealand population includes a large minority population of indigenous people (i.e., Māori) who have special rights in New Zealand law as first nations or tangata whenua (original inhabitants). Since the 1970s, Māori-medium schools (kura kaupapa Māori) and preschools (kōhanga reo) have been developed by Māori communities as a means of preserving and transmitting Māori culture and language to children who largely lived in English-speaking, urban communities with little connection to their historic traditions, customs, and values. In these schools, education was not just in Māori, but also done in what was considered a Māori way, emphasizing Māori cultural priorities and transmission of traditional Māori concepts. The vast majority of students in Māori-medium schooling and even a majority of their teachers have Māori as second language. Less than 10% of the Māori population are fluent speakers of te reo Māori (Māori language) and most are more than 65 years of age. Further, outside of schooling and Māori sacred rituals and sites, there are few opportunities or requirements to be literate or numerate in Māori. Nonetheless, New Zealand has taken a strong stand towards a pluralist educational system in which indigenous Māori have the choice of state-funded schooling in Māori.

Until the development of the Assessment Tools for Teaching and Learning (asTTle), there were no Māori-medium standardized literacy/numeracy assessments in New Zealand. In order to achieve this, a Māori test developer was hired (the first author), a team of Māori item writers was recruited, a series of hui (meetings) were held in the major tribal groups, high-status Māori sponsors were recruited, and extensive resources were allocated to develop Māori-medium school teachers who contributed to writing and reviewing items. These

50 *Peter J. Keegan et al.*

actions achieved acceptance, legitimacy, and benefit for the Māori community whose children were going to provide the data the test developers needed to create the test system.

Creating two versions of the same item for use in different languages and systems is extremely difficult. Consider the extensive development work in the international comparative studies carried out by the OECD PISA, the IEA's TIMSS, and the IAEA's PIRLS systems, which have large financial resources at their disposal to ensure equivalence between countries. In New Zealand, the National Education Monitoring Project (NEMP) made use of activities translated from English in its small-scale surveys of performance in kura kaupapa Māori. However, there were significant issues to do with the equivalence of task language and difficulty in the Māori versions compared to the English tasks (Pereira, 2001; Rau, 2008). In contrast, in the development of the New Zealand assessment system for pāngarau, pānui, and tuhituhi (i.e., mathematics, reading, and writing, respectively) for use in Māori-medium schooling contexts (Hattie et al., 2004), item development was done in Māori and was not dependent on the translation of English materials. From a psychometric point of view, equivalence between two items of the same subject in the one language is difficult to obtain; whereas equivalence across languages, societies, and cultures is much harder to attain (Keegan, Hattie, Brown, & Irving, 2006). As suggested by sociocultural critiques of assessment, translation would have implied that the English version was the standard against which the Māori curricula and performances should have been evaluated. This is simply inappropriate and so the Māori-medium assessments were developed independently in Māori, by Māori, for Māori. Throughout the development of the asTTle Māori-medium assessments, Māori educators were involved in initiating, legitimating, controlling, and designing the content and the reports for the benefit of Māori-medium communities. All the test materials were developed to measure the curriculum statements of te reo Māori (covering pānui and tuhituhi) and pāngarau. Hence, the pluralist approach was to keep the two systems independent of each other, despite covering the same year and curriculum level ranges.

The language difficulty of all Māori-medium materials was checked by experienced teachers of Māori-immersion students to ensure that the vocabulary was within the experience and expectations of second-language-learning Māori students. The materials were checked by panels of teachers around the nation and about half the students in all Māori-medium schools in Years 4 to 12 participated in the field trials and norming of the materials. Furthermore, Māori educationalists identified supplementary teaching materials related to learning needs as detected by the asTTle system.

In order to address the issue that most Māori-medium students are learners of Māori as a second language, and the rapid expansion of Māori vocabulary to cope with specialist registers, the asTTle tool provided additional resources to ensure that students performed at their best. For example, the software generates test-appropriate lists of less common (often technical) vocabulary and provides glossaries so that students and their teachers are adequately prepared. As a language, Māori has had to add or create many new words to deal with phenomena not previously encountered in traditional Māori society, especially in science, mathematics, and technology. Students and teachers may be fluent in te reo Māori, but they may use the English word in their conversation or when answering questions about these phenomena. Where those words are necessary in the asTTle assessment, a vocabulary guide is provided and the English word is provided as a possible correct answer in the answer guide.

The New Zealand English-medium mathematics and Māori-medium pāngarau curriculum statements expect students to think mathematically in the context of real-world situations. Thus, many problems and tasks are embedded in word problems. However, because

Māori students are language learners at the same time as being mathematics students, further accommodations were made. The pāngarau assessments are much less reading dependent than the counterpart assessments in English-medium mathematics. The Māori tasks foregrounded the mathematical computations rather than the linguistic context in which the mathematics was embedded. This was done to better cater for the largely second-language status of the students – their ability to do pāngarau was not so obscured by their ability to read in a second language. Analyses of the asTTle norming data for Māori-medium clearly show that students who speak some Māori at home and who enrol at an early age in the Māori-medium school system achieve more, reflecting the importance of language competence and opportunity as a predictor of academic success (Ministry of Education, 2006b, 2006c, 2006e).

Through embedding the asTTle assessment in the realities of Māori experience and priorities, the Ministry of Education has funded the development of a valid set of standardized assessments for literacy and numeracy in Māori. However, this does not address the needs of the vast majority of Māori students (approximately 85%) being educated in the English mainstream by largely Pākehā teachers. Without a doubt, average Māori student achievement in New Zealand schools is consistently behind that of their Pākehā counterparts. Analysis of the asTTle data seems to suggest the gap is equivalent to about two years of learning and persists across school deciles, though girls are somewhat more advanced than boys (Ministry of Education, 2006a, 2006d, 2006f). This discrepancy is reported consistently in all international surveys of educational achievement conducted in New Zealand and within New Zealand-based surveys. Teachers may be tempted to ignore the difference as a function of the inherent bias within the assessments being used to monitor achievement. However, it is our position that the data clearly point to a fundamental issue within schooling – Māori students do not do as well as might be expected and this is not a consequence of the assessments themselves. Indeed, we argue that the use of assessments to identify the discrepancy forces us to closely re-examine our beliefs and practices and seek changes in schooling. Nonetheless, without further professional learning around the nature of achievement and the role that diagnostic assessments can play in informing changed teaching practices, it is unlikely that the availability of high-quality assessments in and of themselves would be sufficient to change current practices. Certainly, assessments that serve improved teaching are necessary, but not sufficient; teachers do need other support to move towards more culturally responsive and effective teaching strategies, attitudes, and beliefs.

To recap, all assessments must be designed around the type of information required by the teacher, the student, and the parent in order to identify the learning successes and needs of the student. It is up to the classroom teacher to ensure that validity of interpretations and decisions is supported by careful design, administration, and scoring of assessments. Teachers, in collaboration with colleagues, can check their written assignments and tests for sensitivity. They can ensure that assessments align with their curriculum and are appropriately challenging for their students. The notions of constructive alignment between assessment, curriculum, and student and/or cultural responsiveness are key to the success of teaching and thus learning. Teachers can reject presuppositions and stereotypes that children of certain sociocultural backgrounds are fated to low achievement. Certainly one of the advantages of assessment information to teachers is that they can see that students should not be confused with groups – Māori students vary dramatically in learning and are most unlikely to perform similarly as a group. Teachers can analyze performance of their own assessments diagnostically so as to identify strengths and weaknesses of all students regardless of background, and to identify strengths and weaknesses of the success of their own teaching. They

52 Peter J. Keegan et al.

can seek advice and further professional training, especially around the educational, rather than rank ordering, use of assessments.

We have provided an example of a successful assessment system for Māori-medium education that was based on psychometric theories of validity and which was developed in a culturally responsive and sensitive manner. It is important that teachers of socioculturally different students are aware of sociocultural critiques of assessment and, perhaps more importantly, consider how their own beliefs, perceptions, and actions may hinder student achievement. At the same time, they need to know that high-quality assessment systems, which ought to include their own classroom and school-based assessments, can contribute to resolving differential achievement.

References

Awatere, D. (1974). *The development of ethnic awareness and ethnic attitudes in a sample of Auckland primary school children* (unpublished Master's thesis). University of Auckland, Auckland, NZ.

Biddle, D. (2005). *Adverse impact and test validation: A practitioner's guide to valid and defensible employment testing* (2nd ed.). Aldershot, UK: Ashgate.

Bishop, R., & Berryman, M. (2006). *Culture speaks: Cultural relationships and classroom learning.* Wellington, NZ: Huia.

Bishop, R., Berryman, M., Cavanagh, T., & Teddy, L. (2007). *Te Kotahitanga Phase 3: Establishing a culturally responsive pedagogy of relations in mainstream secondary school classrooms.* Wellington: Ministry of Education.

Bishop, R., Berryman, M., Tiakiwai, S., & Richardson, C. (2003). *Te Kotahitanga: The experiences of Year 9 and 10 Maori students in mainstream classrooms.* Hamilton, NZ: University of Waikato.

Bishop, R., & Glynn, T. (1999). *Culture counts: Changing power relations in education.* Palmerston North, NZ: Dunmore Press.

Bourdieu, P., & Passeron, J. C. (1977). *Reproduction in education society and culture* (R. Nice, Trans.). London-Beverly Hills: SAGE.

Brown, G. T. L., Irving, S. E., & Keegan, P. J. (2008). *An introduction to educational assessment, measurement, and evaluation: Improving the quality of teacher-based assessment* (2nd ed.). Auckland, NZ: Pearson Education NZ.

Brown, G. T. L., & Ngan, M. Y. (2010). *Contemporary educational assessment: Practices, principles, and policies.* Singapore: Pearson Education South Asia.

Chang, G. L., & Wells, G. (1988). The literate potential of collaborative talk. In M. MacLure, T. Phillips, & A. Wilkinson (Eds.), *Oracy Matters: The development of talking and listening in education* (pp. 95–109). Milton Keynes, UK: Open University Press.

Collier, V. P. (1989). How long? A synthesis of research on academic achievement in a second language. *TESOL Quarterly, 23*(3), 509–531.

Cummins, J. (1984). *Bilingualism and special education: Issues in assessment and pedagogy.* Clevedon, UK: Multilingual Matters.

Dunning, D., Heath, C., & Suls, J. M. (2004). Flawed self-assessment: Implications for health, education, and the workplace. *Psychological Science in the Public Interest, 5*(3), 69–106.

Ferdman, B. M. (1991). Literacy and cultural identity. In M. Minami & B. P. Kennedy (Eds.), *Language issues in literacy and bilingual/multicultural education* (pp. 347–371). Cambridge, MA: Harvard Educational Review.

Fordham, S., & Ogbu, J. U. (1986). Black students' school success: Coping with the burden of acting white. *The Urban Review, 18*, 176–206.

Gipps, C. (1999). Sociocultural aspects of assessment. *Review of Research in Education, 24*, 355–392. doi:10.3102/0091732X024001355

Hattie, J. A. C., Brown, G. T. L., Keegan, P. J., MacKay, A. J., Irving, S. E., Cutforth, S. . . . Yu, J.

(2004, December). *Assessment Tools for Teaching and Learning (asTTle) Manual* (Version 4, 2005). Wellington, NZ: University of Auckland/Ministry of Education/Learning Media.

Irvine, J. J., & York, D. E. (1995). Learning styles and culturally diverse students: A literature review. In J. A. Banks & C. A. M. Banks (Eds.), *Handbook of research on multicultural education* (pp. 484–497). New York: Macmillan.

Jones, A. (1991). *At school I've got a chance. Culture/privilege: Pacific Islands and Pakeha girls at school.* Palmerston North, NZ: Dunmore Press.

Keegan, P. J., Hattie, J. A., Brown, G. T. L., & Irving, S. E. (2006, July). *Developing and adapting test materials for Maori, the indigenous language of Aotearoa/New Zealand.* Paper presented at the 5th Annual Conference of the International Test Commission (ITC) Conference, Brussels, Belgium.

May, S., & Hill, R. (2008). Māori-medium education: Current issues and challenges. In N. H. Hornberger (Ed.), *Can schools save indigenous languages?* (pp. 66–98). New York: Palgrave.

Messick, S. (1989). Validity. In R. L. Linn (Ed.), *Educational measurement* (3rd ed., pp. 13–103). Old Tappan, NJ: MacMillan.

Ministry of Education. (2006a). *Achievement in mathematics: In focus.* Wellington, NZ: Research Division.

Ministry of Education. (2006b). *Achievement in pangarau: In focus.* Wellington, NZ: Research Division.

Ministry of Education. (2006c). *Achievement in panui: In focus.* Wellington, NZ: Research Division.

Ministry of Education. (2006d). *Achievement in reading: In focus.* Wellington, NZ: Research Division.

Ministry of Education. (2006e). *Achievement in tuhituhi: In focus.* Wellington, NZ: Research Division.

Ministry of Education. (2006f). *Achievement in writing: In focus.* Wellington, NZ: Research Division.

'Otunuku, M., & Brown, G. T. L. (2007). Tongan students' attitudes towards their subjects in New Zealand relative to their academic achievement. *Asia Pacific Education Review, 8*(1), 117–128. doi:10.1007/BF03025838

Padilla, A. M., & Lindholm, K. J. (1995). Quantitative educational research with ethnic minorities. In J. A. Banks & C. A. M. Banks (Eds.), *Handbook of research on multicultural education* (pp. 97–113). New York: Macmillan.

Pereira, J. A. (2001). *Culture, language and translation issues in educational assessment: Maori immersion students in the National Education Monitoring Project* (Master's thesis). University of Otago, Dunedin, NZ.

Rau, C. (2008). Assessment in indigenous language programmes. In E. Shohamy & N. H. Hornberger (Eds.), *Encyclopedia of language and education* (2nd ed., Vol. 7: Language Testing and Assessment, pp. 319–330). Boston, MA: Springer Science.

Reynolds, C. R. (2000). Why is psychometric research on bias in mental testing so often ignored? *Psychology, Public Policy, and Law, 6*(1), 144–150. doi:10.1037//1076-8971.6.1.14

Rogoff, B. (1991). The joint socialization of development by young children and adults. In P. Light, S. Sheldon, & M. Woodhead (Eds.), *Learning to think: Child development in social context 2* (pp. 67–96). London: Routledge.

Rogoff, B., Gauvain, M., & Ellis, S. (1991). Development viewed in its cultural context. In P. Light, S. Sheldon, & M. Woodhead (Eds.), *Learning to think: Child development in social context 2* (pp. 292–339). London: Routledge.

Steele, C. (1988). The psychology of self-affirmation: Sustaining the integrity of the self. In L. Berkowitz (Ed.), *Advances in experimental social psychology* (Vol. 21, pp. 261–302). New York: Academic Press.

Steele, C., & Aronson, J. (1995). Stereotype threat and the intellectual test performance of African-Americans. *Journal of Personality and Social Psychology, 67,* 797–811.

Stobart, G. (2005). Fairness in multicultural assessment systems. *Assessment in Education: Principles, Policy & Practice, 12*(3), 275–287. doi:10.1080/09695940500337249

54 *Peter J. Keegan et al.*

Sutton, R. (2001). Cultural equity issues in mass student testing. *Management in Education, 14,* 29. doi:10.1177/089202060001400111

Vygotsky, L. S. (1978). *Mind in society: The development of higher psychological processes* (M. Cole, V. John-Steiner, S. Scribner, & E. Souberman, eds.). Cambridge, MA: Harvard University Press.

Vygotsky, L. S. (1991). Genesis of the higher mental functions. In P. Light, S. Sheldon, & M. Woodhead (Eds.), *Learning to think: Child development in social context 2* (pp. 32–41). London: Routledge.

Werner, O., & Campbell, D. T. (1973). Translating, working through interpreters, and the problem of decentering. In R. Naroll & R. Cohen (Eds.), *A handbook of method in cultural anthropology* (pp. 398–420). New York: Columbia University Press.

Zumbo, B. D. (1999). *A handbook on the theory and methods of differential item functioning (DIF): Logistic regression modeling as a unitary framework for binary and Likert-type (ordinal) item scores.* Ottawa, ON: Directorate of Human Resources Research and Evaluation, Department of National Defense.

Part 3
Institutional plane

5 Classroom chronotopes privileged by contemporary educational policy
Teaching and learning in testing times

Peter D. Renshaw

Introduction

Sociocultural theory proposed by Vygotsky during his lifetime (1896–1934) focused predominantly on the cultural, tool-mediated nature of human thinking, particularly on the mediating role of speech and other semiotic systems that are deployed by members of a society to communicate their different viewpoints and construct understandings together. Vygotsky (1929) also considered the cultural and historical contexts within which people learn, and contrasted his view of the historically situated "cultural child" with the Piagetian notion of the universal "biological child" (Vygotsky, [1929] 1994). Vygotsky proposed the "cultural child" to foreground his conviction that mental capacities and forms of reasoning are made possible by specific socio-historical conditions of work and life. However, Vygotsky did not research in detail how socio-historical contexts might influence the development of thinking, but with Alexander Luria, he had begun to explore how the revolutionary social and economic changes occurring in the Soviet Union in the 1920s and 1930s were transforming the everyday life and work practices of people in various agrarian communities and, simultaneously, transforming their thinking. Luria later wrote about his discussions with Vygotsky on the socio-historical context of human thinking:

> It seems surprising that the science of psychology has avoided the idea that many mental processes are social and historical in origin, or that important manifestations of human consciousness have been directly shaped by the basic practices of human activity and the actual forms of culture.
>
> (Luria, 1976, p. 3)

In this chapter, the notion of socio-historical contexts is deployed to examine the nexus between current educational policies that rely on high-stakes testing of students, and concomitant changing patterns of classroom activity and curriculum emphases. Tests are assuming ever greater importance to policy makers as a means of tracking the quality of education systems within and between nations (Lingard, 2010). One question considered below, therefore, is why tests have become so central to education policy initiatives at this socio-historical moment. Another issue considered below is how the broad implementation of testing regimes is changing the kinds of learning outcomes and learner characteristics that are valued in schools. Robin Alexander (2010) recently reviewed evidence to show that high-stakes tests are a powerful influence on the allocation of time and curriculum resources in classrooms and tests reframe the kinds of learner attributes and aptitudes that are regarded as valuable.

58   *Peter D. Renshaw*

In order to theorize and analyze socio-historical contexts, I deploy in this chapter Mikhail Bakhtin's (1981, 1984) concept of *chronotope* – specific space–time configurations that are the grounds on which activity occurs, including activities in the classroom. *Chronotope* is being used by sociocultural researchers to study the learning cultures of classrooms (Leander, 2001; Mahiri, 2004; Renshaw, 2007), to analyze ideological assumptions inherent in current educational policy (Hirst & Vadeboncoeur, 2006), and to reveal the different assumptions made by researchers about the process of educational inquiry (Kamberelis & Dimitriadis, 2005).

Analyzing socio-historical contexts: The chronotope

Chronotope was devised by Bakhtin (1981, 1984) to analyze literary texts. Chronotopes within texts are the grounds on which authors build the common cultural sense and accepted local logics of different times/places. Chronotopes enable complex texts with their characters, plots, relationships, motives, and identities to be readily understood by the reading audience. Bakhtin (1981, pp. 243–250) considered a range of chronotopes, such as the following: (i) being on the road (a journey) and encountering another; (ii) routine predictable life in a provincial town; (iii) being on the threshold of a decision with its associated sense of crisis and a break in normal life; (iv) carnivals and holiday time; (v) the cycles of nature; (vi) the idyll of family life; (vii) peasant labor; and (viii) biography or a lifetime. Each of these chronotopes creates a different sense of time, from the slow and predictable passing of time for a peasant, or for community members in a provincial town, to the cyclical time of nature and the seasons, to exciting and unpredictable time at carnivals, to the leisurely time of holidays, or to the crisis time at the point of a life-changing decision. Each chronotope also conjures up a sense of the places within which activity unfolds, with a cast of possible characters and varying emotional tones underlying the activity. Carnivals and "decision points on the road" are emotionally charged chronotopes, whereas laboring as a peasant, or living the slow life in a provincial town, are emotionally understated chronotopes.

As Morson and Emerson (1990) note, "chronotopes are not so much visibly present in activity as they are the ground for activity" (p. 369). Analytically, chronotope draws attention to the temporal dimension of activities and the way that time is segmented, scheduled, and controlled. It draws attention to the pace of passing time, the span of time, and how past, present, and future activities are connected and represented by participants. It also draws attention to the spatial dimension of activities and how particular spaces are designed through the activities of participants. The concept of space is not to be understood as restricted to the actual layout of a physical space or the design of buildings. The chronotopic notion of space concerns how participants create relationships of proximity and distance, of formality and informality, of intimacy and indifference, of authority and deference, and how particular spaces are imbued with human intentions.

Classrooms, with their predictable, but not uniform, time schedules, spaces, furniture, artifacts, characters, and inherent goals and purposes are powerful and readily understood chronotopes. Every classroom is similar in many respects, yet there are subtle and significant variations in the construction of times/spaces and in the associated possibilities for learning, relationships, and identities. By applying chronotope to the analysis of classrooms at different historical moments, consideration is directed at the taken-for-granted time/space through which particular educational policies, practices, and student identities were made possible.

Chronotope is not just background or passive context in which classroom activity occurs, but is active in forming the kinds of characters (teachers and students) and ideologies on which understanding and meaning-making are constructed. This chapter describes only the dominant classroom chronotopes at different historical moments and necessarily has to foreground only the main direction of educational policy and the classroom practices that were privileged within the policy frame. This approach downplays the complexity of specific classrooms where multiple chronotopes are evoked in the interaction between the teacher and students and compete for privilege. For example, a classroom may be organized as a community of learners where collaboration is valued, yet at certain times, when mandated national testing occurs, it may resemble a competitive marketplace between autonomous individuals where collaboration is regarded as cheating. This micro-analytical approach is an important complement to the broader analytical approach offered in this chapter.

Diverse chronotopes of the classroom

In a previous paper (Renshaw, 2003), I outlined four versions of learning in the classroom that were proposed at various times in the twentieth century, each version grounded on a distinctive theory of learning, as well as a configuration of assumptions about the qualities of effective learners and workers for the requirements of the social and economic system at that time. These historical moments, and the shift from one moment to the next, were not primarily based on scientific discoveries about the process of learning per se, but on aligning the requirements of the economic system with systems of schooling and the production of learners and citizens who had the requisite attributes for the times. In other words, learning in the classroom at different historical periods was based on the formation of privileged classroom chronotopes that reflected assumptions about learning per se, as well as assumptions about the workplace, the future life-worlds of the students, and the kinds of citizens envisaged within shifting economic, political, and ideological fields. This brief historical overview of differing chronotopes deepens our understanding of how classrooms are grounded in different configurations of assumptions about, and synchronies between, learning, society, citizenship, and the economy, and it provides insights into how we have reached the present moment of educational policy where classrooms have been framed as testing times/places within a competitive market approach to education.

The relationship between these historically shifting classroom chronotopes and particular actual classrooms in different locations and times is complex, and from Bakhtin's theoretical perspective should be regarded as an ongoing dialogic process between actual and possible classrooms. At every time period, from the late nineteenth century to the twenty-first century, classrooms can be readily identified as similar, with certain core features conserved, such as the distinctive roles of teachers and students, segmented time allocation to learning tasks and curriculum topics, and specific space configurations and furniture for learning to occur. So, the chronotopes described below should be understood as possibilities for change and as options available for promotion by policy makers and for appropriation by practitioners. The embodied practices of teachers and students in classrooms are grounded on an interaction between competing and hybridized chronotopes in specific places. In this chapter, I am not addressing this complex and detailed dialogic process but rather simply sketching the emergence of a range of alternative classroom chronotopes that were produced at different times. For each chronotope, I describe the learning theory that found favor with a sympathetic audience of policy makers and practitioners at that time, and the typical conditions of workplaces, and the kinds of schooling that were promoted as necessary for social and economic progress to be made. Particular attention is given to the way time and space was managed in the organization of classrooms at that time.

Chronotope 1: Classrooms as factory time/spaces

In the early decades of the twentieth century, the scientific study of learning was based on positivist philosophical assumptions and the methodologies and experimental techniques devised by behaviorists to demonstrate various forms of conditioning in animals and humans. Zygmunt Bauman (2001) wondered why nobody much objected to the suggestion that learning for rats-in-mazes was equivalent in principle to learning for humans. Bauman suggested it was because: "The behaviourists' laboratory setting was so strikingly similar to the human predicament as visualized at the time. . . . The contrived plight of the rats-in-a-maze seemed a faithful laboratory replica of the daily predicament of humans-in-the-world" (p. 44).

Work in factory production lines and learning in classrooms were characterized by external constraints and authority regimes, and by extrinsic rewards for the timely completion of assignments and tasks. Workers and students were tracked into hierarchically arranged social roles and opportunities, where development of skills and knowledge (at work and school) was limited by social position, and where attitudes of dogged persistence and compliance with time on task, rather than interest or enthusiasm, characterized engagement in activities. This "bundy-clock" sense of contingent time was entirely compatible with the image of the learner (rat and human) provided by behaviorists. This classroom chronotope was based on inflexibly organized spaces with fixed hierarchical and distal relationships between teachers and learners, and highly regimented and segmented time schedules that defined exactly when activities began and ended.

Chronotope 2: Classrooms as individualistic, inventive time/spaces

By the late 1960s, behaviorist learning theories were being reconsidered and challenged by constructivist ideas drawn from Piaget, Kohlberg, and Bruner. The research focus shifted from determining whether the learner would comply with regimes of external rewards and punishments, to observing, cataloguing, and celebrating their constructive insights and discoveries, and responding to their needs. This shift coincided with the race for technological superiority between East (Soviet bloc) and West (USA and allies), and the associated rekindled interest in scientific inquiry and advancement. Central to this ideological and political project was the production of creative thinkers, both learners and workers, who could be inventive and constructive contributors to scientific discoveries. Jerome Bruner, for example, promoted the notion of discovery learning that relegated adults and teachers to a secondary role in the educational process (Bruner, 1961). Likewise, Piaget was suspicious of external and adult influence on children's learning – he attached primary importance to the constructive activity of individuals. These ideas were influential in supporting the proponents of the open classroom, where learner-guided activities predominated and where teachers became diagnostic observers and facilitators of classroom activities. Based on their observations, teachers were expected to design experiences that could support further learner engagement. The prominence given to personal insights, to creative and constructive thinking and to the fulfillment of personal needs, at this time, was entirely consistent with constructivist theory.

The classroom chronotope of this time, therefore, was grounded on quite flexible time allocation to tasks, since it was based on following up learner interest and enabling intrinsic motivation. Space was designed to be more flexible and open to myriad adjustments related to learner-initiated activities. Space became negotiable and flexible as a way of supporting a more conversational, informal, and egalitarian set of relationships between teachers and students.

Contemporary educational policy 61

Chronotope 3: Classrooms as self-regulated time/spaces

In the following decades, the ideal of the constructive inventive and creative learner shifted to privileging a more self-monitoring and self-regulating learner who had internalized external forms of control. It coincided with a change in political direction in Australia, as well as in the UK and USA, where political conservatives were elected in the late 1970s and early 1980s. The ideal of the self-regulated learner coincided with a different workplace imperative, characterized by the increasing competitiveness of the open market, the privatization of previously publicly run enterprises, and the outsourcing of functions in large bureaucracies. External control and monitoring of workers were less necessary. Middle management was offered redundancy, as the key roles of monitoring and organizing workers, and was devolved to workers themselves. Their performances could now be regulated within the constraints of competitiveness. The ideal worker and the ideal learner were conceived as self-guiding, self-regulating, and self-responsible individuals within a competitive marketplace – the epitome of the neo-liberal citizen. Likewise, the ideal school was the "self-managing" school, led by a principal whose key skills were seen as those of a business executive rather than a member of a professional community of teachers. It is not just chance that learning theorists became fascinated with self-regulated learning during this period. There was a configuration of economic, political, and policy factors that privileged this theorization of learning.

In summary, the self-regulated classroom chronotope assumed that time should not be wasted but its regulation was to be managed by learners who had internalized strategies (scaffolded by teachers) that enabled them to be self-monitoring and self-regulating. Likewise, space could be re-organized and flexibly designed as long as it enabled effective engagement in learning and did not lead to time-wasting. Inefficiency and ineffectiveness could be addressed through more general accountability systems, such as audits. This chronotope placed heightened value on processes of internalization so the spatial order and timeliness of activity in the classroom appeared to occur without overt imposition of authority from the teacher. The emotional tone and relationships between teachers and students were reflective, cordial, and neutral, rather than close and intense. It was a space governed by quiet self-control, rather than active interest or explicit authority.

Chronotope 4: Classrooms as relational time/spaces

At about the same time as learning theory was taking the "meta-turn" outlined above, it was also beginning to be influenced by the "relational turn" based on notions of community (Lave & Wenger, 1991) and the associated notion of a classroom community of learners developed by Ann Brown, and others, in the 1980s and 1990s (Brown & Campione, 1994). Why did the notion of community and relational learning become privileged at that time? One answer is provided by Gee, Hull, and Lankshear (1996), who analyzed the way key concepts from sociocultural learning theory were appropriated by the business community to promote new regimes of work and new types of workers. They characterized the economic changes occurring then as "new fast capitalism", where enterprises were being established on a smaller scale, producing specialist goods for niche markets, using high-tech processes that engage workers in highly interdependent production teams. For such workplaces, the ideal worker required certain dispositions, skills, and knowledge, such as being a team player, ready to share their expertise in a distributed system, committed to joint projects but flexible and adaptive, and motivated by team success. In their monograph, *New Learning*, the Australian Council of Deans of Education (2001) echoed Gee et al. (1996) by suggesting

62   *Peter D. Renshaw*

that new economic imperatives and workplaces demand new types of learning, new forms of citizenship, and new identities for learners. The Deans wrote:

> The new economy requires new persons: persons who can work flexibly with changing technologies; persons who can work effectively in the new relationship-focussed commercial environment; and people who are able to work within an open organisational culture and across diverse cultural settings.
>
> (Australian Council of Deans of Education, 2001, p. 33)

The kinds of classrooms that were seen as compatible with the new economy resembled the ideal promoted under the banner of a community of learners. As I (Renshaw, 2007) proposed elsewhere, the relational approach to learning at schools provides a stark contrast for policy makers to consider at the current time when learning in schools is being framed as the attainment of marketable expertise and tradable skills in an increasingly globalized system of work and production.

In summary, within Chronotope 4, classroom time is assigned to enable productive relationships to be formed and reformed around learning activities. Space is also flexibly formed around community-related activities and the specific requirements of those activities, taking into consideration the number of participants, the learning processes in play, and the tools being deployed. Relationships between the members of these classrooms are close (proximal rather than distal) but task-oriented, rather than playful and informal. Close relationships are valued as a means to the goal of the development of expertise.

Chronotope 5: Classrooms as trading time/spaces

Hirst and Vadeboncoeur (2006) identified the current moment as grounded on a chronotope of economic rationalism and managerialism, where classrooms are created as trading places and learning is treated as a commodity. The chronotope of the classroom as a trading place treats the attainment of specific learning outcomes for students as commodities to be acquired and represented in a portfolio of achievements that can be bartered in the future for other commodities and for access to the labor market. Teachers' work is managed through the detailed regulation of curriculum content, the allocation of time to privileged content areas, and accountability measured through specific assessment tasks and tests. Teachers are provided with resources, curriculum frameworks, and guides in order to make their work "more manageable" but the push for efficiency and production of better student outcomes means that teachers have little time to complete day-to-day work and engage in professional relationships with either their colleagues or the community. For students who are learning at school within the trading chronotope, the emphasis is on their future role in the economic life of society. At the core of new managerialism is a similar emphasis on regulating young people as they are diverted into particular economic roles, with more systems and measures for accounting and monitoring (Hirst & Vadeboncoeur, 2006).

Testing times and classrooms: Case study of Queensland

The increasing power of tests to determine classroom learning activities can be exemplified vividly by considering the recent history of educational policy in Queensland. The classroom chronotope for this moment in Queensland history can be described as Testing Times/

Spaces. It is a variation of Chronotope 5 Trading Times/Spaces, and reflects an intensification of the policy discourses of teacher accountability and testing. These discourses are having a profound effect on the classroom practices of teachers and how they are adapting in order to maintain their reputations and positive professional identities. In a recent address in Australia, Robin Alexander (2010) reflected on his report (Cambridge Primary Review) to the British Government:

> Of all the so-called "levers" of systemic reform, tests seem to be the instrument of choice in policy-makers' efforts to do the two things which they believe they must always be seen to do: raise educational standards and call teachers and schools to account. This means that tests are high stakes not just for children and teachers but also for politicians, and that they may be as much about political capital as educational progress.
>
> (p. 1)

Alexander (2010) criticized the influence of the educational testing culture and its distorting effect on the curriculum. In the Cambridge Primary Review (Alexander, 2009), he argued that children were receiving an education that was "fundamentally deficient". Part of the deficiency arises from the distorting effects of tests on the curriculum. Testing distorts the allocation of classroom time and influences teachers to focus too intensely on those limited aspects of the curriculum that are tested. Alexander and his colleagues found that 10 and 11-year-olds were spending around half their time in the classroom studying English and mathematics and this emphasis had "squeezed out" other subjects from the curriculum. They recommended that the English and mathematics tests be abandoned and that league tables of schools comparing performance on these tests be axed as well. Similarly, a study by the Centre on Education Policy (McMurrer, 2008) showed that since 2001, when *No Child Left Behind* policies were introduced in the USA to require more testing and reporting for reading and mathematics, average class time allocated to reading increased by 47% and for mathematics by 37%. In contrast, time on science, art, music, social studies, and physical education was cut by an average of two and a half hours per week. Time for play and peer interaction at recess was cut by nearly 30%. In terms of cognitive processes, testing regimes also lead teachers to value memorization and recall over deeper understanding and inquiry. The later types of higher-level cognition are regarded as quite time-consuming to enhance and therefore as an inefficient teaching focus for raising test scores when accountability is required in the immediate future rather than in the longer-term overall development of students.

In Australia, national testing for literacy and numeracy in Years 3, 5, 7, and 9 was introduced in 2007 and since then these tests have become high stakes in the terms described by Robin Alexander above. The National Assessment Program – Literacy and Numeracy (NAPLAN) scores of each state and territory are compared in the media annually and there have been quite significant consequences from this comparative process for the direction of educational policies and the work of teachers in schools. For example, in Queensland, following the NAPLAN results of 2007 and the negative media attention to the apparently poor performance of students in Queensland, the Masters Report (Masters, 2009) was commissioned and recommended a range of initiatives to assist Queenslanders to perform better on the NAPLAN tests. At that time, there was a large turn-over of senior administrative staff in Education Queensland and a new leadership team was appointed to implement the recommendations of the Masters Report. Many of the senior officers in the bureaucracy were personally held accountable for the apparent failure of the Queensland education system to prepare students adequately for the basic tests of literacy and numeracy. In particular, a

64   *Peter D. Renshaw*

range of established classroom and assessment practices were questioned. These are explored further below, beginning with the questioning of progressive and moderated assessment that had characterized the system in Queensland since the 1970s.

Queensland had established in 1971 a moderated and scaled teacher-based assessment system for describing the performance of graduating Year 12 students. This progressive assessment approach has been lauded internationally (Maxwell & Cumming, 2011), yet it was recast as problematic following NAPLAN results in 2007. Queensland students were now viewed as lacking test-taking expertise and *nous*, so in preparing for NAPLAN testing in 2008, and thereafter, teachers were advised to teach their students how to be strategic test-takers. Students were encouraged to be serious, to concentrate and try hard in the test situation, and to attempt all questions. Teaching for test-taking became part of the mandated approach in Queensland classrooms.

Game-playing strategies to improve test results were also reported across the states as accountability pressures mounted on principals and teachers to ensure that students improved their NAPLAN results from the previous year. Cobbald (2010) summarized a number of these strategies, including the exclusion of low-performing students from the tests, providing help and assistance to students during the tests, and leaking of test questions to some teachers and schools.

New categories of students were constructed in the light of the NAPLAN distributions of relative performance. In addition to considering who might be excluded entirely from the tests, in the lead-up to the annual NAPLAN tests, teachers were advised to concentrate on those students most likely to show improvement rather than on those students whose performance was far below average and who would require sustained and long-term support to develop their numeracy and literacy skills. NAPLAN has segmented and concentrated time, with intense teaching to the test and certain students, occurring from term one (February to April). The temporal dimension of the NAPLAN classroom has become shortened and focused rather than long-term and developmental. From these considerations, specific types of NAPLAN-framed students emerge: (i) students who should be excluded if possible from the tests; (ii) students on the cusp of improvement who are worth the investment of teaching time; and (iii) students mired in poor performance for whom time investment is unlikely to yield a NAPLAN dividend. Time becomes *capital* to be differentially invested depending on the likely NAPLAN outcome.

In summary, a Testing Classroom Chronotope has been forged in the past five years as NAPLAN annual testing and the associated comparison of performance within and between schools has become engrained practice in Queensland and across Australia. Testing has redefined the temporal dimension of classroom activities. Those curriculum areas and skills associated with the annual tests are now receiving more attention, and so too are specific students who are seen to be worth the investment of quality teaching time. Students who require too much time are being placated rather than given intensive support, and those likely to depress overall performance scores are being invited to absent themselves strategically. This is the kind of oppressive performativity identified by Ball (2008) as undermining the authenticity of teachers' professional work in the current era.

Different temporal cycles for politics/policy, media, and educational processes

Timing – the intersection of different temporal cycles related to the field of politics and policy, to the field of educational practices, and to the world of the media – is crucial in understanding why certain educational policies were devised and implemented. The political cycle hinges on an election every three to four years, and this provides the context for a rapidly churning policy agenda with the need for quick results, for averting crises, and for positive performance to be demonstrated. Politicians and their policy advisors occupy a crisis time/space where decisions and actions need to be initiated quickly and followed through in relatively short periods of time regardless of the ambiguity and uncertainty surrounding the evidence for, or efficacy of, their plans.

The media cycle for any particular event or issue has limited temporal currency, varying from the typical norm of a day of media interest and fame, to (in rare cases) a week of coverage, to (only with regard to major historical events) a month or more of regular media coverage. With regard to NAPLAN testing, the media cycle is now predictable if short-lived. Annually, as the NAPLAN results are reported for each state and territory, and regardless of actual performance or outcomes, the coverage is couched in terms of crisis and risk. Outcomes for top-performing states and territories are interrogated to reveal negative trends or plateaus in performance. Performance of other lower-ranked states and territories is negatively evaluated even if they show improvement because their relative ranking compared to others remains unchanged. The requirement for a media angle to grab the attention of the public heightens the likelihood that results will reinforce a sense of crisis and negativity, which in turn engenders the conditions for unremitting anxiety in practitioners as they strive to maintain or improve performance.

In contrast to the policy/political cycle of 3–4 years, and the media cycle of a few days to a few months, the reform of educational practices cycles according to a much longer time frame. I suggest that a reasonable temporal cycle to evaluate the qualities of an educational system is about 10 years, or the time it takes for a cohort of students to graduate through the system from their foundation year to their graduation. What is happening with the annual review of the quality of educational systems by comparing NAPLAN results is an instance of Goodhart's law, where the intention to determine quality by using certain measures loses authenticity and validity because the measure itself has become the target rather than an indicator of underlying features of the qualities of the system. When the measure becomes the target, those at risk, be they politicians, bureaucrats, teachers, or students, will mobilize resources to avoid appearing to fail.

The highly significant intersection of these different temporal cycles can be seen at the moment that the initial national NAPLAN results were reported in late 2007. They were treated as an educational disaster by the Queensland Government and the Director of the Australian Council for Education Research (ACER), Geoff Masters, was commissioned to provide a report on how the situation should be addressed. His report was commissioned just prior to the state election in March 2008. The coincidence of the timing of the NAPLAN test results and the state election was crucial in the way educational policy subsequently was framed. The Premier, Anna Bligh, oversaw the implementation of the Masters Report and personally engaged in some stakeholder meetings and consultations. This high-level political management reveals how the NAPLAN tests themselves became powerful political forces that could not be ignored with an election looming.

The temporal dimension entered also as part of a historical narrative regarding schooling in Queensland. Masters referenced Rosier (1980) to suggest that Queensland had outperformed all the other states in one of the initial international testing programs. He used this information to suggest that standards had fallen over time and this powerful and nostalgic story was taken up by senior bureaucrats to position current teachers and teacher educators as failing to maintain the high quality of Queensland schools. However, this historical

66 Peter D. Renshaw

narrative is misleading. It is based on a lack of attention to the way sampling was conducted in the 1970s for the test and the contrasting way sampling was conducted for NAPLAN in 2007. In the 1970s, the students to be tested were sampled on their age (14-year-olds), not on their grade of schooling. In Queensland, students at equivalent ages to the other states were one year advanced in terms of their grade level. So when the students were tested in the 1970s, the Queensland students were on average one grade-level advanced compared to their interstate peers. This gave them an advantage in terms of covering more advanced topics in the curriculum and being able to attempt more difficult test items. In 2007, for NAPLAN, the exact opposite sampling procedure was implemented. Students were sampled on the basis of grade level, and this meant that at each of the NAPLAN grade levels (3, 5, 7, 9) Queensland students were younger and had fewer years of schooling, since there had been no compulsory "prep" year in Queensland.

The different demographic characteristics of the Queensland population were also down-played in interpreting the NAPLAN results, but such non-school factors are crucial in understanding the results. Compared to states that performed well on NAPLAN, such as New South Wales, Australian Capital Territory, and Victoria, Queensland has more of its population in regional, rural, and remote locations, it has a higher percentage of low socio-economic status families, and it has more indigenous students. The students taking the tests were also slightly younger and had one year less of schooling. However, these facts, and their clear implications for understanding the national pattern of NAPLAN results, did not prevent a major change in policy and significant changes in how classroom time was allocated and what activities were mandated. I suggest that this contradiction arises because of the differential temporal cycles that govern policy, the media, and educational processes

Alternative narratives and classroom chronotopes

There are alternative narratives to that of poor performance and decline noted above. The first alternative actually arises from looking at change in the Program for International Student Assessment (PISA) scores for Queensland students compared to other states in the period 2000–2009. As Figure 5.1 shows, in the 2009 PISA results, Queensland students performed better than other states except for Western Australia and the ACT. When change from 2000 to 2009 is considered (see Figure 5.2), then Queensland performed better than any other state, notably in improved science scores but also in reading and mathematics. This is a remarkable set of data that runs entirely counter to the narrative of historical decline and poor performance. The question for policy decision makers is to consider the kinds of initiatives that were put in place during this 10-year period. Interestingly, it was a time of significant innovation in Queensland education when the "New Basics" project was launched and Education Queensland adopted a new approach to pedagogy, namely Productive Pedagogies, and a new approach to assessing the complex knowledge and skills that students were developing, namely Rich Tasks. The classroom chronotope most compatible with this reform agenda is the relational chronotope (Chronotope 4), where classrooms are constructed as spaces for developing deeper understanding and higher-level knowledge through collaboration with peers and teachers, and where students are supported to engage in authentic complex learning tasks that have significance for their future lives as active citizens.

The PISA results have had no discernible impact on policy or practice. There has been no celebration of the "New Basics" project or attempt to evaluate why Queensland might have performed so positively during the 2000–2009 period. Rather, the testing chronotope

Contemporary educational policy 67

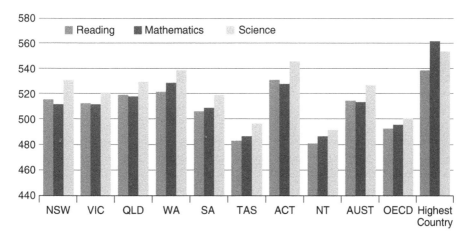

Figure 5.1 PISA mean scores for 15-year-old students in mathematics, reading, and science for Australian states and territories compared to QECD average and the highest country

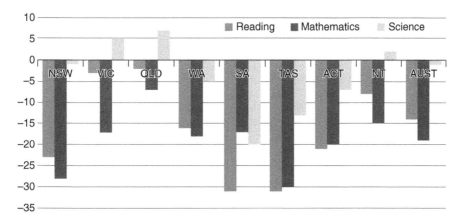

Figure 5.2 Change in PISA mean scores for 15-year-old students from 2000 to 2009 for Australian states and territories

continues to frame the direction of classroom activities and direct the attention of teachers to teaching to the test, avoiding failure and public shaming.

Another alternative arises from considering how schools and teachers might respond more proactively to the demands (that seem relentless in the current era) for more testing and accountability. Schooling is about much more than enhancing test results, and a myopic concern with tests produces a sparse and reductive educational experience. Making schooling a richer experience for all students will indirectly enhance test results, while a reductive focus on test results will reduce even further the benefits that the most at-risk students gain from schooling, both academically and socially (Rose, 1995). Alternative rich forms of accountability are concerned with a broader range of educational purposes that capture the real achievements of students and schools, as well as reveal options for improving outcomes for students. Rich accountabilities focus on how schools relate to students and their

68   *Peter D. Renshaw*

communities in multi-faceted ways over time, and how they enable students to extend their repertoires of practice and learning resources in productive ways for their futures. The notion of rich accountabilities builds on the sociocultural pedagogy of Luis Moll (Moll, 1990; Moll, Amanti, Neffe, & Gonzales, 1992), whose scholarship has been focused on developing classroom teaching strategies that extend and build upon students' funds of knowledge and create bridges between students' life-worlds and the more abstract and generalized knowledge incorporated in curriculum frameworks. This alternative approach to accountability also adopts Moll's ethnographic methods and ethic of being interested in and open to researching the diverse resources that students might have access to in their communities. In many communities, the resources students bring to school are seen as deficient and problematic, rather than as the foundations for future learning. The ethnographic spirit and values inherent in Moll's approach challenges this deficit assumption and asks that teachers enter into a period of respectful inquiry to really understand the life-worlds of their students and build connections and bridges that are likely to be productive and expansive in students' future lives. The chronotope emerging here is richly hybridized, involving, as it does, a dialogue between policy makers, curriculum designers, teachers and students in schools, and their communities. It involves breaking away from engrained distinctions and established boundaries between these fields of activity (policy, curriculum design, pedagogy, and community engagement) in order to create a new classroom chronotope that is open and richly accountable to its stakeholders at all levels.

References

Alexander, R. J. (2009) (Ed.). *Children, their world, their education: Final report and recommendations of the Cambridge Primary Review*. Abingdon, UK: Routledge.

Alexander, R. J. (2010). *The perils of policy: Success, amnesia and collateral damage in systemic educational reform*. Miegunyah Distinguished Visiting Fellowship Program Public Lecture, 10th March (www.primaryreview.org.uk/downloads/Alexander_Miegunyah_lecture_FINAL.pdf).

Australian Council of Deans of Education (2001). *New learning: A charter for Australian education*. Canberra: Australian Council of Deans of Education.

Bakhtin, M. M. (1981). *The dialogic imagination: Four essays* (M. Holquist, Ed.; C. Emerson & M. Holquist, Trans.). Austin: University of Texas Press.

Bakhtin, M. (1984). *Rabelais and his world* (H. Iswolsky, Trans.). Bloomington: Indiana University Press.

Ball, S. J. (2008). *The education debate*. Bristol, UK: Policy Press.

Bauman, Z. (2001). *Community: Seeking safety in an insecure world*. Cambridge, UK: Polity Press.

Brown, A., & Campione, J. (1994). Guided discovery in a community of learners. In A. Brown, J. Campione, & K. McGilly (Eds.), *Classroom lessons: Integrating cognitive theory and classroom practice* (pp. 229–270). Cambridge, MA: MIT Press.

Bruner, J. (1961). The act of discovery. *Harvard Educational Review, 31*, 21–32.

Cobbald, T. (2010). *Rorting and cheating of school results is the future under My School*, Save Our Schools Education Policy Brief (www.saveourschools.com.au/file_download/40).

Gee, J., Hull, G., & Lankshear, C. (1996). *The new work order: Behind the language of the new capitalism*. St. Leonards, NSW: Allen & Unwin.

Hirst, E., & Vadeboncoeur, J. A. (2006). Patrolling the borders of otherness: Dis/placed identity positions for teachers and students in schooled spaces. *Mind, Culture and Activity, 13*(3), 205–227.

Kamberelis, G., & Dimitriadis, G. (2005). *Qualitative inquiry: Approaches to language and literacy research*. New York: Teachers College Press.

Lave, J. & Wenger, E. (1991) *Situated learning: Legitimate peripheral participation*. Cambridge, UK: Cambridge University Press.

Leander, K. M. (2001). This is our freedom bus going home right now: Producing and hybridizing space–time contexts in pedagogical discourse. *Journal of Literacy Research, 33*(4), 637–679.

Lingard, B. (2010). Policy borrowing, policy learning: Testing times in Australian schooling. *Critical Studies in Education, 51*(2), 129–147.

Luria, A. R. (1976). *Cognitive development: Its cultural and social foundations* (M. Cole, Ed.; M. Lopez-Morillas & L. Solotaroff, Trans.). Cambridge, MA: Harvard University Press.

Mahiri, J. (2004). New teachers for new times: The dialogical principle in teaching and learning electronically. In A. F. Ball & S. W. Freedman (Eds.), *Bakhtinian perspectives on language literacy and learning* (pp. 213–231). Cambridge, UK: Cambridge University Press.

Masters, G. (2009). *A shared challenge: Improving literacy numeracy and science learning in Queensland primary schools*. Melbourne: Australian Council for Educational Research.

Maxwell, G. S. & Cumming, J. J. (2011). Managing without public examinations: Successful and sustained curriculum and assessment reform in Queensland. In L. Yates, C. Collins, & K. O'Connor (Eds.), *Australia's curriculum dilemmas: State perspectives and changing times* (pp. 202–222). Melbourne: Melbourne University Press.

McMurrer, J. (2008). *NCLB Year 5: Instructional time in elementary schools: A closer look at changes for specific subjects*. Washington, DC: Center on Education Policy (www.cep-dc.org).

Moll, L. (1990) (Ed.) *Vygotsky and education: Instructional implications and applications of sociohistorical psychology*. New York: Cambridge University Press.

Moll, L., Amanti, C., Neffe, C., & Gonzales, N. (1992) Funds of knowledge for teaching: Using a qualitative approach to connect homes and classrooms. *Theory into Practice, 32*(2), 132–141.

Morson, G. S., & Emerson, C. (1990). *Mikhail Bakhtin: Creation of prosaics*. Stanford, CA: Stanford University Press.

Renshaw, P. (2003). Community and learning: Contradictions dilemmas and prospects. *Discourse Studies in the Cultural Politics of Education, 24*(3), 355–370.

Renshaw, P. (2007). A commentary on the chronotopes of different 'cultures of learning': Transforming classrooms from trading-places into relational-places of learning. *International Journal of Educational Research, 46*, 240–245.

Rose, M. (1995). *Possible lives: The promise of public education in America*. New York: Penguin.

Rosier, M. J. (1980). *Changes in secondary school mathematics in Australia, 1964–1978*. Melbourne: ACER.

Vygotsky, L.S. (1994 [1929]). The problem of the cultural development of the child. In R. van der Veer & J. Valsiner (Eds.), *The Vygotsky Reader* (pp. 57–72). Oxford, UK.: Blackwell. Originally published in 1929 in *Journal of Genetic Psychology, 36*, 415–432.

6 Teacher self-efficacy
Internalized understandings of competence

Janet Draper

Introduction

Teachers are understood to be key shapers of the social context in which students learn, and key sources of guidance and support for student learning. They are commonly regarded as critical to academic achievement, with teacher quality, although sometimes ill- or variously defined, regularly pinpointed as the most influential factor in student learning. This chapter explores an area which is somewhat different from the other chapters in this book in that it focuses on the *teacher* as learner in the social context of working in schools and classrooms, on the development of teachers' cognitions about their competence as teachers and on the links between those cognitions, teacher behaviors and professional actions and student achievement.

Student behavior as well as peer support and the impact of major reforms will also be considered as factors in teachers' social learning contexts which contribute to perceptions of competence.

The sociocultural perspective

Vygotsky's sociocultural perspective leads us to consider the social contexts in which learners learn and the interactions which underpin learning as the main vehicles for learning. A key feature of sociocultural theory is that higher-order capacities derive from social interaction and that, within that social interaction, learning is supported by guidance from more experienced others. Applying sociocultural thinking to teachers' own learning and professional development will therefore require an exploration of the social context in which teachers develop their professional practice and a consideration of the guidance and support which is critical to their acquisition of new behaviors and cognitions. Vygotsky argues that all cognitions effectively occur twice, initially in interaction and then becoming internalized (Vygotsky, 1978). Once internalized, they act as mediators influencing behavioral choices. Competent behavior, seen to have successful outcomes, will contribute to an internalized belief in competence.

Vygotsky (1978) also proposes that, beyond the area of current development where the learner can operate independently, there exists a zone of proximal development (ZPD), the area of potential development within which the learner can cope when aided by others and with which over time s/he may then learn to cope alone. For Vygotsky, within the ZPD experts guide the learner and scaffold or frame learning and development. We shall return later to the possibility that the more experienced guide, in setting the parameters for learning, may simultaneously reduce the scope for learners to derive their own novel ways forward.

What is self-efficacy?

The notion of internalized cognitions or beliefs of competence has been much explored through the development of work on self-efficacy, which was first developed in Bandura's work on social cognitive learning in the late 1970s. It is usually defined as "beliefs in one's capacities to organize and execute the courses of action required to produce given attainments" (Bandura, 1977, p. 3). Put more simply, it refers to one's perceptions of one's capacity to bring about a desired outcome (am I able to do this?). Bandura posited that our behaviors and our successes and failures are strongly affected by our understanding of our abilities.

Self-efficacy concerns *cognitions* of competence, and does not necessarily accord with actual level of competence or with external measures of performance. The cognitions mediate behavior, shaping choices and decisions about actions, and are influenced by the individual's evaluation of prior performance. Bandura (1977, 1994) argues that since efficacy is a consequence of reflections on past behavior, the standards which are used to evaluate performance are highly significant. Those who seek to perform at a very high level, or perfectly, will be more likely to develop low efficacy, while those with more realistic standards will be more likely to develop a positive sense of their competence. These standards are not purely internal creations: Expectations of significant others and of the context shape the feedback which the individual receives.

Bandura (1977) further suggested that self-efficacy might vary in strength (how confident am I that I can do X?), in magnitude (what level of outcome can I achieve?) and generality (how broad a set of outcomes can I achieve – for example, I am an effective teacher with most students/more motivated students/only with bright, highly motivated students?).

The significance of self-efficacy may be seen in the evidence which flowed in during the 1990s of links between academic performance and self-efficacy, and between self-efficacy and motivation (Schunk, 1991; Hackett, 1995; Zimmerman, 1995; Graham & Weiner, 1996).

Where does it come from?

Bandura (1997) suggested four sources for the information and feedback which are the building blocks of self-efficacy: verbal (or social) persuasion (feedback from others, especially significant others), vicarious experiences (learning from the experiences of others, observing behavior modeled by others), physiological arousal (joy at a successful outcome, distress at a poor outcome) and mastery experiences (direct experience of successful accomplishment). Of these, mastery experiences were thought by Bandura to be most influential and this has been confirmed by Tschannen-Moran and Hoy (2007). Bandura posited that all four sources are processed by the individual and thus subject to further subjective evaluation and that only some experiences have major impact, while some may be rejected. For example, some success may be rejected because it is considered to have been too easy; positive evaluations by others may be regarded as emanating from kindness rather than legitimate judgment, and so on, or critical comment may be rejected ("she doesn't like me" or "his standards are too high"). Bandura suggested that, once self-efficacy cognitions are established, they may be sustained by selective absorption of new information, especially if the person remains in the same context. However, moving to a new context opens up self-efficacy to change (Tschannen-Moran & Hoy, 2007).

72   Janet Draper

Teacher self-efficacy

Vygotsky would argue that teacher self-efficacy is internalized from perceptions of effective teaching developed in interaction; that perceived effective practice leads to higher self-efficacy. It follows that if teachers are supported and enabled to develop effective practice, they are likely to develop self-efficacy and, taking a sociocultural view, that support for teacher learning – scaffolding to enable teacher learning – is key to successful teaching. Within the sociocultural perspective, the social environment is understood to be a key shaper of our internalized cognitions, including our abilities. These cognitions are shaped by the support and guidance we are offered and the nature of the interaction within which that support and guidance is given, by our achievements and those of others and by the judgments made and communicated to us by others. Teacher self-efficacy is above all a socially constructed entity. Teachers build their beliefs from a range of experiences, experiences in which students and colleagues play a central role.

What impact does teacher self-efficacy have?

The evidence suggests that teachers with high self-efficacy behave differently from those with little self-efficacy. Efficacious teachers show more enthusiasm and put more effort into planning and preparation (Guskey, 1988; Allinder, 1994). They persist longer when they find their work particularly challenging (Gibson & Dembo, 1984; Podell & Soodak, 1993). Research findings also show associations between teacher self-efficacy and teacher commitment (Coladarci, 1992), their willingness to try new teaching strategies (Fuchs, Fuchs & Bishop, 1992) and levels of teacher stress, burnout and absenteeism (Imants & Van Zoelen, 1995; Brissie, Hoover-Dempsey & Bassler, 1988; Glickman & Tamashiro, 1982).

Teacher efficacy has been found to relate to the goals teachers set for themselves, the effort expended in trying to achieve their goals and their resilience in the face of difficulties. Tschannen-Moran and Hoy (2001) highlight the cyclical nature of the relationship. Regardless of the starting point, higher self-efficacy links to higher goals and greater effort, which in turn link to higher self-efficacy and so on: a self-fulfilling process. The issue of direction of effect becomes less important in a cyclical system since both may affect each other. They also found that the cycle may work negatively, with diminishing results, as well as upward.

Clear evidence also exists of a link between teacher self-efficacy and classroom management, with those with higher self-efficacy beliefs, and hence more confidence in their capacity to manage the class, behaving in ways which are more effective and being more resistant to abandonment when problems arise. A sense of mastery for the teacher is more likely to follow if a class is calm and focused on learning and in contrast, difficult to achieve if there is student misbehavior or inattention at levels which preclude effective learning. Creating a suitable environment for learning is a key part of the teacher's role as a facilitator of learning. Brouwers and Tomic (2000) argue that teachers are aware of the significance of effective classroom management and lose confidence if "confronted by their incompetence every day" (p. 243), thus suggesting that effective classroom management is central to the development of teacher self-efficacy. They also found that "teachers who doubt their ability to maintain classroom order also do less to solve the order problem" (p. 249). This is again cyclical and self-fulfilling, illustrating the power of mediating beliefs, and highlighting the issue of teacher expectations (as explored many years ago by Rosenthal & Jacobson, 1968). Where teachers are convinced they can have little effect, they behave in line with that belief. This is a logical and understandable strategy, albeit one which may lead to educational detriment. It seems that a close link exists between teacher self-efficacy and teacher behavior, and that in turn they influence student motivation, learning and achievement. An exploration of teacher self-efficacy is therefore appropriate within a volume seeking to deconstruct student achievement.

Teachers' understandings of their competence in facilitating student learning and behavior, their capacity to teach more or less effectively, their self-efficacy, are internalized from their experiences of teaching and learning. Teacher self-efficacy influences teacher behavior and shapes learning opportunities for students (Fencl & Scheel, 2005) and the early years of teaching have been found to be critical for the development of teacher efficacy (Guskey, 1988; Fuchs et al., 1992; Hoy & Burke-Spero, 2005). The extent to which the social context of beginning teachers is characterized by the provision of support, guidance and scaffolding which facilitate teacher competence and shape teachers' learning about their own competence and their subsequent professional actions therefore needs to be considered.

While considerable attention has been given by both academics and governments to the technicalities of teaching, the role of teachers' internalized understandings of their own competence is less widely acknowledged. However, in studies of teaching and learning, teacher self-efficacy has been identified as a key element in effective learning in school (Margolis & McCabe, 2006). There is a strong and growing body of evidence showing that teacher self-efficacy is related to student motivation and achievement (Moore & Esselman, 1992), student self-esteem (Cheung & Cheng, 1997) and student self-efficacy (Ashton & Webb, 1986; Anderson, Greene & Loewen, 1988). Brouwers and Tomic (2000) claim a clear causal link between self-efficacy and personal accomplishment, suggesting that self-efficacy may be regarded as the independent variable. However, this link may operate in both directions; for example, student achievement may lead to enhanced teacher self-efficacy and teacher self-efficacy may lead to student achievement, especially for beginning teachers, whose self-efficacy is under construction. In studies of beginning teachers in Scotland, teachers reported that their main source of feedback for reflection and professional learning was their students' receptions of their teaching and their academic progress. In less supportive situations, it was indeed sometimes their only source of feedback during their first year (Draper, Fraser, Smith & Taylor, 1991; Draper, Fraser & Taylor, 1997). Their beliefs in their capacity to teach grew from their students' learning.

While noting the link between teacher self-efficacy and immediate student achievement, it can also be argued that the promotion of teacher self-efficacy is justifiable as a longer-term end in itself, as a significant contributor to teacher motivation and development, commitment and retention and hence to a stable learning environment in schools, as well as offering a secure base to support experimentation for innovation in teaching.

The assessment of self-efficacy as an internalized cognition is inevitably complex. This is especially the case when beginning teachers are involved, whose understanding of their role is broadening and deepening. In a very real sense, one is seeking to measure a moving target. There is some evidence from Scottish research on beginning teachers (Draper et al., 1991) that in their first year of teaching many focused on difficulties with class management and organization and later with time management. Only once they survived these early challenges and moved on were they able to perceive individual needs of students, hence their early beliefs would not have reflected this as an area in which they believed themselves to be more or less capable. A later study (Draper et al., 1997) comparing teachers in settled employment with those with multiple short contracts in different schools yielded the curious finding that those in multiple employment rated themselves as having few needs for further development. The latter group also had less support and less feedback, including from

74   Janet Draper

students. Following further investigation it seemed that, as they moved frequently from school to school and class to class, they became skilled at the early survival challenges they faced and perceived themselves to be accomplished teachers. Those in more settled employment generally had more support and feedback and developed a deeper, more complex cognition of themselves as teachers. The support of mentors and colleagues coupled with extended experience in one school had helped them to have a fuller, deeper understanding of the challenges of teaching in the long term. A sociocultural perspective helps us to understand that scaffolding and feedback from colleagues and feedback from familiar students/pupils had shaped these teachers' different understandings of the work of teaching and also their internalizations of competence and professional development needs.

Teacher development

As noted above, initial teacher education (teacher training) and the early years of teaching are understood to be critical periods in teacher development. The immediate social contexts for learning about teaching are the classroom, with its students and their progress as learners as key sources of feedback, and the school, with colleagues and their expertise, especially those acting as mentors.

To be successful, teachers must develop teaching strategies which work for them both as individuals and in the situated context of the specific learners in a class in a particular school. Learning to teach effectively is not simply a matter of imitating experts, adopting solutions or following instruction but of deriving personally workable teaching and learning strategies in specific contexts. Successful teaching and learning thus involves teachers identifying individually relevant effective practice ("what works" with those involved). Modeling and advice from others simply offer starting points for the development of individual strategies. This is underlined by the findings of Burbank and Kauchak (2003), who found that expert teachers think about and discuss their teaching in ways which novice teachers may have difficulty both in understanding and in applying.

The sociocultural perspective lays great store by the social context in which learning takes place. It argues that the social environment is not simply a setting but is a central component of the learning experience, the vehicle through which learning occurs as a collaborative activity between learner and supporter/facilitator. In a school context, the teacher is a key mediator of the learning experience for the student, and can be understood as a supporter or a director of the child's learning, through scaffolding. Within this perspective, the teacher frames learning opportunities and guides learning. Paralleling this, in exploring the teacher as learner, issues of context and scaffolding require attention to the experiences of beginning teachers and the extent to which these may facilitate the development of teacher self-efficacy.

Student teacher learning in school

Hoy and Burke-Spero (2005) suggest that student teacher experiences in school and the early years in teaching are crucial shapers of teacher self-efficacy, and that this early period in teaching is a critical time when the foundations of teacher identity are established. During initial teacher education (or teacher training), the nature of school placement experiences, shaped by class allocation and level and type of support, are important (Fallin & Royse, 2000). A well-supported student teacher given timely advice and sympathetic guidance for teaching an accommodating class has more chance of success. Trying to handle an unfamiliar, difficult class and/or teaching with little support and advice both decrease the likelihood of experiencing mastery and developing a sense of self-efficacy. Research on student placement/practicum experiences has shown that poor experiences in school can lead to more negative attitudes toward teaching and feelings of inadequacy (Fallin & Royse, 2000).

Starting work as a teacher: Scaffolding support?

New teachers generally receive significant feedback or evidence on competence, either directly through mentors and students or indirectly through student achievement, classroom ethos and contract renewal.

Perhaps unsurprisingly, beginning teachers have been found to have lower self-efficacy than more experienced teachers (Tschannen-Moran & Hoy, 2007). Two reasons for this seem evident: Beginning teachers are learning their craft as well as coping with a new work context, while experienced teachers have had time to build up situated skills and understandings, as well as possibly having more influence on the demands made of them in school. In addition, there is the possibility of survivor bias in relation to more experienced teachers. Teachers who find the work very stressful, very difficult or simply unsatisfying are more likely to leave and those who remain are more likely to be those who feel positive about their capacity to teach successfully.

However, Ghaith and Yaghi (1997) suggest that, as teachers accrue experience, so their self-efficacy diminishes. They argue this is due to coming to believe that their scope to shape student learning is less than they had originally thought and that other factors also significantly influence student learning. This is one interpretation but it could also be the case that, as they come to have a deeper understanding of their role, and engage with student learning over a longer period, they perceive new levels of challenge, like sustaining student motivation in the face of difficulties in learning, and particularly so if there is a shared and labeled understanding in the school that students are highly challenged by their personal and social circumstances. However, there is contradictory evidence which suggests that, as student teachers build their skills, so their beliefs in their competence rise (Hoy & Burke-Spero, 2005). As a beginning teacher in a post for the first time, some research suggests that self-efficacy falls (Cantrell, Young & Moore, 2003) and this has been attributed to beginning teachers having to cope without the scaffolding of support offered by their tutors and the need to deal with the "real job" in all its complexity: a very different task from teaching some lessons to someone else's classes already "up and running". Is it possible to avoid this drop in confidence?

Contextual antecedents of self-efficacy

Schein (1988) argues that an important element of induction into any new work should be planning and support for the new member of staff, which enables early success in the job. Such early success should help develop an internalized positive conviction that one has the potential to do the job well and an expectation of being able to cope with its challenges: the rudiments of self-efficacy. I have argued before that good induction is enabling, while poor induction is disabling (Draper & O'Brien, 2006). For student teachers, such elements as class allocation and support vary their chances of success, as mentioned above, and poor provision of information, little support and feedback, and little encouragement make starting work harder, less likely to be rewarding and less likely to generate perceptions of effectiveness. As Brouwers and Tomic (2000) emphasize, when things do not go well in teaching, there is

76 Janet Draper

continuing negative feedback on a day-to-day basis: The classroom cannot be avoided. Hence self-efficacy may change, but either positively or negatively. Webb and Ashton (1987) found that teacher efficacy could be reduced by poor conditions of service, the absence of recognition and excessive workload. Faced with diminishing circumstances and little confidence in being able to work effectively, it is no surprise that a number of education systems have found themselves faced with real difficulties over the retention of expensively trained teachers.

There is a substantial tranche of evidence on problems encountered by new teachers which relate to the "reality shock" of taking up the role (Veenman, 1984; Draper et al., 1991). The response to these difficulties has increasingly been a recognition that the initial period as a teacher is key in shaping perceptions of competence, and that poor early experiences threaten commitment, retention and teacher development. This has led to the development of induction programs for new teachers in many countries, with a focus on the provision of helpful information and supportive guidance to create a positive social context for both the student and new teacher learning. Hong Kong has been among those which have developed policies on special induction schemes for beginning teachers (see www.edb.gov.hk/FileManager/ EN/Content_2227/pamphlet-eng-final.pdf).

Underpinning these developments would appear to be two beliefs:

- that teachers will teach better if they are well-supported in the early years and that this will engender a positive approach to their own development, encourage collaboration and innovation
- that student learning will be enhanced by teachers who experience a good start (early success) in their work, have appropriate and relevant support, who have a positive attitude to their work and to their own improvement, and a high level of motivation.

Perhaps most importantly, both of these imply that effective teaching is not a matter of personality characteristics or inherent behaviors but, in a truly sociocultural way, is a consequence of the social context in which teachers and students learn. They also imply that teacher motivation and attitude to development follow not simply from a vocational commitment to teaching and student learning, but that they are shaped by how teachers are treated. This shift away from taking teacher motivation for granted and toward something to be fostered by careful support represents a real shift in the perception of teaching in the wider context.

Creating a context for positive professional learning

Since the development of effective teaching is not simply a matter of more experienced teachers sharing how it is done, but requires an individual construction of effective strategies in specific environments with specific learners, effective support for teacher development must offer support for the individual development of practice. That support will require both guidance from experience and scope for uniquely relevant strategies to evolve.

Although induction may be provided, this is no guarantee of positive teacher development. A comparative study of induction in Scotland and Hong Kong derived a model of forms of teacher induction from which it seemed that teachers may acquire different orientations to their work, their development and their colleagues (Draper & Forrester, 2004, 2009; Draper & O'Brien, 2006). The induction experience of teachers varied between schools and systems and there were inconsistencies between policy and actual practice, not only in Scotland and in Hong Kong but, the wider research suggests (e.g., Flores, 2007; Zulijan & Vogrinz, 2007), in other systems also. Although the provision of support had been identified as available, the form it took varied (seen in the model as high or low support; high direction or high autonomy) and reflected different degrees of both autonomy and support. These were captured in a model of induction as the combination of level of support and degree of direction/autonomy, for each could be combined with extremes of the other. Some had received high support for developing their teaching and high autonomy, while some had high support and low autonomy, and so on. Different combinations offer different experiences of induction with different outcomes in terms of internalized understandings of their role as teachers. Each combination represents a different start to professional learning in a post, offering teachers different relationships with their supporters and different opportunities to innovate, or accommodate, experiment alone, or learn without guidance in a setting which has specific unshared expectations ("learning in the dark").

Some new teachers find themselves in learning contexts which more or less effectively support their individual learning as teachers, while others struggle to fit the expectations and practices of others with or without clear guidance on what is expected. Figure 6.1 shows the four quadrants of the model.

Induction, even when in place, does not therefore guarantee a context that supports the development of positive cognitions of competence and effective professional development. The supportiveness of mentors coupled with the autonomy of the beginning teachers are suggested as significant dimensions of effective induction. The model points out that it is the complex interactions of those involved, coupled doubtless with additional factors, which shape the learning experiences of the new teacher, not simply the capability of the teacher or the availability of a mentor. The nature of the interactional context, the sociocultural vehicle for learning, the supportiveness of the interactions and the autonomy they allow will be important for positive teacher development. The beginning teacher's learning will reflect how much scope the interactions in the learning context offer for autonomous professional practice and the extent to which colleagues are a source of support and guidance. In addition, those aspects of teaching which are given high priority by the context and immediate mentors – for example, exam results, or parental contentment – are likely to shape the standards against which beginning teachers evaluate themselves. All these elements of learning will set teacher focus and expectations for later development.

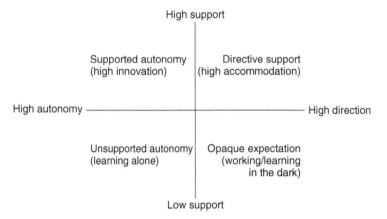

Figure 6.1 Model of four contrasting types of induction experience (adapted from Draper & O'Brien, 2006)

In reflecting on a sociocultural approach to beginning teacher learning, a number of issues emerge. Guidance by an expert may encourage or preclude the beginning teacher in constructing their own understandings and solutions. Therefore, arrangements for the support of new teachers need to be examined regarding whether there is scope for the beginner to develop their own style and try new ways, not simply to accept guidance. Effective support should enable the development of individual practice which is unlikely to imitate the supporter's own practice. In addition, as new teachers begin to work independently, so the scope offered to make a contribution, as well as be guided by others, will shape their sense of being independent professionals. This suggests that scaffolding by a more experienced learner needs sensitive application within the mentoring of new teachers.

In addition, good intentions to support are not sufficient, as found by Burbank and Kauchak (2003), whose research revealed real discontinuities in understanding when expert teachers shared their teaching in ways from which beginning teachers had difficulty learning. The expert offerings were, in Vygotskian terms, beyond the ZPD of the beginning teachers, and the preparation of mentors must include a recognition of guidance shaped to the current and immediately possible areas of development for beginning teachers. Positive teacher efficacy is a more likely outcome with well-tailored support. There is thus a need for the effective selection and training of those who developmentally interact with new teachers (Forde & O'Brien, 2011; Draper & O'Brien, 2006), which will inevitably require resources.

Summarizing the research reviewed overall, it seems that several factors in the social context will shape the self-efficacy of beginning teachers and will impact upon student achievement. These are illustrated in Figure 6.2 and include experience of teaching, effective induction, experience of early success, feedback from mentors and students, and classroom management.

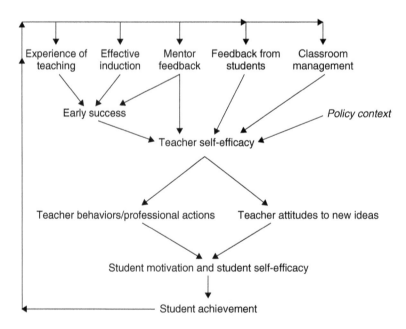

Figure 6.2 Factors affecting the development of self-efficacy of beginning teachers and student achievement

Once established, does teacher self-efficacy change?

As noted above, the selective absorption of feedback (verbal persuasion in Bandura's term) is likely to contribute to maintenance of the established level of self-efficacy. Several pieces of research suggest that efficacy beliefs of experienced teachers show little change (Anderson, Greene & Loewen, 1988; Tschannen-Moran, Hoy & Hoy, 1998), especially if teachers remain in the same context, and that substantial long-term professional development is needed to effect significant changes in practice. Changes in practice seem to be more likely if teachers are engaged in participatory action research (Cochran-Smith & Lytle, 1990). This fits with review findings (EPPI, 2003, 2005a, 2005b) that effective professional development is most likely to impact on teacher practice when it is collaborative, sustained and perceived to be relevant to current needs by teachers themselves. These findings have clear implications for the professional development offered to teachers, especially experienced teachers, and underpin the significance of the social context and of collegial interaction in supporting learning.

Internalized teacher self-efficacy as a goal

While teacher self-efficacy has been strongly evidenced as a factor in student achievement, it is also important as an outcome worth pursuing in its own right, for its impact on teachers and on schools. Effective teaching requires confidence in one's own abilities and a sense of self-efficacy is related to positive approaches to new ideas, learning and development and fuels professional action. Teachers' intrinsic motivations cannot be taken for granted in the face of top-down change processes, for such changes may disturb the link between teacher and practice, and major reform may impact on teacher self-efficacy.

The policy context of teaching and learning and teacher efficacy

In an era of global education reform, education systems need teachers who are open to new ways and willing to experiment and test new teaching strategies, moving out of comfort zones to innovate and to try new ways. However, centrally conceived and implemented reforms, especially those which demand significant changes in professional practice, may also reduce self-efficacy, leaving teachers with a less secure base of confidence in their practice from which to draw strength to cope with change. External imposition of standards and competence frameworks may undermine experienced teachers who, while confident of their competence in the past, are less sure about their competence in the new environment. Rigid frameworks of expectations may also socialize and narrow the internalized understandings of beginning teachers about their work. Ballet, Kelchtermans and Loughran (2006), among others, have suggested that teacher autonomy is reducing, although Tatto's (2007) comparison of reforms across systems suggests this is not inevitable. Tatto distinguished reforms *through and with* teachers and reforms *of* teachers and found the former sustained teacher autonomy and confidence and enabled teachers to make a contribution to reform.

The scope given to teachers to experiment and the ways that teachers are treated in the system are therefore also important. Rigid working contexts, inflexible monitoring and accountability procedures, low status of teachers and limited or "contrived" consultation procedures all contribute to a context in which teachers learn to see themselves as relatively insignificant. The construct "collective teacher efficacy" is useful here, defined by Goddard, Hoy and Woolfolk Hoy (2000) as "the perceptions of teachers that the efforts of the faculty

80 *Janet Draper*

of a school will have a positive effect on student achievement" (p. 486) and links the perception of school culture and climate to teacher self-efficacy. It highlights dangers inherent in teachers losing confidence in being able to make a difference to student learning.

Developing this further, the additional construct of system or professional teacher efficacy is proposed here. Like collective teacher efficacy, this is not an aggregation of individual teacher efficacy but the perception of individual teachers about the scope for teachers as a whole to make a difference within a system or society, to fulfill their "moral purpose" (Fullan, 2001). This highlights perceptions of the system in which they work, the extent to which they are acknowledged and consulted, the extent to which change and reform are top-down or teacher-led, and so on. Taking Goddard's definition of collective teacher efficacy and Bandura's proposals of the origins of self-efficacy (verbal persuasion, vicarious experiences, physiological arousal and mastery experiences) against a backdrop of governmental messages that teachers need to radically change their pedagogical practice in order to be effective, teachers' comments about reduced autonomy, centrally directed continuing professional development and highly competitive exam result comparisons requiring constant improvement, then the prospect for positive teacher efficacy seems discouraging.

Bandura (1997) argued long ago that positive changes in self-efficacy come from "compelling feedback that forcefully disrupts the pre-existing disbelief in one's capabilities" (p. 82). While this may be true, it seems from the relatively recent history of teacher morale in Hong Kong, England (Ball, 2003) and elsewhere that it also applies to negative shifts in teacher efficacy and that pressure for reform has emphasized inadequacies in teachers' practices in a sufficiently compelling way to reduce teachers' beliefs in their capacity to make a difference. The research suggests that, once established, teacher efficacy is not easy to change. It behooves education systems at the level of supporting individual new teachers in school, teachers' immediate social and learning contexts, and at the wider level of supporting teachers as a professional group and in their subsequent professional development, to ensure that teacher learning contexts are constructive enough to support positive internalizations of competence and that change management processes do not undermine those cognitions.

Conclusion

A substantial body of research provides evidence of teacher self-efficacy being significantly related to student achievement through its impact on teacher behavior, teacher and student motivation and the development of student self-efficacy.

The argument then is that, if teacher efficacy relates to student motivation and achievement and, longer term, to a belief in personal efficacy, then measures to support or enable the development of teacher efficacy require significant consideration. This consideration should involve paying due attention to the social context in which student and beginning or novice teachers learn and the constructiveness of the learning opportunities they are offered. It should also include serious planning for effective induction, for the evidence suggests that ensuring beginning teachers are adequately and positively supported is necessary in order to establish positive teacher efficacy. This in turn is more likely to create a positive learning context for students and teachers, a mutually constructive learning environment. The facilitation of such positive learning environments is likely to require careful leadership and management, effective mentoring and good support and appropriate induction for teachers in their early years. However, teachers' learning experiences do not rest solely with peers, school leaders and the wider society alone. Students also play a significant role and their behavior and engagement with learning will shape teachers' perceptions of their effectiveness. Whole-school arrangements to support positive behavior management and student commitment to learning are therefore likely to be also relevant.

In a period of major reform, when teacher change is considered necessary to foster the types of learning required for the future, the evidence on the impact of teacher efficacy is both too sound and too consistent to be ignored. It highlights the importance of a teacher's own perception of capability as a key mediator in their teaching. The sociocultural perspective emphasizes the centrality of the learning context and the importance of the relationships and interactions which make up that context. Technicist definitions of teaching, which define teaching in terms of individual skill and subject knowledge and which commonly underpin policy makers' models of teaching and teacher development, take no real account of the intrapersonal and interpersonal dimensions of teaching which determine learning for students and teachers and overlook the areas where teachers need most support in order to sustain effective teaching and learning. Sustaining a more complex analysis of teachers' roles will be necessary in order to exploit the full potential of teacher efficacy to support student and school achievement.

The sociocultural perspective usefully draws attention to the interactions between new teachers and those who support them and the model of induction offered here highlights the diverse nature of that interaction. Careful selection, training and resourcing of those who support or mentor new teachers will be important if the interactions which support fledgling teachers are to be most effective for their professional development.

References

Allinder, R. M. (1994). The relationships between efficacy and the instructional practices of special education teachers and consultants. *Teacher Education and Special Education, 17*, 86–95.

Anderson, R., Greene, M. & Loewen, P. (1988). Relationships among teachers' and students' thinking skills, sense of efficacy, and student achievement. *Alberta Journal of Educational Research, 34*(2), 148–165.

Ashton, P. T. & Webb, R. B. (1986). *Making a difference: Teachers' sense of efficacy and student achievement.* New York: Longman.

Ball, S. J. (2003). The teacher's soul and the terrors of performativity. *Journal of Education Policy, 18*(2), 215–228.

Ballet, K., Kelchtermans, G. & Loughran, J. (2006). Beyond intensification towards a scholarship of practice: Analyzing changes in teachers' working lives. *Teachers and Teaching: Theory and Practice, 12*, 209–229.

Bandura, A. (1977). Self-efficacy: Toward a unifying theory of behavioral change. *Psychological Bulletin, 84*, 191–215.

Bandura, A. (1994). Self-efficacy. In V. S. Ramachaudran (Ed.), *Encyclopaedia of human behavior* (Vol. 4, pp. 71–81). New York: Academic Press.

Bandura, A. (1997). *Self-efficacy: The exercise of control.* New York: W. H. Freeman.

Brissie, J. S., Hoover-Dempsey, K. V. & Bassler, O. V. (1988). Individual situational contributors to teacher burnout. *Journal of Educational Research, 82*(2), 106–112.

Brouwers, A. & Tomic, W. (2000). A longitudinal study of teacher burnout and perceived self efficacy in classroom management. *Teaching and Teacher Education, 16*(2), 239–253.

Burbank, M. D. & Kauchak, D. (2003). An alternative model to professional development: Investigations into effective collaboration. *Teaching and Teacher Education, 19*, 499–514.

Cantrell, P., Young, S. & Moore, A. (2003). Factors affecting science teaching efficacy of preservice elementary teachers. *Journal of Science Teacher Education, 14*(3), 177–192.

Cheung, W. M. & Cheng, Y. C. (1997). *A multi-level analysis of teachers' self belief and behavior and students' educational outcomes.* Paper presented at the annual meeting of the American Educational Research Association, Chicago.

Cochran-Smith, M. & Lytle, S. (1990). Research on teaching and teacher research: The issues that divide. *Educational Researcher, 19*, 2–11.

Coladarci, T. (1992). Teachers' sense of efficacy and commitment to teaching. *Journal of Experimental Education, 60*, 323–337.

Draper, J. & Forrester, V. (2004). *Early teacher development in the 21st century: Contested and contrasted.* Paper presented at Scottish Educational Research Association, Dundee.

Draper, J. & Forrester, V. (2009). The induction of beginning teachers in Scotland and Hong Kong: Getting it right? *Journal of Comparative and International Education, 4*(1), 74–86.

Draper, J., Fraser, H., Smith, D. & Taylor, W. (1991). *A study of probationers.* Edinburgh: Moray House Institute of Education.

Draper, J., Fraser, H. & Taylor, W. (1997). Teachers at work: Early experiences of professional development. *British Journal of In Service Education, 23*(2), 283–295.

Draper, J. & O'Brien, J. (2006). *Induction: Fostering development at all career stages.* Edinburgh: Dunedin Press.

EPPI (2003). *How does collaborative continuing professional development (CPD) for teachers of the 5–16 age range affect teaching and learning?* London: Evidence for Policy and Practice Information Centre (EPPI), Institute of Education (www.eppi.ioe.ac.uk).

EPPI (2005a). *The impact of collaborative continuing professional development (CPD) on classroom teaching and learning – Review: How do collaborative and sustained CPD and sustained but not collaborative CPD affect teaching and learning?* London: Evidence for Policy and Practice Information Centre (EPPI), Institute of Education (www.eppi.ioe.ac.uk).

EPPI (2005b). *The impact of collaborative continuing professional development (CPD) on classroom teaching and learning – Review: What do teacher impact data tell us about collaborative CPD?* London: Evidence for Policy and Practice Information Centre (EPPI), Institute of Education (www.eppi.ioe.ac.uk).

Fallin, J. & Royse, D. (2000). Student teaching: *the Keystone experience. Music Educators Journal, 87*(3), 19–22.

Fencl, H. & Scheel, K. (2005). Research and teaching: Engaging students – an examination of the effects of teaching strategies on self-efficacy and course in a non-majors physics course. *Journal of College Science Teaching, 35*(1), 20–24.

Flores, M. A. (2007). Looking at induction of beginning teachers in Portugal: Meanings and paradoxes. In M. V. Zulijan & J. Vogrinz (Eds.), *Professional inductions of teachers in Europe and elsewhere.* International scientific monograph (pp. 236–259). Llubjana: European Social Fund/Ministry of Education, Slovenia.

Forde, C. & O'Brien, J. (Eds.). (2011). *Coaching and mentoring.* Edinburgh: Dunedin Academic Press.

Fuchs, L. S., Fuchs, D. & Bishop, N. (1992). Instructional adaptation for students at risk. *Journal of Educational Research, 86*, 70–84.

Fullan, M. (2001). *Leading in a culture of change.* San Francisco, CA: Jossey-Bass.

Ghaith, G. & Yaghi, M. (1997). Relationships among experience, teacher efficacy, and attitudes toward the implementation of instructional innovation. *Teaching and Teacher Education, 13*(4), 451–458.

Gibson, S. & Dembo, M. (1984). Teacher efficacy: A construct validation. *Journal of Educational Psychology, 76*, 569–582.

Glickman, C. D. & Tamashiro, R. T. (1982). A comparison of first year, fifth year and former teachers on efficacy, ego involvement and problem solving. *Psychology in the Schools, 19*, 558–562.

Goddard, R. D., Hoy, W. K. & Woolfolk Hoy, A. (2000). Collective teacher efficacy: Its meaning, measure, and impact on student achievement. *American Educational Research Journal, 37*, 479–507.

Graham, S. & Weiner, B. (1996). Theories and principles of motivation. In D. C. Berliner & R. C. Calfee (Eds.), *Handbook of educational psychology* (pp. 63–84). New York: Simon & Schuster Macmillan.

Guskey, T. R. (1988). Teacher efficacy, self-concept, and attitudes toward the implementation of instructional innovation. *Teaching and Teacher Education, 4*, 63–69.

Hackett, G. (1995). Self-efficacy in career choice and development. In A. Bandura (Ed.), *Self-efficacy in changing societies* (pp. 232–258). New York: Cambridge University Press.

Hoy, A. W. & Burke-Spero, R. (2005). Changes in teacher efficacy during the early years of teaching: A comparison of four measures. *Teaching and Teacher Education, 21,* 343–356.

Imants, J. & van Zoelen, A. (1995). Teachers' sickness absence in primary schools, school climate and teachers' sense of efficacy. *School Organisation, 15*(1), 77–86.

Margolis, H. & McCabe, P. (2006). Improving self-efficacy and motivation: What to do, what to say. *Intervention in School and Clinic, 41*(4), 218–227.

Moore, W. & Esselman, M. (1992). *Teacher efficacy, power, school climate and achievement: A desegregating district's experience.* Paper presented at the annual meeting of the American Educational Research Association, San Francisco, April.

Podell, D. & Soodak, L. (1993). Teacher efficacy and bias in special education referrals. *Journal of Educational Research, 86,* 247–253.

Rosenthal, R. & Jacobson, L. (1968). *Pygmalion in the classroom.* NJ: Holt, Rinehart & Winston.

Schein, E. H. (1988). *Organizational psychology* (3rd ed.). Englewood Cliffs, NJ: Prentice Hall.

Schunk, D. H. (1991). Self-efficacy and academic motivation. *Educational Psychologist, 26,* 207–231.

Tatto, M. T. (Ed.). (2007). *Reforming teaching globally.* Oxford, UK: Symposium Books.

Tschannen-Moran, M. & Hoy, A. W. (2001). Teacher efficacy: Capturing an elusive concept. *Teacher and Teacher Education, 17*(7), 783–805.

Tschannen-Moran, M. & Hoy, A. W. (2007). The differential antecedents of self-efficacy beliefs of novice and experienced teachers. *Teaching and Teacher Education, 23*(6), 944–956.

Tschannen-Moran, M., Hoy, A. W. & Hoy, W. K. (1998). Teacher efficacy: Its meaning and measure. *Review of Educational Research, 68,* 202–248.

Veenman, S. (1984). Perceived problems of beginning teachers. *Review of Educational Research, 54,* 143–178.

Vygotsky, L. S. (1978). *Mind in society: The development of higher mental processes* (M. Cole, V. John-Steiner, S. Scribner & E. Souberman, Eds.). Cambridge, MA: Harvard University Press.

Webb, R. & Ashton, P. T. (1987). Teachers' motivation and the conditions of teaching: A call for ecological reform. In S. Walker & L. Barton (Eds.), *Changing policies, changing teachers: New directions for schooling* (pp. 22–40). Milton Keynes: Open University Press.

Zimmerman, B. J. (1995). Self-efficacy and educational development. In A. Bandura (Ed.), *Self-efficacy in changing societies* (pp. 202–231). New York: Cambridge University Press.

Zulijan, M. & Vogrinz, J. (Eds.). (2007). *Professional inductions of teachers in Europe and elsewhere.* International scientific monograph, Llubjana: European Social Fund/Ministry of Education, Slovenia.

Part 4
Social plane

7 Parental expectations
The influence of the significant other on school achievement

Sivanes Phillipson

Introduction

Parental involvement consists of multilayers of interactions that integrate various aspects of family dynamics. These multilayers at the macro level include parental values, cultural and religious background, and social capital. At the micro level, parental expectations deriving from their values, cultural and religious background, and social capital have been considered as a major influence on their children's development and achievements. It has been found that parental expectations, in particular as transmitted through their involvement, have a high impact on children's school achievements (Yamamoto & Holloway, 2010).

How parents, through their expectations, have an effect on their children's school achievement can be interpreted through Vygotsky's paradigm of the mediation and internalization process within sociocultural theory (1978). The goal of this chapter, using the Vygotskian paradigm, is to question and illustrate the functions parents take in the process toward the development of their children's achievements.

Parents and Vygotsky's significant other

Vygotsky (2004) observed that "The path from the thing to the child and from the child to the thing lies through another person" (p. 532). The "another person" is also referred to as the significant other. The significant other can be a parent who is involved in the processes of mediation and internalization that takes place between the child and the social plane, resulting in the cultural process of learning and development. The significant other's position in the social plane where the child interacts enables them to assist the child to internalize cultural and psychological schemes that are essential for cognitive development (Vygotsky, 1978). In this instance, the significant other is the mediator who is perceived as an expert who frames, filters, and interprets the perceived data from the environment to transfer selected messages and ideas to the child to internalize (Vygotsky, 1981). When a child internalizes the transferred messages or ideas, it is a process "whereby certain aspects of patterns of activity that had been performed on an external plane come to be executed on an internal plane" (Wertsch, 1985, pp. 61–62). In other words, the child processes the information and reorganizes that information into their cognitive structure and acts upon them when needed.

Vygotsky suggested that mediation and internalization processes with the significant other exposed children to "mature cultural forms of behavior" which linked the external and internal plane in a "genetic" relationship (1981, p. 151). In practice, this means that parents who presumably have more knowledge and experience of the sociocultural environment act as filters for their children's learning and cognitive development. A child with guidance and instructions from their parents, then, absorbs and internalizes the information and thinking tools provided to them at different levels and in different ways within the family plane (Rogoff, 1990).

This process requires the existence of a social plane where mediation by parents creates the opportune moments, through available artifacts that children are able to use, to internalize parental expectations that result in their optimum performance. How and where parents place themselves in familial interactions is crucial as the precise placement within the continuum of a child's thinking and performance is helpful in ascertaining proper mediation and internalization of expectations. Parental expectations in this instance have a focal position in children's pathways to their school performance as, on one hand, it is derived from parental motive and involvement as influenced by their children's ability and performance and, on the other hand, it feeds back into parental motives and involvement to influence children's internal actualization of their abilities into actual performance.

Studies have shown that parental expectations have two important positions in children's school achievements. The first and most common position is as a predictor of school achievement, where the higher the expectations of parents are for their children's school achievement, the better the child's achievement (e.g., Neuenschwander, Vida, Garrett, & Eccles, 2007; Phillipson & Phillipson, 2007). The second position of parental expectations is as a mediator of children and family variables that result in academic achievement (Phillipson & Phillipson, 2012; Yamamoto & Holloway, 2010). These two roles that parental expectations have in relation to school achievement support the focal position that I proposed earlier. As such, family settings that create opportunities for optimum transfer and mediation of parental expectations would seem of importance to a child's successful school performance. Accordingly, family settings that do not provide proper access to parent–child interactions that mediate to their children essential psychological and cultural schemas are seen to produce low-achieving children (cf. Feuerstein & Gross, 1997). It is imperative, then, to have an overview from the existing literature of the kinds of parent–child interactions that transfer parental expectations.

Parent–child interactions and expectations

Parent–child interactions are broadly understood as parental involvement, especially in the context of school achievement (Epstein, 2006; Seginer, 2006). Parents can be involved at home and/or at school in many ways to help their children achieve.

Homework

The literature shows that one of the dominant ways parents are involved with their children at home is by helping them with their homework. The summaries of Jeynes (2005, 2007), Hill and Tyson (2009), and Patall, Cooper, and Robinson (2008) showed that parents are generally involved by assisting with their children's homework, by reading to them (for younger children), by monitoring their homework, and by setting rules about homework completion. Parents' assistance in homework is seen to be quite arbitrary, depending on the context of the interactions. In some cases, children gained academic improvement through direct help with homework and setting rules about homework completion (Patall et al., 2008), whereas, in other cases, homework assistance exerted excessive pressure on the children and interfered with their autonomy, which in turn negatively affected children's academic performance (Hill & Tyson, 2009).

In other cases, where parents provided appropriate artifacts and enriching educational activities to stimulate their children's learning interaction, such efforts provided positive impact. In instances where parental assistance with homework had to do with poor prior performance, there seemed to be no improvement in those children's achievements (Jeynes, 2005). This outcome has been attributed to parent–child interaction and communication of beliefs of children's abilities and the associated expectations that affected their children's own self-efficacy and performance (Phillipson, 2009b).

In addition, it was found that parent–child interaction in learning activities led to an increase in parental and children's expectations, as well as an increase in agreement of their expectations (Hao & Bonstead-Bruns, 1998). It also appears to be dependent on the children's age or grade level, where younger children tend to be more accepting and inclined to parental assistance, as opposed to older children, who are more independent (Jeynes, 2007).

Attendance at school events

Other ways parents are involved in their children's development are through attendance and participation in educational activities outside of home and/or school events. The impact of parental attendance and participation in school functions is usually smaller than direct involvement at home (Hill & Tyson, 2009; Jeynes, 2005). Such involvement seems to work as a platform for parents to communicate their expectations, especially in terms of academic concerns that parents have for their children's schooling and school achievement. Wu (2003) found that parental expectations related through their participation at school and other educational activities are quite effective, especially when they are able to voice their academic concerns to their children via such involvement. Yang (2007), furthermore, suggested that parental expectations that were communicated through parent–child interactions during educational activities helped their children self-regulate their learning habits and methods.

Parental motive

When parents help with their children's work or get involved in any event or activities, they do it presumably with a motive to ensure success on their children's part. If that motive is lacking or missing, then parent–child interactions would not have the desired impact on the outcomes in schooling and achievement. The motive in this instance can be interpreted as being associated with the affordance of parental expectations that are being conveyed (Li, 2003) and these include goal or mastery orientation and future attainment. These types of parental expectations are measured and defined in different ways in many studies, and it is vital to delineate their functions in relation to school achievement.

Types of parental expectations

Parental expectations of grades

The first definition used in much research is parental expectations of their children's immediate school achievements in the form of grades or marks (e.g., Phillipson & Phillipson, 2007). This type of parental expectations has been found to predict school achievement either directly or indirectly. Where parental expectations directly predicted school achievement, the relationship was positive and of high impact (Neuenschwander et al., 2007).

In other words, when parental expectations were higher, their children had higher school achievements and, conversely, lower parental expectations led to lower achievement. Parental expectations were also found to have a stronger association when their children were at middle primary and secondary school than when they were very young or much older (Ji, Jiao, & Jing, 1993).

Parental expectations that indirectly predicted school achievement usually acted as a mediator. Parental expectations of children's school grades were found to positively mediate their children's cognitive abilities to perform well in school tests (Lohrfink, 2002; Phillipson, 2010b; Phillipson & Phillipson, 2012). Other research also found that parental expectations of their children's grades mediated their socio-economic status (SES) and resulting achievements (Glick & White, 2004) or parental educational level in predicting achievement (Davis-Kean, 2005). Unreasonable parental expectations were found to mediate children's anxiety to achieve at the adolescent stage (Salimi, Mirzamani, & Shahiri-Tabarestani, 2005).

Parental aspirations

The other common definition of parental expectations has to do with parents' future aspirations for their children. For example, a number of studies asked parents to predict or anticipate their children's highest attainment in terms of schooling and tertiary studies. These studies found a positive relationship between parental aspirations and school achievement (Goldenberg, Gallimore, Reese, & Garnier, 2001; Stern, 2007). However, the relationship strengths were usually lower than parental expectations of children's grades. This was apparent in Stern (2007), where the correlation strengths were lower for parental aspirations as opposed to parental expectations in predicting achievement-related outcomes. In some cases, the relationship between parental aspirations and achievement was insignificant. This could be explained by the lack of proximity in time and space in terms of children's current achievement and future achievements in connection to parental desires for their children's future, which are usually higher than realistically anticipated (Goldenberg et al., 2001).

Children's perceptions of parental expectations

Another way parental expectations are defined is when their children perceive parental expectations and interpret them from their point of view. These kinds of parental expectations have been found to have a positively moderate relationship with achievement, especially at the primary school level (Yang, 2010). Children's perceptions of expectations had a weaker and, in some instances at the secondary school level, negative correlation with school achievement (Yazedjian, Toews, & Navarro, 2009). These findings suggest that older children's perceptions of high parental expectations lower their own performance in school achievement. The contradictory findings between primary and secondary school contexts perhaps have to do with the kinds of measurements used and even the interpretation of parents' motives through their expectations.

To obtain a succinct overview of parental motives as shown in the types of parental expectations and the impact the variable has on achievement, I draw upon meta-analysis data of cross-sectional studies from 20 years of research on parental expectations in relation to school achievement, spanning from primary to secondary schooling. A point to note at this stage is that the following meta-analysis provides an indication of the kinds of parental expectations and their effect sizes, and therefore the report does not fully conform to the traditional reporting scheme of a meta-analysis.

Meta-analysis

The first stage in finding studies that examined the relationship between parental expectations and children's achievement involved a computer search of major databases, including PsycINFO, Sociological Abstracts, ProQuest Dissertations and Theses, ERIC, ProQuest Education Journal, Scopus, Wiley InterScience Journals, and China and Taiwan Databases, using either a single or a combination of keywords. The search terms included: parents/parental expectation(s), parents/parental expectancies, parents/parental goal(s), parents/parental aspiration(s), beliefs, perception, educational expectation(s), goal(s), academic expectation(s), parents' predictions, children's achievement, attainment, performance, and achievement outcome. Both published and unpublished manuscripts, which contained the above keywords in either the title or the abstract, were reviewed. Furthermore, some articles that were not available on the electronic databases were obtained from libraries of universities in Hong Kong as well as other countries – for example, the British Library. Additional journals or dissertations were obtained by examining the reference sections from journal articles on parental expectations.

In the next stage of the selection process, I only included the documents that met all the following selection criteria:

1   The cross-sectional research must have been published between the years 1990 and 2011.
2   The sample in each document must include children of ages 5–12 (kindergarten to grade 6) and 13–20 (grade 7 to early college). I specified this wide range of ages to ensure that more studies could be included in the meta-analysis since not many cross-sectional studies have been completed in this area and also to avoid possible publication bias. I argue that heterogeneity of sample and the random effect on the parent–child relationship are different even when pre-school or post-secondary samples are taken off as rationalized by some meta-analyses (cf. Patall et al., 2008).
3   The research must include a measure of parental expectations/aspirations and school achievement and an indication of the relationships between these variables.
4   The research must fulfill the research question: How do parental expectations affect their children's achievements at the primary and secondary school levels?

The meta-analyses were conducted using the Comprehensive Meta-analysis V.2 (Borenstein, Hedges, Higgins, & Rothstein, 2005), where the synthesis used correlation indexes from research papers that fulfilled the set criteria in this chapter. A total of 12 primary-level and 14 secondary-level research papers were found. Out of the 12 primary-level researches, five were research dissertations and the rest were journal articles, and there were also five dissertations among the 14 papers at the secondary level. While this shows that both published and unpublished researches were included in the synthesis, I realize that there might still be more research that is not included in this synthesis. Duval and Tweedie's (2000) trim and fill funnel plot-based method was used to ascertain whether distribution of effect sizes used in the analysis was consistent with that of normally distributed estimates.

The average effect size, correlation matrix r, is calculated weighted to the sample sizes with 95% confidence intervals (CI). If the CI falls outside of zero, the null hypothesis that parental expectations have no relationship with achievement is rejected. Furthermore, both fixed-error and random-error assumptions are analyzed separately for each of the primary- and secondary-level studies. A comparison analysis is also conducted between different measures/types of parental expectations within each cohort of parental data.

Results

How strongly parental expectations affect their children's school achievements could first be discussed by comparing primary school-level studies and secondary school-level studies in relation to the school achievement measures. The second way of interpreting the parental expectations effect on school achievement is by discerning the types of parental expectations with the highest impact. Table 7.1 presents the details of the studies at the primary school level, including the authors, type of publication and year, sample size and grade levels and/or ages, type of parental expectations measured, and achievement outcomes. Table 7.2 provides the same details for selected studies at the secondary level. Each table also includes computed effect size (r) of the relationships between parental expectations and achievement measures.

School achievement

The correlation effect of parental expectations on primary school achievement, from a total of 56 samples, varied between –0.36 and 0.78 in the 95% CI. With the fixed-error model, the weighted mean r index was 0.387 and was significantly different from zero (0.370, 0.405); whereas with the random-error model, the weighted mean r was 0.369 and again significantly different from zero (0.329, 0.407).

The heterogeneity test of Q (indicated with I^2) showed a significant result, suggesting that effects were not estimating the same underlying population and hence the random-error model was considered most appropriate for this data. However, neither the funnel plot nor Duval and Tweedie's trim and fill procedure pointed at a significant publication bias. The effect sizes indicating the difference between different outcome measures and the effect size after adjustment for publication bias were exactly the same. A repeated analysis with each study removed to ascertain any outliers revealed no difference in effect sizes. This gave confidence for an assumption that the studies of primary-level school achievement were of high quality and supported the moderately high effect size of parental expectations on achievement measures. Language and mathematics achievement measures yielded similar effect sizes of 0.368 and 0.388, respectively, with no zero CI, whereas grade point averages (GPAs) tended to be lower, with the random model yielding an average r of 0.23. Table 7.3 presents the overall results for both the primary and the secondary levels.

At the secondary school level, parental expectations from a total of 26 samples varied between –0.55 and 0.53 in the 95% CI. With the fixed-error model, the weighted mean r index was 0.282 and was significantly different from zero (0.276, 0.288). The random-error model, on the other hand, yielded a conservative weighted mean r of 0.186 and was still significantly different from zero (0.127, 0.243). The heterogeneity test of Q showed a significant result, suggesting that effects were not estimating the same underlying population and therefore the random-error model was taken as the indicative result for the current data. As in the primary school-level data, neither the funnel plot nor Duval and Tweedie's trim and fill procedure pointed at a significant publication bias. The effect sizes indicating the difference between different outcome measures and the effect size after adjustment for publication bias were similar for the random-error model. A repeated analysis with each study removed to ascertain any outliers revealed no difference in effect sizes. This gave confidence for an assumption that the studies of secondary-level school achievement were of quite high quality and supported the moderate effect size of parental expectations on achievement measures.

Table 7.1 List of cross-sectional studies completed at primary school levels

Author (year) and publication type	Sample size	Grade	Age (years)	Type of parental expectations	Type of instrument	Outcome measures (correlation r)		
						Language/ reading/ literacy	Math	GPA
Thordardottir (2000) Dissertation	100	4	—	Parental expectations	Students' standard scores on the national examinations in Icelandic and mathematics	0.22	0.24	—
Goldenberg, Gallimore, Reese, & Garnier (2001) Journal article	81 81 80 80 79 68	Kinder 1 2 3 4 5	—	Parent aspirations/ expectations and perceptions	Standardized math and reading achievement tests	0.16 0.08 0.10 0.15 0.31 0.17	— 0.15 0.17 0.06 0.27 0.22	—
Wu (2003) Dissertation	513	5 & 6	—	Child's perceived parental expectations	School mid-term test scores	0.23	—	—
Englund, Luckner, Whaley, & Egeland (2004) Journal article	187 187	1 3	—	Parental expectations	Teachers' rating of child's overall academic progress	0.28 0.32	—	—
Davis-Kean (2005) Journal article	N = 868 n = 744 n = 741	—	8–12	Parents' educational expectations	WJ-Reading variable WJ-Broad math variable	0.44 —	— 0.44	—
Y.-P. Liu, (2006) Dissertation	653	6	—	Child's perceived parental expectations	School test scores	0.355	—	—
Phillipson & Phillipson (2007) Journal article	N = 158 n = 43[a] n = 58[b] n = 57[c]	5 & 6	10.54 10.9 10.9 9.9	Parental expectations	School test scores	0.616 0.446 0.568	0.508 0.401 0.501	—
Stern (2007) Dissertation	94 87 94 87	3 & 4	—	Parents' expectations Parents aspirations	WJ-III EOG Reading comprehension test WJ-III EOG Reading comprehension test	0.43 0.48 0.16 0.17	—	—
H.-Y. Liu (2008) Dissertation	104	1–6	—	Mothers' expectations	School test scores	0.30	—	—
Phillipson (2009a) Journal article	N = 215 n = 58[g]	5 & 6	8.8– 13.8 8.8–	Parents' expectations	School test scores	0.325 —	0.38	—

94 *Sivanes Phillipson*

Table 7.1 Continued

Author (year) and publication type	Sample size	Grade	Age (years)	Type of parental expectations	Type of instrument	Outcome measures (correlation r)		
						Language/ reading/ literacy	Math	GPA
	n = 58[g]		11.6			0.51	—	
	n = 54[h]		9.8–			—	0.49	
	n = 54[h]		12.0			0.45	—	
	n = 45[i]		8.8–			—	0.50	
	n = 45[i]		12.1			0.59	—	
	n = 58[j]		9.8–			—	0.38	
	n = 58[j]		13.8			0.46	—	
	n = 103 boys					—	0.44	
	n = 103 boys					0.53	—	
	n = 112 girls					—	0.48	
	n = 112 girls					0.45	—	
Phillipson (2010a) Journal article	N = 780	1–6	—	Parental expectations	School test scores			—
	n = 161[d]					0.43	—	
	n = 161[d]					0.25	—	
	n = 161[d]					—	0.43	
	n = 152[e]					0.57	—	
	n = 152[e]					0.47	—	
	n = 152[e]					—	0.55	
	n = 467[f]					0.54	—	
	n = 467[f]					0.52	—	
	n = 467[f]					—	0.43	
Phillipson (2010b) Journal article	215	5 & 6	8.8– 13.8	Parental expectations:	School test scores	— 0.51	0.45 —	—

Notes
a Chinese school I
b Chinese school II
c British School
d High-ability students
e Low-ability students
f Average-ability students
g English school
h Chinese English-medium school
i Chinese school 1
j Chinese school 2

Unlike in the primary school level, language achievement measure for the random-error model yielded effect size of 0.402 with no zero CI. Mathematics yielded an effect size of 0.125 but with a zero CI; whereas GPAs still tended to be lower, with the random model yielding an average r of 0.152 and a zero CI, which indicated a non-significant overall relationship. Studies that had history and science as their outcome measure had moderate effect sizes with significant CI. Importantly, the difference in language and mathematics could be explained by the presence of more negative correlations in mathematics achievements, and the same explanation could also be applied to GPAs.

Table 7.2 List of cross-sectional studies completed at secondary school levels

Author (year) and publication type	Sample size	Grade	Age (years)	Type of parent expectations	Outcome measures (correlations)			
					Type of instrument	Language/ reading/ literacy	Math	GPA/ Others
Ainley, Foreman, & Sheret (1991) Journal article	3045	9–11	—	Child-perceived parental expectations	The average standardized scores in a mathematics test and a reading comprehension test.	0.25		—
Cheng & Wong (1991) Journal article	894	7–13	—	Child-perceived parental expectations	Teachers' ratings of the child's academic performance in comparison to others in the same classroom	—	−0.14	—
Crystal et al. (1994) Journal article	N = 4266	11		Child-perceived parental expectations	47-item test of mathematics achievement			—
	n = 1386 American		17.2			—	−0.07	
	n = 1633 Taiwanese		17.3			—	−0.05	
	n = 1247 Japanese		17.0			—	0.05	
Dai (1998) Dissertation	N = 336	9–10	—	Parental expectations	Math, English, or Chinese grades/GPA from past school records		—	
	n = 81 American		0.53					
	N = 255 Chinese		0.20					
Keith, Keith, Quirk, Sperduto, Santillo, & Killings (1998) Journal article	15,703	10	—	Parental aspirations	Students' self-reported grades in English, mathematics, science, and history in ninth and tenth grades	0.30	0.21	0.33[h] 0.28[s]
Thordardottir (2000) Dissertation	N = 322		—	Parental expectations	Students' standard scores on the national examinations in Icelandic and mathematics			—
	n = 100	7				0.32	0.37	
	n = 122	10				0.53	0.45	

Table 7.2 Continued

Author (year) and publication type	Sample size	Grade	Age (years)	Type of parent expectations	Outcome measures (correlations)			
					Type of instrument	Language/ reading/ literacy	Math	GPA/ Others
Li (2004) Dissertation	558	8	—	Child-perceived parent expectations	Mean grades of three monthly English exams in the first semester	0.524	—	—
Kobayashi (2005) Dissertation	203	—	19.8	Parental expectations	GPA	—		−0.08
Lin (2006) Dissertation	809	8	—	Parental expectations	School test scores		0.037	
Mistry, White, Benner, & Huynh (2009) Journal article	426 (two-times data collection – T1 and T2)	—	12.2–15.7	Mothers' educational expectations	Teachers' rating of the child's academic performance in comparison to others in the same classroom at T1		0.11	
					Teachers' rating of the child's academic performance in comparison to others in the same classroom at T2		0.30	
					WJ Achievement Test at T1	0.25	—	—
					WJ Achievement Test at T2	0.37		
					School records at T2	—	—	0.33
Nicols, Kotchick, Barry, & Haskins (2010) Journal article	130	—	16.76	Child-perceived parental expectations	—	−0.055		—

Spera, Wentzel, & Matto (2009) Journal article	13,577	51% (middle school) 49% (high school) students	—	Parental aspirations	Parents' reporting of their child's approximate grade average	—	—	0.44
Yazedjian, Toews, & Navarro (2009) Journal article	N = 883	First year college	18.4	Child-perceived parental expectations	GPA of the first semester of the freshman year			
		n = 694 White students				—	—	−0.05
		n = 189 Hispanic students				—	—	−0.09
Chen & Gregory (2010) Journal article	59	9	—	Child-perceived parental expectations	End-of-year GPA	—	—	0.31
				Child-perceived parental aspirations				0.36

Notes
If not specified, GPA/Others = GPA
h History grades
s Science grades

98 Sivanes Phillipson

Table 7.3 Overall effect of parental expectations on language, mathematics, and GPA outcomes at primary and secondary levels

			95% CI		
	Primary school level				
Outcome measure	k	$\bar{r}$	Low estimate	High estimate	I^{2a}
Language	2	0.297	0.135	0.444	0
Language/mathematics	33	0.368	0.311	0.422	81.23*
Mathematics	20	0.388	0.334	0.439	53.94*
GPA	1	0.230	0.146	0.310	0
	Secondary school level				
Language	4	0.402	0.178	0.587	96.65*
Mathematics	7	0.127	−0.054	0.300	98.85*
GPA	6	0.152	−0.137	0.418	98.25*
Overall academic	7	0.125	−0.032	0.277	95.59*
History	1	0.280	0.266	0.294	0
Science	1	0.330	0.316	0.344	0

Notes
* $p < 0.00001$
a The p-value in this column indicates whether the Q statistic was significant or not.

Types of parental expectations

There were four types of parental expectations in the studies of the meta-analysis. The prominent one used in 40 samples, out of which 31 were from the primary school level, was parental expectations of their children's school grades. The second type was parental aspirations for their child's future, followed by child's perception of parental expectations. The least common one was mother's expectations of their children's grades.

A repeated analysis with each study removed to remove outliers revealed no difference in effect sizes. This analysis was done to ensure that the studies of both the primary- and the secondary-level school achievement were of quite high quality and supported the effect sizes of types of parental expectations on achievement measures. Table 7.4 presents the comparative results between the types of parental expectations and their impact on achievement-related outcomes.

At the primary school level, parental expectations of their children's grades from 31 samples had a high effect size of 0.479 with non-zero CI (with the random-error model). The Q statistics showed a non-significant index, which suggested that the estimates measured the same underlying population and the fixed model would suffice in this instance. However, the conservative random-error model was still taken as appropriate as there was only a small difference in effect sizes between the fixed model and random model. Meanwhile, at the secondary school level with nine samples, the effect size was also positive and significant; however, with a decreased strength in association (r = 0.299) between this type of parental expectations and school achievement.

Parental future aspirations from 17 samples at the primary level had an effect size of 0.192, while six samples from the secondary level yielded a stronger effect size of 0.317. Both associations were significant with non-zero CIs. The third type of parental expectations is the child-perceived parental expectations, and this had contradictory results between primary and secondary levels. At the primary level, child-perceived parental expectations in

Parental expectations on school achievement 99

Table 7.4 Overall effect of types of parental expectations on achievement at primary and secondary school levels

			95% CI		
			Primary school level		
Type of parental expectations measure	k	$\bar{r}$	Low estimate	High estimate	I^{2a}
Parental expectations of grades	31	0.479	0.455	0.503	1.50
Parental future aspirations	17	0.192	0.093	0.287	83.92*
Mother's expectations	1	0.300	0.114	0.466	0
Child-perceived parental expectations	7	0.302	0.254	0.343	14.44
			Secondary school level		
Parental expectations of grades	9	0.299	0.145	0.439	90.23*
Parental future aspirations	6	0.317	0.245	0.385	99.04*
Mother's expectations	2	0.207	0.015	0.384	88.07**
Child-perceived parental expectations	9	−0.007	−0.156	0.143	98.07*

Notes
* $p < 0.000$
** $p < 0.005$
a The p-value in this column indicates whether the Q statistic was significant or not.

seven samples yielded a significant effect size of 0.302. On the other hand, the same parental expectations in nine samples resulted in a non-significant and very small negative effect size of −0.007. Mother's expectations on one sample at the primary level and two samples at the secondary level had positive and moderate effect sizes.

Discussion

Earlier in this chapter, I concluded that parental expectations have an effect on their children's school achievements and this can be interpreted within Vygotsky's paradigm of the mediation and internalization process within sociocultural theory (1978). Vygotsky's (2004) observation that "The path from the thing to the child and from the child to the thing lies through another person" (p. 532) places the role of parents as one of a significant other in the processes of mediation and internalization that take place between the child and the social plane. I showed that parent–child interaction forms the process of mediation where children are able to internalize much of their parents' values and expectations. However, the kind of function that parental expectations take in the process, and whether this function is effective or not for the development of children's achievements, is the question I set out to answer. The approach taken was through a meta-analysis of the available research.

One consistent point that is established throughout the literature and the meta-analysis results is that parental expectations do impact on their children's school achievements regardless of the type of measures of achievement: language or mathematics. Studies like Neuenschwander et al. (2007) and Stern (2007) show that there is a direct and rather strong relationship between parental expectations and school achievement. Other studies showed that parental expectations mediate other variables to lead to school achievement. What is important though is the question of how effective the role of parents is as the significant other in these relationships.

Parents as the significant other: Are they effective?

In one sense, parents do play the role of significant other when specific types of their expectations are transferred to their children. The meta-analysis results showed that parental expectations that have to do with immediate or near-future school achievement in the form of school grades had positive and higher effect sizes. One explanation for this result might be that this type of parental expectation is communicated effectively to children, to be internalized to result in achievement. As expectations are raised, so is the achievement of the children. I argue that, when parents communicate their expectations for their immediate future school grades, these expectations are more specific and succinct for their children to absorb, especially when channeled through artifacts and involvement (e.g., Jeynes, 2005). Such a process could be further driven by parental motives in seeing to their children's success and they provide the time and space for parental expectations to take effect on their children's actualization of their performance.

Parental expectations for younger and older children

Strong and positive effect sizes are found more at the primary school level than at the secondary school level. This finding is consistent with previous synthesis of parental involvement, where their involvement is more widely accepted by younger children than older children (Patall et al., 2008). Involvement by parents in educational activities or assistance with homework is usually practised with younger children and, hence, interaction during these times leads to provision of time and space that enables communication of expectations. Parents' function as a significant other in this instance is effective, especially when children absorb the expectations in a positive manner and realize their potential into successful performance. Parents' role as a significant other also is effective when their parenting practices through home and school activities promote an "agreement" of understanding of the kinds of realistic expectations that they have for their children (Hao & Bonstead-Bruns, 1998).

As children grow older, their own perception of their parental expectations seems to become distorted, as the meta-analysis results showed that more negative and weaker relationships arise by the time children reach college age. For example, 16-year-old children's perceptions of their parental expectations were negatively correlated to their performance (Nichols, Kotchick, Barry, & Haskins, 2010).

Parental expectations relating to different cultural backgrounds

Of course, different sociocultural contexts in the different studies could also contribute to different outcomes of mediation and internalization of parental expectations. Crystal et al. (1994) demonstrated that American and Taiwanese college students interpreted the relationship between the meaning behind their parental expectations and their academic achievement differently from their Japanese counterparts. In these instances, parental expectations seem to have arbitrary effects on children's school performances.

Could different levels of motive, involvement, and time and space in the process of parent–child interaction explain the arbitrary effect of parental expectations as perceived by their children? This could happen presumably because of lack of proper mediation and internalization of expectations – and hence lack of "agreement". When parental expectations are communicated within the time and space that allows for conducive mediation and internalization, then children should perceive the correct expectations communicated by parents. When parental practices do not create such interactions that encourage development of "mature cultural behaviors", such practices do not make parents' role as one of a significant other.

One possible explanation of parents' failure to be a significant other is provided by the meta-analysis result where parents communicate future aspirations; such aspirations are found to have weaker correlation than expectations that communicate specific goals for the near future. Such future aspirations are far in time and space – perhaps sometimes can be misunderstood by their children, and thus lead to a different or even opposite outcome (Goldenberg et al., 2001). In other words, aspirations can be communicated without specific motive or involvement by parents and no affordance of expectations is conveyed to these kinds of aspirations (Li, 2003). Consequently, parental expectations for the future may not have a mediation structure that creates opportunities for interaction and internalization. The other possible explanation comes from studies that have shown that unnecessary pressure from parents causes children to react in a negative way toward their own ability to perform (Chan, 2006; Watkins, 2009).

Conclusion

Ultimately, I argue that, for parents to be a significant other, the parental focal position in children's pathways to their school performance must derive from a positive parental motive and optimum involvement that influence children's actualization of their potential into performance. This pathway must have time and space for mediation and internalization to ensure "agreement" of expectations. A close proximity in time and space toward an agreed goal is within this pathway. This pathway must also have the artifacts and parental practices that do not provide unrealistic expectations and pressure that distort the real aim of the parental role as a significant other.

References

Ainley, J., Foreman, J., & Sheret, M. (1991). High school factors that influence students to remain in school. *The Journal of Educational Research, 85*(2), 69–80.

Borenstein, M., Hedges, L., Higgins, J., & Rothstein, H. (2005). *Comprehensive meta-analysis, version 2.* Englewood, NJ: Biostat.

Chan, D. W. (2006). Adjustment problems, self-efficacy, and psychological distress among Chinese gifted students in Hong Kong. *Roeper Review, 28*(4), 203–209.

Chen, W.-B., & Gregory, A. (2010). Parental involvement as a protective factor during the transition to high school. *The Journal of Educational Research, 103*(1), 53–62.

Cheng, S. C., & Wong, N. Y. (1991). The attitude towards learning mathematics among secondary school students in Hong Kong. *Education Journal, 19*(1), 13–18.

Crystal, D. S., Chen, C., Fuligni, A. J., Stevenson, H. W., Hsu, C.-C., Ko, H.-J., . . . Kimura, S. (1994). Psychological maladjustment and academic achievement: A cross-cultural study of Japanese, Chinese, and American high school students. *Child Development, 65*(3), 738–753.

Dai, Y. (1998). Relationships among parenting styles, parental expectations and attitudes, and adolescents' school functioning: A cross-cultural study. (Unpublished PhD). Purdue University.

Davis-Kean, P. E. (2005). The influence of parent education and family income on child achievement: The indirect role of parental expectations and the home environment. *Journal of Family Psychology, 19*(2), 294–304.

Duval, S., & Tweedie, R. (2000). Trim and fill: A simple funnel plot-based method of testing and adjusting for publication bias in meta-analysis. *Biometrics, 56,* 276–284.

Englund, M. M., Luckner, A. E., Whaley, G. J. L., & Egeland, B. (2004). Children's achievement in early elementary school: Longitudinal effects of parental involvement, expectations, and quality of assistance. *Journal of Educational Psychology, 96*(4), 723–730.

Epstein, J. L. (2006). Families, schools, and community partnerships. *Young Children, 61*(1), 40.

Feuerstein, R., & Gross, S. (1997). The learning potential assessment device. In D. P. Flanagan, J. L. Genshaft, & P. L. Harrison (Eds.), *Contemporary intellectual assessment: Theories, tests and issues* (pp. 297–313). New York: Guilford.

Glick, J. E., & White, M. J. (2004). Post-secondary school participation of immigrant and native youth: The role of familial resources and educational expectations. *Social Science Research, 33*(2), 272–299.

Goldenberg, C., Gallimore, R., Reese, L., & Garnier, H. (2001). Cause or effect? A longitudinal study of immigrant Latino parents' aspirations and expectations, and their children's school performance. *American Educational Research Journal, 38*(3), 547–582.

Hao, L., & Bonstead-Bruns, M. (1998). Parent–child differences in educational expectations and the academic achievement of immigrant and native students. *Sociology of Education, 71*(3), 175–198.

Hill, N. E., & Tyson, D. F. (2009). Parental involvement in middle school: A meta-analytic assessment of the strategies that promote achievement. *Developmental Psychology, 45*(3), 740–763.

Jeynes, W. H. (2005). A meta-analysis of the relation of parental involvement to urban elementary school student academic achievement. *Urban Education, 40*, 237–269.

Jeynes, W. H. (2007). The relationship between parental involvement and urban secondary school student academic achievement: A meta-analysis. *Urban Education, 42*(1), 82–110.

Ji, G., Jiao, S., & Jing, Q. (1993). Expectancy of Chinese parents and children's cognitive abilities. *International Journal of Psychology, 28*(6), 821–830.

Keith, T. Z., Keith, P., Quirk, K., Sperduto, J., Santillo, S., & Killings, S. (1998). Longitudinal effects of parent involvement on high school grades: Similarities and differences across gender and ethnic groups. *Journal of School Psychology, 35*, 335–363.

Kobayashi, E. (2005). Perceived parental expectations among Chinese American college students: The role of perceived discrepancy and culture in psychological distress. (Unpublished PhD). The Pennsylvania State University.

Li, C.-h. (2004). A study of the influence of the parent on junior-high-school students' achievement in learning English [父母對國中生英語成績之影響]. (Unpublished PhD). National Kaohsiung Normal University.

Li, J. (2003). Affordances and constraints of immigrant Chinese parental expectations on children's school performance. *Alberta Journal of Educational Research, 49*(2), 198–200.

Lin, W.-C. (2006). A study on self-efficacy, parental expectancies, classroom structure perceptions and academic achievement of junior high school students [國中學生自我效能、父母期望、教室結構知覺與學業成就之研究]. (Unpublished Master's thesis). National Changhua University of Education.

Liu, H.-Y. (2008). Exploring the relationship between newly Taiwanese children's English performance and their mothers' expectations [探究新台灣之子的英語學習成果與其母親期望之關係]. (Unpublished Master's thesis). Chaoyang University of Technology.

Liu, Y.-P. (2006). Sixth graders' English learning achievement and its relationship with social economic situation, parents' participation and parents' expectation [家庭社經地位、父母參與、父母期望與國小六年級學生英語學習成就之相關研究]. (Unpublished Master's thesis). National Taipei University of Education.

Lohrfink, K. J. F. (2002). Parental expectations and parenting behavior as mediators of the relation between family structure and child cognitive development. Dissertation Abstracts International: Section B. The Sciences and Engineering, 63(6-B), 3043.

Mistry, R. S., White, E. S., Benner, A. D., & Huynh, V. W. (2009). A longitudinal study of the simultaneous influence of mothers' and teachers' educational expectations on low-income youth's academic achievement. *Journal of Youth and Adolecence, 38*(6), 826–838.

Neuenschwander, M. P., Vida, M., Garrett, J. L., & Eccles, J. S. (2007). Parents' expectations and students' achievement in two western nations. *International Journal of Behavioral Development*, *31*(6), 594–602.

Nichols, T. M., Kotchick, B. A., Barry, C. M., & Haskins, D. G. (2010). Understanding the educational aspirations of African American adolescents: Child, family, and community factors. *Journal of Black Psychology*, *36*(25), 25–48.

Patall, E. A., Cooper, H., & Robinson, J. (2008). Parental involvement in homework: A research synthesis. *Review of Educational Research*, *78*(4), 1039–1101.

Phillipson, S. (2009a). Context of academic achievement: Lessons from Hong Kong. *Educational Psychology*, *29*(4), 447–468.

Phillipson, S. (2009b). *Parent and children voices: Beliefs and expectations of academic achievement.* Köln, Germany: LAP LAMBERT Academic Publishing.

Phillipson, S. (2010a). Modeling parental role in academic achievement: Comparing high-ability to low- and average-ability students. *Talent Development and Excellence*, *2*(1), 83–103.

Phillipson, S. (2010b). Parental role and students' cognitive ability: An achievement model. *The Asia-Pacific Education Researcher*, *19*(2), 229–250.

Phillipson, S., & Phillipson, S. N. (2007). Academic expectation, belief of ability and involvement by parents as predictors of child achievement: A cross-cultural comparison. *Educational Psychology*, *27*(3), 329–348.

Phillipson, S., & Phillipson, S. N. (2012). Children's cognitive ability and their academic achievement: The mediation effects of parental expectations. *Asia Pacific Education Review*, *13*(3), 495–508.

Rogoff, B. (1990). Apprenticeship in thinking: Cognitive development in social context. New York: Oxford University Press.

Salimi, S.-H., Mirzamani, S.-M., & Shahiri-Tabarestani, M. (2005). Association of parental self-esteem and expectations with adolescents' anxiety about career and education. *Psychological Reports*, *96*(3), 569–578.

Seginer, R. (2006). Parent's educational involvement: A developmental ecology perspective. *Parenting: Science and Practice*, *6*, 1–48.

Spera, C., Wentzel, K. R., & Matto, H. C. (2009). Parental aspirations for their children's educational attainment: Relations to ethnicity, parental education, children's academic performance, and parental perceptions of school climate. *Journal of Youth and Adolescence*, *38*(8), 1140–1152.

Stern, M. H. (2007). Parents' academic expectations, children's perceptions, and the reading achievement of children at varying risk. (Unpublished PhD). University of North Carolina.

Thordardottir, I. B. (2000). Student achievement and the national examinations in Vestfirdir, Iceland. (Unpublished PhD). The Pennsylvania State University, PA.

Vygotsky, L. S. (1978). *Mind in society: The development of higher mental process.* Cambridge, MA: Harvard University Press.

Vygotsky, L. S. (1981). The genesis of higher mental functions. In J. V. Wertsch (Ed.), *The concept of activity in Soviet psychology* (pp. 144–188). Armonk, NY: Sharpe.

Vygotsky, L. S. (2004). Scientific legacy: The problem of practical intellect. In R. W. Rieber & D. K. Robinson (Eds.), *The essential Vygotsky* (pp. 513–537). New York: Kluwer Academic/Plenum Publishers.

Watkins, D. A. (2009). Motivation and competition in Hong Kong secondary schools: The students' perspective. In C. K. K. Chan & N. Rao (Eds.), *Revisiting the Chinese learner – changing contexts, changing education* (pp. 71–88). Hong Kong: Springer: Comparative Education Research Centre, The University of Hong Kong.

Wertsch, J. V. (1985). *Vygotsky and the social formation of mind.* Cambridge, MA: Harvard University Press.

Wu, M. C. (2003). The relationship of self efficacy, parental expectations, teacher expectations, academic performance and behavior disturbance of students in elementary schools [國小高年級學童自我效能、知覺父母期望、教師期望與行為困擾、學業表現之相關研究]. (Unpublished Master's thesis). National Taiwan Normal University.

Yamamoto, Y., & Holloway, S. D. (2010). Parental expectations and children's academic performance in sociocultural context. *Educational Psychology Review, 22*(3), 189–214.

Yang, H.-Y. (2007). A study of the relationship among perceptions of parenting styles, parents' expectations, and self-regulated learning of senior elementary school students [國小高年級學生知覺父母管教方式、父母期望與自我調整學系關係之研究]. (Unpublished Master's thesis). National University of Tainan.

Yang, Y.-F. (2010). The correlation of family factors to new immigrant children's English learning attitude and English learning achievement in Taoyuan county [新住民學童家庭因素對其英語學習成就與學習態度的影響—以桃園縣某國小為例]. (Unpublished Master's thesis). National Taipei University of Education.

Yazedjian, A., Toews, M. L., & Navarro, A. (2009). Exploring parental factors, adjustment, and academic achievement among white and hispanic college students. *Journal of College Student Development, 50*(4), 458–467.

8 Examining the relations between a play motive and a learning motive for enhancing school achievement

Doing "school" at home

Marilyn Fleer

Introduction

Whilst longstanding research into motives and motivation has provided the fields of education and psychology with a plethora of evidence and directionality for studying human behaviour, there has in recent times been a distinctly different theorization emerging which draws upon cultural–historical theory (see McInerney, Walker & Liem, 2011). Central to these different conceptualizations is whether a child comes into the world *driven by personal motives* or is seen as *acquiring collective motives* through their participation in human society (Fleer, 2011). These are diametrically opposed positions. Reber and Reber (2001) have stated that, traditionally, the concept of motive has been conceptualized as either the *internal state* of a person which "impels it into action" (p. 447) or a state "specific to particular drives and needs" which are related directly to specific goals and directions (p. 448). In the former, personal motives are internal. In the latter view, it is argued that:

> Motivational states result from multiple interactions of a large number of other variables, among them being the *need* or *drive* level, the *incentive* value of a goal, an organism's *expectations*, the availability of appropriate responses (i.e. learned behaviours), the possible presence of conflicting or contradictory motives and, of course, unconscious factors.
>
> (Reber & Reber, 2001, p. 448; original emphasis).

Hedegaard (2011) has put forward a third conception – motive as a *dynamic interplay* between collective motives and personal motives. It is the *relations* between the personal and the collective that is the focus of her theorization and analytical work.

The differing assumptions underpinning motives and motivation have been instrumental in shaping how research activity is formulated and this has a direct relationship to learning theory. According to Reber and Reber (2001), motivation has been clustered into three theoretical areas, *physiological, behavioural* and *psychosocial*. The former is underpinned by neurological and biochemical analysis, examining primary drives such as pain avoidance. The behavioural research into motives "is concerned largely with elaborations and refinements of drive theory and learning theory" (p. 448), whilst *psychosocial* research seeks to find explanations of learned human behaviours.

Hedegaard (2011) has also noted how learning theories have framed the ways motives and motivation are conceptualized, finding three clusters. She has suggested that the "role of drives, needs, motivation and motives has been formulated in different theories as *forces giving rise to how persons relate to the world and how this relation develops*" (my emphasis;

p. 13). In line with Reber and Reber (2001), the first theory sees motives as an inborn drive, which can be modified, such as is exemplified by psychoanalytical, humanistic and behaviourist approaches. The second clustering foregrounds societal demands, which are appropriated for cognitive outcomes, as seen in cognitive anthropological and sociological approaches. These two perspectives also sit comfortably with that suggested by Reber and Reber (2001).

However, Hedegaard (2011) goes one step further and puts forward a wholeness approach, which is conceptualized as the dynamic relation between the person and their world where the central force is both in the person and in the environment, and together these relations create the dynamic conditions for a person's activity and learning. That is, a motive develops through this dynamic interplay, becoming what Reber and Reber (2001) have termed "a state of arousal that impels an organism to action" (p. 448) and what Hedegaard (2011) has called the relations between *demands and initiatives* and *activities and practices*. It is this latter conceptualization of motives and motivation by Hedegaard (2011) that is of special interest because it allows for both individual and social dimensions of human activity to be examined in ways that Stetsenko and Arievitch (2004) have termed as "non-dichotomizing". This conception of motives is useful for studying how children's dominant motives change from play to learning in the early years because this conception offers a non-reductionist ontological vision of human nature.

This chapter explores the employment of cultural–historical theory to examine how social practices within family homes create the conditions for the development of a school child's learning motive, whilst at the same time analyzing how the child's personal play motive contributes to the new practices introduced as a result of the child commencing school. The overarching theme of this chapter is to show the relations between play and learning motives, avoiding an individualistic paradigm for conceptualizing motives, and to theorize how motives change when a child begins school. Whilst this conceptualization of the dialectical relations between play motives and learning motives is central to the work of teachers for supporting student achievement, less is understood about how a learning motive is realized in the family home. Through examples of everyday family practices of doing homework, a theoretical discussion of how children and their families create the conditions for the development of a learning motive is put forward with a view to examining the interplay between play and learning.

A cultural–historical reading of motives

In drawing upon the work of Lewin, Leontiev and Vygotsky, Hedegaard (2011) has put forward a wholeness approach to children's learning and development of motives. In Hedegaard's (2011) model, she foregrounds the relations between the personal motives of a child, the motives that develop through a child's participation in institutional practices, such as schools or families, and motives that are formed through a family's engagement with societal expectations and rules. These differing levels of participation concurrently create different demands upon a child, and these often peak when a child moves or transitions between institutions, such as when starting school. For instance, Hedegaard (2011) argues that "Demands in these settings by objects or persons can be seen as conditions for as well as motivating activities. For home practices this can be the meals, homework and preparation for going to bed. In school it can be the different subject matter sessions and recess" (p. 10). Hence, it is possible to see how a child can develop multiple motives, which may be conflicting, resulting in what Leontiev (1978) termed a *hierarchy of motives*. This concept captures the juxtaposed activities that children meet, and that they need to prioritize, in order to make decisions about their active, or not, participation in society.

What is important for a child at one point in their life can change because the child gains new experiences as they engage in daily life at school and at home. Hence the motive hierarchy is not stable. For example, a preschool child who enters into school may begin with a motive for play but as a result of a more formal schooling experience may subordinate their play motive for a motive for learning how to read. As Hedegaard and Chaiklin (2005) remind us, "This does not imply that a child's earlier dominant motive disappears; only that it gets another position in the child's motive hierarchy" (p. 65). In this conceptualization, it is possible to see how a child's personal motives are related to one another. Through a wholeness perspective (Hedegaard, 2011), we are able to better understand the relations between a child's personal motives and how these develop or change. This is noted as a child participates in, and transitions between, institutions, where practice traditions are shaped by societal goals and expectations which afford differing kinds of experiences for children and develop different kinds of motives. What this means for the relations between the child and the teacher in the preschool or school setting is critical for the development of a learning motive: "For the teacher it is important to focus on this change in dominating motives, supporting the learning motive if it is there, and helping the child to acquire this motive if it is not developed" (Hedegaard & Chaiklin, 2005, p. 65).

School practices have a profound effect on home practices (see Hedegaard & Fleer, 2013) as is evident when children are asked to participate in homework (Hedegaard, 2011), or are required to engage in after-school tuition or weekend school (Wong & Fleer, 2012). How these home-based practices develop a learning motive is not well understood, especially when play may still be the child's leading motive (Vygotsky, 1966). In order to understand the relations between a motive for play and a learning motive, we must first examine a cultural–historical conception of play. In this chapter, the term cultural–historical is adopted because the literature drawn upon for the arguments presented uses this term, rather than the term sociocultural. However, it is noted that both terms represent the seminal theories first outlined by Vygotsky.

The development of a play motive

It was argued in the previous section that the development of a motive is conceptualized as the "dynamic relation between person and practice" (Hedegaard & Chaiklin, 2005, p. 64). In this theorization, we must focus on the relations *between* the child and the social environment when examining how a child's personal motives for play develop. However, much of the traditional early childhood education literature on play has made central an internal model of motives, as discussed in the introduction, suggesting that children come into the world *driven by a play motive* (Fleer, 2011). Elkonin (2005a, b) has put forward a convincing historical analysis of the development of play, suggesting that play as a human activity has been culturally constructed and arose historically through the changing societal conditions where the introduction of technologies changed the position the child held in the community. That is, as family bands began to use technologies for food production, such as digging sticks, later ploughs, or spears for fishing, later fishing nets, that increased strength and skills were needed to work these technologies, thus not allowing children until they were much older to participate in direct food production. Children needed time to grow stronger and to learn valued skills, such as knot work for creating fishing nets, before they could productively contribute to the survival of the family unit. Consequently,

108 *Marilyn Fleer*

communities gave time, space and resources to children to practise these needed skills, resulting in models and later toys and games being developed for repetitive skills development, such as string games in fishing communities so that children could learn how to mend and build fishing nets. Elkonin (2005a) has argued that these games and toys have stayed in communities over time, even though their original purpose or societal need was no longer relevant. Participation in society was the central need and, through this, a motive for playing with games and toys developed. As societies became more urban, and children began to be isolated from the community work of adults, by being put into schools, children began to engage in social pretend play or role-play. The societal conditions created the need for more complicated imaginary play and, through these new practices, developed a motive for play prior to attending school. For instance, Elkonin (1978) has stated:

> The world of adults becomes very attractive for children, and they are looking forward to becoming a part of this world. In industrialised societies, however, children cannot fulfil their desire directly: They cannot be doctors or firefighters, that is why they "penetrate" the world of adults by imitating and exploring social roles and relations in the course of sociodramatic play, Thus, *the motive of sociodramatic play is "to act like an adult"*.
>
> (cited in Karpov, 2005, pp. 139–40; my emphasis)

If we are to accept Elkonin's position that everyday life is the source of imaginary play themes for children, we would expect to see play activities related to children's specific communities emerging. For instance, in a rural community located near the waterways where a large number of boats can be found, boat play and market gardening play is likely to be evident in the local preschool. In the following play observation made in a preschool within a boating and market gardening community, a group of four preschool children are manipulating a set of dinosaurs in a water trolley. The children do not focus on the dinosaurs themselves, but rather are engaged in role-playing "boating":

> One child who is holding a magnifying glass that he had brought over to the water trolley says "this can be an island". He places the dinosaur on to the magnifying glass. Jamie rejects this suggestion, stating that it is a boat game. Jamie continues to move the dinosaurs in and out of the water, singing "Sailing on a boat". The first child says "It fell out" as the dinosaur falls off the magnifying glass. The child picks up the magnifying glass and studies the dinosaurs. A third child joins the group and puts the cellophane into the water, announcing that it is an island. Jamie indicates he wishes to also have some cellophane. The first child passes him some wet cellophane (not the dry piece he has in his hand). Jamie says "I want that one. I want a good one. Not that one". The newcomer goes and finds more cellophane and drops it into the water. The children continue to move their dinosaurs in and out of the water, and onto cellophane and the magnifying glass, labelling these objects as islands, boats and beaches (Video observation of Rural Preschool, 1 Aug morning).
>
> (Fleer, 2012, p. 85)

In this example, we see that the children have changed the meaning of the objects and the associated actions in their play from what was visible – the plastic dinosaur models – to what was relevant to their community – boating on the waterways. In the same preschool, the children also took plastic water bottles and systematically pretended to poison all the plants in the outdoor area of the centre, suggesting that the observed practice of chemical weeding in the community was being enacted within the preschool. Once again, the children changed the meaning of the objects in relation to community practices and potentially the family activities observed. Vygotsky (1966) has argued that children in play create imaginary situations where they change the meaning of objects and actions. He cites the example of how a child changes the meaning of a stick to a hobbyhorse, giving it new meaning and action. Vygotsky (1966) also argued that the source of children's play did not come from within, but was socially produced, often enacted with others. A cultural–historical reading of play defines actions and activities as play when an imaginary situation is created, and objects and actions are given new meaning, and children take on new roles.

Elkonin (2005b) suggested that children move closer to reality in role-play because they test out the rules and roles of others in society, gaining insights into how their world works. In this theorization of play, it is possible to see how the content of the play is constructed from the child's world, and hence the motive for play is developed through children's interactions with their social and material environment. This is a very different reading of play and is diametrically opposed to the dominant traditional thinking, where the child is viewed as biologically primed for play (i.e., play motive is internally driven), and where the pedagogy of play has been conceptualized as being free of adults (see Fleer, 2010, for a critique of this area). Similarly, Hedegaard (1989) in citing Elkonin (1971) states that "In the preschool/play period and the early school period, the development of the child's motives for mastery of the adult world and acquisition of methods for analysing goals and means thereof characterize the child's relation to the world" (p. 35). A cultural–historical theory of play affords a very different perspective of the concept of motive development. However, Elkonin's (2005a) theorization of the development of a play motive does not show how a motive for play becomes subordinate to a motive for learning.

The development of a learning motive

It has been argued by Hedegaard (2002) that a learning motive develops through the child's participation in schooling. She states that a learning motive "can become connected to subject-matter concepts . . . The learning motive develops from the child's participation in teaching activity, *but the interest the children bring* to this teaching has to be a starting point for their development of motivation" (p. 21; my emphasis). In this reading of a learning motive, it is possible to see that both the child's participation in the new institutional practice of school, alongside what the child brings to this practice, interact and create the conditions for the development of a learning motive. But it is not just the school context that creates these conditions. The development of a learning motive can also be possible through the child's participation in school-type activities that occur in the home, such as when a child does homework (Hedegaard & Fleer, 2013). But these activities and practices need to be conceptualized within a system of social relations that make up the child's environment (Bozhovich, 2009). As noted by Vygotsky (1994), "we can only explain the role of the environment in child development when *we know the relation* between the child and his [sic] environment" (p. 399; my emphasis).

In the following example (discussed empirically in Hedegaard & Fleer, 2013), it is possible to see how a learning motive for homework develops. Here we examine the child's intentions within the family practice of homework. We do this so we can determine the development of a learning motive, as noted by Hedegaard (2011): "It is only through the analyses of the child's intentional actions that we can catch the child's activities and motives" (p. 22).

110　*Marilyn Fleer*

The researchers (Marilyn and Gloria) arrive at the family home and all of the children run to the front door to greet them. Mandy (18 months) shows the researchers the lollipops that Nan (grandmother) has given her, whilst Cam (3 years) shows the researcher (Marilyn) a tennis ball, inviting her to play ball in the kitchen. Cam throws the ball and all the children join in throwing the ball around the kitchen area. Whilst this occurs, Mandy finds another ball, and Nan supports her with ball throwing. Cam, Mandy, Alex (4 years), and Nan continue to throw balls whilst Mum calls Jason (5 years) back to the table to read his school reading book. Jason does not appear to be happy about this. Mum sits at the table. Jason sits down next to his mother. Whilst homework is occurring at the kitchen table a range of activities take place in and around the kitchen area.

Uncle Matthew is playing and discussing computer games with the father. Whilst Nan and Mandy are playing ball, Gran tries to engage Uncle Matthew in ball play too, but he says he is busy. However, he takes the ball from the floor and then passes it to Mandy. Mandy accidently threw the ball at Jason who is reading his book, word by word, with his mother pointing to each word as he reads, and Gran says "You can't give it to Jason, he is busy reading". When Jason struggles with a word, Gran asks him about the book, saying "Is that a book about the creepy crawlies that Nan doesn't like?" This gives Jason the contextual information he needs to work out what the word is. Jason then continues to read. Although there is a lot of activity going on around him, Jason stays focused on his reader. Eventually Jason indicates he wants to leave the table, but his mum says "You have to do your red words" [flash cards to be rote learnt]. Jason kicks his feet and makes disagreeable noises, showing clearly he does not wish to participate. At this point Gran asks if she can look at his reader. As she looks at the book she says "Oh what a beautiful reader". Jason says "No those aren't creepy". His mother takes the pack of red flash cards from their bag that contains single words related to the text in the reader, and puts them on the table. Jason says he wants his father to do the words with him. The father immediately agrees. Gran moves closer to Jason and says she wants to play too. The dad shuffles the flash cards, and when Jason reads the word correctly, the father says "Hi Five" as he puts his hand into the air. Jason responds immediately with a return "Hi Five" clapping his father's hand. Jason smiles and goes back to reading the cards. Gran pretends she is disappointed that she is not as fast as Jason, and also praises Jason. Jason appears to take great delight in the game. When Jason reads all of the words correctly his mother hugs him, and all the adults cheer. Gran offers Jason a lollipop for reading all of his words correctly. Cam who has been observing the homework, says he wants to put all the cards into the plastic bag, when his father starts to pack up the cards. Because the father continues to pack up, Cam now yells out that he wishes to do this. His father stops packing up, and lets Cam play with the cards and then to pack up the cards.

(Observation Period 3 Visit 2, 15th of December)

As noted by Hedegaard (2011), when we study motives from a cultural–historical perspective, we must direct our analysis to understandings the child's intentions. For instance, Hedegaard (2011) writes "to understand and research children's motives we have to follow the child in his or her activities as intentional actions *and interactions with others in activity settings*" (p. 24; my emphasis). In this example of Jason doing schoolwork at home, he was taken away from his play activity and asked to sit at the kitchen table with his mother and to do the homework that the school had given him. Jason was reluctant to stop playing, making resistant noises and facial expressions of disapproval. His intention was to continue to play in the lounge room. Play was the preferred activity for Jason in the system of relations in his family.

Jason's intentionality within his family was also evident when the homework task was intentionally transformed by the grandmother into a competitive game of who could recognize the words on the flash card first. Through the grandmother's game, a new social configuration was emerging, and the reading of the flash cards took on a new emotional tone. Jason responded positively to the homework becoming a game. Although the content remained the same, the social relations changed. On the commencement of this game, Jason changed his level of engagement in the task and changed his emotion, and began to smile, to laugh and to show eagerness in participation. The relations between Jason's play motive and the family's need to have Jason do homework created the conditions by which both play and learning were being enacted concurrently so that Jason would become oriented towards homework. As noted by Hedegaard and Chaiklin (2005):

> During school age the child's motives are dominated by the learning motive which both lets the child orient himself [sic] to knowledge about the world in general, and to specific skills appreciated in his community. The schoolchild becomes oriented to topics that are valued by his parents, by the community, or that the child finds new and exciting to explore. The schoolchild's social motives and play motives are still important.
>
> (p. 80)

The negotiations between the grandmother and Jason provided the conditions for Jason to have more experience of interacting with literacy and, through this, creating opportunities for him to gain more competence in word recognition.

Research by Wong and Fleer (2012) has shown that increased competence through practice can over time lead to the development of a learning motive and a change in the emotional engagement in practice tasks. This has also been noted by Hedegaard and Chaiklin (2005), who state that:

> Motives and knowledge are dialectically connected because knowledge gives content to motives and motives determine knowledge appropriation. A pupil's motive for learning and acquiring specific skills and knowledge does not develop independently of instruction. Motives develop as a relation between the pupil and the activities in which he [sic] participates.
>
> (p. 79)

In the example of Jason, it is possible to see that a motive can be seen both as relating to the institution of the school and to the child, but also as a new social configuration within the family. That is, from the school's perspective, motives are built on institutional values and purposes – to learn to read, and to support this, to practise rote learning of sight vocabulary. From the child's perspective, Jason's intention was to not participate in homework. However, the traditions of the school dictated that each child take home a reading pack each night, which included a reading book and a series of flash cards, which the family was expected to use to help Jason to recognize specific words, and to engage him in the practice of nightly book reading. The pack contained a folder, which required the parents to sign off that this practice had been done, thus making the parents complicit in the practice tradition of schooling. For this new practice to occur and for Jason to develop a motive for homework, a new form of social relations had to develop within the home environment. As Vygotsky (1994) notes:

112 *Marilyn Fleer*

environment should not be regarded as a condition of development which purely objectively determines the development of the child by virtue of the fact that it contains certain qualities or features, but one should always approach environment from the *point of view of the relationship which exists between the child and its environment* at a given stage of his [sic] development.

(p. 339; my emphasis)

Importantly, the demands made upon Jason have to be also understood in relation to the demands that he makes upon his family. Jason participated reluctantly. Through his reluctance, Jason placed demands upon his family to consider other ways of presenting homework to him. The grandmother initially tried to engage Jason in participating in the school reader by commenting upon its contents – creepy crawly things – in order to motivate Jason to look at the reader. This was met with a mild response. Her continued comment in relation to each page helped Jason to focus on the illustrations, as content, to help him with predicting the words in the reader. It also created an external interest, so that the task of reading was being jointly constructed, and seen as a central and important activity for Jason, which meant he was not to be disturbed by the others playing around him. Concurrently, his status as a reader was being built, and his position within the family as doing something important was being established. The social configuration was changing. The interest by the other children in what he was doing was created by the grandmother, and was evident through their keen observation, and later Cam's desire to use and pack up the flash cards. Having access to speciality school resources was valued by Cam, as it represented the new social configuration that was emerging within the family. The siblings' interest in Jason's homework also provided the conditions for changing the emotional engagement in the activity. Reber and Reber (2001) state that the concept of motivation is intertwined with the concept of emotions, arguing that "motivational properties and the energising elements of a motivational disposition often have a strong emotional tone to them" (p. 448). Bozhovich (2009) has also suggested that "the nature of the child's experience must be understood" as "the nature of their affective relationship to the environment" (p. 66). Children develop an affective relationship to their environment, and this emotional experience is conceptualized as the child's social situation of development (Vygotsky, 1998). In the social situation of development, emotional experience becomes the unit "that preserves in simplest form of properties intrinsic to the whole" (Bozhovich, 2009, p. 66). In this reading, we see that "experience is like a node where the varied influences of different external and internal circumstances come together" (Bozhovich, 2009, p. 67) as a system of social relations. This orientation to the development of motives is also evident in the writings of Hedegaard (2011), who illustrates the child and the institutional perspective when she states:

> Through anchoring the child's social situation in activity settings in institutional practice, a double perspective can be put on the child's activity. From the perspective of the child's social situation of development it is how the child experiences the activity emotionally and acts in the situation; while from the institution's perspective it is how the activity takes place in recurrent activity settings. This dialectic is the key to understanding the dynamic of a specific child's learning and development through participating in a specific practice. *Motive development can then be seen as a movement initiated by the child's emotional experience related to the activity setting. To catch this movement the tradition of practice within which a person's activities takes place has to be analysed* as encompassing activity settings that contain recurrent demands for activities.
>
> (Hedegaard, 2011, p. 21; my emphasis)

Relations between play and learning motives 113

Jason's homework developed into a central and esteemed activity because this activity required the whole family's attention, and this attention changed the social relations between family members in the after-school period. Jason demanded that his father, and not his mother, use the flash cards with him. The father responded instantly to this request and sat down next to him, leaving what he was doing. The mother stayed close by, observing. The grandmother also stayed close by but interacted with him for the full duration of the homework activity. Homework made demands upon Jason, but through this, Jason made demands upon his family. "Emotions, in Vygotsky's understanding, are not an organism's passive state, they stimulate activity, stimulate and regulate its relationship with the environment, and every time carry out a sort of 'dictatorship of behavior'" (Bozhovich, 2009, p. 69). Importantly, Jason's emerging new social position within his family, as a school child, with schoolwork responsibilities, positioned him favourably within his family, with the "hi five" from the father when he successfully completed his homework denoting this new status. Bozhovich (2009), in writing in relation to children's environmental attitude or motive, states that motives arise under two circumstances: "on the extent to which learning actually determines children's position among those who surround them and their relationship with them and the extent to which children are capable of meeting the demands the learning places on them" (pp. 75–76).

Jason held a new social position in his family as a school child, and this new social position created the possibility for the development of new psychological resources in different moments within the activity setting. This was most evident because Jason had to engage in homework and participate in the learning demands that resulted due to the school sending home a homework pack with the expectation of Jason doing this work at home. Bozhovich (2009) agreed with Leontiev's:

> underscoring the thought that the forces that drive development have a dynamic nature and are tied with subjects' activity that is with the means by which they interact with the environment. But the concept of activity cannot be divorced from the concept of position, since activity itself determines the children's position within the environment and is only a means for satisfying the needs associated with this position.
>
> (p. 84)

Bozhovich (2009) argues that learning creates new social positions for children, and the example cited above begins to make visible the ways in which this occurs for some children. The new social status within the family is important for the change in motive hierarchy where play becomes subordinate to learning. Beginning school has a lasting effect on not just the child, but also the family.

> [S]tarting school inaugurates a breaking point in children's lives, characterized first and foremost by the fact that, by becoming schoolchildren, they receive new rights and responsibilities and for the first time enter into a serious, socially significant activity, their level of achievement in which will determine their place among and their relationship with those around them.
>
> (Bozhovich, 2009, p. 76)

Doing homework makes this new social status visible within a family, which in turn creates new demands upon a family, opening up possibilities for the development of new psychological resources for Jason. Homework becomes a whole-family activity, ruling what occurs within the after-school period until the set tasks are completed. Through the activity of homework nestled between snack time and dinnertime in Jason's family, playtime was reduced and schoolwork was made public. A new configuration of social relations began to develop, especially between Jason and his grandmother. Through these school demands, and the new social position it afforded to Jason, a learning motive was slowly developing for Jason as he became oriented towards homework and developed a need for becoming a successful school child who could read. The family used Jason's motive for play to begin the transition from play to learning. Consequently, it is possible to see the importance of the relations between a play motive and a learning motive when we examine how homework is being introduced to Jason, and how new family practices are created, and new social configurations emerge to support the goals of schooling.

The family pedagogy (Hedegaard & Fleer, 2013) provided additional opportunities for Jason's participation in school activities at home, thus contributing to the goals of schooling. The broader research literature suggests that the greatest effect on student achievement results when *some* time is devoted to homework, rather than too much, or none at all. US and UK policies tend to advocate ten minutes in the first year of school, increasing by a further ten minutes for each year of schooling, with a net amount of two hours being suggested by the final year of post-compulsory school (The Queensland Government, Department of Education and the Arts, 2004). Jason's participation in homework in his first year of school falls within this recommended band. A systematic review undertaken by the Canadian Council on Learning (2009) indicates that there is mostly a medium effect on achievement noted for children who participate in after-school enhancement activities designed to promote school achievement, and a medium-to-high effect on parent involvement in homework. The latter finding is consistent with other reviews and studies reported (Cooper, 2008). The Canadian Council on Learning (2009) also noted that, where students attend schools which regularly assign homework, these children generally outperform students who attend schools where less homework is assigned. Frequency and quality of homework assigned has a statistically significant effect on achievement, particularly where attention on compliance of homework completion occurs, this being the best predictor of achievement. Jason's grandmother's attention to his homework established a safe and engaging interaction pattern around homework that resulted in Jason completing his homework. A systematic review of the literature shows that homework quality, completion and frequency are the best predictors of student achievement, suggesting that the learning motive being developed by Jason will result in his increased chances of being a successful achiever in school.

Conclusion

Stetsenko and Arievitch (2004) in citing Marx (1888/1955, p. 3) have stated that "human 'essence' is not something abstractly inherent in an individual" but rather it is "'the totality of all social relations'" (p. 483). Homework is one example of such activity that carries with it institutional expectations and values that are collectively enacted in society through family practices. Homework is an explicit example of how a learning motive can be introduced into family practice in order to support the societal goal for children to grow up well educated. Yet, as was shown in this chapter, the child is not a passive agent in homework practice. That is, homework must become part of the system of children's own needs, before they serve as real factors in development. Stetsenko and Arievitch (2004), like Hedegaard (2011), have sought to overcome the theoretical dualisms of a conception of motives, and to give voice to child agency (Stetsenko & Arievitch, 2004) or child interest (Hedegaard & Chaiklin, 2005) and, through this, show how a learning motive is developed through the interplay between family pedagogy and child agency.

In writing against a backdrop of a cognitive agenda, where human functioning is viewed as context free, Stetsenko and Arievitch (2004) theorize how individuals contribute to new cycles of practice through the unity of social and individual human development, naming this as "self as a leading activity" where "both individual (agentive) and social dimensions of the self" (p. 476) are addressed in the development of a motive. In this chapter, I have gone one step further by examining the relations between a motive for play and the motive for learning when the school practice of homework is introduced to children by their parents affording a new social position for the child (Jason) within the family, as a school child with the real need to learn to read. This is consistent with the outcomes of the literature on school achievement generally, where a modest but statistically significant effect has been noted in science and mathematics results in TIMSS (Falch & Ronning, 2011), for achievement in test scores of high and low achievers (Canadian Council on Learning, 2009) and in comparisons of achievement results between those who are given homework and those who are not (Cooper, 2008).

The other reading we must pay attention to is in relation to the traditional assumptions within early childhood pedagogical theory about play, where a play motive is viewed as biologically determined and as something contained within the individual child. This theorization, by its very nature, creates a dualism between play and learning, which is not productive for creating the conditions that develop a personal motive for learning. Reconceptualizing motives as the "dynamic relation between person and practice" (Hedegaard & Chaiklin, 2005, p. 64) affords a very different reading of the motivated child. As observed by Hedegaard (2011), it is through anchoring the child's activity within institutional practices that we can begin to take a double perspective on the child's activity. It is through studying the dynamic zone or interplay between people and practice, and between play and learning, that we have a double view on how Jason is developing a motive for school learning through his new social position in his family as a school child, increasing his participation in the practice tradition of homework, and resulting in the possibility for greater school achievement. Yet how to do this as part of a family's pedagogy is still to be determined. Established cultural family capital that allows for time and space to be devoted to homework, when this is not universally available to all children, must be central in our minds when we consider student achievement results (see Vadeboncoeur, Chapter 2, this volume).

Acknowledgements

I would like to acknowledge the Australian Research Council (Discovery Grant), which funded some of the research that is cited in this chapter, and to thank Avis Ridgway for acting as a senior research assistant in that project. I would also like to acknowledge the Lillian de Lissa Foundation for the research scholarship that allowed for the employment of Gloria Quinones, who supported the data gathering for the second empirical example cited in the chapter.

References

Bozhovich, L. I. (2009). The social situation of child development. *Journal of Russian and East European Psychology, 47*, 59–86.

116 *Marilyn Fleer*

Canadian Council on Learning. (2009). A systematic review of literature examining the impact of homework on academic achievement. Canada: Canadian Council on Learning.

Cooper, H. (2008). Homework: What the research says? *Homework. Research Brief.* Virginia: The National Council of Teachers of Mathematics.

Elkonin, D. B. (1971). Toward the problem of stages in the mental development of children. *Voprosy psikhologii, 4*, 538–563.

Elkonin, D. B. (2005a). The psychology of play. *Journal of Russian and East European Psychology, 43*(1), January–February, 11–21.

Elkonin, D. B. (2005b). The subject of our research: The developed form of play. *Journal of Russian and East European Psychology, 43*(1), January–February, 22–48.

Falch, T. & Ronning, M. (2011). Homework assignment and student achievement in OECD countries. Working paper series, No. 5. Department of Economics, Norwegian University of Science and Technology, Norway. www.svt.ntnu.no/iso/wp/wp.htm. Retrieved 1 February 2012.

Fleer, M. (2010). *Early learning and development: Cultural–historical concepts in play.* New York: Cambridge University Press.

Fleer, M. (2011). Motives as a central concept for learning. In D. M. McInerney, R. A. Walker & G. A. D. Liem (Eds.), *Sociocultural theories of learning and motivation: Looking back, looking forward, Volume 10 in Research on sociocultural influences on motivation and learning* (pp. 65–86). Charlotte, USA: Information Age Publishing, Inc.

Fleer, M. (2012). The development of motives in children's play. In M. Hedegaard, A. Edwards & M. Fleer (Eds.), *Motives in children's development. Cultural–historical approaches* (pp. 79–96). New York: Cambridge University Press.

Hedegaard, M. (1989). Motivational development in school children. *Multidisciplinary Newsletter for Activity Theory, 3*(4), 30–38.

Hedegaard, M. (2002). *Learning and child development: A cultural–historical study.* Aarhus: Aarhus University Press.

Hedegaard, M. (2011). The dynamic aspects in children's learning and development. In M. Hedegaard, A. Edwards & M. Fleer (Eds.), *Motives in children's development. Cultural–historical approaches,* (pp. 7–27). New York: Cambridge University Press.

Hedegaard, M. & Chaiklin, S. (2005). *Radical-local teaching and learning: A cultural–historical approach.* Aarhus, Denmark: Aarhus University Press.

Hedegaard, M. & Fleer, M. (2013). *Play, learning and children's development: Everyday life in families and transition to school.* New York: Cambridge University Press.

Karpov, Y. V. (2005). *The neo-Vygotskian approach to child development.* New York: Cambridge University Press.

Leontiev, A. N. (1978). *Activity, consciousness, and personality.* Englewood Cliffs, NJ: Prentice-Hall.

Marx, M. (1888/1955). Theses on Feurerbach. In K. Marx & Engels, *Collected works* (2nd ed., Vol. 3, pp. 1–4). Moscow: IML Press (original work published 1888).

McInerney, D. M., Walker, R. A. & Liem, G. A. D. (Eds.) (2011). *Sociocultural theories of learning and motivation: Looking back, looking forward, Volume 10 in Research on sociocultural influences on motivation and learning.* Charlotte, USA: Information Age Publishing.

The Queensland Government, Department of Education and the Arts (2004). *Homework literature review: Summary of key research findings.* Queensland: Department of Education and the Arts.

Reber, A. S. & Reber, E. S. (2001). *The Penguin dictionary of psychology* (3rd ed.). London: Penguin Books.

Stetsenko, A. & Arievitch, I. M. (2004). The self in cultural–historical activity theory: Reclaiming the unity of social and individual dimensions of human development. *Theory and Psychology, 14*(4), 475–503.

Vygotsky, L. S. (1966). Play and its role in the mental development of the child. *Voprosy psikhologii, 12*(6), 62–76.

Vygotsky, L. S. (1994). The problem of the environment. In R. van der Veer & J. Valsiner (Eds.), *The Vygotsky reader* (pp. 338–354). Cambridge: Blackwell.

Vygotsky, L.S. (1998). Child psychology. In *The collected works of L.S. Vygotsky, vol. 5* (M. J. Hall, Trans.; Robert W. Rieber, Ed. English translation). New York: Kluwer Academic and Plenum Publishers.

Wong, P. L. & Fleer, M. (2012). A cultural–historical conception of child development: Understanding a Hong Kong immigrant child's development within everyday family practices in Australia. *Mind, Culture and Activity, 19*(2), 107–126.

9 Peer co-regulation of learning, emotion, and coping in small-group learning

Mary McCaslin and Ruby Inez Vega

Introduction

Our work builds upon three basic tenets of Vygotskian theory: multiple functions of language, social origins of higher psychological processes, and the integration of the affective and intellectual in human activity. First, Vygotsky asserted that word meaning was the basic unit of analysis that mediated the relationships among the cultural, historical, and personal planes in human development. He considered language a uniquely human characteristic that allows mastery of nature and, thus, mastery of the self (Leontiev & Luria, 1968, p. 342). Vygotsky focused on the development of multiple functions of language – from communication with others to self-direction of one's own thinking and action. Communication with others is about transforming one's thoughts into words; self-directive language is about turning words into thoughts (Vygotsky, 1962, p. 131). Vygotsky considered self-directed speech an indication of self-awareness and instrumental to seeking and planning solutions to problems.

The developmental sequence of these two functions of language is from social or *inter*personal to self-directive or *intra*personal. Thus, the social environment is the source of each. Self-direction is made possible by language learned through communication by and with others; it is made necessary by problematic events and situations. Self-directive speech is not necessarily covert or "inner" speech; problematic situations can require inner speech to become overt to scaffold self-direction. Sometimes you need to "hear yourself think."

Second, in the Vygotskian perspective, mind is the product of social life, a form of activity originally shared by two people through communication that, as a result of mental development, later becomes a form of behavior within one person (Luria, 1969). Thus, higher psychological processes begin in the social world. The social origins of language and the developmental progression of its multiple functions locate the emergent capacity for what today is called "self-regulation" in the interpersonal realm.

Third, Vygotsky asserted a dynamic relationship between affect and intellect. He considered their separation a major weakness of traditional psychology: Thoughts do not think themselves; people do. People have needs, strengths, feelings, and interests and are engaged in the fullness of living. Vygotsky (1926/1997) agreed with James (1884, in Vygotsky 1926/1997) on what constitutes an emotional episode, a sequence that allows one's own awareness of physical expression (e.g., tears) to become part of the emotional experience (e.g., sadness). Thus, he argued that the appropriate sequence of an emotional episode is A (perception)–C (physical expression)–B (emotion, where emotion now includes as well self-awareness of one's own reactions to/relationship with the environment). This sequence is of particular importance in our study of how students mediate and co-regulate their own and others' emotion and coping in small peer groups. In small groups, students (potentially) are not only aware of their own physical expression and emotional experience, they also are aware (and to varying degrees are concerned) that this has happened in the presence of others (and vice versa). One of Vygotsky's expressed (but unmet) goals made possible through the integration of affect and intellectual was to trace the path from need to thought to activity. Modern researchers on emotional regulation address this challenge.

Related modern constructs

Our work builds upon these basic Vygotskian tenets and four related strands of recent scholarship in particular: activity theory, co-regulation dynamics, emotion regulation, and children's coping.

Activity theory

Vygotsky's focus on word meaning as the basic unit for understanding the dynamic relationship between the individual and the social world has been challenged as too narrow (e.g., Zinchenko, 1985). Activity theory asserts in its place human "activity," defined as "tool-mediated, goal-directed action," as the basic unit that links the individual and society. Activity theorists adhere to the social origins of these practices and situate motives and goals in the social realm rather than as properties of the individual (Kozulin, 1986; Leontiev, 1974–1975, 1978). Wertsch and Stone (1985) extended activity theory into the study of internalization dynamics, and posited "emergent interaction" as the mechanism by which the social becomes personal through mediation and internalization. In our work, we directly examine student activity and emergent interaction dynamics in the here-and-now of small learning groups.

Co-regulation model of the learner

The co-regulation model (e.g., McCaslin, 2009; McCaslin & Lavigne, 2010; McCaslin, Vega, Anderson, Calderon, & Labistre, 2011) posits learners who are social by nature and nurture, have a basic need for participation and validation (McCaslin & Burross, 2008), and differ in how and what they participate – their adaptation. The co-regulation model addresses the reciprocal press among personal, social, and cultural influences that together co-regulate – challenge, shape, and guide – student identity. It guides our elaboration on the fusion of the affective with the intellectual in the reciprocal presses among social and personal influences in small-group learning.

Emotion regulation

Research on emotions, and how to regulate and cope with them, is not explicit in the Vygotskian tradition, but it informs and is informed by it. Temperament researchers, for example, assert the biological basis of emotional reactivity and regulation of attention (e.g., Calkins & Makler, 2011) and the key role of parent mediation and socialization in children's emergent social competence (e.g., Eisenberg, Hofer, & Vaughan, 2007).

Emotion researchers continue to tackle what happens in an emotion episode, the function of emotion in adaptation, and the role of cognitive appraisals (e.g., Frijda, 2008; Gross &

120 Mary McCaslin and Ruby Inez Vega

Thompson, 2007; Weiner, 2005, 2010). Gross and Thompson (2007) identify the emotion episode as comprised of four components of antecedent conditions (situation selection, situation modification, attention deployment, cognitive appraisal) that are followed by response modulation/response. Frijda (2008) identifies the potential role of emotional dispositions, "concerns," or interests in the situational experience of an emotion episode. Concerns and threats to them get attention; attention affords appraisal. We are persuaded that individual differences in what students care about are important to consider, particularly in understanding emotion co-regulation in small groups.

Research on children's coping strategies

Our focus is primarily on situational antecedent, coping response, and interpersonal consequence relationships in small peer-group interaction. We examine how students co-regulate small-group learning and emotion; how they cope with learning and interpersonal stress in the presence of others, within an overall context of accountability. Skinner and colleagues (e.g., Skinner, Edge, Altman, & Sherwood, 2003) have conducted extensive reviews of research on coping, identified families of coping strategies and their assessment, and examined their developmental expression. Skinner and Zimmer-Gembeck (2007) reviewed 44 studies of coping during childhood and adolescence. They identified 12 coping strategies that appeared most often across articles. In order of frequency, they were: support seeking (can include help-seeking), escape (cognitive or behavioral), distraction (cognitive and/or behavioral), problem solving and instrumental action, accommodation, opposition and denial, self-reliance, aggression, social isolation, negotiation, helplessness, and positive cognitive appraisal. They note that only the four most frequent strategies have been researched enough to allow developmental interpretation.

Skinner and Zimmer-Gembeck (2007) found that support-seeking, the most frequently studied coping strategy, appears to change during childhood such that there is a decline in seeking support from adults and an increase in seeking support from peers into middle adolescence. Our tabletalk data suggest that peer co-regulation may "help" or perhaps "pressure" this change. Consider the following. Students are struggling with the task; one student wants to ask the teacher for help.

1. *L:* (Whining) Miss (Teacher), we need help over here!
2. *A:* (Said with force) Just go to the next one!
3. *L:* Uh.
4. *R:* (Overlapping) Kay.
5. Pause
6. *R:* (Reads) List other names for 2/3.
7. *A:* Okaaaay. 2/3. (pause) Kay, 4/6.
8. *L:* (Said slowly, as if writing it down) Four sixes.
9. *A:* 6/9.
10. *L:* 6/9. Ok.
11. *A:* (Overlapping) And 8/12.
12. *L:* (slowly and quietly) Eight . . . (pause) Miss (Teacher)!
13. *A:* (L), we'll just go on and at the end we'll ask her.
14. *R:* (Overlapping; inaudible) . . . let's do it ourselves.
15. *L:* (Overlapping; reading) Ok, circle the . . .

Escape (behavioral or cognitive) is the second most frequently studied child coping strategy. Skinner and colleagues describe an overall slight decrease in escape strategies in response to specific stressors among adolescents. Our findings, like those of Band and Weisz (1988), suggest that researchers frequently study strategies that children do not typically use. "Escape" is the second most frequently studied children's coping strategy; however, it is likely the least implemented by them. Children do not necessarily enjoy the level of control necessary to actually leave a situation; however, cognitive escape to avoid direct action does not appear to be the strategy of choice either.

The third most studied child coping strategy, distraction, also emerged as among the most common strategies reported by or observed in children studied by Band and Weisz (1988). Distraction strategies, like support seeking, are related to inescapable/uncontrollable stressors. Band and Weisz found that cognitive distractions, or diversionary thinking strategies, were used more often as children got older; older children also had a larger array of distraction strategies to implement. Our tabletalks suggest that fifth-grade students certainly engage in distraction. Three of the four groups we studied engaged in off-task distraction in 60% (on average) of the 30-second coding intervals. In comparison, the remaining group averaged 26%. Lesson differences in off-task distractions suggest that some task activities, at least in this math curriculum, invite distractions. For example, attempts to make fractions more "relevant" or "meaningful" by posing problems in which children must divvy up favorite foods like pizza and cake resulted in an average of 61% off-task activity compared with 41% off-task activity in concept development and 40% in estimation lessons. Thus, even within inescapable or uncontrollable situations, some task activities likely afford more distraction coping than others.

Finally, Skinner and Zimmer-Gembeck (2007) identified children's problem solving and instrumental action as the fourth most studied coping strategy. Across 28 studies, when cognitive problem solving was assessed, it was used as frequently as support-seeking and distraction strategies by older children and adolescents. Problem solving as cognitive activity is developmentally related; however, the authors suggest that the adolescent transition (ages 11–12) is an especially important period in which to research these strategies.

Band and Weisz (1988) directly studied coping and stress management among children. Children aged 6, 9, and 12 were interviewed about their experiences of stressful everyday events across six domains. Two coding systems were used to analyze the children's reports. The first, based on the ways of coping model proposed by Folkman and Lazarus (1980), distinguishes specific problem- or emotion-focused strategies. The second system was the primary–secondary coping model developed by Weisz and colleagues (e.g., Weisz, Yeates, Robertson, & Beckham, 1982). Primary coping is aimed at influencing objective conditions/events; secondary is about making it work as is, "maximizing one's goodness of fit with condition as they are" (p. 3). Band and Weisz integrated these two models of coping and applied them to specific situations.

Children's reports of coping with peer relation difficulties and school failure are of special interest. Overall, the authors report that the primary coping responses, including direct problem solving, problem-focused aggression, and problem-focused avoidance, were more represented (by far) than the secondary coping approach (i.e., accommodating to the situation). In addition, reported problem solving in peer relation difficulties was age-related. Twelve-year-olds reported *less* direct problem solving and problem-focused avoidance strategies and *more* peer aggression than younger participants. In contrast, when coping with school failure events, older children reported *more* direct problem solving and *less* problem-focused aggression and avoidance strategies than the younger children. These results suggest the key roles of context and development in children's use of coping strategies.

Small learning groups are a potential stressful mix of these two contexts: peer relation and learning difficulties. How students respond to stress in small learning groups may provide insight into what their primary concerns are, academic and/or social. Band and Weisz's (1988) data suggest that these behavioral displays of concern may differ among students in different grades.

Summary

Small learning groups provide an ideal context for research on theory and constructs related to Vygotskian perspectives. Small groups are inherently social. In principle, small groups are aligned with cultural expectations for learning and are personally relevant for individual members, although just what makes small groups meaningful likely differs among participants. Small-groups involve co-regulation among peers engaged in non-automatic and potentially stressful activity. Non-automatic activity affords the need for co-regulation of other- and self-awareness, other-communication, and self-direction among students. As one sixth-grade student put it, how can you be a friend and be your own person in a small group? Can a good student be a good friend? (McCaslin & Good, 1996b, p. 61).

We expected small groups to include incidents and expectations that students identify as meaningful and problematic and in need of a solution. We consider these instances fusions of affective/intellectual demands that require intellectual/affective solutions. Thus, we consider demands to be meaningful because they are affectively charged challenges to competence, be it academic and/or social, and their solutions require conscious, or mindful, pursuit of goal attainment. When optimal solutions are found wanting and goal attainment not possible, we expect that some students will struggle more, in part because they care more, know less, and/or are less adapted to academic or interpersonal failure. We also expect students to differ in how they cope with their own and others' emotions, negotiate conflict with peers, and struggle to approximate, or at least convincingly substitute, the assigned task or adopted goal (McCaslin, 2009).

Research on small-group learning

Small-group learning formats and activities are common practices in many elementary classrooms, particularly in mathematics. McCaslin and colleagues have conducted multiple studies on small-group learning that, taken together, align with Vygotsky's perspective on the integration of the affective and intellectual in human functioning (Florez & McCaslin, 2008; McCaslin, Burggraf, & Olson, 2011; McCaslin et al., 1994; McCaslin, Vega et al., 2011). The studies vary in question and design to capture student experiences in and perceptions of small-group learning from an array of perspectives: implicit motives or dispositions; explicit motivation and beliefs; actual real-time verbal activity; reconstructions of small-group activity and emotion; and individual differences in the emotional costs of being in small groups. In this chapter, we focus on student stress and coping in small groups using real-time "tabletalk" data.

Our first attempt to capture student (verbal) activity in small-group learning is described in McCaslin, Vega et al. (2011). The current portrayal of student emotional regulation in small groups is a continuation of that work. Variables from the Group Behavior Checklist (GBC) (Vega & McCaslin, 2010) and Group Environment Summary (GES) (McCaslin & Vega, 2010) coding systems are used. Results are first presented at the overall group/lessons level, followed by an extended example of a micro stream of student co-regulation of emotion and coping episodes.

Method

Researchers in self- and social-regulation typically agree that "real-time" data are essential for understanding student regulation and emotional adaptation (e.g., Boekaerts & Corno, 2005; Volet, Vaurus, & Salonen, 2009; Azevedo, Moos, Johnson, & Chauncey, 2010). The work we describe accepts this challenge with fifth-grade students learning fractions in small groups, and their teacher.

Context and participants

Participants attended a school serving moderate socioeconomic status families in the Mid-western United States. One fifth-grade classroom (N = 22 students) and their teacher participated. We focus on four of the seven (unsystematically selected) possible small-learning groups (n = 15; 11 girls, 4 boys) engaged in six fraction lessons (two each in concept development, problem solving, and estimation, respectively). Student "tabletalk" was recorded during group activity; activity worksheets were collected and scored for correctness.

Data source

In each lesson, students engaged in task activities in small groups after the teacher presentation. Tape recordings of students in their small groups, "tabletalks," provide the real-time data. Tabletalks were transcribed verbatim and verified. Variable codes were applied to typescripts that were read while listening to the digitalized recording.

Instrumentation

Group Behaviors Checklist (GBC). GBC captures the range of on- and off-task behaviors that students display when working with others in small groups. Coding is completed in 30-second intervals. The training inter-rater agreement among project staff (N = 5), working independently and coding two complete typescripts, averaged 91% exact agreement. This study uses three GBC variable domains that, along with group affect (described subsequently), define the *social/instructional context*: getting organized (i.e., how is it done and who is responsible), getting help (i.e., types of questions asked), and getting that help right (i.e., clarification and confirmation seeking). These variables represent the mindful or conscious activity students engage in that is relatively more task-related and other-involved.

Group Environment Summary (GES). GES captures student interpersonal and affective dynamics and expressed intrapersonal coping strategies that are categorized as other-involved communication and self-involved somatic complaints. These variables represent processes that, although observable by others, are relatively non-conscious for the individual student. They are part of the everydayness, the affective "informal curriculum" of small-group learning (McCaslin & Good, 1996a). GES is coded at lesson mid-point and end. Training inter-rater agreement among project staff (N = 5), working independently and coding two complete typescripts, averaged 86% exact agreement.

Student achievement. Student activity worksheets were scored for correctness and represent student small-group learning of the lesson material. (See McCaslin, Vega et al. (2011) for more complete documentation of study design and procedures.)

124 Mary McCaslin and Ruby Inez Vega

Data organization

Table 9.1 contains the means (mean proportion of dichotomous presence/absence scores) and standard deviations (based on all groups and all lessons, N = 22) of the three variable domains: social/instructional context; expressed coping strategies; and worksheet percent-

Table 9.1 The big picture: Variable descriptives

Variable domain	Mean	Standard deviation
Social/instructional context		
Group affect		
Playful	0.18	0.36
Business-like/purposeful	0.52	0.45
Indifferent/non-cohesive	0.25	0.40
Argumentative	0.00	0.00
Responsibility for task structure		
Group members	0.77	0.12
Teacher	0.11	0.09
No one (no discernible structure)	0.30	0.16
Type of task structure		
Directions	0.73	0.17
Turn taking	0.13	0.14
Role taking	0.05	0.12
Expressed coping		
Task-involved questions		
Explanation[a]	0.05	0.04
Information[a]	0.29	0.11
Procedures[a]	0.15	0.09
Clarification	0.18	0.10
Confirmation	0.11	0.07
Other-involved communication		
Protective		
Brag	0.36	0.35
Giggle	0.70	0.40
Defend	0.43	0.36
Excuses	0.09	0.25
Aggressive		
Blame	0.30	0.33
Sarcasm	0.32	0.39
Mean/rude	0.50	0.41
Argue/fight	0.61	0.34
Regressive/escape		
Tattle	0.18	0.29
Act infantile	0.52	0.39
Give up	0.09	0.20
Escape/withdraw	0.02	0.11
Self-involved somatic complaints		
Somatic[b]		
Sick	0.30	0.40
Pain	0.11	0.31
Tired	0.07	0.18
Achievement		
Task activity percent correct	77	20

Notes

a Dual-coded for further consideration of seeking clarification or confirmation.

b Variables that did not meet the 5% representation threshold for subsequent analyses are not included.

age correct. How students cope with task engagement concerns is our focus; however, the very existence of student concerns (Frijda, 2008) is an important indication that these students are invested in the task activity.

Social/instructional environment (SIE): Group organization and affect

SIE consists of group affect and task organization responsibility. Group affect was defined as: playful (e.g., share jokes, playfully spar), business-like/purposeful (e.g., get along and work well together), indifferent/non-cohesive, or as a whole argumentative/rude to each other. Task structure organization included: (a) how students organize themselves to do the activity (use the directions, take turns, and assign roles) and (b) who is responsible for initiating or maintaining that organization (group members, teacher, or no organization apparent). There was limited variation in how students organized themselves; they mostly transferred the individual strategy, "follow the directions," to the group context (mean = 0.73). Therefore, we focus on responsibility for that organization.

Expressed coping strategies: Task-involved questions, other-communication, self-involved somatic complaint

Expressed coping strategies are verbally reported actions in response to apparent concerns of (at least) one group member. Coping strategies represent an extension of an intrapersonal emotion regulation episode (defined as an aroused concern, emotional response, and action tendency stream; after Frijda, 2008) in which the focus on the self in relation-to-the-other(s) is a heightened feature of each member's interpersonal affective context. Our analyses of how students cope begin where most research on emotion regulation leaves off. Thus, we are inferring that students have made a given stimulus or demand personally meaningful, transforming it into a concern with an associated stress potential. We do not know the intrapersonal regulation dynamics, including emotional reactivity and its modulation, which may have preceded the expressed coping behavior. In effect, we are "seeing," or more accurately "hearing," what Vygotsky (1926/1997) and James (1884, in Vygotsky 1926/1997), termed event C in the A (stimulus)–C (response)–B (emotion) sequence. In comparison, our small-group participants are personally involved in event B while, like us, witnessing (and being witnessed as) event C among their group members. We categorize student apparent coping responses (event C) into task-involved questions, other-involved communication, and self-involved somatic complaints.

Task-involved (TI) questions. Task-involved questions voluntarily focus or shift focus of attention to regulate task or peer challenges. TI questions include seeking task-related explanation (to understand concepts), information (specific, factual), or procedures (how to do or complete process steps), after Good, Slavings, Hartel, and Emerson (1987). Questions that also sought further clarification or confirmation of the student's own contribution were noted.

Other-involved (OI) communication. Three types of verbal exchange are coded: protective, aggressive ("fight"), and regressive/escape ("flight"). Protective behaviors include brag (boast), giggle (a sort of affective burst of recognition of the state of things), defend (assert blame is not warranted), and excuse (redirect responsibility to an external source other than a person). Aggressive behaviors include blame (redirect responsibility to another person), sarcasm (ironic comment to make others feel less adequate), mean/rude (negative comment toward another), and argue/fight (at least two members in a charged negative exchange).

126   *Mary McCaslin and Ruby Inez Vega*

Regressive/escape behaviors include tattle (bring incorrect or inappropriate peer behavior to the teacher's attention), act infantile (whine or baby talk), give up (no longer willing to participate), and physical escape/withdraw (peer comments that a member is sleeping, left the group).

Self-involved (SI) somatic complaints. SI includes student-reported physical distress of being sick, in pain, and tired.

Achievement

The specific subject matter purpose of learning the assigned curriculum is represented with percent correct task activity achievement scores at the group level and averaged over the lessons for each group.

Results

Data were analyzed across groups and lessons and reported as descriptive and correlational statistics. An example of the give-and-take within a typical activity stream of emotional co-regulation episodes is parsed to illustrate the more fine-grained analyses of student co-regulation that real-time data afford.

Basic trends

Table 9.1 indicates students typically co-regulated their group SIE such that they were in control of organizing how they would go about the task activity (follow directions) and did so within an arena of good working relationships. Even so, challenges to maintaining task structure and interpersonal relationships were evident. In nearly one-third of the (30-second) intervals, no organizational structure was discernable; one-fourth of group affect codes (at mid- and end-points) involved student indifference or non-cohesion. Group affect, however, was never described as "argumentative/rude."

Students coped with challenges of group activity in more and less adaptive ways. TI help-seeking involves voluntary focus of attention; it also can indicate interpersonal trust: I ask you for help because I trust you to help me and I believe that you are competent to do so. Students typically sought relatively basic information and procedural help from each other, often checking that they understood correctly. Students did not use one another as resources for more substantive help or understanding.

The three most frequent OI communications were distributed across categories. First, there was a whole lot of (protective) giggling going on. The second most frequent exchange was (aggressive) argue/fight and the third, (regressive/escape) act infantile (0.70, 0.61, 0.52, respectively). SI somatic complaints primarily consisted of being sick (0.30) or in pain (0.11).

The only significant relationship among the five categories of expressed coping was SI somatic reports and TI questions ($r = 0.69**$). Trends included aggressive and protective ($r = 0.37, p = 0.10$) talk and somatic reports and protective talk ($r = 0.41, p = 0.06$). Patterns suggest we have organized student expressed coping coherently and that somatic reports might serve a strategic buffer function in small-group coping.

Peer co-regulation in small-group learning 127

Relationships among expressed coping variables

The intra-correlations among expressed coping behaviors are available in Table 9.2.

Correlations associated with TI questions suggest that explanation questions are infrequent for good reason. They are correlated with argue/fight (0.54**) and associated with a pattern trend (p = 0.10) – brag (0.33), express sarcasm (0.33), give up (0.34) – that is not particularly reinforcing. In contrast, asking for basic information appears safe for all involved. It is correlated with confirmation (r = 0.47*), which further acknowledges the need of the help-seeker and the expertise of the other. Information questions also are associated with a supportive pattern trend (p = 0.10) that suggests what others do *not* do in this context – giggle (r = –0.31), defend (r = –0.36), blame (r = –0.37), mean/rude (r = –0.40), and escape/withdraw (r = –0.33), itself a low-frequency occurrence consistent with Band and Weisz (1988, 1990). Procedural question-asking is yet a different matter. Asking for help about how to go about doing something (e.g., make a number line, cut a circle into quarters) apparently requires a certain hardiness and ability to see the humor in it all or have a pretty good reason not to do so. Procedural questions are correlated with clarification requests (in effect, seeking further help) (r = 0.59**), giggle (r = 0.43*), sick (r = 0.59*), and pain (r = 0.46*). Associated pattern trends (p = 0.10) include defend (r = 0.33) and escape/withdraw (r = 0.31).

OI communication relationships suggest possible packaging of protective buffers (e.g., giggle, defend [r = 0.52*]) and aggressive "triggers" (e.g., blame, mean/rude [r = 0.70**]; mean/rude, argue/fight [r = 0.43*]). Apparent compensatory relationships among the different category variables include brag (protective) and argue/fight (r = 0.43*), a potential equalizer that may not be what the braggart was looking for – or what the aggressor expected. Giggle (protective) apparently can cushion blame (aggressive) or invite it (r = 0.51*), just as making excuses (protective) may do for tattling (regressive) and reported pain (somatic) (r = 0.58**, r = 0.48*, respectively), and being tired (somatic) does for blaming others (aggressive) (0.45*) and arguing/fighting (0.45*).

Social/instructional environment and expressed coping

As Table 9.3 suggests, responsibility for group organization matters. There is one significant relationship associated with students being responsible for task organization (brag, r = 0.46*); the sole trend suggests a fairly smooth time of it (blame, r = –0.41, p = 0.06). Teacher responsibility for task organization differs. Along with students' procedural questions of how to go about the task (r = 0.43*), teacher responsibility (i.e., intervention) corresponds with student excuses, blaming, mean/rude comments, and some students actually gone (r = 0.42*, r = 0.66**, r = 0.47*, r = 0.51*, respectively). Consider as well the added noise of a pattern trend (p = 0.10) of giggling (0.37), tattling (0.36), and reported pain (0.37) and you have to wonder where the teacher could start to bring the group back in control of their task activity. Many have argued that small groups are very difficult to manage; these findings help us understand why.

Social/instructional environments, expressed coping, and achievement

The culture, social policy makers, and No Child Left Behind (NCLB) care about students learning the assigned curriculum. This is the question we now address: How do small-group SIEs and student coping relate to achievement? Table 9.4 contains the relationships associated with the averaged percent correct on the task activity worksheets students completed as a group. There is one positive relationship between social/instructional context and achieve-

128 *Mary McCaslin and Ruby Inez Vega*

Table 9.2 Intra-correlations within the expressed coping variable domain

Variables	1	2	3	4	5	6	7	8	9
1. Explanation	—								
2. Information	-0.304	—							
3. Procedures	0.308	-0.337	—						
4. Clarification	0.361	-0.104	0.590**	—					
5. Confirmation	-0.313	0.470*	-0.042	-0.158	—				
6. Brag	0.325	-0.013	0.145	0.189	-0.069	—			
7. Giggle	0.35	-0.312	0.430*	0.527*	-0.450*	0.294	—		
8. Defend	0.134	-0.364	0.328	0.288	-0.584**	0.399	0.524*	—	
9. Excuses	0.064	-0.057	0.086	-0.057	-0.086	0.148	0.163	0.073	—
10. Blame	0.09	-0.368	0.34	0.302	-0.109	-0.046	0.510*	0.178	0.376
11. Sarcasm	0.332	-0.043	-0.103	-0.142	-0.03	0.07	0.172	-0.008	0.175
12. Mean/rude	0.215	-0.399	0.125	-0.018	-0.117	0	0.293	-0.082	0.349
13. Argue/fight	0.543**	-0.209	0.227	0.201	-0.041	0.432*	0.345	0.067	0.151
14. Tattle	0.11	-0.152	0.087	0.035	0.053	-0.095	-0.028	0.01	0.580**
15. Act infantile	0.226	-0.008	-0.079	-0.208	-0.112	0.024	0.121	0.268	-0.143
16. Give up	0.335	-0.267	0.123	0.296	-0.23	0.359	0.055	0.263	0.306
17. Escape/ withdrawal	-0.11	-0.325	0.309	0.052	0.006	-0.231	0.166	0.043	-0.081
18. Sick	0.122	0.011	0.593**	0.283	-0.109	0.132	0.126	0.318	-0.043
19. Pain	0.321	0.195	0.446*	0.455*	0.021	0.373	0.289	0.294	0.480*
20. Tired	0.265	-0.128	0.023	0.356	-0.067	-0.228	0.132	-0.113	0.123

ment: business-like group affect (r = 0.42*). Business-like affect also is the only SIE in which members both agree (r = 0.42*) and disagree (r = 0.42*) with each other. That tension, rather than interfere with learning, appears to support it. In contrast, group affect intervals of indifference/non-cohesion and teacher responsible for task structure were negatively related to achievement (-0.42*, -0.72**, respectively). OI communication also is negatively related to achievement: making excuses, blaming others, mean/rude, and escape/withdraw (r = -0.50*, -0.53*, -0.54*, and -0.50*, respectively). These relationships suggest that at least some students are not adaptively coping with learning difficulty in the presence of peers. This is certainly not the peer-as-resource that promoters of small-group learning envision and it seems an especially important area for further research.

Co-regulation illustration: Expressed coping episodes

Our findings, based upon group/lesson-level data, provide a compelling argument for the importance of better understanding what happens in small-group learning. We now consider what we can learn from a more micro analysis of student co-regulation of affective and intellectual demands within the social–personal press of small groups.

We define a particular coping episode within a stream of episodes by three events: an **A**ntecedent, a **B**ehavior, and a **C**onsequence. Antecedents are the circumstances related to task or interpersonal requirements that set the stage for a coping event to occur. They "trig-

10	11	12	13	14	15	16	17	18	19	20
—										
0.156	—									
0.700**	0.295	—								
0.213	0.248	0.425*	—							
0.403	0.094	0.201	0.022	—						
0.037	0.028	−0.074	−0.02	−0.142	—					
0.115	−0.083	0	0.192	0.321	−0.028	—				
0.472*	−0.18	0.274	−0.074	−0.14	0.271	−0.103	—			
−0.241	−0.248	−0.293	−0.171	0.028	−0.197	−0.055	−0.166	—		
0.005	−0.018	0	0.325	0.158	0.077	0.215	−0.083	0.298	—	
0.453*	0.187	0.166	0.261	0.445*	−0.196	0.156	−0.087	−0.132	−0.151	—

ger" or demand the attention of someone who is disposed to care about and interpret them. Behaviors of interest are task- or social/interpersonal-related actions that occur immediately after antecedents. Consequences include (continued) student interpersonal coping that follow from the **AB** sequence. Consequence completes the sequence of events in the episode; however, consequence can also serve as the Antecedent in subsequent episodes.

Segments of recorded group work were identified for analysis if (1) one or more of the three most frequent coping behaviors (giggle/laugh, argue/fight, and act infantile) occurred, (2) the interval was previously coded in GBC analyses as students talk/utter loudly, express disagreement, or express agreement, and (3) the intervals were representative of the typical SIE (i.e., students structured the task and followed directions). In short, we selected a typical representative example of a stream of expressed coping episodes.

Example group and lesson

This group is a mixed achievement-level group (1 High, 2 Medium, 1 Low) of girls. One student was absent; present students worked on a fractions concepts worksheet for 13 minutes, 30 seconds. Students spent 7 minutes, 51 seconds struggling to answer the last question, which reads:

> *The fraction $\frac{7}{18}$ does not appear on your sheet. Do you think it is smaller than $\frac{1}{2}$ or larger than $\frac{1}{2}$? Explain how you decided.*

130   Mary McCaslin and Ruby Inez Vega

Table 9.3 Social/instructional context and expressed coping

Expressed coping	Group members	Teacher
Task-involved questions		
Explanation (a)	0.259	0.065
Information (a)	0.124	−0.169
Procedures (a)	−0.272	0.426*
Clarification	−0.222	0.328
Confirmation	0.04	0.35
Other-involved communication		
Protective		
Brag	0.455*	0.187
Giggle	−0.233	0.367
Defend	−0.126	−0.005
Excuses	−0.307	0.421
Aggressive		
Blame	−0.414	0.657**
Sarcasm	−0.032	−0.094
Mean/rude	−0.133	0.467*
Argue/fight	0.322	0.288
Regressive/escape		
Tattle	−0.309	0.356
Act infantile	0.293	−0.095
Give up	0.179	0.129
Escape/withdraw	−0.331	0.507*
Self-involved somatic complaints		
Somatic (b)		
Sick	−0.19	−0.055
Pain	−0.065	0.368
Tired	−0.112	0.12

Notes
* Correlation is significant at the 0.05 level (two-tailed).
** Correlation is significant at the 0.01 level (two-tailed).

At first, students disagreed over the correct answer. Once this was resolved (with teacher intervention), students then struggled with articulating how they decided on their answer. Two group members determined that the solution to this problem was to have a different member, the academic leader (A), write the answer. This was done. The stream of expressed coping sequences below is from the final 1 minute, 22 seconds of recorded work. We have not edited the sequence of exchanges.

> *Episode One: I think I know it.*
> A: Students struggle to write answer to question.
> B: Students express disagreement. (Lines 1–6)
> C: Student talk pauses. (Line 7)
>
> 1. *A:*   Okay. *(reads answer)* By looking at 7/12 at that the box . . . of 7/16 would be smaller than . . .
> 2. Pause
> 3. *L:*   Twelfths.
> 4. *A:*   No. Than . . . *(pause then continues reading)* By looking at 7/12 that the box of 7/16
> 5. would be smaller than . . .
> 6. *L:*   7/12.
> 7. Pause

Peer co-regulation in small-group learning   131

Table 9.4 Variable domain and achievement correlations

Variable domain	*r*
Social/instructional context	
Group affect	
Playful	−0.082
Business-like/purposeful	**0.424***
Indifferent/non-cohesive	**−0.423***
Responsibility for task structure	
Group members	0.324
Teacher	**−0.717****
No one (no discernible structure)	−0.25
Type of task structure	
Directions	−0.04
Turn taking	−0.073
Role taking	0.188
Expressed coping	
Task-involved questions	
Explanation (a)	−0.011
Information (a)	−0.028
Procedures (a)	−0.096
Clarification	0.068
Confirmation	−0.187
Other-involved communication	
Protective	
Brag	−0.007
Giggle	−0.342
Defend	0.087
Excuses	**−0.502***
Aggressive	
Blame	**−0.525***
Sarcasm	−0.172
Mean/rude	**−0.535***
Argue/fight	−0.143
Regressive/escape	
Tattle	−0.266
Act infantile	−0.18
Give up	0.128
Escape/withdraw	**−0.499***
Self-involved somatic complaints	
Somatic (b)	
Sick	0.272
Pain	−0.365
Tired	0.149

Notes
* Correlation is significant at the 0.05 level (two-tailed).
** Correlation is significant at the 0.01 level (two-tailed).

In episode one, students cope with learning difficulties by remaining task-focused, directly attempting to solve the problem, consistent with the findings of Band and Weisz (1988). The ending pause suggests that students are at a potential turning point: block or break-through.

Episode Two: Well you don't know it either.
A: Student is mean/rude. (Line 8)
B: Student defends herself. (Line 9)
C: Students argue/fight. (Lines 11, 12, 13)

  8. *R:*   See, she knows how to, she knows what to put.
  9. *L:*   Excuse me if I don't. Sorry. But you can't talk.
10. *R:*   Huh?
11. *L:*   You can't talk. *(mumbles)* 'Cause you don't even know your fractions.
12. *R:*   Yes I do.
13. *L:*   No you don't. Then how come you didn't do that one?

In episode two, the two students who are not the answer-writer/academic leader turn on each other, arguing about one another not knowing fractions.

Episode Three: Got it now. . . .
A: Students argue/fight. (Lines 11, 12, 13 above)
B: Student redirects others to task. (Line 14)
C: Student stops argument/fight. (Line 17)

14. *A:*   *(Overlapping loudly)* Ok, this is what I put. *(reads)* By looking at 7/12 that the box of
15.   7/16 . . . would be smaller than the box of 7/12 so it would be smaller than 1/2.
16. *R:*   *(Overlapping)* What one?
17. *L:*   *(Overlapping)* Never mind.

In episode three, the answer-writer/academic leader pulls the arguing students into the task and away from each other.

Episode Four: . . . . or maybe not.
A: Student uncertainty about answer. (Lines 18–20)
B: Student giggles at herself. Student is still uncertain. (Line 19)
C: Student resignation. (Line 21)

18. *L:*   That's true.
19. *A:*   *(Giggles)*
20. *R:*   Yeah.
21. *A:*   It still kinda don't make sense but, oh well.

In episode four, the academic leader (still) does not understand why their answer (obtained earlier with teacher help) is correct. She gives up. Other group members appear satisfied with the correct answer.

Episode Five: Done is good, or not.
A: Resignation. (Line 22)
B: (Differential) Goal substitution. (Lines 23–25)
C: Self-affirmation. (Lines 26–27)

22. *Big overlapping sigh.*
23. *L:*   Okay.
24. *R:*   Make sense.
25. *A:*   Miss Teacher! We're finished, do we turn it off?
26. *L:*   *(Overlapping – re-reading quietly)* By looking at 7/12 . . .
27. *A:*   Okay, ready? Stop.
RECORDER OFF

In episode five, students differentially cope with their less-than-satisfying task completion. The academic leader, A, shifts her concern from completion to compliance, checking with the teacher to stop recording. L continues to perseverate on (re)reading directions and R is fine with done, if that is what A says. A re-asserts her authority in the group by taking charge of "stop."

Summary and conclusion

The reciprocal press among group SIE (group affect, activity organization, and responsibility), students' expressed coping behavior, and achievement demands differentially influences student concerns. Students' regulation strategies in the service of those concerns also play a considerable role in how group members subsequently co-regulate one another. For example, imagine that I do not understand what I am supposed to do for my part of the task. I say something mean/rude; you take the bait and now we argue/fight, no longer worried about the task. Or perhaps I do not understand what I am supposed to do and I talk instead about the pain I am in; you allow that as a reasonable excuse and ask someone else. How students co-regulate these emotion regulation streams is a key issue in small-group learning of the formal – i.e., the intended – and informal curricula. Note the antecedent demand in each of these examples was learning difficulty. There was enough task challenge in our study to capture student concern; the average percent correct on the task activity worksheets was 77%. Expressed coping strategies suggest that students on the whole also struggled with self and each other. The frequency of students' aggressive coping behavior further suggests that these fifth-grade students mediated learning difficulty as peer-related rather than school-failure related difficulty (Band & Weisz, 1988).

Real-time co-regulation analyses convey the complexity of small-group events and provide one way to better understand when, why, and how students engage, struggle, negotiate, escalate, compromise, and settle in small groups. We are interested in how we might harness small-group co-regulation dynamics for the promotion of student learning and well-being. Practically, teachers need help in identifying amidst the chatter what are meaningful cues that curricular learning is indeed in progress and that students are learning to appreciate and validate their own and others' participation. How students mediate co-regulation dynamics and appropriate personally meaningful experiences that become part of their disposition toward learning with peers and identity as learners and social beings are the next foci of our work.

Acknowledgement

The authors acknowledge and thank Erin Anderson, Lauren Ballard, Christine Calderon, and Angela Labistre for their contributions to this project. This research was supported in part by the National Science Foundation, Grant # TPE 9145-493 to Good, McCaslin, and Reys, and the Center for Research on Classrooms, College of Education, University of Arizona.

References

Azevedo, R., Moos, D. C., Johnson, A. M., & Chauncey, A. D. (2010). Measuring cognitive and metacognitive regulatory processes during hypermedia learning: Issues and challenges. *Educational Psychologist, 45*, 210–223.

Band, E. B., & Weisz, J. R. (1988). How to feel better when it feels bad: Children's perspectives on coping with everyday stress. *Developmental Psychology, 24*, 247–253.

Band, E. B., & Weisz, J. R. (1990). Developmental differences in primary and secondary control coping and adjustment to juvenile diabetes. *Journal of Clinical Child Psychology, 19*, 150–158.

Boekaerts, M., & Corno, L. (2005). Self-regulation in the classroom: A perspective on assessment and intervention. *Applied Psychology: An International Review, 54*, 199–231.

Calkins, S. D., & Mackler, J. S. (2011). Temperament, emotion regulation, and social development. In M. K. Underwood & L. H. Rosen (Eds.), *Social development: Relationships in infancy, childhood, and adolescence* (pp. 44–70). New York: Guilford Press.

Eisenberg, N., Hofer, C., & Vaughan, J. (2007). Effortful control and its socioemotional consequences. In J. J. Gross (Ed.), *Handbook of emotion regulation* (pp. 287–306). New York: Guilford Press.

Florez, I. R., & McCaslin, M. (2008). Student perceptions of small group learning. In M. McCaslin & T. L. Good (Eds.), *Teachers College Record, Special Issue: School Reform Matters, 110*(11), 2438–2452.

Folkman, S., & Lazarus, R. S. (1980). An analysis of coping in a middle-aged community sample. *Journal of Health and Social Behavior, 21*, 219–239.

Frijda, N. H. (2008). The psychologists' point of view. In M. Lewis, J. M Haviland-Jones, & L.F. Barrett (Eds.), *Handbook of emotions* (3rd ed.) (pp. 68–87). New York: Guilford Press.

Good, T. L., Slavings, R. L., Hartel, H. H., & Emerson, H. (1987). Student passivity: A study of question asking in K-12 classrooms. *Sociology of Education, 60*, 181–199.

Gross, J. J., & Thompson, R. A. (2007). Emotion regulation: Conceptual foundations. In J. J. Gross (Ed.), *Handbook of emotion regulation* (pp. 3–24). New York: Guilford Press.

Kozulin, A. (1986). The concept of activity in Soviet psychology: Vygotsky, his disciples, and critics. *American Psychologist, 41*, 264–274.

Leontiev, A. N. (1974–1975). The problem of activity in psychology. *Soviet Psychology, 13*, 4–33.

Leontiev, A. N. (1978). *Activity, consciousness, and personality.* Englewood Cliffs, NJ: Prentice Hall.

Leontiev, A. N., & Luria, A. R. (1968). The psychological ideas of L. S. Vygotsky. In B. B. Wolman (Ed.), *Historical roots of contemporary psychology* (pp. 338–367). New York: Harper & Row.

Luria, A. R. (1969). Speech development and the formation of mental processes. In M. Cole & I. Maltzman (Eds.), *A handbook of contemporary Soviet psychology* (pp. 121–162). New York: Basic Books.

McCaslin, M. (2009). Co-regulation of student motivation and emergent identity. *Educational Psychologist, 44*(2), 137–146.

McCaslin, M., Burggraf, S., & Olson, A. M. (2011, June). The role of social/instructional context in elementary students' reported emotional adaptation. Paper to be presented at the biennial meetings of the SELF Conference, Quebec City, Quebec, Canada.

McCaslin, M., & Burross, H. (2008). Student motivational dynamics. *Teachers College Record, 110*(11), 2319–2340.

McCaslin, M., & Good, T. L. (1996a). The informal curriculum. In D. Berliner & R. Calfee (Eds.), *Handbook of educational psychology* (pp. 622–673). New York: Macmillan.

McCaslin, M., & Good, T. L. (1996b). *Listening in classrooms.* New York: HarperCollins.

McCaslin, M., & Lavigne, A. L. (2010). Social policy, educational opportunity, and classroom practice: A co-regulation approach to research on student motivation and achievement. In T. Urdan and S. Karabenick (Eds.), *The decade ahead: Applications and contexts of motivation and achievement* (Vol. 16B, pp. 215–253). London: Emerald Publishing Group.

McCaslin, M., Tuck, D., Waird, A., Brown, B., LaPage, J., & Pyle, J. (1994). Gender composition and small-group learning in fourth-grade mathematics. *Elementary School Journal, 94*, 467–482.

McCaslin, M., & Vega, R. I. (2010). Observation of small-group learning: The Group Environment Summary. Unpublished manuscript. Tucson, AZ: University of Arizona.

McCaslin, M., Vega, R. I., Anderson, E. E., Calderon, C. N., & Labistre, A. M. (2011). Tabletalk: Navigating and negotiating in small-group learning. In D. M. McInerney, R. Walker, & G. A. Liem (Eds.), *Sociocultural theories of learning and motivation: Looking back, looking forward. Research on sociocultural influences on motivation and learning* (Vol. 10, pp. 191–222). Charlotte, NC: Information Age Publishing.

Skinner, E. A., Edge, K., Altman, J., & Sherwood, H. (2003). Searching for the structure of coping: A review and critique of category systems for classifying ways of coping. *Psychological Bulletin, 129*, 216–269.

Skinner, E. A., & Zimmer-Gembeck, M. J. (2007). The development of coping. *Annual Review of Psychology, 58*, 119–144.

Vega, R. I., & McCaslin, M. (2010). Observation of small-group learning: The Group Behavior Checklist. Unpublished manuscript. Tucson, AZ: University of Arizona.

Volet, S., Vauras, M., & Salonen, P. (2009). Self- and social regulation in learning contexts: An integrative perspective. *Educational Psychologist, 44*(4), 215–226.

Vygotsky, L. S. (1926/1997). *Educational psychology.* (R. Silverman, Trans.). Boca Raton, FL: St. Lucie Press.

Vygotsky, L. S. (1962). *Thought and language.* Cambridge, MA: MIT Press.

Weiner, B. (2005). Motivation from an attributional perspective and the social psychology of competence. In A. J. Elliot & C. S. Dweck (Eds.), *Handbook of competence and motivation* (pp. 73–84). New York: Guilford Press.

Weiner, B. (2010). Development of an attribution-based theory of motivation: A history of ideas. *Educational Psychologist, 45*, 28–36.

Weisz, J. R., Yeates, K. O., Robertson, D., & Beckham, J. C. (1982). Perceived contingency of skill and chance events: A developmental analysis. *Developmental Psychology, 18*, 898–905.

Wertsch, J., & Stone, C. (1985). The concept of internalization in Vygotsky's account of the genesis of higher mental functions. In J. Wertsch (Ed.), *Culture, communication, and cognition: Vygotskian perspectives* (pp. 162–182). New York: Cambridge University Press.

Zinchenko, V. P. (1985). Vygotsky's ideas about units for the analysis of mind. In J. Wertsch (Ed.), *Culture, communication, and cognition: Vygotskian perspectives* (pp. 94–118). New York: Cambridge University Press.

10 Teacher–student relationships and students' learning outcomes

Atara Sivan and Dennis W. K. Chan

Teacher–student relationships in a sociocultural perspective

Sociocultural theory, which has been developed from the work of Vygotsky (1978), highlights the significant contribution of social context to children's development. It puts much emphasis on the interaction between people and the culture in which they live, as well as on the ways in which their attitudes and beliefs affect teaching and learning. Within classroom contexts, teachers play a profound role in children's development by acting as agents of culture and providing the social interaction necessary for their learning. In his work *Tool and Sign*, Vygotsky described human development as a process which involves the use of various culture tools that allow people to embody their collective experiences in external forms, patterns of behavior and modes of acting, thinking, and communicating in everyday life (Stetsenko, 2004). According to Vygotsky, the existence and growth of what he called "human culture" contribute to human development through the teaching and learning processes which encompass passing collectively accumulated experiences from one generation to the other. Vygotsky further emphasized the significant role of collaborative shared activities with more experienced adults. In the context of education, these adults are teachers. Much has been said within sociocultural theory about teachers' uses of different pedagogies and their contribution to students' cognitive learning outcomes (Goldstein, 1999). Despite the importance of teacher–student relationships and non-cognitive learning outcomes to children's development, scant attention has been paid to the relational dimension of teaching and learning, as well as to learning outcomes that go beyond the cognitive domain. In the present chapter, we aim to fill this gap by providing an integrative examination of the nature of teacher–student interactions in the classroom and its relationship with students' cognitive, affective, and moral learning outcomes. Specifically, we examine teacher–student interactions with reference to the Model for Interpersonal Teacher Behavior and the research findings using this model, including our recent study in Hong Kong (Sivan & Chan, in press). We take a special look at the relationships between teacher–student interactions and students' learning outcomes, particularly in the affective and moral domains as they are highlighted in our study.

Teacher interpersonal behavior – examining the relational dimension

Research on teacher–student interactions in the classroom pertains to the interpersonal and relational dimension of teaching and learning (Brekelmans, Sleegers, & Fraser, 2000; Petegem, Creemers, Rossel, & Aelterman, 2005). It shifts from focusing on the instructional-methodological aspect that portrays teaching styles and offers technical strategies and pedagogies to the interpersonal sphere, which "has to do with interpersonal actions which create and maintain a positive classroom atmosphere" (Wubbels, Creton, Levy, & Hooymayers, 1993, p. xiv). While the two aspects are interconnected in that one could affect the other, the interpersonal dimension seems to be more represented in the affective climate of the classroom than in teachers' instructional techniques. The importance of examining the interpersonal aspect lies in its possible effect on the classroom environment and thus on teaching and learning. As Wubbels et al. (1993) stated "if the quality of classroom environment does not meet certain basic conditions, the methodological aspect loses its significance" (p. xiv). The increasing interest in the psychosocial characteristics of the classroom learning environment over the past few decades has brought with it a growing attention to the interpersonal interactions between teachers and students. Of particular relevance to the examination of teacher–student relationships is the Model for Interpersonal Teacher Behavior (MITB), which was developed to examine teacher–student interactions based on students' perceptions of these relationships (Wubbels & Brekelmans, 2005; Wubbels & Levy, 1993). Students' perceptions of interpersonal teacher behavior are important because they mediate between teachers' teaching and student learning outcomes. Furthermore, students' perceptions provide a comprehensive picture of teachers' patterns of behavior and point out some distinctive features which otherwise may not be discovered (Wubbels & Levy, 1993).

Measuring interpersonal teacher behavior in the classroom is concerned with the relationship dimension of the classroom environment. This dimension provides an interpersonal perspective on teaching which can "create and maintain a positive and warm classroom atmosphere conducive to learning" (Petegem et al., 2005, p. 35). Based on Leary's (1957) classic examination of dialogues and group discussion in clinical situations and adapted to the context of education, the MITB maps the behavior of a teacher on two dimensions: Proximity and Influence. While the Proximity dimension refers to cooperation and opposition practices which show the teacher's approval and disapproval of students and their behavior, the Influence dimension varies between dominance and submission practices which indicate whether students' activities are determined by the teacher or by students themselves. These two dimensions can be portrayed in a two-dimensional plane that can be further subdivided into eight categories representing different kinds of teacher interpersonal behavior: Leadership, Helpful/Friendly, Understanding, Student Responsibility/Freedom, Uncertain, Dissatisfied, Admonishing, and Strict. The model is presented in Figure 10.1. While the Proximity dimension is associated with Understanding, Helpful/Friendly, Dissatisfied, and Admonishing types of behavior, the Influence dimension is related to Leadership, Strict, Student Responsibility/Freedom, and Uncertain kinds of behavior. A teacher who is characterized by Leadership tends to lead and organize the classroom situation, to set tasks and to determine procedures, and to structure the classroom situation. A teacher who is depicted as Helpful/Friendly shows interest in students and behaves in a friendly and considerate manner. A teacher who is described as Understanding shows concern and care for students, and is patient and open to them. A teacher who exhibits Student Responsibility/Freedom is giving students opportunities to assume responsibility for their own activities. Unlike the above four types of behavior, which represent cooperative teacher interactions, the other four types of behavior tend to be identified with more opposition practices. For example, while a teacher showing Uncertain type of behavior tends to exhibit uncertainty and keep a low profile, a teacher who is characterized by Dissatisfied type of behavior shows unhappiness and dissatisfaction with students. In the other two types of behavior, Admonishing and Strict, the teacher shows anger and impatience in class and is strict and demanding with the students respectively.

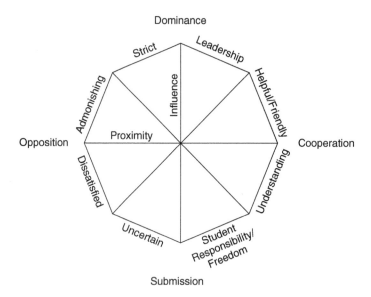

Figure 10.1 The Model for Interpersonal Teacher Behavior

These eight types of interpersonal teacher behavior are measured by the Questionnaire on Teacher Interaction (QTI) (Wubbels et al., 1993), which was originally developed in the Netherlands in Dutch (77 items) (Wubbels, Brekelmans, & Hooymayers, 1991), translated into English, and followed by an American version (64 items) and an Australian version (48 items) on a five-point Likert scale (Wubbels & Levy, 1993). Since its development, it has been translated into various languages and widely used in different countries, including those in the Asia-Pacific regions, such as Australia (den Brok, Fisher, Wubbels, Brekelmans, & Rickards, 2006), Singapore (Goh & Fraser, 1995, 1998), India (den Brok, Fisher, & Koul, 2005), and Korea (Kim, Fisher, & Fraser, 2000). Studies showing its reliability and validity include Dutch (Brekelmans, Wubbels, & Creton, 1990), American (Wubbels & Levy, 1993), Australian (den Brok et al., 2006), Singaporean (Goh & Fraser, 2000), and Indonesian (Soerjaningsih, Fraser, & Aldridge, 2001) samples. In a recent study conducted in Hong Kong (Sivan & Chan, in press), we validated the Chinese version of the QTI. Results of this study provided evidence supporting its cross-cultural validity and reliability in the Hong Kong context and indicating consistency with previous research conducted in other places, such as Singapore, Brunei, and Australia (den Brok et al., 2006).

An examination of the studies on teacher–student interactions as measured by the QTI shows similarities in students' perceptions regarding the nature of teacher interpersonal behavior. For example, a study conducted among Korean secondary school science students (Kim et al., 2000) found that students assigned higher scores to teachers who were perceived as exhibiting Leadership, Helpful/Friendly, and Understanding behaviors and lower scores to those demonstrating Uncertainty, Dissatisfaction, and Admonishing and Strictness. Similar results were found among secondary school students in Hong Kong, where teachers were perceived by their students as scoring high on the Leadership, Helpful/Friendly, Understanding, and Student Responsibility/Freedom scales but as scoring low on the Uncertain, Dissatisfied, Admonishing, and Strict scales.

On the whole, while studies have indicated similarities in the nature of interpersonal teacher behavior with the prevalence of more cooperative types of behavior, some differences were found in students' perceptions between different countries. A comparison between Korean, Australian, and Singaporean science students revealed that Korean students tended to assign lower scores to their teachers' cooperative types of behaviors, such as Leadership, Helpful/Friendly, and Understanding, and higher scores to their Student Responsibility/Freedom, Uncertainty, and Dissatisfaction types of behavior than did their Australian and Singaporean counterparts (Kim et al., 2000). These differences were attributed to the greater emphasis on the constructivist approach to the national curriculum of science in Korea (Kim et al., 2000).

In their cross-national examination of teacher interpersonal behavior, den Brok et al. (2003, 2006) identified differences between countries in the positioning of some types of behavior on the two dimensions of Proximity and Influence. The researchers suggested that these differences could reflect differences in meanings or connotations attached to certain teacher behaviors. They further suggested that these between-countries differences could reflect different ways in which students observe their teachers' behaviors while referring to different cues which could be looked at differently in terms of their importance. In this regard, the differences could possibly be attributed to the different contexts of learning, which have been emphasized as important aspects in sociocultural theory. Teacher–student relationships are one of the areas which could possibly be affected by both the context and the culture in which it is practised.

Further support to the importance of the sociocultural context is provided in the study by den Brok et al. (2006), which found differences in the dimension scores between teachers in Brunei and those in Australia, with the former rated lower on Proximity and higher on Influence than did the latter. These differences were attributed to the context of learning in Brunei, which is characterized by a collectivist tendency existing in many Asian contexts. In these contexts, teachers possess a lot of power and are expected to exercise it in their interactions with students (den Brok et al., 2006; Watkins & Biggs, 1996).

Teacher interpersonal behavior and student learning outcomes

Learning outcomes refer to what students know and are able to demonstrate as a result of their learning experience. An integrative approach to learning outcomes focuses on "the essential and enduring knowledge, abilities (skills) and attitudes (values, dispositions) that constitute the integrated learning needed by a graduate of a course or program" (Battersby, 1999, p. 8). In recent years, there has been a growing interest in measuring students' learning outcomes as a way to indicate the success of the learning process in terms of student development. An examination of numerous definitions of learning outcomes shows that they refer to both the cognitive and the affective domains. While it is not uncommon to find a greater emphasis among researchers on students' learning outcomes in the cognitive domain (Savickiene, 2010), studies examining student–teacher interactions in the classroom have investigated both domains. Specifically, interpersonal teacher behavior as measured by the QTI was found to be related to students' cognitive and affective learning outcomes. Furthermore, research indicated a significant relationship between students' perceptions of the eight types of interpersonal teacher behavior and their cognitive and affective learning outcomes, and highlighted that particular types of interpersonal behavior are more effective for certain learning outcomes than others (e.g., Wubbels & Brekelmans, 2005).

Cognitive learning outcomes

Cognitive learning outcomes have been mainly measured by achievement tests in a specific subject. Relationships were found for both the Influence and Proximity dimensions of teacher–student interactions and their related types of behavior. Brekelmans (1989, as cited in Wubbels & Brekelmans, 2005) found a positive relationship between students' perceptions of interpersonal teacher behavior and their scores on a physics test. The higher the teacher was perceived on the Influence dimension, the higher were students' scores. In regard to the types of teacher behavior, Goh and Fraser (2000) found positive relationships between the Leadership type of behavior and students' scores on a mathematics test. They further found positive relationships between Helpful/Friendly, Understanding, and Student Responsibility/Freedom types of behaviors and students' scores on the test. Similar findings were reported in relation to the cognitive domain measured by problem solving in physics (Brekelmans et al., 1990; den Brok, Brekelmans, & Wubbels, 2004). While the above studies were conducted among science-related subjects, few studies undertaken among other subjects found similar results. For example, a study by den Brok et al. (2004), which examined interpersonal teacher behavior in teaching English as a foreign language, found positive relationships between the Proximity dimension and students' cognitive learning outcomes as measured by reading comprehension. In our study on secondary school students in Hong Kong (Sivan & Chan, in press), we extended the investigation to include the subjects of Chinese, English, and mathematics. Results of our study indicated that, on the whole, students' cognitive learning outcomes were positively correlated with the more cooperative types of teacher behavior and negatively associated with the less cooperative ones.

Affective learning outcomes

Besides examining cognitive outcomes, increasing attention has been paid to the affective domain, with the underlying belief that it is as important as the cognitive domain. In relation to sociocultural theory, it has been argued that, despite the lack of scholarly attention to the role of the affective domain, Vygotsky understood its centrality in cognitive development (Goldstein, 1999). In his publication *Thought and Language* (Vygotsky, 1962, p. 8), Vygotsky emphasized the importance of "the existence of [a] dynamic system of meaning in which the affective and intellectual unite". Vygotsky (1962) further wrote: "The separation of the intellectual side of our consciousness, from its affective, volitional side is one of the fundamental flaws of traditional psychology" (as cited in Wertsch, 1985, p. 189). Affective learning outcomes include, among others, the attitudes students develop about the subject, the topic, and the teacher. Russo and Benson (2005) indicated that, when students have positive affect about these targets, they are more likely to complete courses, become involved intellectually with the material and the others in the class, and are more satisfied. Similarly, Cheng (1994) argued that students' attitudes toward learning could potentially affect their academic achievement.

Studies on teacher–student relationships employing the QTI have found a very consistent pattern of associations between teacher interpersonal behavior and students' attitudes toward specific subjects, such as those related to science (e.g., physics, biology, chemistry, and mathematics). Students' attitudes were measured in terms of various dimensions, including subject motivation, liking, enjoyment and leisure, and career interest (e.g., Brekelmans, Wubbels, & den Brok, 2002; den Brok et al., 2004; Goh & Fraser, 2000). A study by den

Brok, Fisher, and Scott (2005), investigating the enjoyment in science classes using Test of Science Related Attitudes (Fraser, 1978, 1981), indicated that the more enjoyment or pleasure students experience in science, the more they see the relevance of their study for their future education and occupation and the more they have confidence in performing well in the subject. Students' enjoyment was also found to be positively related to the development of interest in science and to their willingness to invest more effort in learning this subject. These associations between teacher–student interpersonal behavior and students' attitudes toward science were found across different countries, including the Netherlands, Australia, Singapore, Korea, and Brunei. Brekelmans et al. (1990), for example, found an association between the Proximity dimension and students' attitudes toward physics. The stronger students' perceptions of this dimension in teacher interpersonal behavior in the physics classroom, the more positive their attitudes toward this subject. Khine and Fisher (2004) found a significant positive relationship between Leadership, Helpful/Friendly, Understanding, and Student Responsibility/Freedom types of behavior and secondary school students' attitudes toward their sciences classes in both Australia and Singapore. At the same time, the Uncertain, Dissatisfied, Admonishing, and Strict types of behavior were significantly and negatively correlated with students' attitudes in both countries. A similar pattern was found among primary school students in Singapore, where positive students' attitudes were found in classes with an emphasis on a teacher's Leadership/Friendly and Understanding behaviors (Goh & Fraser, 2000). In addition, den Brok, Fisher, and Scott (2005) found that both the Influence and the Proximity dimensions positively affected students' attitudes toward science, and that the more students perceived their teachers to be dominant and cooperative, the higher was their enjoyment in science.

In another study among physics students in the Netherlands, den Brok et al. (2004) found strong positive relations between students' perceptions of their teacher's interpersonal behavior on the Proximity dimension and their subject-specific motivation. More specifically, results indicated that students' perceptions of the cooperativeness of their teachers affected their motivation toward studying physics. In their review of studies on teacher–student relationships using the QTI, Wubbels and Brekelmans (2005) pointed out that, while students' affective learning outcomes were positively associated with the two dimensions of teacher interpersonal behavior, the association was somewhat stronger for the Influence than the Proximity dimension.

Most of the studies on teacher–student interactions and students' affective learning outcomes measure the latter by students' subject-specific attitudes. Even though teachers have been recognized as one of the factors contributing to student learning, little attention has been given to students' attitudes toward their teachers in studies on interpersonal teacher behavior. In order to fill this gap, we (Sivan & Chan, in press) have extended the conventional ways of measuring the affective domain by devising a five-item inventory (SATT: Student Attitudes toward Their Teachers) in our studies of secondary school students in Hong Kong. Students were asked to indicate their attitudes toward their subject-specific teacher on a five-point scale (Cronbach's alpha = 0.93). To obtain a more comprehensive view of students' affective learning outcomes, we also included a 10-item modified Enjoyment subscale of the Test of Science Related Attitudes (TOSRA; Fraser, 1978, 1981) to measure students' enjoyment of specific subjects (Cronbach's alpha = 0.92). Results of our study indicated that, among the QTI scales, Leadership, Helpful/Friendly, and Dissatisfied were significantly correlated with both SATT and TOSRA. Furthermore, on the whole, the QTI scales were found to be better predictors of SATT than their enjoyment of specific subjects (TOSRA).

142 *Atara Sivan and Dennis W. K. Chan*

Learning values and attitudes – adding the moral outcome

Although both students' cognitive and affective learning outcomes have been studied extensively in relation to teacher interpersonal behavior in the classroom, scant attention has been given to their moral learning outcomes. According to Vygotsky (1962), formal education is one of the ways in which adults pass on to their children the ways in which their culture interprets the world. This transfer is done by teachers who impart ideas and concepts through their teaching (Vygotsky, 1962). The importance of culture has been emphasized by Vygotsky as a source of attitudes. As stated in Taylor (1992) in relation to Vygotsky's perspective: "A person's attitude (including feelings, thoughts, and actions) is affected by his/her environment. This includes experiences within the environment as well as the culture of the environment itself" (p. 13). As role models who influence their students' development, teachers are those who transmit the culture to their students. Brekelmans et al. (2000) maintain that teaching can be studied from different perspectives to better understand its different functions. These perspectives include: subject-content perspective, learning activities perspective, interpersonal perspective, organizational perspective, and moral perspective, with the latter being defined as "describing teaching in terms of the values a teacher is communicating to pupils" (Brekelmans et al., 2000, p. 228). The need to investigate the moral perspective is further supported by Lovat and Clement's (2008) argument for the interdependent relationships between values education and quality teaching and their positive impact on student learning and development. They grounded their argument on research illustrating how students' cognitive and affective development has been enhanced through the inclusion of values education as part of quality teaching.

Guided by the above arguments and in an attempt to attend to the local needs of the Hong Kong educational context, we have added the moral dimension to the cognitive and affective domains in our investigation of interpersonal teacher behavior. The need for placing more emphasis on values education in Hong Kong has been raised in its recent education reform. The reform, which was launched in 2001 (Curriculum Development Council, 2001), signifies a move to a more progressive system and brings about pedagogical changes to better suit student needs and to adapt to changes in society. These changes include a shift from a separate subject-based curriculum to the establishment of several key learning areas which aim to develop generic skills, values, and attitudes. As part of this reform, the Hong Kong Curriculum Development Council (2001) has proposed a list of values and attitudes for incorporation into the school curriculum.

In recent studies of primary and secondary school teachers and students in Hong Kong, using observation and interviews, we identified the significant role of teachers in inculcating values in their classrooms (Sivan & Chan, 2008, 2010). Teachers were found to use various direct and indirect ways of imparting values and attitudes in the classroom and students indicated that they had learned a wide range of personal and social values from their teachers. Results of these studies, together with our aim to investigate the moral perspective of student learning outcomes, have prompted us to examine the possible relationships between teacher–student interactions and students' learning of values and attitudes. While the former was measured by the QTI, the latter was assessed by a 26-item questionnaire on a five-point scale (Sivan & Chan, 2008). This scale (SLAV: Cronbach's alpha = 0.97) measured students' learning of a set of attitudes and values from their subject-specific teachers. This set of attitudes and values was developed from a list put forth by the Hong Kong Curriculum Development Council (2001, Appendix II) for incorporation into the school curriculum. Some of these attitudes and values include, among others, honesty, courage, independence, perseverance, equality, tolerance, rationality, liberty, respect for others, and optimism. A high score on the SLAV indicates high levels of student agreement regarding the learning of values and attitudes from their teachers.

In our study, we identified two patterns of relationships. First, the more cooperative types of behaviors (e.g., Leadership, Understanding, and Student Responsibility/Freedom) were positively associated with the student moral learning outcomes as measured by the SLAV, while the less cooperative behaviors (e.g., Dissatisfied) were negatively correlated with these learning outcomes. Second, the above-mentioned QTI scales were also found to be significant predictors of students' moral learning outcomes.

Discussion

The present chapter has shed some light on the relational aspect of teaching and learning and its relationship to students' learning outcomes. Results of studies undertaken in different countries on teacher–student relationships confirmed that students' perceptions of their interpersonal teacher behavior in the classroom are related to their learning outcomes. Overall, previous studies indicate that teachers are perceived as possessing more cooperative types of behavior than less cooperative ones. Teachers are favorably perceived as demonstrating leadership in organizing and structuring their lessons, behaving in a considerate manner, inspiring confidence and trust, showing empathy and understanding, as well as giving freedom and responsibility to students. These perceptions are associated with positive learning outcomes. Teachers are perceived less as demonstrating unhappiness and dissatisfaction, as showing anger, and as being demanding and strict with students.

Regarding the association between teacher interpersonal behavior and students' learning outcomes, it can be seen that cooperative teacher–student interactions are positively associated with students' cognitive and affective learning outcomes as measured by test results and subject-specific attitudes, respectively. Our study in Hong Kong has contributed to the field of knowledge by extending the affective domain to include students' attitudes toward their teachers, as well as by introducing the moral domain of learning values and attitudes from their teachers. Results indicated that cooperative teacher–student interactions were positively associated with student learning outcomes and were significant predictors of students' learning in both the affective and the moral domains. These findings strongly suggest that teachers' positive interpersonal behavior will have profound implications for student learning not only in the cognitive domain but also in the affective and moral ones. Therefore, it would be useful to include students' attitudes toward their teachers and their learning of values and attitudes when examining their learning process.

Values education has been acknowledged as a significant part of the socialization process in school which contributes to students' development (Cooper, Burman, Ling, Razdevsek-Pucko, & Stephenson, 1998). Furthermore, the role of teachers in this process has been emphasized, especially in the messages they convey through teacher–student interactions (Halstead, 1996). Studies on the value-and-attitude messages conveyed by teachers in the classroom have further alluded to the importance of this process (Brint, Contreras, & Matthews, 2001; Sivan & Chan, 2008). Since values education is a significant component of quality teaching, the findings of our study on secondary school students (Sivan & Chan, in press) suggest that the former could be enhanced through positive student–teacher interactions. Students will be more inclined to learn values and attitudes from their teachers who convey socializing messages and exhibit cooperative interpersonal behaviors, especially those related to Leadership, Understanding, and Student Responsibility/Freedom. The identification of specific types of teacher interpersonal behavior which could positively affect student learning of values and attitudes is significant in view of the important role of the teacher as an agent of culture in general and in the process of values education in particular (Brint et al., 2001; Halstead, 1996; Sivan & Chan, 2008).

In his review of Vygotsky's perspectives, Smagorinsky (2011) refers to the process of appropriation through which people make use, adopt, and modify the tools available in their social environment and develop ways of thinking which are common to specific cultural practice. This process, which has also been referred to as internalization, depends on the congruence of the learner's values and prior experience and goals with those that are more experienced in the culture. According to Smagorinsky, one of the factors that affect this appropriation is the social context of learning, which provides the environment in which one learns to use tools. Apart from its physical structure, the context includes also a set of human values and serves as "structures that are products of cultural history in which individual histories converge and are thus inherently relational and value-laden" (2011, p. 35). Results of the examination of the moral perspective of teaching and learning, as it is illustrated through learning of values and attitudes by students and its relationship to teacher–student interactions, carry some practical implications as to how the appropriation could be supported. While the classroom is regarded as the physical structure of the context of learning (Smagorinsky, 2011), the values and attitudes learned by students and the positive relationship between this learning and students' perceptions of their teachers' interpersonal behavior, which was found in Hong Kong classrooms (Sivan & Chan, in press), could further facilitate students' processes of appropriation, which is of significance to their development.

While results of studies on interpersonal teacher behavior portray similarities in its nature, some differences in students' perceptions of their teacher behaviors were found between different countries. The between-countries differences further illustrate the importance of attending to the sociocultural context, which has been emphasized by sociocultural theory, when examining students' learning in the classroom. In view of the relatively small number of cross-cultural studies on teacher interpersonal behavior in the classroom (den Brok et al., 2006), it would be useful to extend such examination to different cultural contexts.

The examination of interpersonal teacher behavior has been made with reference to sociocultural theory. In line with Vygotsky's emphasis on the importance of the environment which comprises the people and their culture, this chapter lends support to the importance of teacher–student interactions to student learning. It also suggests some positive patterns of teacher interpersonal behavior as additional means to those suggested by Vygotsky (1978) for enhancing student development.

According to Goldstein (1999), while scholars building on Vygotsky have been emphasizing the important role of the context in cognitive development of children, they have been paying scant attention to the significant role of interpersonal relationships in this context. In her analysis, Goldstein provided numerous examples where "interpersonal relationships are simply an assumed, implicit contour of the contextual terrain" (p. 654) and argued that they must be considered explicitly when examining the context of learning. Goldstein further asserted that the affective qualities of teacher–student relationships, which she labeled as an interrelational dimension, are an important part of the teaching–learning process and need to be attended to explicitly in order to strengthen children's educational experiences. In line with Goldstein's emphasis on the interrelational dimension and her theorizing the nature and different elements of this dimension, this chapter points out the various patterns of interpersonal relationships which were positively associated with students' learning outcomes, particularly within the affective and moral domains.

Two recommendations for future research on interpersonal teacher behavior can be made. First, since most previous studies employing the QTI were conducted among science-related subjects, with only few including non-science subjects (den Brok, Levy, Brekelmans & Wubbels, 2005; Sivan & Chan, in press), it would be useful to extend this investigation to include additional subjects. This inclusion could provide a more holistic picture of the influence of interpersonal teacher behavior on student learning by examining different classroom contexts, adding the subject-content and possibly the learning activities perspectives of teaching and learning (Brekelmans et al., 2000) to the interpersonal and moral domains which have been portrayed in this chapter. Second, future research could extend the methodology by adopting a qualitative approach to studying interpersonal teacher behavior, rather than solely employing a quantitative approach. Students in different sociocultural contexts may have different perceptions and interpretations of interpersonal teacher behavior, which the quantitative approach does not examine. Research based on these recommendations could facilitate a better understanding of the role teachers play in students' learning and development and identify differences in the interpretation of interpersonal teacher behavior in various sociocultural contexts.

References

Battersby, M. (1999). *So, what's a learning outcome anyway?* Vancouver, BC: Centre for Curriculum, Transfer, and Technology (ERIC Document Reproduction Service No. 430611).

Brekelmans, M., Sleegers, P., & Fraser, B. J. (2000). Teaching for active learning. In P. R. J. Simons, J. L. van der Linden, & T. Duffy (Eds.), *New learning* (pp. 227–242). Dordrecht, the Netherlands: Kluwer Academic Publishers.

Brekelmans, M., Wubbels, T., & Creton, H. A. (1990). A study of student perceptions of physics teacher behavior. *Journal of Research in Science Teaching, 27*, 335–350.

Brekelmans, M., Wubbels, T., & den Brok, P. (2002). Teacher experience and the teacher–student relationship in the classroom environment. In S. C. Goh & M. S. Khine (Eds.), *Studies in educational learning environments: An international perspective* (pp.73–100). Singapore: New World Scientific.

Brint, S., Contreras, M. F., & Matthews, M. T. (2001). Socialization messages in primary schools: An organizational analysis. *Sociology of Education, 75*, 157–180.

Cooper, M., Burman, E., Ling, L., Razdevsek-Pucko, V., & Stephenson, J. (1998). Practical strategies in values education. In J. Stephenson, L. Ling, E. Burman, & M. Copper (Eds.), *Values in education* (pp. 161–194). London: Routledge.

Cheng, Y. C. (1994). Classroom environment and student affective performance: An effective profile. *Journal of Experimental Education, 62*(3), 221–239.

Curriculum Development Council. (2001). *Learning to learn, life-long learning and whole-person development.* Hong Kong: Hong Kong Special Administration Region of the People's Republic of China.

den Brok, P., Brekelmans, M., & Wubbels, T. (2004). Interpersonal teacher behavior and student outcomes. *School Effectiveness & School Improvement, 15*(3), 407–442.

den Brok, P., Fisher, D. L., Brekelmans, M., Rickards, T., Wubbels, T., Levy, J., & Waldrip, B. (2003, March). *The cross national validity of students' perceptions of science teachers' interpersonal behavior.* Paper presented at the Annual Meeting of the National Association for Research in Science Teaching, Philadelphia.

den Brok, P., Fisher, D. L., & Koul, P. (2005). The importance of teacher interpersonal behavior for secondary science students' attitudes in Kashmir. *The Journal of Classroom Interaction, 40*(2), 5–19.

den Brok, P., Fisher, D. L., & Scott, R. (2005). The importance of teacher interpersonal behavior for student attitudes in Brunei primary science classes. *International Journal of Science Education, 7*(3), 765–779.

den Brok, P., Fisher, D. L., Wubbels, T., Brekelmans, M., & Rickards, T. (2006). Secondary teachers' interpersonal behaviour in Singapore, Brunei and Australia: A cross-national comparison. *Asia Pacific Journal of Education, 26*(1), 79–95.

den Brok, P., Levy, J., Brekelmans, M., & Wubbels, T. (2005). The effect of teacher interpersonal behavior on students' subject-specific motivation. *The Journal of Classroom Interaction, 40*(2), 20–33.

Fraser, B. J. (1978). Development of a test of science related attitudes. *Science Education, 62*(4), 509–515.

Fraser, B. J. (1981). *TOSRA test of science related attitudes handbook.* Hawthorn, Victoria, Australia: Australia Council for Educational Research.

Goh, S. C., & Fraser, B. J. (1995, April). *Learning environment and student outcomes in primary mathematics classrooms in Singapore.* Paper presented at the Annual Meeting of the American Educational Research Association, San Francisco, California.

Goh, S. C., & Fraser, B. J. (1998). Teacher interpersonal behavior, classroom environment and student outcomes in primary mathematics in Singapore. *Learning Environments Research, 1,* 199–229.

Goh, S. C., & Fraser, B. J. (2000). Teacher interpersonal behavior and elementary students' outcomes. *Journal of Research in Childhood Education, 14*(2), 216–231.

Goldstein, L. S. (1999). The relational zone: The role of caring relationships in the co-construction of mind. *American Educational Research Journal, 36*(3), 647–673.

Halstead, J. M. (1996). Values and values education in schools. In J. M. Halstead & M. J. Taylor (Eds.), *Values in education and education in values* (pp. 3–14). Washington, DC: Falmer Press.

Khine, M. S., & Fisher, D. (2004). Teacher interaction in psychosocial learning environments: Cultural differences and their implications in science instruction. *Research in Science and Technological Education, 22*(1), 99–111.

Kim, H. B, Fisher, D. L., & Fraser, B. J. (2000). Classroom environment and teacher interpersonal behavior in secondary science classes in Korea. *Evaluation and Research in Education, 14*(1), 3–22.

Leary, T. (1957). *An interpersonal diagnosis of personality.* New York: Ronald Press Company.

Lovat, T., & Clement, N. (2008). Quality teaching and values education: Coalescing for effective learning. *Journal of Moral Education, 37*(1), 1–16.

Petegem, K. V., Creemers, B. P. M., Rossel, Y., & Aelterman, A. (2005). Relationship between teacher characteristics, interpersonal teacher behaviour and teacher wellbeing. *The Journal of Classroom Interaction, 40*(2), 34–44.

Russo, T., & Benson, S. (2005). Learning with invisible others: Perceptions of online presence and their relationship to cognitive and affective learning. *Educational Technology & Society, 8*(1), 54–62.

Savickiene, I. (2010). Conception of learning outcomes in the Bloom's taxonomy affective domain. *Quality of Higher Education, 7,* 37–59.

Sivan, A., & Chan, W. K. D. (2008). Values education in Hong Kong classrooms. *Learning and Teaching, 1*(2), 75–85.

Sivan, A., & Chan, W. K. D. (2010). Values in education: A comparison of students' and teachers' views. In S. T. Menon (Ed.), *Competing values in an uncertain environment: Managing the paradox* (pp. 640–648). Shreveport, LA: International Society for the Study of Work & Organizational Values, Department of Management and Marketing, Louisiana State University Shreveport.

Sivan, A., & Chan, W. K. D. (in press). Teacher interpersonal behavior and secondary students' cognitive, affective and moral outcomes in Hong Kong. *Learning Environments Research.* doi: 10.1007/s10984-012-9123-5

Smagorinsky, P. (2011). *Vygotsky and literacy research: A methodological framework.* Rotterdam, the Netherlands: Sense Publishers.

Soerjaningsih, W., Fraser, B. J., & Aldridge, J. M. (2001, December). *Student-teacher interpersonal behaviour and student outcomes among university students in Indonesia.* Paper presented at the Australian Association for Research in Education, Fremantle.

Stetsenko, A. (2004). Scientific legacy, tool and sign in the development of the child. In R. W. Rieber & D. K. Robinson (Eds.), *The essential Vygotsky* (pp. 501–537). New York: Kluwer Academic/ Plenum Publishers.

Taylor, L. (1992). Mathematical attitude development from a Vygotskian perspective. *Mathematics Education Research Journal, 4*(3), 8–23.

Vygotsky, L. S. (1962). *Thought and language.* Cambridge MA: MIT Press.

Vygotsky, L. S. (1978). *Mind in society: The development of higher psychological processes.* Cambridge, MA: Harvard University Press.

Watkins, D. A., & Biggs, J. B. (Eds.). (1996). *The Chinese learner: Cultural, psychological and contextual influences.* Hong Kong: Comparative Education Research Centre, Faculty of Education, University of Hong Kong.

Wertsch, J. V. (1985). *Vygotsky and the social formation of the mind.* Cambridge, MA: Harvard University Press.

Wubbels, T., & Brekelmans, M. (2005). Two decades of research on teacher–student relationships in class. *International Journal of Educational Research, 43*, 6–24.

Wubbels, T., Brekelmans, M., & Hooymayers, H. (1991). Interpersonal teacher behavior in the classroom. In B. J. Fraser & H. J. Walberg (Eds.), *Educational environments: Evaluation, antecedents and consequences.* Oxford: Pergamon Press.

Wubbels, T., Creton, H. A., Levy, J., & Hooymayers, H. P. (1993). The model for interpersonal teacher behavior. In T. Wubbels & J. Levy (Eds.), *Do you know what you look for? Interpersonal relationships in education* (pp. 13–28). London: Falmer Press.

Wubbels, T., & Levy, J. (Eds.). (1993). *Do you know what you look like? Interpersonal relations in education.* London: The Falmer Press.

11 Social learning, language, and instruction for adult learners where English is their second language

Ian Hay, Rosemary Callingham and Frederick Wright

Introduction

There is a reported association between individuals' language development, reasoning ability, and their social and academic success in educational settings (Bishop, 1997; Catts & Kamhi, 2005; Goswami & Bryant, 2007; Hay, Elias, Fielding-Barnsley, Homel, & Frieberg, 2007). In addition, there is a growing belief that appropriate ongoing and supplemented language, learning, and reasoning experiences can act as protective factors that have a positive influence upon individuals' cognitive and social development and so help alleviate low educational achievement (Enfield & Levinson, 2006; Paul, 2007; Wertsch, 2008). Much of the research has come from educators and researchers working within a developmental framework and with students at risk of failure. There is evidence that an individual's language and vocabulary competencies underpin the transition into comprehension of instruction, information processing, and reasoning (Goswami & Bryant, 2007; Hay & Fielding-Barnsley, 2012; Mercer & Littleton, 2007). Perceiving language, thinking, and comprehension development as linked with parts of a person's cognitive development is the basis for Vygotsky's (1962, 1978) social learning theory.

From this perspective, language development occurs within a social learning context, based on the notion that children's vocabulary development takes place along with their cognitive and semantic (meaning) framework. Vygotsky's (1978) hypothesis is that social interaction, cognition development, and language development are interactive in an iterative way, and his approach has shifted the focus of instruction away from the traditional view of a teacher as a transmitter of information to students. From a Vygotskian perspective, learning is promoted in a context in which individuals play an active role in their own learning, interacting with others in the learning enterprise. In this context, a more knowledgeable other (i.e., parent, peer, or teacher) collaborates and has a dialogue with the individual in order to help that person form new thinking and understanding of the topic under review (Mercer & Littleton, 2007; Nuthall, 2005; Rogoff, 1990).

Although the Vygotskian theory (1978) has a strong developmental focus, it does have application to adult learners because, regardless of age, a person's learning is likely to be enhanced through the reciprocal interactions between the learner and a more informed other person (Lövdén, Bäckman, Lindenberger, Schaefer, & Schmiedek, 2010). For Vygotsky, this formation and construction of new knowledge occurs first in a social setting between the individual and the other person (the inter-psychological level). At a second level (the intra-psychological level), the individual is able to assimilate this new information, link it to other knowledge, and apply it to new contexts. The role of the teacher or instructor is therefore important and active in the student's learning. Based on a Vygotskian perspective, the teacher aims to facilitate the student's learning and the formation of new reasoning through a dialogue that is focused on the student gaining a greater understanding of the topic being discussed and reviewed (Wertsch, 2008). For Vygotsky (1978), this learning occurs within a "zone of proximal development" (ZPD) for the student. This zone is the distance or difference between an individual's ability to understand and perform a task under direction or guidance and with support, compared with the individual's ability to perform the task independently (Guk & Kellogg, 2007). The ZPD is dynamic and changes as the task demands change – for example, a child may be able to understand the physical characteristics of an apple, a carrot, and a tomato, but may not understand how these three items are the same or are different (Hay & Fielding-Barnsley, 2012). This ongoing re-classifying, reasoning, and reviewing of a previous concept is a life-long process, activated by the task requirements and by the questions asked. For example, an adult may have to re-conceptualize his/her understanding about the differences between an apple and a tomato if someone asks: How is a fruit defined?

Vygotsky's social learning theory has been explored by Marion Blank (2002) and her colleagues. In particular, they focused on young children's early language and the children's ability to use reasoning (Blank, Rose, & Berlin, 2003). For Blank et al., language and reasoning are two skills that are interactive and self-enhancing, such that, as children's understandings of vocabulary and concepts improve, so too does their ability to reason, which further enhances their ability to use the words in more complex settings. It is the social dialogue that helps to transmit the meaning of the vocabulary to the child and it provides the child with the opportunity to practise the language and concepts in situations that require more reasoning. Blank et al. assert that teachers and others can improve an individual's language and reasoning development by enhancing their own dialogue, questioning, and conversation with that individual (Blank, 2002; Blank & Franklin, 1980). This assertion is closely aligned with the Vygotskian theory (1978) that a person's development of thought and reasoning occurs through dialogue and language. Although Blank's research (2002) has to date had a child focus, it is based on the Vygotskian theory that learning interactions occur across the life span (Lövdén et al., 2010), making it suitable for application with adult learners.

Blank and her colleagues (Blank, 2002; Blank & Franklin, 1980; Blank et al., 2003) have proposed four levels of dialogue complexity, where the students are active participants in the learning interchanges. In such a communicative context, the teacher initiates and shapes the dialogue so that the students respond at a more appropriate and advancing level of linguistic complexity. The four basic levels of questions and interactions are outlined in terms of their complexity in Table 11.1. Students who have limited mastery of the lower levels of complexity will generally have difficulty with the more advanced levels (Blank, 2002; Blank & White,

Table 11.1 Blank's four levels of language complexity

Level of complexity and proficiency	Language complexity to the experience	Example of teacher discourse
1	Directly supplied information (characteristics)	What do you see?
2	Classification (selective analysis of experience)	Group the shapes by colour. How is this different from this?
3	Reorganization (reordering the experience)	Re-tell me the story. What is your experience with this topic?
4	Abstraction and inference (reasoning about the experience)	What made it happen? Why do they do this?

1999; Elias, Hay, Homel, & Freiberg, 2006). Teachers can use these four levels to introduce and review topics for discussion and learning, and can move backwards or forwards across the levels depending on the responses provided by the student (Hay & Fielding-Barnsley, 2012).

From Vygotsky's (1978) perspective, the three elements that Blank is organizing into a hierarchy are: (i) language proficiency; (ii) social skills proficiency; and (iii) reasoning proficiency, which are considered to be related because they stem from a common underlying cognitive source that manifests all three proficiencies. It is speculated that the core cognitive proficiency of language and reasoning is working memory (Baddeley, 2007), along with processing speed and capacity (Goswami & Bryant, 2007). From this perspective, people's reasoning, language, and social development cannot be easily separated from their ongoing and developing cognitive skills to store, organize, and retrieve information into long-term memory (Baddeley, 2007; Enfield & Levinson, 2006; Hattie, 2009). This cognitive enhancement of the individual is considered to continue throughout the life-long learning process (Paul, 2007). There is ongoing cognitive research in support of this perspective by Lövdén et al. (2010), who noted that a person's language usage, knowledge, memory, and processing efficiency are all highly interconnected within a person's brain functioning. This interconnection is critical for an individual to be a flexible learner and problem solver. Hence, Blank's (2002) framework should also have application with adults because it is based on Vygotsky's (1978) social learning theory. To date, however, there has been little research that has applied Blank's framework to adults.

Second-language learners

Second-language learners have more difficulty with fast and effective language processing and this difficulty is related to the cognitive links between language and thinking (Barrera, 2006; Wertsch, 2008). Wertsch's sociocultural theory focuses on language as a tool that mediates the internal metacognitive system. That is, mediated explicit language use is thought to develop into an internalized inner speech, which is used to intervene with an individual's reasoning ability (Wertsch, 2008). It is likely, however, that individuals will develop ways to self-regulate, or use higher-order strategies that are more commonly used in their culture of origin. If students of different cultural backgrounds come into an education system that is based on different ways of entering into thinking about how to solve problems, then these students are likely to have to adapt to these differences, or struggle with the programme they have entered.

Guss and Wiley (2007) asserted that, although reasoning and metacognition have been widely studied in Western-orientated countries, such as North America, there has been less research completed cross-culturally. They compared reasoning usage and metacognition strategies for individuals located in India, Brazil, and the United States. Although they observed some similarities, they also reported differences in the choice of reasoning and thinking strategies used by individuals across the three countries. In particular, speed of processing was more important to Indians, whereas USA participants rated critical thinking as the most important reasoning skill compared with the other cultures. Brazilians rated their ability to synthesize ideas as more important than did people who lived in India or the USA. Guss and Wiley commented that "apparently the individual skills required for specific metacognitive strategies differ between cultures" (p. 20).

De Guerrero (2005) alleged that adults and older children learning a second language have to develop a second inner speech. This need may delay their ability to process oral information and to reason quickly in the second language. This process is different for young children who might learn two languages and adapt inner speech based on the multiple languages the child is exposed to. De Guerrero also suggested that, as a part of an adult learning a second language, the individual goes through a period of private speech development similar to a child's learning of a language. Private speech development was identified in adult second-language students, who reported rehearsing and saying back to themselves words, vocabulary, and concepts with which they had metalinguistic difficulties (Lantolf & Appel, 1994). From a Vygotskian (1978) perspective, inner speech brings together explicit and implicit reasoning through a central executive functioning within the brain that is manifested by external speech.

From the research quoted here, it is likely that delays in processing information caused by lack of immediate recognition of vocabulary, concepts, and social cues may have a detrimental impact on students' learning in a second language, especially where the context of learning and examination is unfamiliar and hence more stressful. This impact may be compounded by the observation that teachers and lecturers, especially in the higher education sector, tend to introduce abstract ideas too early and cover the content too quickly for many students less familiar with the vocabulary and concepts of that content (Hay & Woolley, 2011; Woolley, 2011). In this situation, second-language learners have a double disadvantage: They lack the language skills needed to process the information efficiently and effectively, and they may not be culturally aware of social processes in the classroom, such as asking questions or requesting help. In this situation, second-language learners can find themselves falling behind in their learning. In many instances, this begins to influence their self-efficacy, which in turn influences their capacity to learn, setting up a cycle of failure (Goldburg, Rueda, & August, 2008; Hay & Ashman, 2012; Hay & Simmons, 2011).

In summary, the research and theoretical framework of Blank (Blank, 2002; Blank & White, 1999), which is based on Vygotsky's (1978) framework, has the potential to be extended to adults who are second-language learners, but to date this extension has not been reported. The second part of this chapter describes an intervention using Blank's approach with young adult learners who were from non-English speaking backgrounds learning in an Australian higher education institution.

Intervention

The study took place in a large metropolitan Technical and Further Education (TAFE) college in Australia. Teachers willing to participate in the study were enlisted from staff who taught international or migrant students in mainstream educational programmes. Three experienced, post-Year 12, TAFE teachers were recruited to take part in the study. Each of the teachers had more than five years' teaching experience, with one holding a PhD, and one having completed studies in teaching English as a second language and a Diploma of Training and Assessment. The third teacher was qualified as a TAFE teacher, holding a Certificate Four in Training and Assessment. The three staff also had workplace experience in their area of teaching. Hence, all teachers had considerable experience and expertise in their own professional domains.

Four classes were involved in the study and all students were doing some form of Diploma in Community Services award course. The TAFE classes were made up of international students, with three having one local student in each. Most international students were from Mainland China. The students were required to have an International English Language Testing System (IELTS) score of Level 5 to gain entry to their Diploma level course. Level 5 users are described as "moderate users" of English.

152 *Ian Hay et al.*

All of the TAFE classes involved students being introduced to new concepts that could have had culturally differing interpretations for the students. Teaching topics introduced included: dealing with domestic violence; counselling at-risk individuals; and understanding disability services.

TAFE teachers interested in the study were provided with a training workshop directly addressing Blank's (2002) four levels of questioning: matching (Level 1); classification (Level 2); reorganization (Level 3); and abstraction and inference (Level 4). Discussion involved the contextual nature of communicating and listening, supported by several practical activities. For example, how different people interpreted the word "family" was considered. Depending on context, people referred to different aspects of family, including differences in the age of group members, such as children. These activities particularly focused on using Blank's second level of dialogue, which is classification.

Reference was made to the complexity of conversation within a classroom and the difficulty of picking up context in a room of 20 or more students, especially when the social context of the classroom was unfamiliar. Adult students who have come from an Asian culture with a focus on respect for the role of the teacher and the teacher's knowledge and the replication of class content knowledge (Kong & Ng, 2005) can be confused by the behaviour of lecturers and teachers in Australia who want to debate and discuss the content and encourage peer group interactions (Houghton & Bain, 1993). The teachers described their current practices and difficulties that some students had with the subjects they were teaching.

The teachers were specifically asked to use Blank's levels of questioning in their classrooms. In particular, they were asked to focus on Levels 2 (classification) and 3 (reorganization) to provide a needed scaffold to the higher levels of thinking. Teachers were asked to classify concepts and meanings of words within the discipline they studied and were encouraged to make definitions explicit and have discussions about interpretations of the concepts used in the classroom. An example of the level of such examination involved words such as disability, continuum of services, and advocacy.

Because many of the students were doing qualifications in welfare, examples of using Blank's levels of questioning in the welfare context were provided. Typically, students in this TAFE course had difficulty with the unit of study on disability and building modifications, and the following is an example of how the welfare studies teachers could use Blank's (2002) levels of dialogue when forming questions to advance the students' level of reasoning on the topic of study.

Level 1 Characteristics of the topic

- What are the characteristics of someone with cerebral palsy?
- Where do the words "cerebral palsy" come from?
- What may a person with cerebral palsy look like?
- How would a person with cerebral palsy speak and move?
- Identify the movements you make in the morning, from getting out of bed to getting to the front gate.

Level 2 Comparison and contrast

- Identify the movements you may make in the morning, from getting out of bed to getting to the front gate, if you had cerebral palsy.
- What are the differences between having cerebral palsy and not having it?
- What are the problems that you would experience in your home if you had cerebral palsy?

Level 3 Reorganization, person reflections, applying new knowledge

- Think about being in a wheelchair. How would you get in and out of your house or in and out of your bathroom? How would you do the cooking?
- What changes would you make to your kitchen cupboards?

Level 4 Higher-order reasoning

- Why modify the home of someone who has cerebral palsy?
- Why is it important to do a home visit when designing a building modification plan for a person with cerebral palsy?

These levels of dialogue are assisting the student to move to a greater level of understanding and reasoning about the topic, whilst the questions help the teacher work within the students' ZPD. Because this zone is dynamic and fluid, the more knowledgeable other (in this case, the TAFE lecturer) asks different types of questions depending on the responses from the student. If the student's responses suggest that the student knows the vocabulary and characteristics associated with the concept being investigated, then the teacher is able to ask more complex reasoning questions. The teacher can move back and forth along this cognitive sequence of questions depending on the students' answers. This movement creates a zone within which new reasoning and learning occurs, but this learning is being enhanced, guided and directed by the TAFE teacher. Blank's (2002) dialogue levels are providing the teacher with a strategy and a tool that can be applied at different times. The focus is on the notion of advancing the students within their own individual ZPD. Blank's dialogue levels are not linked to a specific subject area or curriculum, but are focused on the students' cognitive processes, language, memory, and learning processes. It is not the particular questions that make a difference but the nature of the questioning, moving from lower-level, descriptive questions to those targeting more abstract understanding in a purposeful manner. The low-to-high level structure aids the student in linking to existing understandings, which maximizes the opportunity for students to integrate their new knowledge and develop a richer basis for taking the next step in learning.

Organization and outcomes

Small-group discussion was suggested as one approach to building social relationships in the classroom and this method was modelled during the professional learning session. Forms of questions that might be used as discussion starters were also considered. Teachers were asked to try these ideas in their classrooms and to report back on their success or otherwise. Overall, the intervention lasted nine weeks because this fitted with the operating schedule of the college.

At the conclusion of the units of study, the students whose teachers participated in this project were assessed using the TAFE assessment procedures that had been used in the units in the past. These were principally the writing of a report, which had created many difficulties for past students. Not only did they have to understand the specialist words used, they had to use these in meaningful ways to produce a document of a particular type, which mimicked what would be expected of them when qualified. The major finding was that, whereas in the past about one in three students did poorly on the task and had to re-do it, after the intervention far fewer students (about 5%) had to rewrite their report. The class average for

154   Ian Hay et al.

the assessment also increased, with more students achieving a credit level or above for their unit of study. Informal feedback from the students was also positive, with teachers identified as being able to explain their content knowledge and being responsive to their students.

Teacher interviews

A significant part of the evaluation of the intervention focused on teachers' perceptions of Blank's (2002) dialogue strategies as a form of intervention in TAFE and the level of difficulty in its implementation. During the intervention and afterwards, the participating TAFE teachers were interviewed about their perceptions of their students' responses to the approaches and associated issues.

The teachers are referred to by pseudonyms. Wendy taught a class on dealing with aspects of domestic violence. She was experienced and had been involved in career development through undertaking courses in teaching English to second-language learners and further studies in general teaching. She had two groups of students, one of which she targeted with the language-based approach. The other group she taught as she had always done.

Theresa was involved in teaching a class in counselling. She was also an experienced teacher who had worked in the welfare system for a considerable period and was convener of a number of professional bodies associated with welfare. Theresa used the intervention with a class that was made up of 22 students of Korean, Chinese, Sri Lankan, and Indian backgrounds. One member of the group was a local Australian student. She not only took the group for classes, but also was the pastoral teacher for the group and had known the group for two years in this role. The group was well known to her.

The third teacher, Mary, was an experienced teacher who held a PhD related to hearing deficits. She taught a class in Disability Studies that included words such as "impairment, disability, handicap – words we do use and words we don't use". Mary recognized the importance of language and said that her work with hearing-impaired students helped her communicate with students who were second-language learners.

Each teacher took a different approach to implementing the language intervention in their classrooms, and their perceptions were also varied. Wendy stated:

> with one particular group I used Blank's theory and in the other I did not. So I just went through and explained the unit outline and explained what the assessment would be, read through it, this is what we do, got the nod and they said that this was okay . . . With the second group we dissected every word that was there, like "compare". What does that mean? And then we put it on the board and worked out what their opinion of "compare" was to what I wanted in the word "compare" and at the very end of that particular task they (the group that used Blank) [showed] competency all the way. There was around five I think that . . . did not understand what was being asked in the breakdown of the task.

In contrast, the intervention approach taken by Theresa used small-group discussion. Classes were broken down into peer groups of three and the target word or concept was discussed in the group. The groups were then brought back into the whole class and the word or concept was elaborated. Theresa commented:

> The group became accountable for what was meant . . . when you ask somebody a question and you are asking them to say what they believe or think or know and

asking them to expose that known or unknown, it is daunting for them. To give it to them in groups, and that had all been checked out and everything and discussed, the dauntedness was gone, because they had already spoken about it . . . It doesn't mean they come up with one answer, what they might come up with is some of us in the group thought this and others thought that. It was okay for the group to agree or disagree.

The approach taken by Mary was to introduce a concept through:

look[ing] at case scenario for the assessment about a woman with multiple sclerosis. Question: What is multiple sclerosis? It's a disease, can't move, get worse. Explain. It's a disease of the nerves, two types of nerves, sensory and motor. Explain these differences. Sheath around the nerve is wearing away – sclerosis. Auto immune disease – own body is doing damage – don't know why. Progress of disease can be different for different people – rapid, slow, stop and start.

Mary described writing words on the board and then discussing them with the class, as she usually did. Her practice could be seen as using Blank's Level 4 (abstraction and inference), as seen in her initial question "What is multiple sclerosis?" but she tried to move to lower-level ideas through her explanations. For example, the statement "It's a disease, can't move, get worse" implies comparison (Level 2) and the extension comment "It's a disease of the nerves" appears to reorganize the information somewhat. She commented, however, that she found the Blank approach hard to implement in a classroom situation, stating that she did not feel confident with each level of questioning. Where a word or concept was perceived to not be understood by the class, small-group discussion took place as part of her normal practice.

The focus of the intervention was ensuring that all of Blank's levels were used appropriately to build students' understanding of new ideas. Wendy wrote in her notes:

Group 1
I had a number of students asking me about the assessment task's requirements as they would not understand questions that they had to answer.

Group 2
From this (using Blank's approach) the students were able to rephrase this question so that they had an understanding.

The comment about the group using the language intervention suggests that the students were operating at Blank's Level 3 (reorganization), whereas the group not using the intervention appeared unable to either match (Level 1) the assessment task to previous work or to classify the questions (Level 2). Theresa also indicated that some of her students were developing Level 3 skills through "the exploration of not only what is the definition of the word, but the experience of the word, and the cultural experience of the word, and even awareness to see it in a different light".

The comments that teachers made about in-class interactions were also telling. Students were perceived as more willing to contribute, to ask questions, and to interact in ways that are common in Australian classrooms but less widespread in Asian schools. Wendy stated, for example:

156 *Ian Hay et al.*

> I think that to keep students engaged and to keep students in the course they must feel that they're getting something out of it. I found that the people I did Blank's with had a better glossary and were more prepared to ask and they knew my teaching style was to dissect different things so they felt very comfortable to come to me to say what does that mean.

Theresa similarly commented:

> So the thing about Blank's, that is, it really encourages them to participate and in fact we had a whole discussion on class participation as well, around it, and how do you want to participate in class, and without them even knowing about Blank's stuff, they wanted to do it that way.

Theresa gave the example of a Korean female student who was at risk of failing the course. After the intervention was used in the classroom, this student began to grasp ideas and moved ahead to become one of the best students. The student had apparently benefited from a structured approach that was also supported by the classroom culture.

In contrast, Mary did not report any changes in her students' behaviour. She felt confused by the levels of questioning and did not feel that her teaching style was different from that expected in the intervention. It may be that she had not clearly understood the notion of moving between the levels and, in particular, beginning at the lower levels and moving upwards. Although she had been given an outline of an approach to a lesson using Blank's (2002) levels, her comment was, "the actual process [was] fairly confusing I think. I didn't have a clear idea in my mind as to what the four different stages were." From discussions with Mary, it appeared that she did not have a Vygotskian view of language as an organizer of thought. Instead, her perception was that language was structured and functional, with apparently few cultural overtones. She seemed to expect that, because her students spoke functional English, they would automatically understand the pragmatics of Australian classrooms. It is possible that Mary's previous experience with students who were deaf learning functional English had influenced her notions of language. Mary might have benefited from a more focused summary of the levels and additional practice at framing questions that addressed each level. Her difficulties, however, are a useful reminder that very experienced and successful teachers may take time to absorb new techniques into their practice.

Discussion

The main and important finding of this research is that Vygotsky's (1978) social learning theory, as developed and interpreted by Blank (2002), has application for the successful teaching and learning of adult students who are also second-language learners. This is also, to date, the first reported evidence-based study that validates that Blank's (2002) dialogue framework can enhance the learning outcomes of adults.

In this study, TAFE teachers' knowledge about how to adapt their pedagogical skills to improve students' learning was enhanced when they adapted their levels of questioning within a sequential and cognitive framework. This framework progressed from knowing the vocabulary and the concepts to organizing these words and concepts within an increasingly more complex reasoning structure. The TAFE teachers who applied Blank's level of dialogue questions were better able to operate within their adult students' ZPD. The findings also support the notion that people's vocabulary development takes place along with their cognitive and semantic (meaning) framework (Goswami & Bryant, 2007).

Based on the teachers' comments about the use of Blank's approach in their classrooms, two observations emerged.

1 When provided with opportunities to discuss ideas in small groups using a sociocultural, structured approach, students developed an understanding of words and concepts they were not clear about before.
2 Students developed greater confidence in being able to ask questions, which two of the teachers suggested was not commonplace in their experience before the intervention.

When taken from a socio-learning perspective, the findings indicate that these international students were beginning to develop vocabulary and contextual knowledge of content being taught, along with higher-order reasoning associated with the content. They became more aware of how to engage in a dialogue with others and in a discourse about the concepts and the vocabulary associated with their course of study. In particular, they were able to move along the question sequence, from knowing the vocabulary and the concepts to how to apply those concepts. Encouraging the teachers to focus initially on the vocabulary and the concepts (Blank's, 2002, Level 1 and Level 2 type interactions) enabled the students to better understand the content, rather than be confused by introducing abstract reasoning before the foundation concepts were understood. Asking a person: "What are the typical building modifications for a person with cerebral palsy?" assumes that the person being asked has an understanding of the words "cerebral palsy" and "modification". If that person does not have an "inner speech" understanding of the words, then the question is too abstract for that person at that point in time. From Blank's perspective and Vygotsky's (1978) inner speech notion, the teacher needs to be able to support the student's learning by making the vocabulary and concepts meaningful. Only then can the student better understand the concept and relate this new concept to other ideas and vocabulary (Baddeley, 2007).

Through the use of Blank's (2002) questioning levels, students were more confident and less passive about their learning. For example, Theresa described students coming to her in small groups to ask questions about the subject. Although this behaviour is not surprising in a class of Australian students, it had not occurred at all in Theresa's previous classes with predominantly Asian students. The changed behaviour of the students suggests that they were becoming more able to take on the kinds of classroom expectations that are usual in Australian TAFE classrooms. Since the content knowledge and the teachers associated with the TAFE courses had not changed, and the participating students had similar backgrounds to previous students, the improvement in the students' performance is likely to be a result of the conscious efforts by teachers to use a structured framework of questions to help their students understand both the subject content and the expectations on them as learners.

Vygotsky's (1978) notion that students' ZPD is the place where teachers must operate to enhance their students' learning has been explored in education for some time (e.g., Goswami & Bryant, 2007; Guk & Kellogg, 2007). Students' academic performance is reduced in classrooms where teachers fail to monitor their students' responses to a task and do not adapt and shape their teaching to accommodate their students' performances (Hattie, 2009; Hay, 2000). Further, Nuthall (2005) maintains that too often the dialogue interactions between teachers and their students fall short of enhancing students' learning, reasoning, or thinking. In these classrooms, teacher-directed exchanges become routines and ritualized activities involving the class as a group responding to questions, usually in terms of correct or incorrect, with the teacher then moving on to the next topic or question. Nuthall suggested that, in these classrooms, students absorb these routines, expected behaviours, and group responses and so learn to look as if they are engaged and learning, even when the task they are working on is below or above their ability. This style of teaching is in contrast to that advocated by Vygotsky (1978) and Blank (2002), where teachers need to monitor their own feedback and their interactions with all of their students to actively shape an individual student's learning and reasoning. Compared to Nuthall's ritualized classroom, where a student's "incorrect" response to a question is an error, in the Vygotsky-influenced classroom a student's "incorrect" response to a question is a window into that student's reasoning and an opportunity for the teacher to engage in a dialogue with that student. The student is hence provided with a route to reflection about the topic and enhancement of understanding of the concept, word, or context that the teacher's question is investigating. That is, the teacher initiates and shapes the dialogue so that the student responds at a more appropriate and advancing level of linguistic and reasoning complexity.

Conclusion

This study is supportive of previous research that has argued that teachers need to be engaged with and to be actively involved in shaping their students' learning within a dialogue and reasoning framework (e.g., Mercer & Littleton, 2007; Nuthall, 2005) and that this dialogue focus is beneficial for students whose language of instruction and assessment is other than their first language (Wertsch, 2008). The findings are also supportive of the assertion that better-quality teacher feedback to students is more meaningful and enhances students' opportunities for learning (Hattie, 2009).

There are four main findings from this research. First, the application of Blank's (2002) dialogue framework with adult students who were second-language learners helped these students to bridge the gap between the teachers' use of terms and concepts and the students' understanding and use of those terms. Second, TAFE teachers were able to incorporate Blank's (2002) levels of questioning framework into their regular programme and this enhanced their teaching and their students' learning. Third, the findings are supportive of Vygotsky's social learning theory in the context of young adult second-language learners. Fourth, the findings reinforce the argument that there are strong interactive links between individuals' language development, their cognitive reasoning, and their educational success, and that these links appear to be best facilitated within a learning environment where the dialogue between the teacher and the student is meaningful, planned, and encouraged.

The results of this study have implications for pedagogical practices, the development of teachers' pedagogical knowledge, and the design of better educational practice, particularly for students where the language of instruction and assessment is not in their first language. There is a need to provide pre-service and other teachers with more knowledge and strategies on how to improve their dialogue and questioning techniques within their classrooms. There is also a growing body of evidence that holds that teachers who are introduced to Blank's (2002) dialogue levels and framework are able to transfer this new procedural knowledge into their pedagogical and classroom practices, which in turn has a positive impact on their competency as teachers and on their students' learning.

References

Baddeley, A. D. (2007). *Working memory, thought and action*. Oxford: Oxford University Press.
Barrera, M. (2006). Role of definitional and assessment models in the identification of new or second language learners of English for special education. *Journal of Learning Disabilities, 39*(2), 142–156.

Bishop, D.V. M. (1997). *Uncommon understanding: Development and disorder of language comprehension in children*. Hove, UK: Psychological Press.

Blank, M. (2002). Classroom discourse: A key to literacy. In K. Butler & E. Silliman (Eds.), *Speaking, reading and writing in children with learning disabilities: New paradigms in research and practice* (pp. 151–173). Malwah, NJ: Erlbaum.

Blank, M., & Franklin, C. (1980) Dialogue with preschoolers: A cognitively-based system of assessment. *Applied Psycholinguistics, 1*, 127–150.

Blank, M., Rose, S. A., & Berlin, L. J. (2003). *Preschool language assessment instrument: The language of learning in practice* (2nd ed.). Austin, TX: Pro Ed.

Blank, M., & White, S. (1999) Activating the zone of proximal development in school: Obstacles and solutions. In P. Lloyd & C. Fernnyhough (Eds.), *Lev Vygotsky: Critical assessment* (pp. 331–350). London: Routledge.

Catts, H. W., & Kamhi, A. G. (2005). *The connection between language and reading disabilities*. Mahwah, NJ: Erlbaum.

De Guerrero, M. C. M. (2005). *Inner speech L2: Thinking words in a second language*. New York: Springer.

Elias, G., Hay. I., Homel, R., & Freiberg, K. (2006). Enhancing parent–child book reading in a disadvantaged community. *Australian Journal of Early Childhood, 31*, 20–25.

Enfield, N., & Levinson, S. C. (Eds.). (2006). *Roots of human sociality: Culture, cognition, and interaction*. Oxford: Berg.

Goldburg, C., Rueda, R. S., & August, D. (2008). Sociocultural contexts and literacy development. In D. August & T. Shanahan (Eds.), *Developing reading and writing in second-language learners* (pp. 95–129). New York: Routledge.

Goswami, U., & Bryant, P. (2007). Children's cognitive development and learning. *Research Report 2/1a: The Primary Review*. University of Cambridge.

Guk, I., & Kellogg, D. (2007). The ZPD and whole class teaching: Teacher-led and student-led interactional mediation of tasks. *Language Teaching Research, 11*, 281–299.

Guss, C., & Wiley, B. (2007). Metacognition of problem-solving strategies in Brazil, India, and the United States. *Journal of Cognition and Culture, 7*, 1–25.

Hattie, J. (2009). *Visible learning*. New York: Routledge.

Hay, I. (2000). Cognitive strategies in the secondary school: Investigating Process Based Instruction and students' perceptions of effective teaching strategies. *Journal of Cognitive Education and Psychology, 1*, 164–176.

Hay, I., & Ashman, A. (2012). Self-concept. In R. J. Levesque (Ed.), *Encyclopedia of adolescence* (pp. 2516–2536). New York: Springer.

Hay, I., Elias, G., Fielding-Barnsley, R., Homel, R., & Frieberg, K. (2007). Language delays, reading delays and learning difficulties: Interactive elements requiring multidimensional programming. *Journal of Learning Disabilities, 40*, 400–409.

Hay, I., & Fielding-Barnsley, R. (2012). Social learning, language and literacy. *Australasian Journal of Early Childhood, 37*, 24–29.

Hay, I., & Simmons, N. (2011).The significance of pan-cultural factors of self-concept, friendship and emotional development on students' learning and identity. In T. Lê & Q. Lê (Eds.), *Linguistic diversity and cultural identity: A global perspective* (pp. 189–198). New York: Nova Science Publishers.

Hay, I., & Woolley, G. (2011). The challenge of reading comprehension. In T. Lê, Q. Lê, & M. Short (Eds.), *Language and literacy in a challenging world* (pp. 123–136). New York: Nova Science Publishers.

Houghton, S., & Bain, A. (1993). Peer tutoring with ESL and below average readers. *Journal of Behavioural Education, 3*, 125–142.

Lantolf, J. P., & Appel, G. (1994). Theoretical framework: An introduction to Vygotskian perspectives on second language research. In J. P. Lantolf & G. Appel (Eds.), *Vygotskian approaches to second language research* (pp. 1–32). Norwood, NJ: Ablex.

Lövdén, M., Bäckman, L., Lindenberger, U., Schaefer, S., & Schmiedek, F. (2010). A theoretical framework for the study of adult cognitive plasticity. *Psychological Bulletin, 136*(4), 659–676.

Kong, L. Y., & Ng, P. T. (2005). School-parent partnerships in Singapore. *Educational Research for Policy and Practice, 4,* 1–11.

Mercer, N., & Littleton, K. (2007). *Dialogue and the development of children's thinking.* London: Routledge.

Nuthall, G. (2005). The cultural myths and realities of classroom teaching and learning: A personal journey. *Teachers College Record, 107*(5), 895–934.

Paul, R. (2007). *Language disorders: From infancy through adolescence* (3rd ed.). St. Louis, MI: Mosby.

Rogoff, B. (1990). *Apprenticeship in thinking: Cognitive development in social context.* New York: Oxford University Press.

Vygotsky, L. S. (1962). *Thought and language.* Cambridge, MA: MIT Press.

Vygotsky, L. S. (1978). *Mind in society: The development of higher psychological processes.* Cambridge, MA: Harvard University Press.

Wertsch, J. (2008). From social interaction to higher psychological processes: A clarification and application of Vygotsky's theory. *Human Development, 51,* 66–79.

Woolley, G. (2011). *Reading comprehension: Assisting children with learning difficulties.* Dordrecht, the Netherlands: Springer International.

12 Two instead of one ZPD

Individual and joint construction in the ZPD

Aleksandar Baucal

Introduction

In 1934, Vygotsky (Выготский) published the book "Мышление и речь" (Myslenie i rech), crystallizing his theoretical ideas intended to enable psychology to overcome "the crisis in psychology" – that is, the fact that psychology was divided into different ontological and epistemological approaches (Vygotsky, 1987a, 1934/1986; Yaroshevski, 1989). Nowadays, it seems that psychology is still in crisis since it is divided between different approaches (e.g., biological-evolutionary vs. sociocultural). However, it cannot be said that psychology has spent a century in vain: Now we know much more about both biological and sociocultural–historical aspects of human beings, but it seems that knowing more does not make integration easier.

In my view, Vygotsky really provided a blueprint for an integrative approach and this is why it is proper to qualify him as "the Mozart of Psychology", as was done by philosopher Stephen Toulmin (1978). It is also true that the blueprint leaves some space for different interpretations, giving the impression of being "somewhat cryptic" (Wertsch, 1984, p. 7). However, his ideas do not leave space for *just any kind of interpretation*. In order to find out their meanings, one needs to take into account not only those paragraphs in which the given idea is discussed, but also other key ideas of Vygotsky's theory.

This is the approach I am going to take in this chapter, dealing with a key concept of Vygotsky's theory – namely, the zone of proximal development (ZPD). The main aim is to provide empirical arguments for the claim that both individual construction and joint construction can be involved in the development of new competencies in the ZPD. In the first part, I will analyze theoretical and practical meanings of the ZPD. Then, I will present results of my own research suggesting that ZPD includes both mechanisms of development – individual and joint construction. Finally, I am going to discuss theoretical and practical implications of the extended conceptualization of the ZPD.

ZPD: From a new kind of assessment to a new metatheory

Today, the idea of ZPD is widespread and is the best-known idea from Vygotsky's theory (Palinscar, 1998; Chaiklin, 2003; del Río & Álvarez, 2007). In November 2011, EBSCO's database found 553 articles in the previous 30 years with "ZPD" in the abstract. However, the idea is used in so many different ways that there is a risk that it is "used loosely and indiscriminately, thereby becoming so amorphous that it loses all explanatory power" (Wertsch, 1984, p. 7).

A reason for the combination of high popularity and high risk of misunderstanding lay in Vygotsky's specific writing style: "Vygotsky did not hesitate to put poetic images in his

162 *Aleksandar Baucal*

psychological works" (Kozulin, 1986, p. xiv). Although such writing style contributes to misunderstandings, it can happen only when one takes into consideration isolated pieces of his text. If one builds understanding of certain ideas in relation with other theoretical ideas, it becomes easy to avoid misunderstandings. Discussing the case of ZPD, del Río and Álvarez came to a similar conclusion that "the ZPD is Vygotsky's best-known concept in the Western hemisphere . . . although proper understanding of the ZPD also requires knowledge of his general genetic model" (2007, p. 277).

Chaiklin (2003) identified eight original texts in which Vygotsky discussed the ZPD concept: six stenographic transcripts of lectures, and two texts published as book chapters, including Chapter 6 in the book *Myslenie i rech*. Probably the most quoted passage about ZPD is the following one:

> Having found that the mental age of two children was, let us say, eight, we gave each of them harder problems than he could manage on his own and provided some slight assistance: the first step in a solution, a leading question, or some other form of help. We discovered that one child could, in cooperation, solve problems designed for twelve-year-olds, while the other could not go beyond problems intended for nine-year-olds. The discrepancy between a child's actual mental age and the level he reaches in solving problems with assistance indicates the zone of his proximal development; in our example, this zone is four for the first child and one for the second. Can we truly say that their mental development is the same? Experience has shown that the child with the larger zone of proximal development will do much better in school.
>
> (Vygotsky, 1934/1986, p. 187)

Following the idea of Bakhtin (1984), it is important to take into consideration the dialogical relation within which Vygotsky produced this passage. This passage was a part of Vygotsky's dialogue with the influential psychometric approach to children's abilities, assuming that the child's ability is directly proportional to the number of items *solved independently* (Vygotsky, 1935). A similar belief is still widespread among teachers and lay people, and it is reflected through practice of classroom assessment and assessment practices in other areas of life. Even more, if somebody would be supported during assessment, it would be treated as cheating.

> In the investigation of the cognitive development of the child it is usual to think that indicative of the child's intellect is only that which the child can do himself. We give the child series of tests, series of tasks of varying difficulty, and by the way and the degree of difficulty up to which the child can solve the task we judge the greater or lesser development of his intellect. It is usual to think that indicative of the degree of development of the child's intellect is the independent, unassisted solving of the task by the child.
>
> (Vygotsky, 1935, p. 41)

On the other side, Vygotsky argued that assessment through independent work is only half of the story. The main point of his definition of ZPD is to argue that, although the independent achievement of children indicates abilities that are already developed to the mature stage (zone of actual development – ZAD), children's achievement with certain kinds of assistance is also informative. It indicates abilities in the process of development and that will become mature in future. Thus the ZPD provides a unique window to future development.

The claim that traditional testing needs to be extended by assisted performance had already significant impact on the assessment practice – for example, the dynamic assessment approach was developed (see Lidz & Elliott, 2000; Sternberg & Grigorenko, 2002). However, Vygotsky's agenda behind ZPD was far more ambitious than just to change assessment practice. That was only the first step in sketching a whole new sociocultural theory of development.

From ZPD to a new relationship between learning and development

If the child in collaboration with a more competent partner can overcome more complex challenges than when he performs independently (to be "*a head taller than himself*", Vygotsky, 1967, p. 16), it means that learning can be a source of development. In this way, Vygotsky introduced a new perspective on the relationship between learning and development.

Typically, children's cognitive development is treated as a process that is rather independent from learning. The development is the process of creating something qualitatively new. The learning cannot contribute to the development, but it can rely on its results. Piaget's theory of cognitive development is a good example of this kind of understanding of the relationship between development and learning (Piaget, 1970, 1977). Although Piaget somewhat modified his view on this issue (e.g., Piaget, 1995), he generally assumed that developmental transformation of deep cognitive structure is independent from learning. It is the internal process of equilibration and reflective abstraction that creates new cognitive structures. When the child develops a new cognitive structure, he can learn about more complex phenomena. Therefore, development needs to precede learning because it creates a necessary precondition for learning of more complex phenomena. This kind of understanding of the relationship between learning and development is still very influential, especially in developmental and educational psychology. Moreover, such understanding is an important reason why these two disciplines are typically separated from each other.

With the ZPD notion, Vygotsky turned around the relationship between development and learning (1978a). The ZPD implies that an "essential feature of learning is that it creates the zone of proximal development" (Vygotsky, 1978a, p. 90). Therefore, the learning is a constitutive part of the development, so development can come about from learning.

Does it mean that Vygotsky claimed that *any* kind of learning can have such impact on development – for example, that instrumental learning or conditional learning can lead towards development of new, qualitatively more complex competencies? Although both belong to the general category of learning, from Vygotsky's theory, it follows that they cannot have developmental impact. When he claimed that learning can be the source of development, he referred to a *complex sociocultural kind of learning*. It happens only when the child collaborates with a more competent partner, who introduces cultural tools as mediators (concepts, ideas, strategies, technical tools, etc.) in the joint activity and supports the child to internalize them. Although he used the general term "learning", in fact he meant a very particular kind of collaborative learning that can be found regularly when the child participates in family and community life, as well as in the teaching/learning process.

What is the role of cultural tools in the development of new competencies? Vygotsky provided answers to this question by discussing the critical role of word (речь) in the development of concepts and conceptual/abstract thinking. He assumed that *the functional use of word* has a key role in the development of higher forms of thinking. At the beginning, the word is the instrument for the development of concept (meaning and sense), and then it serves as its symbol. When the child uses the word functionally (within a certain purposeful activity), it supports him to orchestrate different mental functions and resources (namely, attention, analysis, abstraction, synthesis, knowledge, motivation, emotions, etc.), to create

164 *Aleksandar Baucal*

the meaning and sense, enabling communication, collaboration and activity (Vygotsky, 1934/1986). Therefore, during collaborative learning and appropriation of cultural tools, the partner and tools support the child in exploration of how to orchestrate their own psychological functions and resources in such a way to enable him to participate meaningfully and competently in social and cultural activities.

From a new relationship between learning and development to a new metatheory

The concept of ZPD brought not only a new perspective on what needs to be assessed and how to assess it, but also quite a new theory of the relationship between learning and development. However, Vygotsky went further: He put forward a new cultural–historical theory integrating biological, universal and social-cultural–historical constituents of the human mind and activity (Vygotsky, 1934/1986). This ultimate goal of Vygotsky is described in a good way by Ivić:

> Vygotsky's concept of "the proximal zone of development" has first of all theoretical implications. In the sociocultural conception of development children cannot be regarded as cut off from their social and cultural environment like young Robinson Crusoes. Their ties with other people form part of their very nature. . . . In this concept of the proximal zone, the view of the child as a social being engenders a methodological approach with far-reaching implications, since the child's development is regarded as a dynamic and dialectical process.
>
> (Ivić, 1994, p. 772)

One of the key assumptions of the integrative theory of Vygotsky concerns the distinction of two kinds of mental functions: elementary (lower: LMF) and higher (HMF). If we would use a more contemporary term, we could use the "biological-evolutionary based" mental functions for the LMF, and the "socioculturally mediated" mental functions for the HMF. While the former are founded in human biology, making human beings similar to higher primates – that is, not mediated, but universal and relatively stable across historical time – the latter are mediated by cultural tools, relative to cultural groups, changeable through historical time and therefore specific to human beings.

The assumption that human beings are both biological and sociocultural beings was nothing new (e.g., Wundt made a similar distinction much before Vygotsky – see Rieber & Robinson, 2001). What was really the contribution of Vygotsky is his proposal on how LMF and HMF are integrated through mediation and cultural tools. The child is a sociocultural being from the beginning; he is networked with others and in constant dialogical relationship with others, even when he is alone (Bakhtin, 1984). Within shared activities, the child develops HMF from LMF by appropriation of sociocultural tools while being scaffolded (in terms of Wood, Bruner & Ross, 1976) by a more competent partner. Thus, the sociocultural context consists of cultural tools "inherited" from previous generations as well as others with whom the child participates in shared activities. This becomes an integral part of his mind and activities (like prosthetic devices or implants). Ivić (1994) illustrated this idea of Vygotsky's theory by example, using the role of written language:

> Written language and book-based culture have a profound impact on the ways in which perception, memory and thought function. This is because written language contains

within itself a model for the analysis of reality (treatment in discrete units, linearity and temporality in the organization of thoughts, loss of the sense of totality, etc.) and psychological techniques including, in particular, an enhanced power of memory that alters the relationship between memory and thought.

(Ivić, 1994, p. 767)

Being mediated and scaffolded by cultural tools and more competent others, the child orchestrates his own mental functions (both LMF and HMF), creating in Vygotsky's terms "interfunctional systems" (Vygotsky, 1987b), making him a competent participant in different communities, such as family, school, neighbourhood, playground, peer groups, internet groups, work organizations and so on (both Rogoff, 2003 and Bourdieu, 1990, expressed a similar idea by the concept of habitus). These interfunctional systems, composed by orchestration of biological and sociocultural functions, are in the background of child competencies. Therefore, in Vygotsky's framework, child competencies are considered as sociocultural, not individual by "nature", since they are co-constructed through interaction with others and mediated by cultural tools. It means that competencies are constructed first outside of the person and then become constituents of individual mind and activity (general genetic law – Vygotsky, 1978b). In this way, many traditional distinctions, such as internal–external, individual–social, inside–outside and so on, are blurred.

To summarize, the introduction of the idea of ZPD brought a new metatheory intending to integrate biological and sociocultural, individual and social, private and public, inside and outside and other dichotomies that divided psychology into different approaches, creating the "crisis of psychology". The ZPD can be characterized as "the Vygotskian system's 'leading window': it addresses all the basic questions that can be posed regarding any psychological system" (del Río & Álvarez, 2007, p. 281). Thus, the ZPD concept is not an ontologically and/or epistemologically neutral technical innovation, but it encapsulates all basic assumptions and concepts of Vygotsky's theory.

Puzzling research findings about the ZPD

When Vygotsky discussed the ZPD, he did not describe in detail the research studies he used to support theoretical assumptions and claims. Therefore, researchers need first to develop a methodology for studying the ZPD that results in diversity of approaches for studying the ZPD. Although some difficulties arise in terms of integration of findings from studies based on different assumptions, focuses, aims and methodologies, such diversity also provides the opportunity to better understand multiple aspects of the ZPD phenomena (Baucal, Arcidiacono & Buđevac, 2011).

The research study I am going to discuss in detail is motivated by the fact that interaction between the child and the more competent other is by itself a complex phenomenon. Two individuals who collaborate have different personal histories, identities, social status and position, interests, motivation, ways of communication and so on. Moreover, during interaction they negotiate on different grounds and terms, struggling to establish a certain kind of relationship to shape the form and trajectory of the joint activity in a certain way. When one claims that children can develop new competencies through interaction with more competent others, a question is raised as to the role of different aspects of social interaction. For example, is it the cognitive collaboration that provides conditions for the child to develop new competencies (negotiation about definition of the object of discussion, what they need to do together, how to do that, what kind of cultural tools might be relevant, how to use them, etc.) or is it simply being with the other that supports the child to engage more strongly, to explore new ways of thinking about the object and construct new competencies by himself? This dilemma, as with many others, is defined in terms of oppositions, but it helps to make distinct at the analytical level two aspects that are typically interwoven in reality.

These two aspects of social interaction need to be differentiated, especially in relation to the ZPD and the assumption that every HMF is developed through specific kinds of interaction with more competent others. It is worth noting here that, according to Vygotsky, not every kind of interaction with a more competent other can initiate, guide and shape development. Some conditions need to be met in order to have development as a result of the interaction with a more competent other. Vygotsky did not enlist these conditions explicitly, but they can be drawn from his theory: (i) interaction between the child and partner needs to be in the child's ZPD; (ii) it is necessary that the child is actively engaged during interaction; and (iii) the more competent partner needs to allow the child to take gradual control over the activity, to master appropriate mediating tools and to become an independent user of those tools in organization of their own activities. It implies that a kind of interaction in which the other provides only emotional–motivational support to the child, without taking part in the child's struggle to develop new competencies, cannot result in the development of new competencies.

The following study aimed to differentiate the effects of emotional–motivational and cognitive aspects of the interaction with a more competent other.

Motivational and cognitive support during interaction and their impact on the ZPD

In this study, a pre-/post-research design was employed (see Figure 12.1).

In the pre-test, 126 students (8–12 years old) were assessed twice by the Raven matrices. The first assessment was organized in the classroom (group testing: G1). Based on their achievements, students were divided randomly into two equal groups – experimental (EG)

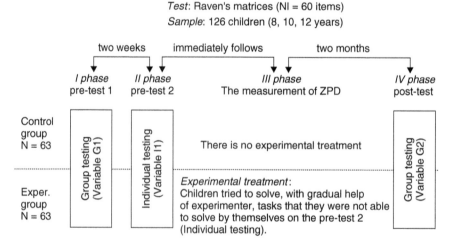

Figure 12.1 Research design

and control (CG) group. Two weeks later, in the second pre-test, students were assessed individually in a separate room. During the session, the researcher evaluated each answer and identified items that were solved correctly (individual testing: I1). When students had finished, those from the CG went back to their classroom while students from the EG were involved in the intervention phase. Two months later, a third assessment was organized in the same way as the first group pre-test (the post-test: G2).

The intervention consisted of standardized gradual support for students from the researcher while they were working on the items they had not solved in previous attempts. First level of support was an *emotional–motivational support*. Each student was encouraged to attempt the item again ("Try again to solve this item, you can do it"). If the student managed to solve the item, the researcher proceeded with the next item. If the student did not make it, the researcher provided the second level of support – the researcher analyzed relations existing between elements in each row of the given item (*cognitive 1 support*). In this way, the researcher supported the student to identify the relation within rows, which is a necessary condition to solve the item. If the student solved the given item with this support, the researcher proceeded with the next one, and if the child was not able to solve it, the next, third level of support was provided – analysis of relations between elements in an item's column (*cognitive 2 support*). If the student made it with the third level of support, the researcher proceeded with the next item, otherwise the fourth and last level of support was provided – integrated analysis of rows and columns of given items to support students to take into consideration both dimensions of the matrix (*cognitive 3 support*). Therefore, for each student from the EG, the following information came as a result of such a procedure: (i) the number of items students solved independently; (ii) information about the number of items students solved with the first, second, third and fourth levels of help; and (iii) the number of items students were not able to solve even with the highest level of support. For students from the CG only, information on the number of items solved independently was available.

Measurement of the ZPD

Based on Vygotsky's theory, the number of items solved individually in the pre-test indicates the ZAD. However, Vygotsky did not provide technical instruction on how the ZPD can be measured. In his famous passage on the ZPD, he only indicated that a student who is able to do more with the same level of support has wider ZPD. Following this, a formula for measurement of the ZPD was developed:

$$ZPD = \left(\frac{H1}{NI - I1} \times 4 \right) + \left(\frac{H2}{NI - I1} \times 3 \right) + \left(\frac{H3}{NI - I1} \times 2 \right) + \left(\frac{H4}{NI - I1} \times 1 \right)$$

where NI is the total number of items (in the case of the Raven matrices, it is 60); I1 is the number of items solved independently in the individual pre-test; and H1, H2, H3 and H4 is the number of items solved with respective level of support (emotional–motivational, cognitive 1, 2 and 3).

Since students solved different numbers of items independently, the number of items solved with a certain level of support is first divided by the number of items the child tried to solve with support. For example, if the student solved 40 (I1) out of 60 items (NI) independently, then he worked on 20 items with support. Then if five of these 20 items were solved with the first level of support, it means that 25% of items were solved with this support. Furthermore, it is assumed that if a student solves a given item with the lower level of support, it means that ZPD for this item is wider. This is the reason why the proportion of items solved with the first level of support is multiplied by four, while the number of items asking for a higher level of support was multiplied with three, two or one, respectively, to the level of support. In short, students who solved more items with lower levels of support had wider ZPD.

Results

The information on the number of items students from EG and CG managed to solve (independently and with support) is presented in Figure 12.2. It shows that both groups solved on average 35–36 items in the pre-test (i.e., the difference is not significant). Students from the EG managed to solve eight additional items with the first level of support, reaching scores of about 44 items, about six items with the second level of support (scoring about 50 items), about four items with the third level of support and two items with the fourth level, coming close to scoring 57 out of 60.

However, two months later, in the post-test, students from the EG had on average 43 points, and students from the CG stayed at about 35 points, as in the pre-test. It suggests that CG participants did not make any improvement during the two months, while students from the EG profited very much from the intervention (t=7.34, df=59, p< 0.000) – about seven items or 20% of items solved independently in the pre-test. Therefore, these findings confirmed that students can do more with support from a more competent other than they can independently.

When Vygotsky discussed the ZPD, he also claimed that ZPD is informative regarding future cognitive levels of children. Results from this study also supported this assumption. The multiple regression analysis showed that the ZPD predicts post-test score over and above the pre-test score ($F_{(1,58)}$=45.631, p< 0.000). It suggests that both ZAD and ZPD contribute to future developmental levels. Although the ZPD can explain small amounts of individual differences (about 2% of variance), it can be treated as a significant effect, since the ZAD accumulates effects of all learning opportunities before the research and the ZPD reflects only specific experience during the intervention.

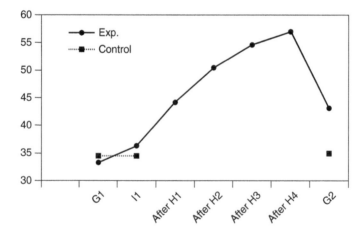

Figure 12.2 The number of items solved in EG and CG in different phases of the study

Now we come to the key research question: What is the impact of different levels of support to the future development of a child? According to Vygotsky, the emotional–motivational support applied in the study could not support cognitive development since it does not include joint thinking and appropriation of cultural tools (in this case, thinking strategies suitable for these kinds of items). Thus, only this kind of cognitive support is supposed to result in development of new competencies in the study.

To get an answer to the question, the following analysis was performed. First, items solved in the post-test, but not in the pre-test, were selected as they indicate competencies developed in between. Then, for each item, the kind of support (emotional–motivational or cognitive) the student needed to solve it during the intervention phase was identified. Assuming that the emotional–motivational support is not a productive one, it was expected that these items asked only for cognitive support during interaction with the researcher. However, the result was somewhat different: Students managed to solve about 50% of items with only emotional–motivational support; about 45% with some kind of cognitive support; and about 5% of items were not solved even with the highest level of cognitive support.

Two instead of one ZPD: Individual and joint construction in the ZPD

What kind of conclusion can be drawn from the results of the above study about the ZPD and Vygotsky's theory of development of new competencies?

First, the finding that students from the EG (involved in interaction with the researcher demonstrating strategies of thinking about Raven matrices) were more successful than students from the CG even two months after fits very well into Vygotsky's theory. It confirms one of the best-known of Vygotsky's claims on the ZPD – that is, that the child can do more through interaction with a more competent other than individually. Furthermore, the impact of the social interaction with a more competent partner in this study is rather strong, especially taking into consideration that students and researchers collaborated on Raven matrices that are supposed to measure fluid intelligence.

The second conclusion is related to the claim that the ZPD is predictive for the future level of cognitive development. As was discussed above, Vygotsky assumed that the future development of two students with the same level of actual development but different ZPDs will not be the same – the student with a higher ZPD is supposed to be more competent in the future than the other one. The research result that showed students with higher ZPD were more successful in the post-test when they did the Raven matrices individually confirms the assumption that the measure of ZPD used in this study is indicative for the future development level of students.

The results of this research study also demonstrate that interaction with a more competent other that includes cognitive support (where the researcher did certain steps in the analysis and thinking about matrices on behalf of the student) has an impact on cognitive development. Some items that students were able to get right with the cognitive type of support were also done correctly in the individual post-tests. This finding is in line with Vygotsky's assumption that during interaction the child appropriates certain cultural tools as mediation tools for his thinking and that it makes him become more competent.

However, two findings do not seem to be in accordance with Vygotsky's theory. First, in a large number of cases, students needed only the emotional–motivational support from the researcher in order to solve items which they were not able to solve independently in the pre-test. Second, half of the items which had been solved by students in the post-test but not in the pre-test (indicating developmental effect) asked only for the emotional–cognitive support during the interaction with the researcher. Both findings lead towards the same conclusion – it seems that even social interaction with no joint cognitive activity can somehow support children's development of new competencies. Without the joint cognitive activity, we cannot call upon the co-construction of the new competencies as an explanation. As we can see when Vygotsky's theory is discussed, the joint cognitive activity and co-construction of the new competencies during joint thinking are core components of the theory. Therefore, these two findings seem to ask for an explanation outside of Vygotsky's theory. Consequently, it is now a question of how to interpret, within Vygotsky's theory, the finding that some items not solved independently in the pre-test were solved only with the emotional–motivational support without cognitive instruction from the researcher.

One interpretation can be that this result indicates that students were somewhat more competent in the pre-test than they managed to demonstrate through independent work. In other words, it assumes that students had some "hidden competencies" in the pre-test – that is, competencies that were not exposed within the arrangements used in that phase of the research. However, when they interacted with a more competent other who supported them emotionally and motivationally, they managed to employ their "hidden competencies" and get some additional items right. Following this interpretation, we can say that interaction with a more competent other can advance meta-cognition of students, making them more capable of using already existing competencies in a more effective way. This results in better achievements of students, which cannot be interpreted as an indication that the new competencies are developed through the interaction with a more competent other, but that already existing competencies are employed in a better way. If this interpretation could be confirmed through subsequent research, then this finding will ask for a small modification of Vygotsky's theory. In this case, we would assume that not all children's competencies could be detected through their independent work. Furthermore, if the child is more successful in collaboration with a more competent other than individually, it might be because of two reasons: (i) the child managed to use his own "hidden competencies" better; and (ii) the child really develops some new competencies together with a more competent other. However, this modification of Vygotsky's theory would not ask for deeper changes in terms of the key assumptions and concepts. It will ask only for improvement in technical terms – that is, to find a better methodology for identifying the "hidden competencies" of children in order to avoid mixing them with the competencies that are co-constructed through the interaction with a more competent other.

An alternative interpretation can be that success with only emotional–motivational support can also be a result of the individual construction of the new competencies during social interaction. In other words, the assumption behind this interpretation is that emotional–motivational support can encourage children to explore and reorganize individually their understanding and their thinking about cognitive tasks. Being supported by the other who is more competent can encourage the child to give additional effort and to engage more, resulting in individual construction of new competencies. Following this interpretation, it means that both individual construction and co-construction can be involved in joint activity and construction of new competence.

Contrary to the first interpretation ("hidden competencies"), this interpretation seems to ask for a modification of Vygotsky's theory in more profound terms. It seems that one of the key assumptions about joint construction of new competencies would need to be modified in order to also include individual construction as the way in which new competencies can emerge through social interaction with a more competent other. Still, this assumption is treated as a cornerstone of Vygotsky's theoretical framework. Namely, in the key referent reviews and introductory books (e.g., Kozulin, 1986; Wertsch, 1988, 1993; Yaroshevski, 1989; van der Veer & Valsiner, 1991; Ivić, 1994; Daniels, 2005), the essential logic of Vygotsky's theory is depicted in the following terms: *higher mental functions are co-constructed through social interaction and appropriation of cultural tools, and then it follows that all higher mental functions are of sociocultural "nature", so the human mind and activity are basically sociocultural and relational phenomena*. This is also the way in which the ZPD concept and its place within Vygotsky's theory are presented at the beginning of the chapter. Taking this into consideration, would it mean that the introduction of individual construction as a possible mechanism of development of new competencies breaks the foundations of Vygotsky's theoretical building?

In my view, this tension between Vygotsky's theory and the second interpretation (assuming that individual construction can also be an explanation of the way new competencies are developed through interaction with a more competent other) can be resolved within the theory because it can be shown that, contrary to the canonical way of its presentation, it already has room for individual construction. For example, when Vygotsky discussed development of different kinds of concepts, he especially stressed pseudoconcepts as developmentally relevant concepts. He defined pseudoconcepts as concepts that look like mature concepts (i.e., the child uses concepts in communication and speech in a similar way to adults), but the kind of thinking and understanding behind pseudoconcepts is not conceptual thinking, but thinking in so-called "complexies" (Vygotsky, 1934/1986). Vygotsky explained this phenomenon as a result of the fact that the child can appropriate the way words are used by others (parents or teachers), but not their way of thinking and understanding. The way others use words is "visible" to the child and the other way around, how the child uses words is "visible" to others, so they can support him to align the use of words with others. However, the way the child thinks and understands what is represented by words does not need to be accessible to others, so they are not in a position to get into dialogue and negotiation. What is relevant for discussion about individual and joint construction is that Vygotsky supposed that pseudo-concepts play a significant role in the development of conceptual thinking. He assumed that the child's functional use of words will frame and guide transformation of his thinking, to align it to the way words are used. In other words, even in Vygotsky's theory, the child might reorganize his own thinking and understanding to back up certain (socioculturally designed) ways of using words. Therefore, it demonstrates that, contrary to the typical presentation of Vygotsky's theory, there is already a place for individual construction within the theory.

Thus, it can be assumed that both individual and social construction can be involved in the interaction with more competent others. It might be supposed that some kinds of interaction might be more supportive to individual construction, and some others to co-construction, but in general terms both kinds of construction are involved in social interaction. If social interaction does not meet conditions for joint construction in the ZPD, it still can scaffold individual construction of the child. In these cases, the child can also be more successful with another than individually and this experience can support him to achieve a higher level of development. Consequently, it would look like a case for ZPD because the child does more with others than individually, and it influences his further development. Nevertheless, cognitive development in these cases would be the result of the individual and not joint construction, as Vygotsky supposed.

Results of the research discussed in this chapter suggest that the ZPD phenomenon as it was portrayed by Vygotsky seems to be more complex and can involve both kinds of construction (individual and social). It means that we can continue to think about the ZPD as a phenomenon in which children can do more when they interact with others as well as one in which this experience can support their cognitive development. However, contrary to before, we need to assume that not only co-construction can explain how the child becomes more developed through social interaction, but we need to take into consideration that individual construction might also be involved in the development of new competencies through social interaction. It makes the ZPD phenomenon more complex, but more interesting. Finally, if the ZPD once-upon-a-time served Vygotsky to build a new theory on sociocultural formation of the mind, it seems that it can now serve as a platform for the integration of two important mechanisms of development into a single theory.

References

Bakhtin, M. M. (1984). *Problems of Dostoevsky's poetics* (C. Emerson, Trans., Ed.). Minneapolis: University of Minnesota.

Baucal, A., Arcidiacono, F. & Buđevac, N. (2011). Reflecting on different views of social interaction: Explanatory and analytic perspectives. In A. Baucal, F. Arcidiacono & N. Buđevac (Eds.), *Studying interaction in different contexts: A qualitative view* (pp. 233–251). Belgrade: Institute of Psychology.

Bourdieu, P. (1990) Structures, habitus, practices. In P. Bourdieu (Ed.), *The logic of practice* (pp. 52–79). Stanford, CA: Stanford University Press.

Chaiklin, S. (2003). The zone of proximal development in Vygotsky's analysis of learning and instruction. In A. Kozulin, B. Gindis, V. S. Ageyev & S. M. Miller (Eds.), *Vygotsky's educational theory in cultural context* (pp. 39–64). Cambridge: Cambridge University Press.

Daniels, H. (2005). *Introduction to Vygotsky*. Hove: Routledge.

del Río, P. & Álvarez, A. (2007). Inside and outside the zone of proximal development: An ecofunctional reading of Vygotsky. In H. Daniels, M. Cole & J. V. Wertsch (Eds.), *The Cambridge companion to Vygotsky* (pp. 276–303). Cambridge: Cambridge University Press.

Ivić, I. (1994). Lev S. Vygotsky. *Prospects, 24*(3/4), 761–785.

Kozulin, A. (1986). Vygotsky in context. In L. S. Vygotsky, *Thought and language* (A. Kozulin, Trans., Ed.) (pp. xi–lvi). Cambridge, MA: The MIT Press.

Lidz, C. & Elliott, J. (2000). *Dynamic assessment: Prevailing models and applications*. Oxford: Elsevier Science Inc.

Palinscar, A. S. (1998). Keeping the metaphor of scaffolding fresh – a response to C. Addison Stone's "The metaphor of scaffolding: Its utility for the field of learning disabilities." *Journal of Learning Disabilities, 31*, 370–373.

Piaget, J. (1970). Piaget's theory. In P. H. Mussen (Ed.), *Handbook of child psychology vol. 1* (pp. 703–732). New York: Wiley.

Piaget, J. (1977). *The essential Piaget* (H. E. Gruber & J. J. Vonèche, Eds.). New York: Basic Books.

Piaget, J. (1995). *Sociological studies*. London: Routledge.

Rieber, R. W. & Robinson, D. K. (2001). *Wilhelm Wundt in history: The making of a scientific psychology*. Dordrecht, the Netherlands: Kluwer/Plenum.

Rogoff, B. (2003). *The cultural nature of human development*. New York: Oxford University Press.

Sternberg, R. & Grigorenko, E. (2002). *Dynamic testing: The nature and measurement of learning potential*. Cambridge: Cambridge University Press.

Toulmin, S. (1978). The Mozart of psychology. *The New York Review of Books*, 28 September, 51–57.

van der Veer, R. & Valsiner, J. (1991). *Understanding Vygotsky: A quest for synthesis*. Cambridge: Basil Blackwell.

Выготский, Л. С. (1934). *Мышление и речь*. Москва-Ленинград: Государсственное социально-экономическое издательство [Vygotsky, L. S. (1934). *Thought and language*. Moscow-Leningrad: State Socio-Economic Publishing House].

Vygotsky, L. S. (1934/1986). *Thought and language* (A. Kozulin, Trans., Ed.). Cambridge, MA: The MIT Press.

Vygotsky, L. S. (1935). Dinamika umstvennogo razvitija shkol'nika v svjazi s obucheniem [The child's intellectual development dynamics connected with instruction]. In L. S. Vygotsky, *Umstvennoe razvitie detef v processe obuchenija [The child's intellectual development in the process of instruction]* (pp. 33–52). Moscow-Leningrad: Uchpedgiz.

Vygotsky, L. S. (1967). Play and its role in the mental development of the child. *Soviet Psychology, 5*(3), 6–18.

Vygotsky, L. S. (1978a). Interaction between learning and development. In M. Cole, V. John-Steiner & E. Souberman (Eds.), *Mind in society: The development of higher psychological processes* (pp. 79–91). Cambridge, MA: Harvard University Press.

Vygotsky, L. S. (1978b). Internalization of higher psychological functions. In M. Cole, V. John-Steiner & E. Souberman (Eds.), *Mind in society: The development of higher psychological processes* (pp. 52–57). Cambridge, MA: Harvard University Press.

Vygotsky, L. S. (1987a). The historical meaning of the crisis in psychology: A methodological investigation. In R. W. Rieber & J. Wollock (Eds.), *The collected works of L.S. Vygotsky – volume 3: Problems of the theory and history of psychology* (pp. 233–344). New York: Plenum Press.

Vygotsky, L. S. (1987b). On psychological systems. In R. W. Rieber & J. Wollock (Eds.), *The collected works of L.S. Vygotsky – volume 3: Problems of the theory and history of psychology* (pp. 91–108). New York: Plenum Press.

Wertsch, J. V. (1984). The zone of proximal development: Some conceptual issues. *New Directions for Child and Adolescent Development, 23*, 7–18.

Wertsch, J. V. (1988). *Vygotsky and the social formation of mind*. Cambridge, MA: Harvard University Press.

Wertsch, J. V. (1993). *Voices of the mind: A sociocultural approach to mediated action*. Cambridge, MA: Harvard University Press.

Wood, D., Bruner, J. S. & Ross, G. (1976). The role of tutoring in problem solving. *Journal of Child Psychology and Psychiatry, 17*, 89–100.

Yaroshevski, M. (1989). *Lev Vygotsky*. Moscow: Progress Publisher.

Part 5
Personal plane

13 When Lev Vygotsky meets Francis Galton

On the nature and nurture of reading development

Simpson W. L. Wong

Reading skills as a foundation for thinking

In modern knowledge-based societies, the importance of reading skills is recognized by people of all ages and those working in various industries. The huge variations in reading abilities observed in all the sampled populations have motivated researchers to examine the two major sources of such individual variation – namely, genes and environment. There are increasing findings of the unique contributions of genetic and environmental influences to reading development reported in scholarly journals and the information is valuable for educators, policy makers and learners. In this chapter, the major methodology used for detecting the genetic and environmental effects and the implication of twin studies on reading development and instructions will be summarized and discussed.

A review of Lev Vygotsky and Francis Galton's work is particularly useful in understanding the two driving forces of reading development: genes and environment. Their viewpoints complement each other and suggest the importance of considering the effects of both genes and environment. More importantly, from the scholarly work of these two great thinkers, it is obvious that neither environmentalism nor genetic determinism on its own is a valid assumption to guide empirical studies.

According to Vygotsky (1978, p. 114), reading ability serves not only as a tool for knowledge transfer and communication but also as a necessary cultural tool for the development of intellectual and self-regulative abilities. Due to its high importance, reading skills, along with rational, abstract and scientific thinking, are defined by Vygotsky and Luria (1994) as one of the highest achievements of human thinking. Without sufficient reading skills, we are unable to acquire knowledge that is in print. As writing systems are a late human invention, our genes have not evolved enough to support the mastery of reading skills as compared with spoken language development (see Geary & Bjorklund, 2000, for a discussion of reading skills as "biologically secondary abilities"). Therefore, huge individual difference is observed among normally developing children and some children are diagnosed with reading disabilities worldwide.

In discussing the effect of genes, Vygotsky focused on the effect of learning experiences on mental changes and the differences in cognitive abilities between ethnicities or age groups. According to his "general genetic law of cultural development" (Vygotsky, 1978, p. 57), the mastery of cultural knowledge is achieved through two levels. The first level of learning occurs when children engage in interpersonal communication. At the second level, learners make use of the inner speech to personalize the knowledge they obtain through social interaction. This law applies to voluntary attention, logical memory and the formation of concepts. This interpretation of genetic effect by Vygotsky refers to the learning mechanism shared among humans. Moll (1994) contended that Vygotsky had attempted in his contemporary work to discuss the biological constraints on human cognitive development. The genetic effect was claimed to act upon a child's organic development, which affects the degree of mastery in the use of tools and, in turn, determines a child's system of activity (Vygotsky, 1997). However, Vygotsky did not set up any empirical research to verify his theory on genetic effects. Rather than individual difference, Vygotsky discussed whether genes accounted for the cross-ethnic and cross-age difference in learning. He argued that social history and education lead to the differential learning outcomes observed across ethnic and age groups (Vygotsky & Luria, 1994). The two interpretations of "genetic effects" made by Vygotsky had restricted the study of the effect of genes on reading development because his interpretation did not take "individual variations" into consideration. Alternatively, if genetic effects are interpreted in terms of familial resemblance and at the interpersonal level, more testable hypotheses can be formulated and then tested with scientific studies. This research gap was filled by Francis Galton.

Learning behaviors of twin individuals had fascinated Francis Galton and motivated him to conduct studies that tracked the developmental changes in twins from 1876. Using evolution as a theoretical framework, Galton tried to examine if heredity affects human behavior. He invented "correlation", a statistical technique that allowed him to quantify degrees of similarity among family members. For example, Galton (1883) demonstrated a strong correlation between children's height and the average height of their parents. Using other major methods of human behavioral genetics, such as family, twin and adoption designs, he provided further evidence to support the claim that behavioral traits run in families. These studies demonstrated that heritability can be defined both quantitatively (e.g., height is distributed along a continuum) and qualitatively (e.g., the texture of pea plants is either smooth or wrinkled in Mendel's 1866 study). Known as the father of behavioral genetics, Francis Galton laid the groundwork for studying heredity of learning behavior. A proper definition of "heritability" sets the stage for behavioral genetics research.

A well-accepted, logical and operational definition of heritability refers to the degree of genetic contribution to observed individual difference in a particular population at a particular time (Plomin, DeFries, McClearn & McGuffin, 2008). It should be noted that heritability does not concern the phenotype of a single individual. For example, if studies show that the heritability of reading skills is about 80%, this index does not imply that 80% of your reading skills were developed as a result of genes and the remaining 20% was contributed by the environment. Instead, this 80% signifies the extent to which genes account for the difference in reading abilities observed among readers within a particular population. Moreover, heritability has no implication for the cause of average differences between social classes or ethnic groups. It is possible that, even when heritability within a group is extremely high, the average difference between groups could be due solely to environmental differences (Plomin et al., 2008). The study of heritability is irrelevant to any claim made in eugenics. To date, the contemporary behavioral geneticists are mainly concerned with the sources of individual variation and the etiologies of various learning abilities and disabilities. Because of the word limit, this chapter focuses on twin study design and reading abilities. Readers who are interested in adoption study design and reading disabilities may consult Plomin et al.'s (2008) seminal introductory book.

The impact of genes and environment on reading development

Based on the fact that genes and environment are indispensable in human development, the main objective for conducting a study on heritability is to clarify the roles genes and environment play. Our genes are inherited from our parents and are protein in nature. The human genome functions in cells throughout our body. When researchers try to understand the heritability of a complex behavior such as reading, the goal is not identifying a single "reading gene". For one reason, the effect of a single gene is usually not influential unless this small genetic effect combines with the effect of a collection of genes. The summation of genetic effects occurs either within a single locus or across multiple loci, influencing different phenotypic characters. Technological breakthrough in genome-wide association studies supports the examination of hundreds of thousands of single-nucleotide polymorphisms (SNP) in an efficient and economical way (Sham, Bader, Craig, O'Donovan & Owen, 2002). Still, the direct linkage between genes and behavior is hardly traceable. To solve this problem, additional levels of analysis are needed to bridge the relations between genes and behavior. An increasingly common practice is describing and conceptualizing behavior in terms of neural network and cognitive processes. Working models have been proposed by Morton and Frith (1995) and Bishop and Snowling (2004).

The relationships between genes and a behavior depicted in these working models are not one-to-one but one-to-many. A set of genes would be associated with a behavior mediated by several brain regions and cognitive processes. The nature of these relationships is probabilistic rather than deterministic. In other words, the relationships between genes and behaviors are not simply causal but depend on unpredictable contingencies. This characteristic is worth noting as it suggests that reading performances are not solely determined by genes but are liable to the interaction among a set of factors. At each level of analysis, environment also contributes to the changes or stability of development.

The genes–brain–cognition–behavior framework is reasonable because, in the course of brain development, genes are responsible for transcribing and translating DNA into proteins. In cooperation with the environmental input, genes control the formation of the neural networks of the brain and its corresponding cognitive functions (Baker, 2004). Molecular genetic studies, for instance, have shown that IQ is linked with DNA markers in or near candidate genes that are in charge of synaptic transmission and brain development (Plomin et al., 1995). Using pooled DNA and a microarray with 10,000 SNPs, four SNPs associated with general ability (g-factor) were identified in a sample of seven-year-old children (Butcher et al., 2005). Follow-up studies indicated that these g-factor-related SNPs are related to reading ability (Harlaar, Spinath, Dale & Plomin, 2005). These recent discoveries paint a more complete picture of the etiology of reading development. The genes–brain–cognition–behavior framework becomes an essential working model for integrating research findings in the field of reading development. Therefore, the effects of reading instructions can act at multiple levels, and one of the goals of twin studies is to identify and quantify the contributions of genes and environment to phenotypes.

Apart from genetic influences, environment as well plays a significant role in reading development. The critical effect of school environment on reading development was acknowledged by Vygotsky (1978, p. 107). He argued that school instruction promotes reading skills necessary for the advancement of other intellectual abilities. Among a range of environmental factors, classroom teaching style (Foorman, Francis, Fletcher, Schatschneider & Mehta, 1998) and home environment (Whitehurst & Lonigan, 1998) contribute largely to reading success. Children from a high socio-economic status (SES) family often outperform in reading and related cognitive measures compared to their low SES counterparts (e.g., Raz & Bryant, 1990). Collaborative reading, which involves parent-to-child scaffolding, consistently explains on average 8% of the variances of a number of reading outcomes (Bus, van Ijzendoorn & Pelligrini, 1995). Shared book and parent–child reading methods, in particular, enhance children's literacy growth (e.g., Whitehurst et al., 1988).

180 *Simpson W. L. Wong*

It is important to note that a single environmental factor is not stand-alone. Each of the environmental factors is indeed part of an aggregated environmental effect when the reciprocal interaction between environmental factors is considered. The interplay of various environmental factors has been summarized in Bronfenbrenner's (1979) ecological model, and this model has been applied for identifying external factors that impact reading development (McBride-Chang, 2004). This ecological view considers both the immediate environment the child has close contact with (e.g., parents) and the distal factors that influence the immediate learning environment (e.g., national literacy curriculum). Attempts have been made in recent behavioral genetics studies to examine the effect of genes on some factors in the five sub-systems (chrono-, macro-, exo-, meso- and micro-systems) within the ecology of reading. For instance, the number and quality of books in the home influence the rate of reading acquisition (e.g., Scarborough, 1998). Apart from identifying the magnitude of genetic and environmental effects, behavioral-genetics studies examined the notion of "nature of nurture" (e.g., Plomin & Bergeman, 1991). For instance, it seems apparent that books in the home are considered as an environmental factor. However, parents actually play a role in deciding which and how many books to acquire, and therefore we should use caution when interpreting books as an environmental factor. Parents who are genetically prepared to read well may be more likely to be good at reading or have a strong interest in reading and, therefore, they purchase many books and create a stimulating home literacy environment for their children. In this case, the effect of genes and environment intertwines. The genetic disposition of a child may also contribute to the number of books in the home. The twin study is a genetically informed quasi-experimental design that can separate the environmental influences from genetic influences. As discussed below, twin study design enables us to partition two kinds of environmental effects – namely shared and non-shared environmental effects.

Twin study: A method to examine genetic and environmental influences

To handle the nature–nurture debate by a scientific method, the initial step to take is to examine the extent to which the individual variation of a behavior trait (or a cognitive skill) is influenced by genetic and environmental factors (Plomin et al., 2008). In an attempt to estimate genetic influence on general learning ability, the first twin study was conducted in the 1920s (Merriman, 1924). The basic idea of twin study design is to compare the degree of phenotypic resemblance between monozygotic (MZ) and dizygotic (DZ) twins (also known as identical and fraternal twins, respectively). Findings of twin studies are not limited to twin populations but are generalized to non-twin populations. Because MZ twins derive from the same fertilized egg, they are genetically identical. In contrast, DZ twins derive from two separately fertilized eggs and share, on average, half of their segregating alleles (the 0.01% of genes that are not shared among human beings and vary across individuals) with their co-twins. In terms of genetic similarity, MZ twins are twice as similar genetically as DZ twins. Based on this characteristic, MZ twins should resemble each other to a greater extent than DZ twins if a behavioral trait is strongly influenced by genetic factors.

A rough approximation of heritability is made by doubling the difference between the within-pair correlations for MZ and DZ twins. When the MZ twin correlation is substantial and almost doubles the size of the DZ twin correlation, a strong genetic influence is indicated. Following this logic, within-pair similarities that are not due to genetic factors are assigned as *shared environmental influences*, which contribute toward resemblance among individuals growing up in the same environment. Because MZ twins share all their genes and family environment, anything less than a perfect within-pair correlation for MZ twins shows

The nature and nurture of reading development 181

the influence of specific factors that create differences among co-twins from the same family. These so-called non-shared environmental effects are estimated from within-pair differences between MZ twins. For a more accurate estimation of genetic, shared and non-shared environmental effects, a model-fitting technique is adopted. The appendix section of Plomin et al.'s (2008) book is recommended for readers who are interested in the mathematics and statistics for twin analyses.

The phenotypes and endophenotypes of reading

Defining the phenotype of reading is not an easy task because reading is a complex behavior. The three common reading skills being researched are word decoding, reading fluency and reading comprehension. Each of these skills encompasses an array of skills, ranging from perceptual to cognitive skills, and from decoding to syntactic skills. Apart from this multi-componential nature of reading, the improvement of reading with continuous learning and reading experiences requires sensitive measurements that can reliably detect such changes over time or the participants' learning outcome cannot be accurately captured. Interestingly, the building blocks of reading play different roles at different stages of reading development. Thus, genetic effects are studied in respect to various components of reading and also to the timing for when these relations occur.

For a better management of reading measures, Petrill, Deater-Deckard, Thompson, DeThorne and Schatschneider (2006) have proposed two types of reading tasks. First, *content-based* tasks (e.g., word recognition) measure the accuracy in retrieving learnt lexical knowledge stored in long-term memory. Second, *process-based* tasks (e.g., phoneme segmentation) measure the mental manipulation of linguistic information. Other researchers suggest that *content- and process-based* tasks measure linguistic and meta-linguistic skills, respectively. Recently, perceptual skills such as auditory processing and speech perception have been found to be fundamental to reading development. As perceptual skills can be measured at the preliterate period, they are thought to be more closely related to the genetic disposition. Furthermore, the study of the biological basis of reading brings reading behaviors more akin to genotypes.

In the last two decades, a number of neurological markers of reading abilities have been reported in research using electroencephalogram (EEG) and functional magnetic resonance imaging (fMRI) techniques. These neurological markers are better at representing the degree of sensitivity to genetic susceptibility and are specific to the disorder in question (Skuse, 2001). The qualified markers are defined as the endophenotypes of reading abilities/disabilities. Phonological deficit is one of the few cognitive markers that can be qualified also as an endophenotype of developmental dyslexia because it is persistent despite the improved capability of word decoding and learning in dyslexic individuals (Snowling, 2008). Therefore, it has become increasingly popular to develop evidence-based reading instruction programs based on neurological findings.

Twin research of reading ability

Twin studies have enhanced our understanding of how genes and environment contribute to reading ability. Early twin studies of reading measured both accuracies of word reading in isolation and prose reading (Hohnen & Stevenson, 1999). Later studies examined the difference and similarity between the heritability of the abilities of reading words in isolation and reading comprehension. A line of studies has extended to non-word reading and reading fluency (e.g., Byrne et al., 2007; Taylor, Roehrig, Hensler, Connor & Schatschneider,

2010). The twin study method is useful to tackle the multi-faceted nature of reading skills and examine the etiology of reading development as a whole. Because a large sample size is warranted for optimal statistical power, there is only a handful of twin studies on reading around the world. Major twin study projects of reading include the Twins Early Development Study (TEDS) in the United Kingdom, the Florida Twin Project in Reading (FTP-R), the Western Reserve Reading Project (WRRP) and the Colorado Longitudinal Twin Study of Reading Disability (LTSRD) in the United States, the International Longitudinal Twin Study (ILTS) with samples in Australia, the United States and Scandinavia, and the Chinese Twin Study of Reading (CTSR) with samples in Hong Kong, China.

In general, strong genetic influences were found for reading skills (e.g., Chow, Ho, Wong, Waye & Bishop, 2011; Hart, Petrill, Thompson & Plomin, 2009) and rapid naming ability (e.g., Davis, Knopik, Olson, Wadsworth & DeFries, 2001; Petrill et al., 2006). Also, significant genetic effects were indicated for phonological awareness (e.g., Hohnen & Stevenson, 1999). These findings have informed molecular genetics studies of reading (e.g., Lim, Ho, Chou & Waye, 2011). In contrast, shared environmental influences were relatively greater on vocabulary knowledge compared to genetic effects (e.g., Byrne et al., 2002). The findings inform us about which component skills of reading demand more environmental input.

Cross-cultural differences

Identifying the cultural-specific factors in reading development is of no less importance than searching for the universal principles that explain reading development. Among the aforementioned large-scale twin projects, the ILTS has investigated the cultural and country effects systematically in a single twin study. The ILTS of early reading development involves samples of twins recruited in the United States (Colorado), Australia (the Sydney area) and Scandinavia (Sweden and Norway). The cross-country differences in the onset of reading instruction and educational philosophy have an effect on the etiology of reading. According to the established traditions and educational philosophy shared among people in Scandinavia, social, emotional and aesthetic development rather than intellectual preparation for school work should be the core element in the preschool curriculum. Formal or informal reading instruction is not recommended until compulsory education starts when the child is seven years old (Lundberg, 1999). With these values well integrated among most parents in Scandinavia, relatively lower amounts of shared book reading and letter-based activities with parents were observed. As a result, less than half of the Scandinavian twins were able to read a word at the end of kindergarten. An opposite situation was observed in English-speaking countries where early informal and sometimes formal reading instruction in the home and preschool are cherished (Mann & Wimmer, 2002). Comparing English and non-English-speaking children, the reading performances of children from Scandinavia were significantly lower than their American and Australian counterparts (Samuelsson et al., 2008). These studies have demonstrated that a greater intensity and an earlier administration of formal reading instruction create a more homogenous learning environment for child learners. As a result, overall variability will be largely explained by the genetic contribution.

The overlap of genetic/environmental effects among the building blocks of reading

A number of cognitive-linguistic skills have been found to correlate strongly to reading skills at the behavioral-cognitive level. To further determine the extent to which these phenotypic/observed correlations are mediated by the same set of genetic or environmental factors, multivariate twin analyses are needed. The degree of genetic overlap is reflected by genetic correlation, which indexes the extent to which genetic factors influencing one behavioral trait also affect another trait. In other words, it is the probability of a set of genes that influence one measure which will also influence the other measure. A genetic correlation of 1 indicates all genetic effects overlap for the two measures, suggesting a high degree of genetic overlap. In comparison, a genetic correlation of 0 indicates that all genetic effects are independent for the two measures, suggesting a high degree of genetic specificity. This logic applies to the interpretation of environmental overlap. High genetic correlation among componential skills of reading suggests that a set of "generalist genes" control learning of different skills (Plomin & Kovas, 2005). From a cognitive perspective, a high degree of genetic overlap reflects a low degree of modularity, while a high degree of genetic specificity reflects a high degree of modularity. Previous studies have shown genetic overlap between reading skills and rapid naming ability (Davis et al., 2001), phonological memory (Wadsworth, DeFries, Fulker, Olson & Pennington, 1995) and phonological awareness (Petrill et al., 2007). Similar results were obtained in cross-sectional studies including children of a wide age range. Those studies have shown that the component processes of reading, such as phonology, fluency and orthographic skills, were correlated largely via genetic pathways (e.g., Davis et al., 2001). The results of multivariate twin analyses are important because they clarify the sources of phenotypic associations observed among all the component skills of reading. Before that, correlations could still be attributed to reading experience which varies across individual readers and is hard to track. Once the genetic correlations are obtained, early identification of children who are at genetic risk for reading disabilities can be made by referring to the preliterate skills that are associated with later reading abilities at the genetic level (e.g., early phonemic awareness and later decoding skills). Following early screening, practitioners can provide special training to prevent devastating genetic effects from proliferation.

Heritability in second-language acquisition

Genes not only affect our first but also second-language acquisition. Dale, Harlaar, Haworth and Plomin (2010) reported a study conducted on 604 pairs of 14-year-old twins from England and Wales. These adolescent participants speak English at home and had been learning a European language (French, German, Italian or Spanish) as a second language. Their first- and second-language proficiencies were assessed by teachers' rating based on the United Kingdom National Curriculum (NC) criteria (Department for Education and Skills, 2004; National Curriculum Assessments, 2007). Interestingly, the genetic effect of second-language acquisition (0.67) was found to be stronger than that for first-language acquisition, both observed in the same sample (0.41) and previously reported in other samples. Moreover, the results demonstrate that overlap of genetic influences on first- and second-language acquisition were nearly complete (0.99). Conversely, shared environmental effects were weak and the shared environmental overlap between the first and second languages was low (0.07). The acquisition of the first and a second language seems to rely on different environmental supports. We should be cautious when interpreting Dale et al.'s (2010) results because about 10% of the twins were not learning the same second language and their performances were assessed by different teachers. Future studies should consider measuring the actual reading performances of the learners rather than depending on teacher ratings. Doing so can also preclude a sample of learners learning a mixture of second languages.

Education implications

Once again, it cannot be denied that both genes and environment play a significant role in human development and achievement. However, the relationship between the genotype and phenotype of a behavior is deemed probabilistic rather than deterministic. In the realm of scientific pursuits of heritability, it is important to set the right stage for generating testable hypotheses. This chapter first illustrates some of the misunderstandings of "genetic effect" and provides an overview of twin study design that allows us to estimate the relative contribution of genetic and environmental influences for all kinds of behavioral traits. Using reading as an illustration, this chapter demonstrates how the sources of individual difference in a complex behavior and its componential skills can be understood through twin studies. Critically, and seemingly counter-intuitively, a strong genetic effect does not imply that a behavior cannot be altered by the environment. Instead, environmental inputs are particularly essential if the full blossom of a genetically influenced skill is expected. In the meantime, when a strong environmental influence is detected for a skill, the current learning environment is found stimulating enough for the growth of such a skill. The third index, non-shared environmental effect, informs us how unique reading experiences and reading-related strategies affect reading acquisition. A strong non-shared environmental effect indicates that learners' personal experiences and personality traits impact on reading development as well.

All in all, twin studies inform educators of the effect of genes and environment on learning outcomes. The information about the time at which the stimulating learning environment should be catered for students is useful for planning effective education programs. The twin model is potentially important in evaluating the effectiveness of the response-to-instruction (RTI) approach to reading (Samuelsson et al., 2008). One aim of the RTI is to observe age-to-age changes in reading achievement to improve identification of reading disability and the selection of at-risk readers for intervention (Compton, Fuchs, Fuchs & Bryant, 2006). If successful, individual differences in reading skills accounted for by limited reading instruction should be successively reduced. If the twin study method could be integrated with intervention studies of RTI, the training effects attributed to genes and environment could be partitioned.

The genetic estimate serves also as an indirect index of equality. When strong and reliable genetic effects are detected in a twin study, it implies that the country that is being studied has achieved a satisfactory level of equality of education opportunity (Plomin, Haworth & Davis, 2010). The reason is that, if an effective nationwide reading curriculum or universal childhood education is implemented, the environmental range in real life is actually small and therefore individual variations are more likely to be caused by genetic variations. Under this circumstance, each learner's learning potentials, such as their reading outcome, would be maximized.

Conclusion

In conclusion, the roles of environment and genes in human development have been acknowledged by two great thinkers, Lev Vygotsky and Francis Galton, respectively. When we examine the etiology of skill acquisition – for example, reading development – we should consider the effects of environment and genes without overlooking either one of the two. This can be accomplished by the twin study method, a quantitative approach that can partition the additive genetic effects, the shared environmental and non-shared environmental effects on any quantifiable behavioral trait. While the basic univariate twin analysis answers the "nature versus nurture" question, multivariate twin analyses further explore the overlap of genetic and environmental pathways among multiple quantifiable behavioral traits. For example, word decoding and its component skills, such as phonological processing skills, share a significant portion of genetic effects. This and similar results are important for a holistic understanding of reading development, which stimulates the design of reading instruction, diagnostic tools and intervention programs. We all look forward to the future discovery of the genotype–phenotype mappings of typical reading abilities, the idea of which has been foreseen but not actualized in Vygotsky's and Galton's era.

Acknowledgement

The author would like to thank Profs Dorothy Bishop, Connie Ho and Mary Waye for the introduction of Behavioral Genetics, and Ms Hoyee Miao and Vina Leung for their assistance with this chapter.

References

Baker, C. (2004). *Behavioral genetics: An introduction to how genes and environments interact through development to shape differences in mood, personality, and intelligence.* Washington, DC: AAAS Publication Services.

Bishop, D. V. M. & Snowling, M. J. (2004). Developmental dyslexia and specific language impairment: Same or different? *Psychological Bulletin, 130,* 858–888.

Bronfenbrenner, U. (1979). *The ecology of human development.* Cambridge, MA: Harvard University Press.

Bus, A. G., van Ijzendoorn, M. H. & Pellegrini, A. D. (1995). Joint book reading makes for success in learning to read: A meta-analysis on intergenerational transmission of literacy. *Review of Educational Research, 65,* 1–21.

Butcher, L. M., Meaburn, E., Knight, J., Sham, P. C., Schalkwyk, L. C., Craig, I. W. & Plomin, R. (2005). SNPs, microarrays and pooled DNA: Identification of four loci associated with mild mental impairment in a sample of 6000 children. *Human Molecular Genetics, 14*(10), 1315–1325.

Byrne, B., Delaland, C., Fielding-Barnsley, R., Quain, P., Samuelsson, S., Høien, T. . . . Olson, R. K. (2002). Longitudinal twin study of early reading development in three countries: Preliminary results. *Annals of Dyslexia, 52,* 47–73.

Byrne, B., Samuelsson, S., Wadsworth, S., Hulslander, J., Corley, R., DeFries, J. C. . . . Olson, R. K. (2007). Longitudinal twin study of early literacy development: Preschool through grade 1. *Reading and Writing, 20,* 77–102.

Chow, B. W. Y., Ho, C. S. H., Wong, S. W. L., Waye, M. M. Y. & Bishop, D. V. M. (2011). Genetic and environmental influences on Chinese language and reading abilities. *PLOS One, 6*(2), e16640.

Compton, D. L., Fuchs, D., Fuchs, L. S. & Bryant, J. D. (2006). Selecting at-risk readers in first grade for early intervention: A two-year longitudinal study of decision rules and procedures. *Journal of Educational Psychology, 98,* 394–409.

Dale, P. S., Harlaar, N., Haworth, C. M. A. & Plomin, R. (2010). Two by two: A twin study of second language acquisition. *Psychological Science, 21,* 635–640.

Davis, C. J., Knopik, V. S., Olson, R. K., Wadsworth, S. J. & DeFries, J. C. (2001). Genetic and environmental influences on rapid naming and reading ability: A twin study. *Annals of Dyslexia, 51,* 241–258.

Department for Education and Skills. (2004). *The national curriculum: Handbook for secondary teachers in England, key stages 3 and 4 (revised).* London: Department for Education and Skills.

Foorman, B. R., Francis, D. J., Fletcher, J. M., Schatschneider, C. & Mehta, P. (1998). The role of instruction in learning to read: Preventing reading failure in at-risk children. *Journal of Educational Psychology, 90*, 37–55.

Galton, F. (1883). *Inquiries into human faculty and its development* (2nd ed.). London: J. M. Dent.

Geary, D. C. & Bjorklund, D. F. (2000). Evolutionary developmental psychology. *Child Development, 71*, 57–65.

Harlaar, N., Spinath, F. M., Dale, P. S. & Plomin, R. (2005). Genetic influences on early word recognition abilities and disabilities: A study of 7-year-old twins. *Journal of Child Psychology and Psychiatry, 46*, 373–384.

Hart, S. A., Petrill, S. A., Thompson, L. A. & Plomin, R. (2009). The ABC's of math: A genetic analysis of mathematics and its links with reading ability and general cognitive ability. *Journal of Educational Psychology, 101*, 388–402.

Hohnen, B. & Stevenson, J. (1999). The structure of genetic influences on general cognitive, language, phonological, and reading abilities. *Developmental Psychology, 35*, 590–603.

Lim, C. K. P., Ho, C. S.-H., Chou, C. H. N. & Waye, M. M. Y. (2011). Association of the rs3743205 variant of DYX1C1 with dyslexia in Chinese children. *Behavioral and Brain Functions, 7*, 16.

Lundberg, I. (1999). Learning to read in Scandinavia. In M. Harris & G. Hatano (Eds.), *Learning to read: Cross-linguistic perspectives* (pp. 157–172). Cambridge: Cambridge University Press.

Mann, V. & Wimmer, H. (2002). Phoneme awareness and pathways into literacy: A comparison of German and American children. *Reading and Writing: An Interdisciplinary Journal, 15*, 653–682.

McBride-Chang, C. (2004). *Children's literacy development.* New York: Oxford University Press.

Mendel, G. (1866). Experiments on plant hybrids (English translation). In C. Stern & E. R. Sherwood (Eds.), *The origin of genetics: A Mendel source book*, 1966 (pp. 1–48). San Francisco: W. H. Freeman.

Merriman, C. (1924). The intellectual resemblance of twins. *Psychological Monographs, 33*, 1–58.

Moll, L. C. (1994). Literacy research in community and classrooms: A sociocultural approach. In R. B. Ruddell, M. R. Ruddell & H. Singer (Eds.), *Theoretical Models and Processes of Reading* (4th ed.) (pp. 179–207). Newark, DE: International Reading Association.

Morton, J. & Frith, U. (1995). Structural approaches to developmental psychopathology. In D. Cicchetti & D. J. Cohen (Eds.), *Developmental psychopathology* (Vol. 1, pp. 357–390). New York: Wiley.

National Curriculum Assessments. (2007). *Key stage 3 assessment and reporting arrangements 2008.* London: Qualifications and Curriculum Authority.

Petrill, S. A., Deater-Deckard, K., Thompson, L. A., DeThorne, L. S. & Schatschneider, C. (2006). Reading skills in early readers: Genetic and shared environmental influences. *Journal of Learning Disabilities, 39*, 48–55.

Petrill, S. A., Deater-Deckard, K., Thompson, L. A., Schatschneider, C., Dethorne, L. S. & Vandenbergh, D. J. (2007). Longitudinal genetic analysis of early reading: The Western reserve reading project. *Reading and Writing, 20*(1–2), 127–146.

Plomin, R. & Bergeman, C. S. (1991). The nature of nurture: Perspective and prospective. In R. Plomin & G. E. McClearn (Eds.), *Nature, nurture, and psychology* (pp. 457–493). Washington, DC: American Psychological Association.

Plomin, R., DeFries, J. C., McClearn, G. E. & McGuffin, P. (2008). *Behavioral genetics* (5th ed.). New York: Worth.

Plomin, R., Haworth, C. M. A. & Davis, O. S. P. (2010). Genetics of learning abilities and disabilities: Recent developments from the UK and possible directions for research in China. *Behavioral Genetics, 40*, 297–305.

Plomin, R. & Kovas, Y. (2005). Generalist genes and learning disabilities. *Psychological Bulletin, 131*, 592–617.

Plomin, R., McClearn, G. E., Smith, D. L., Skuder, P., Vignetti, S., Chorney, M. J. . . . McGuffin, P. (1995). Allelic associations between 100 DNA markers and high versus low IQ. *Intelligence, 21*, 31–48.

Raz, I. S. & Bryant, P. (1990). Social background, phonological awareness and children's reading. *British Journal of Developmental Psychology, 8*, 209–225.

Samuelsson, S., Byrne, B., Olson, R. K., Hulslander, J., Wadsworth, S., Corley, R. . . . Defries, J. C. (2008). Response to early literacy instruction in the United States, Australia, and Scandinavia: A behavioral-genetic analysis. *Learning and Individual Differences, 18*(3), 289–295.

Scarborough, H. S. (1998). Early identification of children at risk for reading disabilities: Phonological awareness and some other promising predictors. In B. K. Shapiro, P. J. Accardo & A. J. Capute (Eds.), *Specific reading disability: A view of the spectrum* (pp. 74–119). Timonium, MD: York Press.

Sham, P., Bader, J. S., Craig, I., O'Donovan, M. & Owen, M. (2002). DNA pooling: A tool for large-scale association studies. *National Review of Genetics, 3*, 862–871.

Skuse, D. H. (2001). Endophenotypes and child psychiatry. *British Journal of Psychiatry, 178*, 395–396.

Snowling, M. J. (2008). Specific disorders and broader phenotypes: The case of dyslexia. *Quarterly Journal of Experimental Psychology, 61*, 142–156.

Taylor, J., Roehrig, A. D., Hensler, B. S., Connor, C. M. & Schatschneider, C. (2010). Teacher quality moderates the genetic effects on early reading. *Science, 328*, 512–514.

Vygotsky, L. S. (1978). *Mind in society.* Cambridge, MA: Harvard University Press.

Vygotsky, L. S. (1997). *The collected works of L. S. Vygotsky, Vol. 4: The history of the development of higher mental functions* (R. W. Rieber, Ed.; M. J. Hall, Trans.). New York: Plenum.

Vygotsky, L. S. & Luria, A. R. (1994). Tool and symbol in child development. In R. van der Veer & J. Valsiner (Eds.), *The Vygotsky reader* (pp. 99–174). Cambridge, MA: Blackwell.

Wadsworth, S. J., DeFries, J. C., Fulker, D. W., Olson, R. K. & Pennington, B. F. (1995). Reading performance and verbal short-term memory: A twin study of reciprocal causation. *Intelligence, 20*, 145–167.

Whitehurst, G. J., Falco, F. L. Lonigan, C. J., Fischel, J. E., DeBaryshe, B. D., Valdez-Menchaca & Caulfield, M. (1988). Accelerating language development through picture book reading. *Developmental Psychology, 24*, 552–559.

Whitehurst, G. J. & Lonigan, C. J. (1998). Child development and emergent literacy. *Child Development, 69*, 848–872.

14 Education for citizenship

An experiment in leadership development of pupils making the transition from primary to secondary school

Jim O'Brien, Evgeniya Plotnikova and Iain Mills

Education for citizenship in Scotland

Scotland at present is introducing a new curriculum involving much more interactive teacher methodology and, as in other jurisdictions, consulting with and placing responsibilities on school students (Rudduck & McIntyre, 2007). Underpinning this curricular approach is the establishment of four capacities – namely, all young people should become successful learners, confident individuals, responsible citizens and successful contributors. These four capacities not only recognize the importance of individual achievement and self-confidence but also acknowledge the centrality of contribution to society, of playing an active role as a citizen (Hayward, 2007, p. 263). Such acknowledgement reflects elements of Vygotsky's (1978) sociocultural theory, in which the concept of social interaction is key to capacity building.

O'Brien and MacLeod (2009, p. 1), in considering the *Social Agenda of the School*, suggest it "is concerned with the provision of appropriate care for pupils in the school phase of their lives and development by helping them to prepare personally and emotionally for life both within and outside school". The Scottish Executive (2005, p. iii) made the claim that:

> Scottish schools have at their heart a vision of enabling all children and young people to thrive and achieve their full potential as learners and as members of society. Supporting pupils' personal, social and emotional development in school has been a focus of professional commitment and growing expertise for many years.

Among the areas that became the responsibility of guidance systems and personnel was Personal and Social Education (PSE), perhaps one of the more contentious areas of the work that schools do, as it encompasses fundamental matters associated with possible purposes of education. There are tensions evident between the development of the individual and the needs of the social group, or, as Carr (1999) notes in relation to values education, the confusion between education and social engineering. The debate about the scope and nature of citizenship is summarized by Evans (1995, p. 16) thus:

> Minimal interpretations emphasize civil and legal status, rights and responsibilities . . . The good citizen is law-abiding, public-spirited, exercises political involvement through voting for representatives . . . Maximal interpretations, by contrast, entail consciousness of self as a member of a shared democratic culture, emphasize participatory approaches to political involvement and consider ways in which social disadvantage undermine citizenship by denying people full participation in society in any significant sense.

Four overlapping areas of self-awareness, self-esteem, interpersonal relationships and independence/interdependence are readily identifiable in PSE provision and the centrality of personal and social development has been recognized in the "Curriculum for Excellence", where values and citizenship are permeating areas. Maitles (2005) provides an excellent overview and concrete examples of how schools deal with these concepts, while Munn and Arnott (2009) trace the historical development of citizenship education that has come to prominence within PSE approaches adopted in schools. The review report *Education for Citizenship in Scotland: A Paper for Discussion and Development* (Learning and Teaching Scotland, 2002) set out the key purposes of education for citizenship and the ways in which these might be pursued. Education for citizenship was seen as an overarching purpose of the curriculum, not as a separate subject requiring a specific space in the school timetable, as in England. Munn and Arnott (2009, p. 447) provide a summary of important features of the report, including the following:

- The purpose of education for citizenship was to develop young people's capability for thoughtful and responsible participation in political, economic, social and cultural life.
- Children and young people were seen as "citizens now" rather than citizens-in-waiting.
- It emphasized that young people learn most about citizenship by being active citizens.

How citizenship education is developing in practice has been reported (Deuchar, 2003; Ross, Munn & Brown, 2007), and HMIE (2003) have evaluated the effectiveness of citizenship provision and the quality of young people's learning and personal and social development and growth. Citizenship and values education combined with PSE approaches are viewed as important mechanisms for student development in Scottish schools, especially in the period of transition from primary to secondary school.

The challenge of transition from primary to secondary school

Transition from primary to secondary school is characterized as one of the most stressful stages in young people's educational experience (Zeedyk et al., 2003). The age of transition (normally 11–12 years old in Scottish schools) is associated with dynamic physical and psychological changes in growing children. At this stage, children become especially vulnerable as they undergo a complex process of transformation of their self-concept and perception of "others". This process can be accompanied with a range of problems that may be related to students' academic performance, social adaptation and psychological well-being. At least two school-related problems merit mention. First, primary–secondary school transition is associated with difficulties of adjustment to new educational demands (new curriculum subjects, assessment standards, increasing study workload, etc.). Second, transition from the familiar and personal environment of primary school to the unknown, impersonal setting of secondary school with new teachers and normally a greater number of pupils is an important stage in children's socialization. Often this transition period results in problems of social adaptation and integration and can impact on student learning.

Problems associated with primary–secondary school transition are common in other educational systems (Chedzoy & Burden, 2005) and, in Britain, this area has been the subject of research, albeit sporadic and discontinuous, having a different focus and involving different purposes. According to West, Sweeting and Young (2008), the UK research in this field is characterized by:

190   *Jim O'Brien et al.*

- reviews (Galton, Morrison & Pell, 2000; Boyd et al., 2007)
- local education authority reports (North Ayrshire Council, 2000)
- evaluations of "transition projects" (Shepherd & Roker, 2005)
- academic research (Galton, Gray & Ruddock, 1999; Galton, Morrison & Pell, 2000).

To this list, one could also add central government policy documents (DCSF, 2008) and statement papers of non-governmental organizations (North Ayrshire Council, 2000).

Much effort is made by Scottish teachers, responsible for guidance and PSE, to establish arrangements designed to ease the transition of primary students to secondary. There have been a number of initiatives; between 1994 and 2003, West et al. (2008) conducted a longitudinal survey of 2000 Scottish pupils – the key aims of the project were to explore school factors affecting pupil transition and to track long-term effects of transition on pupils' well-being and school attainment. Another study explored concerns and expectations of teachers, parents and pupils prior to and after transition (Zeedyk et al., 2003), and a government-funded evaluation project (Scottish Executive Education Department, 2007) presented the results of pilot initiatives on improving primary to secondary school transitions in three local authorities: North Lanarkshire, East Ayrshire and Glasgow City (2007). The key focus of these initiatives was on strengthening links between primary and secondary schools to improve school attainment, in particular in literacy and numeracy, not on pupil well-being, mirroring current priorities associated with attainment and raising school standards.

Transition from primary to secondary remains a perennial if under-funded area for policy making and research and where those on the ground in schools and local authorities, alert to potential difficulties, attempt to ease the transition in various ways, and it is one of the reasons why our Pupil Leadership Project was located at this juncture. Contrary to previous fragmental research, our project aimed to identify applicable techniques for not only measuring changes in pupil self-perceptions over the period of transition from primary to secondary school but also supporting children during this time. The practical support in implementation of this project was provided by the local authority officer who had been active in pupil involvement and citizenship projects in the area and identified location and timing best for the purpose of the project (Mills, 2004).

Pupil leadership

Leadership is a multifaceted concept and student leadership is normally considered in the broader context of educational leadership. However, studies are emerging that are concerned with student leadership (Dempster & Lizzio, 2007; Frost, 2008). There are several ways of conceptualizing leadership in schools (O'Brien, Murphy & Draper, 2007). We were interested in authentic leadership, which the theoretical literature suggests is characterized by positive social outcomes. For the purposes of the Pupil Leadership Project, we focused on two particular approaches: leadership as individual attribute, "trait theory"; and leadership as dispersed throughout groups and organizations – namely a "distributive" model.

Taking leadership as an individual attribute is a common, if unfashionable, way of defining the concept. It relies on "trait theory" – one of the first explanatory models of leadership developed by Thomas Carlyle in 1841; it is based on the assumption that leadership potential has a strong correlation with a specific type of personality, which is characterized by such traits as achievement, motivation, ambition, energy, tenacity, self-confidence and imitativeness. From this perspective, leadership development is based on the measurement of leadership qualities and provision of leadership training to those with greater potential.

Education for citizenship   191

The "trait theory" approach was partly employed by us at the stage of identification of leaders among pupils in primary schools. However, this was not the only technique applied to measure leadership attributes. The other important components in the identification of leaders included teacher assessments and peer evaluations. Their leader nominations were based mainly on informal indicators, such as charisma, reputation among peers and social position in the class (see description of the methodology below).

The second conception of leadership applied in this research is known as distributed leadership (MacBeath, Oduro & Waterhouse, 2004; Spillane, 2005; Spillane, Halverson & Diamond, 2004). Leadership in this case is understood as a "process and relationship, which is about learning together and constructing meaning and knowledge collectively and collaboratively" (Harris & Lambert, 2003, p. 3). This reflects very vividly the essence of leadership as collective practice that aims at successful performance of the team rather than the individual.

In summary, "trait theory", together with the model of "distributed leadership", was used in measuring leadership skills and designing training sessions for pupils, which aimed at developing and sustaining leadership skills and qualities in the transition period. The leadership training provided consisted mainly of team tasks where pupils were encouraged to become leaders who support and improve performance of the group, and who are able to become active agents in the primary–secondary school transition and to take part in the management of problems arising or related to this period. As for the measurement of leadership skills, there were two key techniques applied: self-evaluation testing and leader nomination by teachers and classmates. Selection of these methodological tools was based on the following theoretical assumptions.

A substantial number of studies on leadership development show its dependency on self-concept, self-identity and self-esteem (Leary & Tangney, 2003). Self-perception is considered to be an important indicator of leadership potential (Hogg & van Knippenberg, 2003). Therefore, pupil self-assessment testing of leadership skills was included in this study as a key component. The other important indicator of leadership potential is the perception of the leader by a social group. In this context, leadership becomes a factor of social interaction, in the Vygotskian way, and could be measured using peer evaluation and sociometric testing which identifies the hierarchy and leadership configuration in a class (Moreno & Jennings, 1938).

Research locale, rationale and methodology

The University of Edinburgh and Inverclyde Council Education Service launched the "Pupil Leadership Project" jointly in 2008–2009. Inverclyde is a mix of rural and large urban areas with a heavy industrial past in shipbuilding and engineering; unemployment and social deprivation are common but the council is proactive and its schools are recognized for performing much better than schools in comparator authorities, and its pupil attainment levels regularly exceed the national average. Fifty percent of students go on to further and higher education after leaving school (www.inverclyde.gov.uk/education-and-learning). For the project, the ambition of the authority was to make further progress with student achievement and attainment and primary–secondary transition was viewed as a key area for experimentation and development. We focused on problems of transition, emphasizing greater attention to students' needs during this period. In particular, leadership training was proposed as a mechanism which may help to "smooth" the impact of social and psychological problems caused by school transition and we posited the view that the long-standing effects of leadership training in the transition period could have a positive impact on students in their subsequent school career and post-schooling life. The study was not specifically designed to explore either the problems of school transition or leadership development among pupils. It aimed to link these concepts by examining how leadership training could be applied as a tool of support during primary–secondary school transition and lead to greater student self-esteem and self-efficacy. A strong practical impetus was incorporated from the beginning. Our aim was to work toward some possible interventions or solutions to the problems that commonly emerge during the transition period. The research project's aims were:

- exploration of the self-perceptions of primary school students in the pre-transitional period
- identification of students perceived as having leadership potential
- evaluation of the effects of training sessions on leadership skills of P7 students in the transition period
- consideration of the role of leadership training as a tool for "smoothing" school transition and proposing links with the education for a citizenship program.

The study applied an experimental method in social psychology. For data collection, a triangulation of methods was used: pupils' self-assessment test, sociometric testing, peer-group evaluation, semi-structured interviews with teachers in primary schools, expert interviews with training course providers, observation of training sessions, after-training evaluation and focus-group discussions with the experimental group.

Three local authority schools were involved in the project: one secondary school and two associated primary schools.[1] At the first stage, the data were collected from the two primary schools and involved interaction with 78 students, five teachers and two leadership course providers. In the general sample of pupils, 32 children were identified as potential leaders. This cohort of pupils (32) was split into experimental and control groups for further pre-training and post-training evaluations. Prior to this, research consent forms were obtained from the head teachers, parents and university ethics committee.

The first phase of the research in the two primary schools involved students in P7 – that is, in their final year of primary education. One hundred percent of the P7 cohorts in both schools were involved: 34 students in one school and 44 in the other. The students were either 10 or 11 years old. A small number of teachers from each school were also involved.

At this stage, researchers visited each school to discuss "what is leadership?" with the students. Various qualities, which may or may not be qualities of leaders, were identified and discussed, including assertiveness, popularity and the ability to get the best out of others. Following this, the students were asked to complete a paper survey where they identified those among their peers who they felt had definite leadership qualities or some leadership qualities. Five teachers from each school – the ones selected being the teachers that knew the students best – went through a similar session on leadership and completed the same paper survey as the pupils. The results were collated, and the 32 students with the highest combined scores from their peers and teachers were selected to be in the training group (the group that would receive further leadership training over the next year) or control group, the two groups of 16 being balanced in terms of their overall scores.

Following this initial identification of "leaders", P7 students completed the test that aimed to identify their self-perceptions in the transition period. The structure of the self-assessment questionnaire was based on the model elaborated by a group of researchers at the University of Maryland (Schneider, Paul, White & Holcombe, 1999) that focuses on the understanding of the origin, development and emergence of student leadership behavior. The questionnaire included assessment of attributes in the following categories: personality, interests, motivation, behavior, skills and ability. Later the self-perceptions were compared for two groups – those identified as "leaders" and "other students". In the next step, the social acceptance of students was explored by means of the sociometric testing that revealed social dynamics in the class and identified positions of leaders in the sociogram of class relations. Finally, at this juncture, semi-structured interviews with teachers involved in leader nomination were conducted to reveal what characteristics they used to identify leaders in their classes. These interviews also explored teachers' views about opportunities for inclusion of leadership training in the school curriculum.

Initial meetings were held with two training course providers, nominated by the local authority, to discuss the design and focus of the training sessions. The researchers' suggestion was to focus training sessions on developing the students' confidence, potential and leadership qualities by means of:

- discussion of good leadership qualities
- practical tasks focused on communication
- team-building and decision-making skills.

After the training events, interviews designed to elicit additional information about the aims and design of the training sessions were conducted with course providers. The training sessions were observed and enriched and deepened the researchers' understandings of class dynamics and students' leadership. Shortly after training sessions, group discussions were held with the participants in order to get their feedback and suggestions for similar initiatives in the future. Additionally, several months after leadership training, the students were asked to complete questionnaires delineating the long-lasting effects of the training.

Four months after all 78 students moved to the same secondary school, the 16 members of the training group received a further full day of leadership training; the control group again received no training. The second training day was focused on consolidating the results achieved during the first, concentrating on practical leadership skills tasks, motivation, teamwork and future life/career planning goals.

The final component of the research involved repeating the survey, with the 78 students (and a small group of teachers) once again being asked to identify those students (from the 78) whom they perceived as displaying definite or some leadership qualities. The results were analyzed to establish how the group that had taken part in the training sessions (the training group) was perceived in comparison with the control group who had received no training. The students were again placed in rank order and changes in their rank position were examined. Also a repeat survey was carried out with both experimental and control groups, evaluating the impacts of the training sessions on their leadership qualities and skills.

Findings

The scale applied for the self-evaluation was elaborated for 8–16-year-old children and consists of 68 statements, based on the children's self-concept scale elaborated by Piers and Harris (1969). They cover children's perceptions of their physical appearance, social behavior, academic status, depreciation and self-satisfaction. On the whole, children with positive self-concepts underlined their intellectual abilities, creativity, progress at school, and communicative and manual skills. In contrast, children with negative self-concepts felt

194   *Jim O'Brien et al.*

unconfident about their appearance and experienced isolation from peers and pressure of parents' high expectations.

In general, there were no crucial distinctions discovered between self-perceptions of "leaders" and "other students". However, there were a few specific differences observed. The results of this test indicated that those who were identified as leaders demonstrated surprisingly less positive self-perceptions compared to their peers.[2]

Further investigation showed that the overall tendency of "leaders" being less positive in their self-perceptions differed across the statements. In their evaluation of some qualities, "leaders" were more positive than their classmates (for instance, in assessing their physical appearance, achievement in sport and communicative skills). However, these differences were not statistically significant.

Compared to "other students", "leaders" are more likely to agree with the statements indicating higher level of anxiety: "I worry a lot", "It is usually my fault when something goes wrong", "I am clumsy", "I am often afraid". At the same time, leaders are more likely to perform higher levels of agreement with the statements expressing their "leading positions": "I usually want my own way", "I am leader in games and sports" (see Table 14.1).

Despite having more negative self-perceptions, "leaders" were more popular among peers and more often were chosen by their classmates for team activities. Based on the observed results, it is estimated that 53% of pupils (nominated as leaders) are chosen by their classmates for school and leisure time activities. Among "other students", only 29% obtained a high score of social acceptance (see Table 14.2).

The results of the self-evaluation and the sociometric test determined the choice of the leadership group for the subsequent training. It was decided to conduct training sessions specifically for leaders for three reasons. First, the data for the self-assessment show that, in general, the self-concepts of the "leaders" and "other students" are quite similar. Therefore, the leaders' responses represent the typical pattern of children's state in the transition period and could be used as a baseline for further analysis of pupil self-perceptions in the transitional period. Second, in some instances, leaders demonstrate distinctive characteristics that identify them in the transition period as a "risk group", with lower self-perceptions and requiring extra support. Finally, based on the results of the sociometric test, leaders are more often

Table 14.1 Children who agree with the following statements (%)

Statement	Leaders	Non-leaders
Level of anxiety		
I worry a lot	32	11
It is usually my fault when something goes wrong	13	7
I am often afraid	10	7
I am clumsy	36	25
Leadership performance		
I am leader in games and sports	25	16
I usually want my own way	31	7

Table 14.2 Distribution of pupils' choices for the group of pupils identified as leaders by teachers' evaluations (%)

	Leaders (in teachers' opinion)	Other students
High score of social acceptance	53.1	28.9
Low score of social acceptance	46.9	71.1

chosen by their classmates for team activities; therefore, their positions could be suggested for future projects as a channel to disseminate learning effects of the leadership training to other children during the next stage of the project if this were to go ahead.

To examine the effect of the training sessions, feedback from children was collected through focus groups and questionnaires. Shortly after training sessions, group discussions were held with participants in order to get their feedback and suggestions for similar initiatives in the future. The following themes were discussed: the most interesting/useful parts of the training sessions, less interesting/useful parts and proposed changes.

Generally, students enjoyed the leadership training as an extra opportunity for teamwork and meeting students from the other primary school. They indicated that both training sessions increased their confidence and flexibility in working with different people and "taking on bigger tasks". In particular, leadership sessions were found helpful in learning how "to be able to speak out more", "to perform creative thinking and to find multiple solutions". Children had learned ideas about the shared and supportive nature of leadership, which they expressed as: "there is not just one leader", "leaders must listen to and involve others", "bullying is 'bad leadership'".

Among the opportunities for leadership development, children recognized some activities at school: school activity week, school shows, sports competitions, participation in class debates and organization of pupil council, monitoring duties, activities in outdoor education centers and during summer school, enterprise events and school charity work. As barriers to leadership development, pupils identify several factors. First, social acceptance of "leaders" is not always positive among peers ("accused of being bossy", "put-downs from others", "people not cooperating", "pupils may not listen to you"). Second, competition with other pupils who are willing to be leaders was also indicated as one of the factors which prevent leadership skill development in the group ("there might be other bossy people, other leaders wanting to take charge as well"). And finally, pressure from "grown-ups" (parents and teachers) is considered as a factor limiting leadership initiatives ("mum and dad like to be in charge", "parents can be over-controlling", "teachers often tend to take over").

Four months later, a questionnaire was distributed to the training group and those who did not take part (control group). Two dimensions were identified for comparison:

- development of leadership skills (How do students evaluate their own leadership qualities and skills since the training session?)
- practising leadership skills (What recent experience do children recognize as their leadership practice? What school activities do pupils consider as opportunities for leadership development)?

The students from the training group showed certain progress in the evaluation of their leadership potential. They are more willing to "participate in teamwork" and "to take initiative when working with the group of other pupils". Pupils from the training group are more confident in leading group activities and gaining support from their classmates (Tables 14.3 and 14.4).

Table 14.3 "I am able to lead group activities well" (%)

	Training group	*Control group*
Agree	80.0	56.3
Disagree	6.7	18.8
Uncertain	13.3	25

196　*Jim O'Brien et al.*

Table 14.4 "My ideas are usually supported by classmates" (%)*

	Training group	Control group
Agree	86.7	50.0
Disagree	6.7	12.5
Uncertain	6.7	37.5

Note
* The differences given in the table are not statistically significant.

In both groups, students were asked to recall their most recent experience of leadership in practice. Pupils from both groups most often referred to sport activities as examples of recent experience of leadership (33% in the training group and 29% in the control group). Children in the training group were also more active in school sales and shows (33%), whereas in the control group only 7% indicated these as part of their leadership experience.

The results of the final peer evaluation test suggest that there were clear differences in how the training and control group members were perceived by their peers (and some of their teachers) one year later. Overall, students originally identified for the training and control groups retained 25 of the top 32 positions in the rank order of 78 pupils from the cohort, and all 16 of the top places. Some changes in overall rank order positions were triggered by a small number of pupils not previously identified as leaders now being perceived as potential leaders by their peers. This caused some pupils from both the training and the leadership groups to slip down the *overall* rank order.

The valuable research result from the data analysis concerns the relative placing of control group and training group members *in relation to each other*. The data in Tables 14.5 and 14.6 show that overall the training group members have risen in rank order placing in comparison with the control group members. Eleven of the 16 training group members now occupy higher rank order placing within the top 32. Training group members have improved their positions by three rank places compared to control group members (both had initial identical overall rank averages). Of the training group members, 68.75% improved their rank order position within the group of 32 first identified. In terms of their peers' perceptions, they are now regarded as having stronger leadership qualities than the members of the control group (who did not undergo leadership training).

Table 14.5 Final results for training group and control group (based on comparison of the P7 and S1 rank order positions of the 32 pupils in the training and control groups)

	Rank position up	No change in rank position	Rank position down
Members of the training group (16)	11	1	4
Members of the control group (16)	6	0	10

Table 14.6 Average rank order places, P7 and S1 (training and control group) where 1 is the highest placing

	Average rank order place in P7	Average rank order place in S1
16 training group members	16.1	14.9
16 control group members	16.1	17.9

When the rank orders for pupil leadership from first and second phases were compared, it was noted that, although most pupils demonstrated similar ranking or a small increase or decrease in rank order, there were a small number of students whose rank order place rose or fell by a far greater extent. Two pupils went up by 17 places or more in the rank order, but five pupils – identified as leaders in P7 – experienced a fall of 14 places or more (four of them were pupils from the control group). Telephone interviews were carried out with members of school staff who knew the pupils best from the secondary school and both primary schools, and staff were asked to suggest possible reasons for this marked change in rank position. In most cases, the suggested reasons put forward – for the same pupil – by the secondary and primary schools were similar. Primary teachers indicated that these larger changes in rank position were not particularly surprising. The transition from primary to secondary school is one that some pupils achieve more easily than others. It is not unexpected that pupils who tend to be quiet or shy or who display behavioral problems may find adjustment more difficult. This appears to be reflected in changes in the way their peers perceive them in terms of their leadership qualities. This has no overall bearing on the assessment of the impact of leadership training, but it does explain some of the anomalies. Overall, the results may suggest that the pupils who undertook leadership training coped better with the adjustment at transition from primary to secondary school.

Discussion and conclusions

Most of the students positively assess their performance at school, at home and in their community of peers. However, some pupils experience isolation from peers, pressure of parents' high expectations and lack of self-confidence during the transition period. In general, there are no crucial distinctions between self-perceptions of leaders and other students during the period of transition, although some observations reveal some specific differences. Leaders tend to be less shy, more confident in their physical appearance, and more independent and successful in sport and communicative skills. Non-leaders are more easy-tempered and less worried. Overall, leaders are more likely to portray negative self-perceptions in comparison to their classmates. The significant differences in pupils' self-evaluations were observed in regard to motivation and level of anxiety. Leaders tend to have higher leadership motivation but at the same time they more often feel worried and stressed. Considering other differences in frequency distributions, leaders are more concerned and anxious about their actions, feelings and parents' expectations.

The evaluation discovered that participants are more willing to take part in group activities and take on leadership roles in teamwork compared to other children. They feel more confident about their ideas, which tend to be more often accepted by their peers. Moreover, participation in the training sessions enlarged children's perspectives on future opportunities for leadership development.

Overall, the information collected by qualitative and quantitative methods indicated that leadership training did have an impact on the "training group" of 16, both in terms of the (changing) way they were perceived by other pupils with regard to their leadership qualities and also in terms of the way they perceived themselves. The extent of this impact and its statistical significance cannot be fully ascertained due to the limited scale of the study.

This was a pilot study but unfortunately funding and prevailing economic circumstances did not permit a larger follow-up and of course generalization is difficult from the data. However, following discussions with children and results of the peer evaluations, it could be concluded that the leadership training had a positive impact on development of leadership skills (team-working skills, self-confidence and leadership initiative) and the related pupils' class rating. Self-esteem and personal capacities appear to have been influenced and, in some instances, enhanced. The data are inadequate in relation to the long-standing effects of the leadership training – that was to have been a major strand in the follow-up. However, the evidence suggests that we may tentatively conclude that the intervention and interaction and dialogue about leadership themes and attributes contributed to greater self-regulation on the part of the students in the experimental group and that teaching such provided these students with greater awareness of their role and influence on others and their sense of social responsibility.

The pilot study could be improved given this experience and offered to a larger sample of pupils, or the leadership training extended to a greater number of pupils to determine its effect, if any, on student self-esteem, awareness of others and their potential to influence others, plus capacity for self-regulation in their daily interactions. Recognizing the restricted financial resources in most schools and authorities, organization of such training days for all pupils could become economically problematic, especially in a time of economic recession, but an alternative approach could be based on the model of sharing and collective learning among peers (a distributed model of leadership), as would be encouraged in a sociocultural model. In this case, the training events could be facilitated and supervised by those pupils who were previously involved in the leadership training. Such events could be successfully integrated into the approach to citizenship education adopted by the school, formally and informally involving everyday school and classroom activities, as well as organized as part of activities already practised in school trips, shows, charity events and community experiences.

Notes

1 The schools were identified by the local authority because almost every student from the two primary schools would move on to that particular secondary school, unlike other clusters where a greater number of parents exercise parental choice and send their children to secondary schools other than the cluster secondary school. This meant that the cohorts from the primaries taking part in the research would be virtually intact when moving on to secondary school, where the second phase of the research took place. The schools involved were from a catchment area – the area their students are drawn from – that was predominantly middle class in character.

2 The index of positive "self-concept" was calculated as the sum of values for all positive statements with subtraction of values for all negative statements. The median value of the index was calculated for the leadership group and other children to compare the distribution of responses in the two groups. The overall test scores gained by "other children" are higher in comparison to the leadership group (median value for the leadership group is 59, which is lower compared to the group of "other children": 65). This difference in median values is not statistically significant. The level of significance is above 0.05 (p = 0.792).

References

Boyd, B., Dunlop A. W., Mitchell J., Logue J., Gavienas E., Seagraves L. . . . Deuchar, R. (2007). Curriculum architecture – a literature review: Report for the Scottish Executive Education Department to inform the implementation of a Curriculum for Excellence. Glasgow: University of Strathclyde.

Carr, D. (1999). Values education in Scotland. In T. Bryce & W. Humes (Eds.), *Scottish education* (pp. 298–303). Edinburgh: Edinburgh University Press.

Chedzoy, S. M. & Burden, R. L. (2005). Assessing student attitudes to primary–secondary school transfer. *Research in Education, 74*(1), 22–35.

Dempster, N. & Lizzio, A. (2007). Student leadership: Necessary research. *Australian Journal of Education, 51*(3), 276–286.

Department for Children, Schools and Families (2008). *What makes a successful transition from primary to secondary school? Findings from the Effective Pre-school, Primary and Secondary Education 3–14 (EPPSE)*. Research Report DCFS-RR019. London: Institute of Education, University of London.

Deuchar, R. (2003). Preparing tomorrow's people: The new challenges of citizenship education for involving Scottish pupils and teachers in participative decision-making processes. *Scottish Educational Review, 35*(1), 27–37.

Evans, K. (1995). Competence and citizenship: Towards a complementary model for times of critical social change. *British Journal of Education and Work, 8*(2), 14–27.

Frost, R. (2008). Developing student participation, research and leadership: The HCD Student Partnership. *School Leadership & Management, 28*(4), 353–368.

Galton, M., Gray J. & Ruddock J. (1999). *The impact of school transitions and transfers on pupil progress and attainment*. DfEE Research Report No. 131, Norwich: HMSO.

Galton, M., Morrison, I. & Pell, T. (2000). Transfer and transition in English schools: Reviewing the evidence. *International Journal of Educational Research, 33*, 340–363.

Harris, A. & Lambert, L. (2003). *Building leadership capacity for school improvement*. Milton Keynes: Open University Press.

Hayward, L. (2007). Curriculum, pedagogies and assessment in Scotland: The quest for social justice. 'Ah kent yir faither'. *Assessment in Education: Principles, Policy & Practice, 14*(2), 251–268.

HMIE. (2003). *How good is our school? Education for citizenship*. Edinburgh: HMIE.

Hogg, M. A. & van Knippenberg, D. (2003). Social identity and leadership processes in groups. *Advances in Experimental Social Psychology, 35*, 1–52.

Learning and Teaching Scotland. (2002) *Education for citizenship: A paper for discussion and development*. Dundee: Learning and Teaching Scotland.

Leary, M. R. and Tangney, J. P. (2003). *Handbook of self and identity*. New York: Guilford Press.

MacBeath, J., Oduro, G. K. T. & Waterhouse, J. (2004). *Distributed leadership in action: A study of current practice in schools*. Nottingham: National College for School Leadership.

Maitles, H. (2005). *Values in education – we're all citizens now*. Edinburgh: Dunedin Academic Press.

Mills, I. (2004). Citizenship: Pupil involvement in Scottish secondary schools. *Pedagogy, Culture and Society, 12*(2), 259–280.

Moreno, J. L. & Jennings, H. H. (1938). Statistics of social configurations. *Sociometry, 1*(3/4), 342–374.

Munn, P. & Arnott, M. (2009). Citizenship in Scottish schools: The evolution of education for citizenship from the late twentieth century to the present. *History of Education: Journal of the History of Education Society, 38*(3), 437–454.

North Ayrshire Council. (2000). *Guidelines for the Transfer of Information from P7 to S1. 'Save the kids'*. Retrieved from www.safekids.co.uk/transition-from-primary-secondary-school.html.

O'Brien, J. & MacLeod, G. (2009). *The social agenda of the school*. Policy and Practice in Education Series. Edinburgh: Dunedin Academic Press.

O'Brien, J., Murphy, D. & Draper, J. (2007). *School leadership* (2nd ed.). Policy and Practice in Education Series. Edinburgh: Dunedin Academic Press.

Piers, E. V. & Harris, D. B. (1969). *The Piers–Harris Children's Self-Concept Scale*. Nashville, TN: Counselor Recording and Tests.

Ross, H., Munn, P. & Brown, J. (2007). What counts as student voice in active citizenship case studies? Education for citizenship in Scotland. *Education, Citizenship and Social Justice, 2*(3), 237–256.

Rudduck, J. & McIntyre, D. (2007). *Improving learning through consulting pupils*. London: Routledge.

Schneider, B., Paul, M. C., White, S. S. & Holcombe, K. M. (1999). Understanding high school student leaders, I: Predicting teacher ratings of leader behavior. *Leadership Quarterly, 10*(4), 609–636.

Scottish Executive. (2005). *Happy, safe and achieving their potential. A standard of support for children and young people in Scottish schools. The Report of The National Review of Guidance, 2004*. Edinburgh: Scottish Executive.

Scottish Executive Education Department (SEED). (2007). *Evaluation of pilots to improve primary to secondary school transitions*. Retrieved from www.scotland.gov.uk/Publications/2007/01/24111206/0.

Shepherd, J. & Roker, D. (2005). *An evaluation of a transition to secondary school.* National Pyramid Trust, Brighton: Trust for the Study of Adolescence.

Spillane, J. P. (2005). Distributed leadership. *The Educational Forum, 69*(2), 143–150.

Spillane, J. P., Halverson, R. & Diamond, J. B. (2004). Towards a theory of leadership practice: A distributed perspective. *Journal of Curriculum Studies, 36*(1), 3–34.

Vygotsky, L. S. (1978). *Mind in society.* Cambridge, MA: Harvard University Press.

West, P., Sweeting, H. & Young, R. (2008). Transition matters: Pupils' experiences of the primary–secondary school transition in the West of Scotland and consequences for well-being and attainment. *Research Papers in Education, 25*(1), 1–29.

Zeedyk, M. S., Gallacher, J., Henderson, M., Hope, G., Husband, B. & Lindsay, K. (2003). Negotiating the transition from primary to secondary school: Perceptions of pupils, parents and teachers. *School Psychology International, 24*(1), 69–79.

15 How encouragement in everyday family practices facilitates Hong Kong–Australian children's motive for learning

Pui Ling Wong

Introduction

The Hong Kong immigrant community is a group with high educational attainment in Australia (DIAC, 2006; Zhao, 2000). Children from this community are one of the high academically achieving groups, outperforming their peers in the classroom (Pe-Pua, Mitchell, Iredale & Castles, 1996). Despite these outstanding achievements, there is little research on this group, especially on children's educational and learning experiences. Nevertheless, this outstanding characteristic has been recently highlighted and brought to wider public attention by SBS, an Australian multi-cultural and multilingual broadcaster, reporting that "migrant school students are topping their classes in literacy and numeracy" in its World News TV program (SBS, 2011a) and setting up a website called "Dragon children" to address and discuss the question "what's behind the success of Chinese–Australian students?" (SBS, 2011b).

Much of the literature, including the experts' opinions expressed in the above-mentioned SBS documentary materials, suggests that the parental support for and emphasis on learning has helped secure the success of Chinese students (Archer & Francis, 2007; Li, 2004; Matthews, 2002; Pearce, 2006). Little is known from the children's perspectives about how they acquire the competencies and develop a learning motive for academic success. While many studies have brought out the essential role of parents in children's academic achievement, increasing research evidence has pointed out that parents' dominant family practices emphasizing academic competence have caused excessive pressures for children and are thus potentially counterproductive to their academic achievement (Li, 2005). The recent energetic debate about the "tiger mother" complicates this seeming contradiction. This mother placed high demands on her daughters, drilling them for academic excellence, yet the eldest daughter wrote to the media to repudiate accusations that the mother had exercised excessive control and to show that she was indeed happy and appreciated her mother's parenting approach (*New York Post*, January 2011). These conflicting outcomes suggest it is important to understand the phenomenon from the children's perspective, since the children's understanding and experience of the situation shapes their motives and attitudes (Bozhovich, 2009; Lawrence & Valsiner, 2003). Van Oers (2011) adverts that, when we study children's development, we should not only focus on the adult's contribution, but more importantly understand the child's perspective of his/her own social situation. He reminds researchers that Vygotsky's powerful understandings of children's learning and development are firmly founded on the importance of social interactions of children with social others and on the children's agency within a cultural–historical context.

Through an in-depth case study of three Hong Kong–Australian families, this chapter discusses and illustrates two important aspects of Vygotsky's cultural–historical approach to

202   *Pui Ling Wong*

studying children's development of an achievement-related learning motive. They are "the environment" and "the child". In respect of the environment, this chapter focuses on productive parent–child interactions, which in this chapter consist of various kinds of encouragement. Regarding "the child", this chapter focuses on the child's perception and personal sense of his/her learning. The chapter reveals the ways encouragement helps forge positive learning motives in relation to children's perceptions and personal sense.

Theoretical perspectives

This chapter builds on the interpretations of a cultural–historical approach to child development, in particular, Vygotsky's (1998) concept of the social situation of development. It focuses on the investigation of family practices as the environment of learning for children. Children's perspectives form the central focus of this chapter, which aims to identify children's perceptions and personal senses of their learning environment. The Chinese concept of learning (Li, 2001), embedded in Chinese family values, is also drawn on to examine Hong Kong–Australian children's development of their motive for learning. Another important concept in this chapter is encouragement, a significant interaction between parent and child that helps children develop a motive for learning. These concepts are discussed in this section and form the theoretical perspectives guiding discussion of the findings.

The social situation of development

Vygotsky's (1998) concept of the social situation of development refers to the role, influence and meaning of the social environment, such as family and school, in relation to child development. The cultural–historical approach to researching a child's social situation of development emphasizes the importance of understanding the mutual and changing relationships between the child and the surrounding reality, and his/her understanding and emotional experience of these social situations (Vygotsky, 1994). Such social situations, together with the child's own subjectivity and agency, constitute the social situation of development for that child. The child's social situation is significant for the child's development because, depending on the ways the child has understood and experienced the situation, different development opportunities are afforded. That is, a child may experience a situation differently at different age periods because the child's ability to generalize his/her social situation varies at different stages or even differs from that of another child in the same situation, such as among siblings (Vygotsky, 1994). This indicates that it is not only the environment and the social others around the child that are important, as most of the literature has emphasized, but also the child him/herself. In fact, Vygotsky paid attention to the ways children's personal characteristics and affect interact with the social situation, creating a dynamic contribution to their own development. Thus, the child's own perspectives need to be foregrounded to achieve a better understanding of the way children develop (Bozhovich, 2009; Gonzalez Rey, 2009; Lawrence & Valsiner, 2003; van Oers, 2011; Vygotsky, 1994).

The child's perception and personal sense

When studying children's learning and development, it is important to take into account the child's perspective because this allows "the researchers to investigate how children contribute to their own developmental conditions" (Hedegaard & Fleer, 2008, p. 5). However, identifying a child's perspective is a problem. In this regard, Hedegaard (2008) suggests focusing on investigating the intentions and motives of the child when s/he participates in his/her everyday activities within institutional practices. By tracing back to Vygotsky's concept of the social situation of development and referring to other relevant literature (Bozhovich, 2009; Gonzales Rey, 2009; Lawrence & Valsiner, 2003; Leontiev, 1978; Vygotsky, 1994), it is possible to gain further insights into the concept of the child's perception (Vygotsky, 1994) and the child's personal sense (Leontiev, 1978) in capturing children's perspectives. In this chapter, a child's perception refers to the child's awareness, interpretation and understanding of the cultural meaning of his/her social situation, which is related to the cognition of the child. The child's personal sense, on the other hand, refers to the child's affective attachment to his/her social situation, and the personal value and meaning of this to the child. It is related to a person's motive, interest, need, will and action. With these conceptual frames, a child's perspective can be understood and captured concretely by looking at the child's affective responses and understandings of the social environment.

Developing a learning motive and its relation to the Chinese concept of learning

Children develop motives within the systems dominated by the values of their social and cultural environment. Leontiev (1978) pointed out that motive is connected to activity and "activity does not exist without a motive" (p. 62). He added that motive drives human activity. When a person has a need, objects or actions that seem to be able to satisfy the need will motivate the person to accomplish activity toward those objects or actions. For example, if a child has the need to acquire knowledge, s/he may see school as the object (or going to school as the action) that can help fulfill this need. Thus the child is motivated to engage in learning at school. According to Hedegaard (2010) and Vygotsky (1998), a child can acquire a motive orientation toward mastering the dominant institutional activity through participation in activities that are interesting or motivating to the child. As a child develops a motive, it is important for him/her to appropriate the institution's or the caregiver's values and meanings (Wong & Fleer, 2012). Many Hong Kong parents value learning highly and structure numerous learning activities in their children's daily lives (Pe-Pau et al., 1996; Wong, 2007).

Van Oers (2008) indicates that "the way people learn depends on the culture they live in" and "the transformation of the learning processes is a cultural process" (p. 8). The Chinese concept of learning, "haoxuexin", means inner desire to learn (Li, 2001, p. 122). Learning in Chinese cultural meaning is not just acquiring knowledge and skill, but also involves effort, persistence, perseverance, conscientiousness and contribution to society (Li, 2001). These concepts are important for understanding how Hong Kong–Australian children develop a learning motive that embraces the Chinese concept of learning for their educational achievement.

Encouragement

The concept of encouragement, conceptualized within the cultural–historical paradigm, has been discussed in Wong and Fleer (2012). In this chapter, this concept is extended to foreground the child's perspective in the process. In relation to Vygotsky's (1998) concept of the social situation of development, encouragement can be further conceptualized as a specific social interaction process, with a parent or a social other via an action with the goal to motivate the child for achievement. In the process of encouragement, the social other tries

204 *Pui Ling Wong*

to communicate to the child the demands or goals needed to be achieved; whether this is perceived by the child as encouraging depends on the child's perception and personal sense toward the action. Encouragement can be carried out by the social other in different forms, such as material rewards, incentive systems, verbal recognition and emotional anticipation (Wong & Fleer, 2012). This external action creates a specific social condition (intervention) for the child; if the child perceives it as being encouraging, the action is internalized by the child, who then develops his/her own new motive, uses his/her agency and creates a new activity to accomplish the task or demand required by the social others, and the child him/herself (Lawrence & Valsiner, 2003). Thus it is clear that encouragement is not merely a behavior of social others; indeed, in the case of parent–child interaction, parents and children contribute dialectically to effective acts of encouragement.

Research design

This chapter examines how Hong Kong immigrant families create conditions for their children's learning and development, with a specific focus on understanding the child's perspective through their perceptions and personal senses of their own social situations. Studies based on quantitative methods have increasingly been criticized for not being able to establish a rigorous causal relationship between parental contribution and the academic performance of their children (Nozaki & Inokuchi, 2007; Wu, Palinkas & He, 2010). To overcome this deficiency, this study adopts a qualitative case study research approach, which follows the cultural–historical paradigm and Hedegaard and Fleer's (2008) dialectical-interactive methodology. The theoretical and methodological approach provides comprehensive and systematic guidance to understand children's perspectives on the development of their achievement-related learning motives and the role of encouragement in family learning environments.

Participants

Three Hong Kong immigrant families in Melbourne, Australia, participated in the study. At the beginning of data collection, all parents were in their late 30s to early 40s. Further particulars are given in Table 15.1.

Data collection

Data were collected for 12 months, resulting in 46 visits (22 for the Chan family, 19 for the Lee family and 15 for the Cheung family), 80 hours of video footage and 18 hours of audio recording. In addition, over 150 photos, 90 video clips and various documents related to the

Table 15.1 Particulars of the participant families

Family	Chan	Lee	Cheung
Parents	Flora and Ivan	Terri and Tony	Linda and Andrew
Migrated	11 years ago	2 years ago	Over 15 years ago
Children	Jessica (6) and Vincent (9)	Simon (newborn) and Steven (7, born in HK)	Micky (5), Betty (7) and Jenny (11)
School attended	Government school	Independent Christian school	Private school

children's learning and education were provided by the participants. These data were gathered through video observations of the children's participation in their everyday activities at different times and days at home and across different institutions, such as school, Chinese language school and the places where the children attended enhancement learning activities. Enhancement learning denotes out-of-school learning aiming to foster and enhance a range of skills and knowledge that will help the child in academic achievement, life skills and multifaceted aspects of development, such as music and sport. The daily activities of the children were filmed to capture a holistic view of their everyday life. Data were also collected through video or audio-recorded interviews with children and parents. In addition, children and parents were asked to take photos or video clips of activities that the children liked and disliked, and that the parents believed were important for children's learning, education and growing up. This method aimed to collect data regarding the participants' perspectives from the data they supplied, thus complementing the data generated from the video observations.

Data analysis

Data analysis sought to reveal the family practices related to the children's learning and education, identify the children's perceptions and personal sense of the family practices and examine the role of encouragement for developing a learning motive in the children in the study. The dialectical-interactive methodological approach was used, with its three levels of analysis (Hedegaard, 2008). A *common sense interpretation* was used to identify patterns that at first glance stood out from the data set. This was followed by a *situated practice interpretation* of each family, applying the framing theoretical concepts to identify categories of significance to the particular family. Finally, *thematic interpretation* was carried out, in which the conceptual categories evolving from the situated practice interpretation were further examined across families and in relation to the research aim to find meaningful themes with evidence from multiple sources across data sets. This layered analysis yielded rich and comprehensive understandings. The concepts discussed in the theoretical perspectives section were used in the analysis to help recognize conceptual and thematic patterns.

Findings

The social situation of children's learning and education

Analysis reveals that the parents in this study had worked actively, according to their values, in "configuring" the social situations for their children's learning and education. Few conflicting or different values come from other institutions, such as school and enhancement learning centers, because those institutions had been chosen to be in line with the parents' values. Thus, this chapter is focused on the investigation of the family practices in relation to the discussion of the social situation of learning and education for the children. The families in this study paid careful attention to choosing the schools, learning centers and after-school activities for the children, as they believed that it was important to provide a favorable environment for their children to learn and develop. In cases where the families found a discrepancy of values and practices between them and the chosen institutions, they would cease their children's participation in the institution and/or actively seek a more suitable one to replace it. The Chan family had chosen a government school with effective family–school communication, and good academic performance and discipline. The Lee family had first sent Steven to a local government school; however, after one year, Steven had changed to an independent Christian school because of the mismatch of family–school values and practices with the first school (see Wong, 2012b).

Findings indicate that the parental values, demands and practices were shaped by their societal, cultural and historical conditions (Wong, 2012a; Wong & Fleer, 2012). All parents in this study were brought up and had their schooling in Hong Kong. All of them had tertiary education qualifications. Despite the fact that five of them had done their tertiary education in Australia, their family practices regarding their children's learning and education were greatly influenced by the Chinese concept of learning (Li, 2001). All three families demanded that their children do practice, be persistent, expend effort and work hard on their education and learning. Related literature suggests that these are the cultural capital that Chinese immigrant children are equipped with by their parents, helping them outperform their peers academically in Australia (Guo, 2006; Mak & Chan, 1995; Matthews, 2002; SBS, 2011a, 2011b). Moreover, because the Cheung family had very high expectations of their children, the children were required to always deliver work of the best quality. Both Andrew and Linda emphasized academic learning strongly, since they wanted their children to be in the top tier in their classes. The enhancement learning arranged for their children aimed mainly at academic enhancement and was linked to assessment. According to the SBS (2011b), the achievement-oriented practice of the Cheungs is commonly found in many Chinese (including Hong Kong) families in Australia. The Lee family was concerned with Steven's academic learning but let him take the initiative to do his homework and revision for tests. Terri would give Steven extra homework during holidays. The Lee and Chan families both wanted their children to try different enhancement activities and experience multi-faceted development. The Lee parents chose some activities according to Steven's desire (e.g., football) and at the same time insisted that he do some activities which he did not like but that Terri and Tony believed were good for him (e.g., Chinese language). Findings reveal that the parental values and family practices of the three families resembled each other and also differed, and this also applied to the social situations for the children in the three families.

Table 15.2 shows in detail the choice of school, parental expectations, demands and involvement, and the family practices for children's academic and enhancement learning in the three families, which formed the social situation for the children's learning and education at the time of this study. As discussed in the theoretical perspective section, to determine whether the social situations "configured" by the parents are effective for their children's development, we need to consider the children's perceptions and personal sense of these social situations. With this consideration, we are able to gain a better understanding of each child's social situation of development.

Children's perceptions and personal sense of their learning and education

Leontiev (1978) argues that "the effects of external action depend on their interpretation by the subject" (p. 47). To capture the children's perspectives, each child's perception and personal sense regarding their learning and education were identified and analyzed by viewing and reviewing the data collected from the related video observations and interviews, noticing and interpreting the child's conversation and interaction with others, his/her expression, and his/her verbal, emotional and physical responses in relation to his/her understanding and affective attachment to the academic and enhancement learning. Examples follow of the perception and personal sense regarding school or enhancement learning as gleaned from the data for Jessica Chan and Jenny Cheung.

How encouragement facilitates motive for learning   207

Table 15.2 The social situation of learning and education for the participant children

	The Chan family	*The Lee family*	*The Cheung family*
Choice of school	Government school	Independent Christian school	Private school
Expectations	High–medium, implicitly delighted if children are top tier	Medium–low, not being the last one in the class is acceptable	Very high, top tier
Demands	Work hard, put in effort, persistence, do practice	Work hard, put in effort, persistence, do practice, concentrate	Work hard, put in effort, do more practice, persistence, always deliver work of the best quality
Involvement	Flora actively involved, Ivan supported	Involved, but preferred not to check and correct Steven's homework	Linda devoted all her time to her children's learning and education, Andrew actively involved
Academic learning	Emphasized but not recognized, monitored and assisted children on tests and homework, gave extra homework in both school term and holidays	Concerned but let Steven take care of his academic learning, gave extra homework only in holidays	Highly emphasized, Linda closely monitored and actively assisted her children to complete their homework and tests to top standard
Enhancement learning	General: Wanted their children to experience multi-faceted development; let them try different activities Activities for Vincent and Jessica: Chinese language school, swimming, musical instruments, Church Sunday school, Children's choir Activities for Vincent only: Boys' brigade Activities for Jessica only: Gymnastics	General: Wanted Steven to experience multi-faceted development; let him try different activities; some activities parents insisted Steven must do, e.g., learning Chinese; at the same time they chose some activities according to Steven's desire, e.g., football training Activities for Steven: Chinese language school, swimming, Church Sunday school, drama, chess, football, English tuition	General: Mainly related to academic enhancement; all activities linked to assessment, e.g., piano grade-level examination; parents chose the type of activities for the children Activities for Jenny, Betty and Micky: Chinese language school, swimming, musical instrument Activities for Jenny and Betty: Kumon, Mandarin tuition Activities for Jenny only: Tuition class

Jessica's perception and personal sense of her academic learning

The video recordings and interviews of Jessica's everyday life showed that she always had a positive personal sense of her academic learning. She valued going to school, seeing it as an opportunity to participate in enjoyable school-related activities and to interact with friends, which she experienced as fun. The meaning of learning well at school for Jessica was about the approval of others. She was happy when teachers praised her and her parents were proud of her. Entirely of her own volition, she prioritized homework (e.g., take-home reading) over play, smiling and laughing as she did the work. Each observation of her at school and home attested to her enthusiastic participation in academic and social activities. Her pleasure at receiving explicit verbal praise from her teachers and parents for the effort she put into her school learning – which seemed to occur regularly – was evident in her smiles. She expressed her perceptions of the value of learning and her positive personal sense of enjoyment in

208 *Pui Ling Wong*

learning explicitly through frequent statements about liking school, and implicitly through her smiles and alacrity in engaging in academic-related tasks.

Jenny's perception and personal sense of her enhancement learning

Analysis of Jenny's data found that she perceived her enhancement activities as valuable because she was learning additional things that school had not provided, which she felt accorded her the advantage of doing extra practice and learning in advance, helping her to get good results at school. She explicitly stated that the amounts and types of learning were just right and they helped her to become good at things and receive awards. She said she also found it interesting and fun to do and complete tuition exercises. Jenny thus expressed her perception of the value of learning from tuition, and also gave voice to her personal sense of its importance for the development of her learning orientation; she felt confident to do well when she put in the effort.

In general, these children have developed an understanding of their learning in the formal education setting, although the degree of awareness and understanding may vary. For example, Jessica's understanding about school learning was still shallow, seeing school as a place to read, do math and play with friends, while Jenny, who was older and more able to generalize the associated meanings, perceived the more long-term benefits of school and had become aware of its value in her personal growth and knowledge. All participant children were able to understand that school is a place to learn and that discipline and practice play a large role in achievement. They also had a positive personal sense of school learning; all of them were happy attending their school and found most school activities fun. As indicated from observations, all children were eager to return to school after the long summer vacation. For example, Jenny and Betty expressed in the interviews that they had missed the learning activities, friends and teachers from school.

The perceptions and personal sense of enhancement learning varied among the children. Jenny was very positive and she had a clear understanding of the enhancement learning her parents had arranged for her. She perceived that her extra-curricular activities had added value to her school learning and equipped her with numerous rewards. Jessica, in contrast, had a simple understanding that these were the activities her parents wanted her to engage in and that by doing so she could acquire different skills and become good at things. She found her enhancement learning valuable, as her mother was always around guiding her to do the homework and practice. She found the activities fun and enjoyed them. The perceptions and personal senses of Betty and Micky on their enhancement learning were similar to those of Jessica but on a few occasions they felt annoyed when required to practise their musical instruments daily and were worried when they had not accomplished the tasks required by their tutors.

Steven and Vincent, on the other hand, were negative toward some of their enhancement learning activities, which they felt were not desired but imposed by their parents. They also found that doing extra homework and practice for the enhancement activities was boring. While they had an understanding that the activities were about learning skills and they needed to keep practising – this was their perception of the learning situation – they felt no affinity with some of their enhancement learning, at least in the beginning, and had not developed a positive personal sense of value for the related learning.

The above analysis clearly illustrates the importance of taking into account children's perspectives for understanding their development. It shows that the different perceptions and personal senses the children possessed led to different experiences and attitudes toward their learning (Bozhovich, 2009; Vygotsky, 1994). For example, because generally all the children had good perceptions and a positive personal sense of their school learning, they had good experiences and strong engagement in it and, as Bozhovich (2009) has argued, this helped the children's school achievements. In contrast, Steven's and Vincent's perceptions and personal senses of some of their enhancement learning activities were negative, and they had negative attitudes toward them. The analysis presented above has also illustrated the interdependent relationship between perception and personal sense (e.g., Jenny's more elaborate perception brought better personal sense and vice versa), and the existence of differences in perception and personal sense for children at different ages, such as Jessica and Jenny, and among siblings such as Jessica and Vincent (Bozhovich, 2009; Vygotsky, 1994).

Development of an achievement-related learning motive

As discussed in the theoretical perspective section, Hedegaard (2010) and Leontiev (1978) indicated that motives are connected to the dominant institutional activities. For school, the dominant activity is learning. This chapter refers to school learning activities as the activities related to academic learning and learning to socialize at school. Providing the school activities can fulfill the child's needs and are interesting or motivating to a child, s/he will develop a motive for learning at school (Hedegaard, 2010; Leontiev, 1978; Vygotsky, 1998). Schools place their expectations and demands on their students, as do families on their children regarding their school learning (Hedegaard, 2010). In the case of the participant children, their schools expected academic achievement and their parents demanded that they behave attentively and make conscientious effort to perform as well as possible. These school and family demands shaped the children's needs regarding their school learning. As can be seen from these children's perceptions and personal senses regarding their school learning discussed in the previous section, generally, the children had the need to feel competent in their knowledge and skills and their value as a social person, as well as to be valued as studious. Findings revealed their needs were able to be fulfilled; they were motivated to "do" school and were interested in the school activities.

The children in this study differed in age and thus in the degree to which their learning motive had been established. However, one thing they had in common was that they had all engaged, at their parents' behest, in enhancement activities and this had nurtured the children's orientation to achievement-related learning. Micky and Jessica were in the early years of primary school (Pre-prep and Grade 1) where their motive for school learning was forming and competence to learn was being acquired. Betty and Steven were in the middle year (both Grade 2), being more engaged and confident in their school learning, and Vincent and Jenny were in the later years of primary school (Grades 4 and 6), demonstrating a developed motive for learning at school and having mastered their school learning well. Findings reveal that all participant children had very good academic performances, especially Jenny, who was the top student in her class.

In the three families, not only at school but after school, the parents valued learning and arranged much enhancement learning for the children, with the embedded demand of acquiring the Chinese concept of learning. It can be reasoned that, if the children were able to understand and appropriate the same meaning as their parents, together with a positive sense of what learning could give them, then gradually they should develop a learning motive which embraces the Chinese concept of learning involving effort, persistence, perseverance, conscientiousness and contribution to society (Li, 2001). Developing a learning motive encompassing the Chinese cultural meaning of learning would require the child to become aware of and understand the idea that learning is not just acquiring knowledge or skill, but also involves the aspects listed above. With this concept and awareness in mind, the child would interpret and generalize learning in this cultural way and this in turn would engender positive emotion to act toward the goal; the child would be more willing to act toward achievement-oriented goals. The findings illustrate that generally this form of learning motive had developed and was continuing to develop among these children. For example, in doing practice, putting in effort, not easily giving up and being hard-working, most of the children (e.g., Jenny and Jessica) showed they had understood the values and were willing to act accordingly. But in some aspects and for some children, like Steven and Vincent, this motive still needed to be further developed. In comparison with the five aspects, the concept of applying what one has learned to contribute to society was not explicitly promoted in the Lee and Cheung families. However, it was clearly found in Vincent's guitar learning experience, when he proudly provided accompaniment for the church choir (see Wong & Fleer, 2012).

Despite the clear progression of these children in their development of a learning motive, the process of this development was not always smooth in enhancement activities. Analysis indicated that the positive sense regarding enhancement learning was not yet highly developed in Steven and Vincent at the beginning of the research. However, subsequent data revealed an important, constructive parent–child interaction – encouragement – that helped these boys develop more positive meanings for learning in enhancement settings.

The role of encouragement

Findings discussed above regarding Vincent and Steven only represented the facts found in the early stage of data collection. When more data were gathered, an important discovery emerged; encouragement from the parents helped Vincent in particular to develop a learning motive. Vincent's guitar learning experience is a good example of the gradual process of development of a learning motive supported by various forms of encouragement, illustrating how Vincent's orientation progressed from a pronounced lack of motive for learning the guitar to developing a motive for guitar playing and then expanded to a learning motive embracing the Chinese concept of learning. This process is closely described by Wong and Fleer (2012).

This chapter foregrounds children's perspectives in the learning process and discusses how encouragement in everyday family practices facilitates learning motives in respect to children's perceptions and personal sense. Analysis reveals that all the parents in this study placed demands on their children's learning and education, but accompanied these demands with various forms of encouragement to help them fulfill the demands and develop a learning motive. The encouragement used by the three families can be classified in six forms: material rewards, incentive systems, verbal explanation and recognition, supportive action, emotional anticipation and self-encouragement. The detail of how the families used encouragement is set out in Table 15.3.

Material reward was the form of encouragement commonly used by all the families to encourage their children to accomplish tasks. It worked to provide an instant encouragement to trigger the child to perform. An analysis of video observation shows that the parents (or one of them) would usually announce to the child what was required to be done and what the reward would be when the task was completed. Since the reward was usually something that the child liked (e.g., candies for the Chan children and stationery for the Cheung

Table 15.3 Different forms of encouragement used by the participant families

Form	The Chan family	The Lee family	The Cheung family
Material reward	Candies	Food, clothing, lunch bag	Stationery
Incentive system	Stickers, everyday task sheet, free time for TV, computer games and Wii	Lego, checklist	Marbles system for small gifts
Verbal	Explanation, recognition	Explanation, recognition	Explanation, reminders
Emotional anticipation	Arranging an important role to perform, role model for sibling	Role model for younger brother	Role model of siblings, giving negative and role model examples
Supportive action	Companionship, scaffolding, supportive manner	Companionship, scaffolding, arranging for favorite activity	Companionship, scaffolding
Self-encouragement	Not applicable	Not applicable	Consciously challenging self and explicit aim to build up competences

children) – and related data showed this was effective – the child was happy and motivated to accomplish the task so as to achieve the reward (Leontiev, 1978). With this prompt and task completion, the child quickly became equipped with a positive personal sense, the reward helping to build up the child's personal value and pleasant feelings about completing the task. However, usually the material reward contributed little to help the child understand the meaning behind the demand. Interview data from the mothers indicated that material rewards usually worked well at the beginning, but the effect gradually diminished when the reward lost its attraction in the child's personal sense. It did not work well as a long-term strategy to encourage their children to build their own sense of responsibility.

All the families had created their own *incentive system* to encourage their children to meet demands. The Chan family found its system very effective, the Lee family used an incentive system on and off and found it useful, while the Cheung family had created a marble system to encourage the Cheung children but stopped using it because the children found it unfair, as the rules set for getting the marbles were loose, and it was easy for the younger children to get a reward but hard for the older children. The incentive system created a "really effective motive" psychologically for the children with the result that a positive personal sense was triggered (Leontiev, 2009, p. 365). With the support of the incentive systems, the family values and meaning system of learning were delivered to the child. Although they initially acted as the "only understandable motive" in the children's consciousness, they gradually came through and constructed a new layer of personal meaning, becoming a new "really effective motive" to drive them to acquire the essence of learning and competence (Leontiev, 2009, p. 365).

Verbal explanation was frequently used in all the three families, although differing in the areas of emphasis from family to family. The parents not only placed demands on their children, but also explained the reasons to them. This is very important for the child to be aware of, understand, generalize and develop the same values as those of the parents (Bozhovich, 2009). Verbal explanation can also foster the development of personal sense through the processes of internalization and externalization during social interactions (Lawrence & Valsiner, 2003). Linda emphasized explaining the pros and cons of meeting the demands; for example, when persuading Betty to engage in Kumon lessons, she explained the benefits of doing extra exercises on math and not wasting time "wandering around" at home. Terri focused on explaining cause and effect to Steven. Through explanation, all the three families also transmitted the essence of the Chinese concept of learning to their children, helping the children understand and come in line with their parents' values. *Verbal recognition* and *supportive action* from parents helped promote affective attachment and positive emotions in the children and through close parent–child interactions helped the children better understand their social situations and acquire the same interpretation of these as their parents.

Another form of encouragement used by the families was *emotional anticipation*. Terri started to encourage Steven to be diligent and perform well both at school and at home to act as the role model for his younger brother, Simon. Betty and Micky saw Jenny as their role model and looked forward to achieving academic success and the desire to learn like Jenny. Linda liked to give examples of role models (e.g., her own siblings worked very hard in their school years and now they had very good careers and good lives) and sometimes she gave negative examples to her children, especially Jenny, to help her realize the adverse consequences and not to follow. Supporting anticipation of a future benefit in the children can help them to get a clear meaning and picture of the "goals" and engender positive emotions to drive the children to work toward these goals (Lawrence & Valsiner, 2003). Having positive perceptions and a personal sense of the social situation of their school and enhancement learning helped the children develop the motive for and competence through their learning.

It was discovered from the case of Jenny that encouragement did not come directly from her parents, although it was certainly related to her parents' provision of a conducive environment for her, such as the tuition classes, Kumon and other enhancement learning, which helped her acquire competencies. She could see with the enhancement learning that she could do things better than her peers and, with that, she felt encouraged because she had the competencies (related to perception) and confidence (related to personal sense) to meet different demands. She had built up a form of self-encouragement whereby she felt she could do many things; for her, a learning motive had become fully developed. This form of self-encouragement resulted from family practices.

In general, the role of encouragement is to match the children's perception and personal sense of learning with the institutional demands. In relation to this chapter, the role of encouragement in its various forms is to eventually help achieve the appropriation of the Chinese concept of learning valued by the parents and to develop a positive personal sense of learning.

Conclusion

The cultural–historical approach to understanding children's development emphasizes the importance of interactions between children and social others – such as parents – in their social settings, and the meanings they give to these. Vygotsky argued that cultural, historical, social, cognitive and affective aspects of this construction of meaning should be taken into account, although the last is often under-researched in this approach, as are the mechanisms supporting positive affect toward learning. This chapter has shown how children perceive and make sense of their learning in the social situations their parents have "configured" for them. It is, after all, not simply the parents' demands and highly structured activities, imbued with their own cultural values, which lead inevitably to high achievement; such outcomes are mediated by the ways their children perceive these demands and activities and respond to them. Children contribute thus to their own achievements. Parents' attention and responses to their children's personal sense of learning activities are also critical in the shaping of their children's learning. This chapter has demonstrated how encouragement played an important role in supporting children's development of an achievement-related learning motive, which embraced the Chinese concept of learning. Moreover, it reveals that such encouragement was most effective when it was responsive to the children's understanding and feelings.

It is important that parents not only place demands but use more encouragement in their everyday family practices to help their children to develop motives and acquire competencies. In using encouragement, parents may also need to be more explicit to their children about how they perceive learning and why they value it. Encouragement in various forms should help align the child's perceptions and personal sense of learning and help children appropriate their parents' values to suit their own desires and goals. This in turn would help sustain the outstanding records of academic success of Hong Kong groups in Australia. Findings from this study indicate that encouragement can be different from family to family; the outcome of encouragement is determined by the affordances of the parents and the perceptions and personal sense of their children. Parents may have to use different forms of encouragement with different children. This chapter provides a better understanding of encouragement as a central concept for Hong Kong–Australian children's development of an achievement-related learning motive, yet there is a need for further research on how encouragement is used across a broader sample set and contexts.

Acknowledgements

The participant families presented in this chapter are gratefully acknowledged for their enthusiastic participation and contribution. The author's sincere gratitude goes to Professor Marilyn Fleer for her extensive support and to Professor Bert van Oers for his insightful discussion.

References

Archer, L. & Francis, B. (2007). *Understanding minority ethnic achievement*. London: Routledge.
Bozhovich, L. I. (2009). The social situation of child development. *Journal of Russian and East European Psychology, 47*(4), 59–86.
DIAC. (2006). *Community information summary Hong Kong-born*. Australian Government, Department of Immigration and Citizenship.
Gonzalez Rey, F. L. (2009). Historical relevance of Vygotsky's work: Its significance for a new approach to the problem of subjectivity in psychology. *Outlines, 1*, 59–68.
Guo, K. (2006). Raising children in Chinese immigrant families: Evidence from the research literature. *Australian Journal of Early Childhood, 31*(2), 7–13.
Hedegaard, M. (2008). Developing a dialectic approach to researching children's development. In M. Hedegaard & M. Fleer (Eds.), *Studying children: A cultural-historical approach* (pp. 30–45). Maidenhead, UK: Open University Press.
Hedegaard, M. (2010). *Children's everyday life across institution and how this influences their learning and development: A cultural-historical perspective on children's development*. Paper presented at the 11th International Readings dedicated to the memory of L. S. Vygotsky, Moscow, November 15.
Hedegaard, M. & Fleer, M. (Eds.) (2008). *Studying children: A cultural-historical approach*. Maidenhead, UK: Open University Press.
Lawrence, J. A. & Valsiner, J. (2003). Making personal sense: An account of basic internalization and externalization processes. *Theory & Psychology, 13*(6), 723–752.
Leontiev, A. N. (1978). *Activity, consciousness and personality*. Englewood Cliffs, NJ: Prentice-Hall.

Leontiev, A. N. (2009). *Development of mind: selected works*. Pacifica, CA: Marxists Internet Archive.

Li, G. (2005). Other people's success: Impact of the "Model Minority" myth on underachieving Asian students in North America. *KEDI Journal of Educational Policy, 2*(1), 69–89.

Li, Jin (2001). Chinese conceptualization of learning. *Ethos, 29*(2), 111–137.

Li, Jun (2004). Parental expectations of Chinese immigrants: A folk theory about children's school achievement. *Race, Ethnicity and Education, 7*(2), 167–183.

Mak, A. S. & Chan, H. (1995). Chinese family values in Australia. In R. Hartley (Ed.), *Families and cultural diversity in Australia* (pp. 70–95). Sydney: Allen & Unwin.

Matthews, J. (2002). Racialized schooling, 'Ethnic success' and Asian-Australian students. *British Journal of Sociology of Education, 23*(2), 193–207.

New York Post. (2011, 18 January). *Why I love my strict Chinese mom.* Retrieved from www.nypost.com/p/entertainment/why_love_my_strict_chinese_mom_ uUvfmLcA5eteY0u2KXt7hM.

Nozaki, Y. & Inokuchi, H. (2007). Quantitative, qualitative, and theoretical conversations: Research on Asian American school experiences. *Asia Pacific Journal of Education, 27*(2), 221–232.

Pearce, R. (2006). Effects of cultural and social structural factors on the achievement of White and Chinese American students at school transition points. *American Educational Research Journal, 43*(1), 75–101.

Pe-Pua, R., Mitchell, C., Iredale, R. & Castles, S. (1996). *Astronaut families and parachute children: The cycle of migration between Hong Kong and Australia.* Canberra: Australian Government Publishing Service.

SBS. (2011a, April 30). *Migrant children performance.* [TV broadcast]. SBS 6:30 p.m. World News.

SBS. (2011b). *Dragon children: What's behind the success of Chinese-Australian students?* Retrieved from www.sbs.com.au/dragonchildren/.

Van Oers, B. (2008). Learning and learning theory from a cultural–historical point of view. In B. van Oers, W. Wardekker, E. Elbers & R. Van der Veer (Eds.), *The transformation of learning: Advances in cultural-historical activity theory* (pp. 3–12). Cambridge: Cambridge University Press.

Van Oers, B. (2011). Where is the child? Controversy in the Neo-Vygotskian approach to child development. *Mind, Culture, and Activity, 18*(1), 84–88.

Vygotsky, L. S. (1994). The problem of the environment. In R. Van der Veer & J. Valsiner (Eds.), *The Vygotsky reader* (pp. 338–354). Oxford: Blackwell.

Vygotsky, L. S. (1998). *The collected works of L. S. Vygotsky, Vol. 5: Child psychology* (M. J. Hall, Trans; R. W. Reiber, Ed.). New York: Plenum Press.

Wong, P. L. (2007). The education values of Hong Kong community in Australia: A review of the literature. *ANZCIES 2007 Conference Proceeding*, pp. 313–326.

Wong, P. L. (2012a). Hong Kong-Australian parents' development of values, expectations and practices for their children's education: A dialectical process. In P. W. K. Chan (Ed.), *Asia Pacific education: Diversity, challenges and changes* (pp. 68–86). Melbourne, Australia: Monash University Publishing.

Wong, P. L. (2012b). Parents' perspectives of the home–school interrelationship: A study of two Hong Kong–Australian families. *Australasian Journal of Early Childhood, 37*(4), 59–67.

Wong, P. L. & Fleer, M. (2012). A cultural-historical study of how children from Hong Kong immigrant families develop a learning motive within everyday family practices in Australia. *Mind, Culture and Activity, 19*(2), 107–126.

Wu, Q., Palinkas, L. A. & He, X. (2010). An ecological examination of social capital effects on the academic achievement of Chinese migrant children. *British Journal of Social Work, 40*, 2578–2597.

Zhao, Z. (2000). *Community profiles 1996 census Hong Kong born.* Canberra: Australian Government Publishing Services, Department of Immigration and Multicultural Affairs.

Part 6
Mental plane

16 Cognitive style and achievement through a sociocultural lens

A new way of thinking about style differences

Elizabeth R. Peterson and Kane Meissel

Introduction

Parents and educators have long attempted to gain an understanding of how students learn best and whether the learning process (the way information is encoded, stored and retrieved) and learning environment (time and space) can be altered to facilitate learning. Those interested in this area often find themselves exploring the notion of cognitive or learning styles, or the idea that people have preferred ways of learning and thinking.

Research and opinions about the value of styles are polarized. Some see style as the key to understanding learning differences and, at an extreme, use this as the foundation for their "quasi evangelical crusade to transform all layers of education" (Coffield, Eccleston, Hall, Meagher & Mosely, 2004, p. 125). Advocates such as Prashnig (2000) argue that teachers have a "duty" to teach in a way that matches a student's style (p. 1) and that failure in schools is not because of a poor curriculum, but because instruction is not matched to individual learners. For this reason she claims that "There are no learning disabilities – only TEACHING DISABILITIES" (p. 1, original emphasis).

For others, the style field is disparate, plagued with problems, has no real evidence of validity, is lacking in scientific rigor and is even pointless. As one researcher said: "There is no point in chasing a chimera" (Tiedemann, 1989, p. 273). A review of styles in the journal *Psychological Science in the Public Interest* (2009) concluded:

> at present, there is no adequate evidence base to justify incorporating learning styles assessments into general educational practice. Thus, limited education resources would better be devoted to adopting other educational practices that have a strong evidence base, of which there are an increasing number.
>
> (Pashler, McDaniel, Rohrer & Bjork, 2009, p. 105)

Hence there is considerable disagreement about the value and importance of style for educational achievement. Style researchers are criticized for being oblivious to, or in denial of, the criticisms (Peterson, Rayner & Armstrong, 2009). However, a recent survey of 94 style researchers found that, like the critics, they also reported strong concerns about poor measurement, lack of construct validation, confusing terminology and definitions, and a lack of coherent theory (Peterson et al., 2009). Yet researchers report having continued in the field because they saw value in the application of styles, particularly the allowances made for learning diversity and potential. These findings suggest a strong continued commitment to the field.

This chapter will briefly review the history of style research and differences between the terms learning style and cognitive style. It will then focus solely on cognitive style, giving details of two major models. Next, drawing on recent research findings, this chapter will explore how using a sociocultural lens can add to our understanding of cognitive style differences. Finally, we look at the educational implications of style and consider whether style can be said to make a difference to student learning and achievement.

Brief history of style research

Kozhevnikov (2007) identified four main historical periods of style development (see also Moskvina & Kozhevnikov, 2011). In the first period, cognitive style research evolved from work in the 1940s that focused on identifying and understanding individual differences in performance on perceptual and cognitive tasks, usually conducted in the laboratory. The second phase centered on examining how these individual differences related to other psychological factors, such as intelligence and personality. Learning style research emerged somewhat later (in the 1970s); this third phase focused on the role of style in applied areas and, importantly, included consideration of preferences for particular learning environments (including the type of instruction and activities and the setup of the classroom). The current period of style research focuses on relating style differences to other psychological constructs, such as metacognition, levels of information processing and neuropsychology. Note that little research has been conducted under the style umbrella looking at how such style preference might develop; instead the focus has been on the impact and assessment of such differences.

Definitions of cognitive style and learning style

Research produced across the four main style phases that Kozhevnikov (2007) identifies spans 70 years and has led not only to numerous models and tests of cognitive style and learning style but also to a multitude of definitions. A recent survey of 65 style researchers attempted to reach consensus on the definitions of cognitive style and learning style (Armstrong, Peterson & Rayner, 2012). This was conducted because of a growing concern among style researchers, and their critics, of a lack of clarity around definitions and terminology and, further, that terms were frequently used interchangeably. The study used the Delphi technique (Rescher, 1997), whereby consensus was elicited over three rounds of anonymous online voting. The definitions of learning and cognitive style that emerged from this process were, respectively:

> Cognitive styles refer to individual differences in people's preferred way of processing (perceiving, organizing and analyzing) information using cognitive *brain-based mechanisms and structures*. They are assumed to be *relatively stable and possibly innate*. While cognitive styles can influence a person's behaviour, other processing strategies may at times be employed depending on task demands – this is because they are only preferences.
>
> (Armstrong et al., 2012, p. 450, emphasis added)

and:

> Learning styles are individuals' preferred ways of responding (cognitively and behaviourally) to learning tasks *which change depending on the environment or context*. They can affect a person's motivation and attitude to learning, and shape their performance.
>
> (Armstrong et al., 2012, pp. 451, emphasis added)

Reflecting their different historical backgrounds, these two definitions vary most in terms of the degree to which style is seen as stable, fixed and innate (cognitive style) versus modifiable and changeable through interactions with the environment (learning styles). This chapter focuses on cognitive styles. Two popular cognitive style models are described below.

Popular cognitive style models

The Field Dependence–Independence cognitive style was the first to be identified (Witkin & Asch, 1948a, 1948b) and remains the most studied and influential cognitive style dimension (Desmedt & Valcke, 2004). Many dimensions of cognitive style are conceptually similar to the Field Dependence–Independence dimension, with each researcher either being oblivious to the existence of similar dimensions disguised under different names, or determined to stamp their mark by naming their own dimensions (e.g., Impulsivity and Reflectivity dimension: Kagan, Rosman, Day, Albert & Philips, 1964; Levellers and Sharpeners: Holzman & Klein, 1954; Divergent–Convergent Thinking: Guilford, 1967; Holist–Serialist: Pask & Scott, 1972; Wholistic–Analytic: Riding, 1991; Global Analytic and Impulsive Reflective dimensions: Dunn, Dunn & Price, 1989, etc.). The observation that there are numerous names for similar dimensions is not new. In 1976, Lewis noted that in style research "we have a situation in which different groups of researchers seem determined to pursue their own pet distinctions in cheerful disregard of one another" (p. 305).

Witkin's field independent and field dependent cognitive style

The Field Dependence–Independence dimension (Witkin & Asch, 1948a, 1948b) has attracted mostly empirical, laboratory-based research. Witkin and colleagues developed three main tests of the dimension. The Rod and Frame test (Witkin & Asch, 1948a) involves the participant trying to orientate a rod that is in a tilted frame to the true vertical position. Differences were found in the extent to which participants could quickly rotate the rod to the actual vertical position (field independent) as opposed to those who rotated the rod so it was in line with the tilted frame (field dependent). This task was similar to the body adjustment task (Witkin, 1950), which involved a person trying to orientate themselves to an upright position while sitting in a chair in a tilted room. Finally, the group Embedded Figures test (Witkin, Oltman, Raskin & Kidd, 1971) is a paper and pencil test that involves detecting shapes within other more complex shapes. Individuals who are faster at finding the hidden shapes were similarly argued to be field independent since they were not overly affected or distracted by the more complex shape. All three tests are argued to be highly correlated (Witkin & Goodenough, 1981).

   Research. A substantial and wide range of research has been conducted on the Field Dependence–Independence dimension, ranging from associations with educational outcomes (e.g., Tinajero & Paramo, 1998) to more specific findings, such as susceptibility to paranormal beliefs (e.g., Hergovich, 2003). With respect to educational outcomes, field independence has been associated with greater levels of academic success than field dependence (e.g., Tinajero & Paramo, 1998; Roberge & Flexer, 1983). Field-independent students also have better problem-posing ability and pose more complex problems (Nicolaou & Xistouri, 2011). The dimension has also been related to academic and career choices (e.g., Goodenough et al., 1979; Guisande, Fernanda Paramo, Soares & Almeida, 2007). While there is substantial research on the correlates with Field Dependence–Independence, the mechanisms by which these preferences are developed has been largely ignored. In part, this is due to the underlying assumption that these style differences are hard-wired and hence not easily changed.

The strongest criticism of the Field Dependence–Independence dimension has consistently been its failure to demonstrate independence from cognitive ability. In a review of the research using the Embedded Figures test, McKenna (1984) concluded that field dependence had substantial and numerous correlates with general intelligence tests, particularly spatial ability and performance (as opposed to verbal) tests. Therefore, it is likely that the associations with educational outcomes may be partially due to the substantial shared variance between field dependence and intelligence.

Riding's cognitive style analysis

Currently popular in the UK and Europe (Rezaei & Katz, 2004), Riding's (1991) cognitive style analysis (CSA) test is a computerized measure of cognitive style and is argued to overcome some of the problems associated with performance-based style tests. This test has typically been used in educational settings and to date has been cited in at least 62 publications by 98 different researchers. Riding's style test developed out of a review of 30 cognitive styles and the conclusion that most of them measured two broad dimensions of cognitive style: the verbal–imagery dimension and the wholistic–analytic dimension. Riding (1998) subsequently proposed a new computerized CSA test to measure these dimensions. The test assesses style by calculating how quickly participants respond to questions involving semantic (verbal) versus color (imagery) relationships and how rapidly they respond to questions that involve either identifying if two figures are the same (wholistic) or identifying if one figure is embedded within another figure (analytic).

Riding argued that their CSA test was a breakthrough because the test: (i) is objectively measured; (ii) fulfills the requirements of a style; (iii) has dimensions which are independent of one another; (iv) has dimensions which are separate from intelligence; (v) is independent of personality; (vi) is related to observed behaviors; and (vii) relates to physiological measures (see Riding & Rayner, 1998). A host of studies has also been conducted to establish these claims (see Riding, 2002, for a review).

In addition, the fact that the CSA's dimensions (wholistic–analytic and verbal–imagery) appear to have grown out of existing style theories is seen as a strength. In particular, the CSA's wholistic–analytic dimension was argued to broadly encompass earlier style theories, such as Field Dependence–Independence, Holist–Serialist, Levelling–Sharpening and Impulsivity–Reflectivity (Riding & Cheema, 1991). The verbal–imagery dimension is historically less established. However, it is argued by Riding and Cheema (1991) to broadly encompass the ideas of Dual Coding (Paivio, 1971), the Verbalizer–Visualizer Questionnaire (Richardson, 1977) and the Verbal–Imagery Code test (Riding & Calvey, 1981; also Riding & Rayner, 1998, for a review).

Research. Riding has published numerous articles exploring the validity of the CSA, including demonstrating that style is not directly related to performance on intelligence tests (Riding & Pearson, 1994) and personality (Riding & Wigley, 1997). However, style may interact with cognitive ability, such that style seems to be more critical when pupils are of a lower ability (Riding & Agrell, 1997).

Performance on the CSA test has also been related to learning preferences, such that imagers reported liking more pictures and less writing than verbalizers, while group work was most popular with wholists, especially lower-ability wholists and imagers (Riding & Read, 1996). The CSA has also been related to behavioral problems, with wholists and verbalizers more susceptible (Riding & Craig, 1999). Finally, Riding and colleagues have provided further evidence of the importance of cognitive style, indicating relationships with preferred structure of learning material (Riding & Sadler-Smith, 1992; Riding & Douglas, 1993), learning content (Riding & Dyer, 1980) and subject (Riding & Staley, 1998), as well as levels of stress (Borg & Riding, 1993) and even localized brain activity, indicated by differing electroencephalogram outputs for individuals with different style preferences (Glass & Riding, 1999). However, like the research on the Field Dependence–Independence dimension, the process by which these preferences may develop has been ignored.

Despite the extensive program of research carried out on the CSA and attempts to demonstrate its validity, Riding has not published the test's reliability. Reliability was finally established in the early 2000s (Peterson, Deary & Austin, 2003; Rezaei & Katz, 2004) and found to be poor. This calls into question how so many papers could be published concerning the test's validity when the underlying measure was so unreliable. This lack of stability led Peterson and colleagues to redesign the verbal–imagery dimension and to lengthen the wholistic–analytic dimension (Peterson, Deary & Austin, 2005a, 2003). Acceptable test–re-test and internal consistency scores for the revised versions were achieved, and the revised test's independence from personality and ability was demonstrated (Peterson, Deary & Austin, 2005b). However, to date, these revised tests of Riding's verbal–imagery and wholistic–analytic style have largely gone unvalidated, despite demonstrating improved reliability.

In summary, while there is an ever-growing body of research on these two key models of style, both have been heavily criticized, particularly for their reliability, which arguably should be attainable if the construct being measured is relatively stable and fixed, and the measurement tool is appropriate. One possible explanation for this is that the construct may not be as stable as researchers think and that social and cultural differences may shape the development and use of particular cognitive styles, making them less stable than researchers have argued. Vygotsky's (1978) sociocultural model of learning may be able to provide some answers or future research directions, if applied to cognitive style research.

Vygotsky's approach to learning and development

The key tenet of Vygotosky's work is that social experiences and culture shape human development from birth (Daniels, 2001) and hence human development cannot be investigated without acknowledging the role of both. Children also play an active role by influencing the forces that shape them (Daniels, 2001; Moll, 1990).

Vygotsky acknowledges that, although individuals are born with a set of basic skills, abilities and reflexes and are actively involved in their own learning, it is by interacting with the environment that the basic mental functions (e.g., attention, sensation perception and memory) are developed into higher mental functions (McLeod, 2007). Hence intellectual development is a mediated process whereby culturally produced tools (e.g., ideas, signs, symbols) develop, shape and are shaped by interactions with the world (Daniels, 2011); in particular, by interactions with "more knowledgeable others", who can help individuals learn the processes required to later independently perform the action. Therefore, how humans think and act (even when alone) is argued to be a function of the beliefs, values and tools of the culture in which they have grown up.

Cognitive style and Vygotsky

To apply a Vygotskian approach to styles, it seems that styles should be studied in terms of how they develop, change and grow in interaction with those around them: They should not be studied in isolation. Indeed, Vygotsky used the analogy of analyzing water in terms of its component parts (hydrogen and oxygen), noting that this level of analysis will never explain the characteristics of the whole (Moll, 1990).

Cognitive styles do not seem to fit well with Vygotskian theory; first because of the focus on biologically based, hard-wired, cognitive preferences, and second because attempts to isolate differences in these preferences are often done within laboratory-based settings using empirical tasks. This seems to be very removed from the idea that the social environment might play a crucial role in cognitive style development.

Even though Vygotsky was primarily interested in studying the individual by examining the whole activity rather than the sub-skills, he did not ignore the role of biological factors, arguing that it is not possible to study higher-order processes without a study of their biological roots and fundamental attributes (Daniels, 2011).

In acknowledging the role of biology and the existence of potentially elementary processes, it seems that cognitive styles should not be excluded from study under a Vygtoskian framework. In fact, research on cultural differences in perceptual processing suggests that this line of research may prove fruitful.

Cultural differences in cognitive styles

Cross-cultural differences have not been investigated for Riding's (1991) CSA test. However, the possibility of such differences was raised for Witkin's cognitive style dimensions as early as 1976 by John Berry, but has received very little attention from style researchers since then. Berry argued that individuals from migratory cultures were more likely to be field independent, whereas those from historically more sedentary, agricultural cultures were more likely to be field dependent. These differences were thought to be due to socialization, whereby the cognitive style that was most appropriate for the environment was the one that developed. Those from more agricultural societies developed close social structures and the need to accommodate others' social needs, whereas those from hunter–gatherer societies focused more on controlling the environment and less on conformity and autonomy (Ji, Peng & Nisbett, 2000). A few studies using Witkin's original style measures have found some support for this general trend (e.g., Engelbrecht & Natzel, 1997; Ji et al., 2000).

More recently, cognition and perception researchers have started to explore how the natural and cultural aspects of development work together to influence cognition using a variety of different perceptual tasks, including face perception, reasoning, Navon stimuli, Stroop tasks and framing tasks (e.g., Kitayama, Duffy, Kawamura & Larsen, 2003; Miyamoto, Yoshikawa & Kitayama, 2011; Nisbett & Miyamoto, 2005; Norenzayan, Smith, Kim & Nisbett, 2002).

For example, in a study by Norenzayan et al. (2002), participants were asked to judge to which group of flowers a target flower was most similar (see Figure 16.1). As shown in Figure 16.1, the Group 1 flowers have many features in common with the target flower on the left, but the flowers in Group 1 have no features that are common across all of them. Hence Group 1 can be argued to be holistically similar to the target. The Group 2 flowers all have the same stem as the target flower on the left, but other than that, are quite different. Hence the flowers in Group 2 have a common unidimensional rule, but are otherwise quite different. Results from this study found that East Asians were more likely to identify the target flower as similar to Group 1 (those with more global family resemblances), while European Americans were more likely to identify the target object as similar to those from Group 2, which shared a common unique feature (the same stem). Multiple studies have

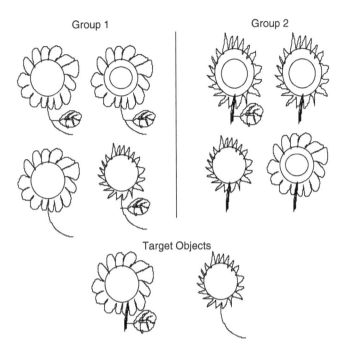

Figure 16.1 Example of stimuli used in the Norenzayan et al. (2002) study

now found a similar pattern to this. That is, East Asian participants notice contextual information and relationships, and are argued to be field dependent or have a global advantage over Caucasian Westerners (Kitayama et al., 2003; Masuda & Nisbett, 2001; McKone et al., 2010; Miyamoto et al., 2011; Nisbett & Miyamoto, 2005). Consequently, it is now well established that cultural differences influence information processing. This research has not been conducted by style researchers, but by cognitive researchers interested in understanding the more fundamental development of cognitive processes and cognitive preferences. Consequently, these cultural differences in traditional cognitive style tests have not been explored.

The question then becomes how these cultural differences came about. Researchers have suggested that the different values placed on independence and interdependence in different cultures are reflected in everyday tasks and activities which serve to reinforce cultural differences in neural activities in the brain (Kitayama & Park, 2010). For example, Miyamoto, Nisbett and Masuda (2006) found that, even in the everyday physical environments in which Westerners and East Asians grow up, there are differences that may encourage different perceptual and cognitive development. Miyamoto et al. (2006) compared photos of schools, hotels and post offices in different Japanese and American cities and found the Japanese perceptual environments were often more complex and ambiguous and contained more objects than the related American environment. They subsequently showed that Japanese students were better at spotting the differences (between two similar pictures of everyday scenes) than American students, due to their ability to spot contextual and relational changes (e.g., the height of a pole or the location of a truck). Similar findings were found by Masuda and Nisbett (2001).

Even from a young age, culture has been argued to affect perception and attention. For example, when labeling toys, Japanese mothers tend to point out relational and contextual aspects, often using toys in rituals of social exchange, whereas American mothers focused more on the toy overall and were more likely to name it when playing with their infants (Fernald & Morikawa, 1993). A review by Park and Huang (2010) concluded that these differences in environments over time seem to be reflected by changes in neural functioning and in particular activation in areas of the brain associated with processing perceptual information. This fits with Vygotsky's idea that the development occurs via the internalization of the cognitive processes explored in this social apprenticeship-type model.

Interestingly, however, these cultural biases in perception have been found to be flexible and may be related to the individual's social orientation at any given time. That is, researchers have found that, when students who are bicultural are reminded of experiences associated with one of their identities (e.g., as an American or an Asian) and are given an attribution task, those who are primed with an American identity tend to make fewer contextual attributions and more physical attributions than those primed toward an Asian identity (Peng & Knowles, 2003). This finding, in particular, questions the fixed nature of cognitive styles.

Overall, Nisbett and Miyamoto (2005) argue that studies on cultural differences in cognition indicate that perception cannot be considered a universal process and that social and cultural differences shape perception and cognition in important ways. Hence, culture and biology interact to affect cognitive outcomes.

These findings, derived from the cognitive psychology field, suggest that researchers investigating cognitive styles need to consider the importance of the social and cultural environment in which learning takes place, as well as a need to move beyond the laboratory to look at how cognitive style differences might develop. By acknowledging the role of the environment and social context in learning, the lack of reliability of many style measures may also be explained. Finally, this research suggests the need to reconsider the degree to which cognitive styles are viewed as hard-wired or fixed.

Style, education and achievement

In this book entitled *Constructing Educational Achievement*, it is appropriate to turn to the question of whether style adds anything to our understanding of student achievement.

Within education, there is an increasing call to acknowledge cultural differences in learning processes (Charlesworth, 2011). This is underscored by the fact that the number of international tertiary students studying abroad has increased more than four-fold in the last 30 years, with 3.7 million OECD students enrolled outside their country of origin in 2009 (OECD, 2011).

Charlesworth (2011) argues that an understanding of styles is one way in which teachers and students can begin to recognize, understand and help deal with our increasingly diverse student population. Similarly, in the field of management and business with increasing globalization, there is a call for managers and business people to work sensitively and manage people across cultures (Yamazaki & Kayes, 2004, 2010).

However, when it comes to academic achievement, and whether style plays a role, to date the research does not support this notion. This is contrary to what many think and is the opposite of what drives many people toward finding out about style in the first place. Indeed, it was hearing a story about a bright university student who was failing miserably until he discovered "how he learnt best" that was the motivator for the first author of this chapter to undertake research in this field. Driving this was the concern that there were many others who were bright, but unaware of how they learnt best. If you are a parent or a teacher looking for an explanation for a low-achieving or struggling student, style certainly seems to be a potential answer and solution.

Unfortunately, the reality is that, despite 60 years of research on cognitive style and 40 years on learning styles, there continues to be no direct evidence that matching teaching to students' styles makes a big enough difference to academic outcomes to warrant the amount of time and money invested. John Hattie's (2009) synthesis of 800 meta-analyses related to achievement concludes that matching to style has an average effect size of 0.41 on student achievement. If we accept Hattie's benchmark that effect sizes greater than 0.4 (the average effect size in education) are worth more attention than those less than 0.4 (note that other factors such as additivity, time required, cost and interaction effects should also be considered), then this suggests that matching to students' learning styles may be of marginal practical value.

In comparison, the effect sizes of factors that look at the more sociocultural influences on achievement are also not as high as might be expected. Hattie's (2009) meta-synthesis found that the average effect size for home factors on achievement was 0.31, for school factors it was 0.23 and for teacher factors it was 0.49. This suggests that the teacher has on average the strongest influence on student academic outcomes and has a larger effect on average than the school or home environment or style type (if 0.41 is taken as the average style effect size). However, caution must be taken when reporting average effect sizes as they can hide much variance associated with individual factors.

However, it is important to note that Hattie's (2009) analysis combines the effects of very different cognitive style and learning style measures. Hattie's synthesis, therefore, collapses across a broad range of style measures, confounds learning style with cognitive style and is dominated by research relating to one particular learning style that has been heavily criticized.

If the measures of cognitive style and learning style are separated out and looked at individually, the picture is even worse. A meta-analysis which included (among others) two cognitive style tests (Witkin's and Riding's) and their relation to achievement in hypertext and technology-enhanced environments found that the average effect sizes ranged from 0.06 to 0.19 and only Witkin's learning style measure found significant interaction between style, learning environment and achievement (Slemmer, 2002). However, both Hattie's (2009) and Slemmer's (2002) meta-analyses only include studies that have looked at matching teaching or learning environments to students' styles and vice versa. Evans and Waring (2009, 2012) have argued that the matching approach ignores the complexity of the style profile of any one individual and hence a meta-analysis based on the impact of matching learning or teaching to an individual's style and its subsequent effect on achievement may be misleading.

Nevertheless, whether a student's style is matched or not, overall, it seems that style research to date has not demonstrated any sizable and practical level of influence on student achievement in over 60 years, and this raises the question of whether the field should be abandoned altogether. Unsurprisingly, style researchers argue it should not. While acknowledging that the style field suffers from issues of reliability and validity (Peterson et al., 2009), they believe it continues to have pedagogical value (see recent edited books by Rayner & Cools, 2011; Zhang, Sternberg & Rayner, 2012). A common justification is that learning about styles reminds us of the diversity of approaches people take to any given task and, as such, it helps people to be more accepting, tolerant and sensitive of differences we face in the home, school, workplace and beyond (Peterson, Carne & Freear, 2011). Having a questionnaire or tool that makes these differences salient (however accurate), if used appropriately, can be a useful way to start thinking about individual differences. As a practical example, teachers, before doing large assignments that require considerable team or group work, may find that some discussion of different styles and ways of learning and thinking may help to increase respect for the differences in the approaches taken to the tasks. On the individual level, a student who takes the time to reflect on their own style of learning and the fact that others approach learning differently can be encouraged to try out alternative ways of learning material (e.g., using mind maps rather than writing notes). In doing this, students also become more metacognitively aware, self-regulating and may also adopt a deeper approach to learning (Evans & Waring, 2012).

Evans and Waring (2012) also argue that, with respect to education, future style research needs to take into account the complex nature of learning. That is, rather than looking at single styles and their impact on, for example, achievement, researchers need to look at the interactions between styles themselves and also between styles and cognitive strategies, learning approaches and learning environments. Hence, future style researchers may need to adopt a broader view of the learner and explore style as a potential moderator or mediator of achievement outcomes.

In summarizing the research on style and achievement, it seems that style can help students to understand that people approach learning and everyday tasks differently and that these differences are largely unrelated to their knowledge, abilities and personalities. Style helps draw attention to these often unnoticed everyday differences. It is important to remember that these style preferences are subtle and not fixed, and it is vital that people are not seen as being placed in discrete categories, with style preference used as an excuse for poor learning outcomes. As Yates (2000) said:

> the documented evidence of such natural tendencies does not indicate the need for differential educational planning or curriculum implementation . . . however, the concept of cognitive style can play a major role in helping educators become sensitive to naturally occurring individual differences in encoding and reacting tendencies.
>
> (p. 362)

Conclusion

In this chapter, we have established that there are both strong advocates and strong critics of style research. At face value, styles seem to exist: We see them in our classroom, our workplaces and across cultures, but the tools designed to assess them continue to have measurement challenges and there is little evidence that matching style preferences improves student achievement. Instead, the best advice seems to be to use style as a way of making alternative approaches to learning salience and in doing so increase metacognition. This in turn is likely to help increase sensitivity, tolerance and understanding for learning differences.

Finally, to date, style research has largely occurred in isolation from other cognitive psychology research and has tended to focus on measurement and applications, rather than on understanding their development. In taking a sociocultural lens to the style construct, we find that cognitive preferences seem to be shaped, at least partially, by the sociocultural environments in which we live and grow. Taking a more sociocultural lens to style, therefore, allows us to engage with the important question of how style differences develop and why they might change, potentially making their measurement less stable. This ultimately lays the foundations for new and significant directions for cognitive style researchers to explore.

References

Armstrong, S. J., Peterson, E. R. & Rayner, S. G. (2012). Understanding and defining cognitive style and learning style: A Delphi study in the context of educational psychology. *Educational Studies, 38*, 449–455.

Berry, J. W. (1976). *Human ecology and cognitive style: Comparative studies in cultural and psychological adaptation.* New York: Halsted Press, Sage Publications.

Borg, M. G. & Riding, R. J. (1993). Teacher stress and cognitive style. *British Journal of Educational Psychology, 63*(2), 271–286.

Charlesworth, Z. M. (2011). Cultures of learning: Cultures of style. In S. Rayner & E. Cools (Eds.), *Style differences in cognition, learning and management: Theory, research and practice* (pp. 224–236). New York: Routledge.

Coffield, F., Eccleston, K., Hall, E., Meagher, N. & Mosely, D. (2004). *Learning styles and pedagogy in post-16 learning: A systematic and critical review.* London: Learning and Skills Development Agency.

Daniels, H. (2001). *Vygotsky and pedagogy.* London: Routledge Falmer.

Daniels, H. (2011). Vygotsky and psychology. In U. Goswami (Ed.), *The Wiley-Blackwell handbook of child cognitive development* (pp. 673–696). Oxford: Blackwell Publishers Ltd.

Desmedt, E. & Valcke, M. (2004). Mapping the learning styles "jungle": An overview of the literature based on citation analysis. *Educational Psychology, 24*(4), 445–464.

Dunn, K., Dunn, R. & Price, G. E. (1989). *Learning styles inventory.* Lawrence, KS: Price Systems.

Engelbrecht, P. & Natzel, S. G. (1997). Cultural variations in cognitive style – field dependence vs field independence. *School Psychology International, 18*(2), 155–164.

Evans, C. & Waring, M. (2009). The place of cognitive style in pedagogy: Realizing potential in practice. In L. F. Zhang & R. J. Sternberg (Eds.), *Style differences in cognition, learning, and management: Theory, research and practice* (pp. 188–203). New York: Routledge.

Evans, C. & Waring, M. (2012). Applications of styles in educational instruction and assessment. In L. F. Zhang, R. J. Sternberg, R. J. Rayner & S. G. Rayner (Eds.), *Handbook of intellectual styles* (pp. 295–328). New York: Springer Publications.

Fernald, A. & Morikawa, H. (1993). Common themes and cultural variations in Japanese and American mothers' speech to infants. *Child Development, 64*(3), 637–656.

Glass, A. & Riding, R. J. (1999). EEG differences and cognitive style. *Biological Psychology, 51*(1), 23–41.

Goodenough, D. R., Oltman, P. K., Friedman, F., Moore, C. A., Witkin, H. A. & Raskin, E. (1979). Cognitive styles in the development of medical careers. *Journal of Vocational Behavior, 14*(3), 241–351. doi:10.1016/0001-8791(79)90062-9

Guilford, J. P. (1967). *The nature of human intelligence.* New York: McGraw-Hill.

Guisande, M. A., Fernanda Paramo, M., Soares, A. P. & Almeida, L. S. (2007). Field-dependence-independence and career counseling: Directions for research. *Perceptual and Motor Skills, 104*(2), 654–662.

Hattie, J. A. C. (2009). *Visible learning: A synthesis of over 800 meta-analyses relating to achievement.* London: Routledge.

Hergovich, A. (2003). Field dependence, suggestibility and belief in paranormal phenomena. *Personality and Individual Differences, 34*, 195–209.

Holzman, P. S. & Klein, G. S. (1954). Cognitive systems principles of levelling and sharpening: Individual differences in visual time-error assimilation effects. *Journal of Psychology, 37*, 105–122.

Ji, L., Peng, K. & Nisbett, R. E. (2000). Culture, control, and perception of relationships in the environment. *Journal of Personality & Social Psychology, 78*(5), 943–945.

Kagan, J., Rosman, B., Day, D., Albert, J. & Philips, W. (1964). Information processing and the child: Significance of analytic and reflective attitudes. *Psychological Monographs, 78*(1), 1–37.

Kitayama, S., Duffy, S., Kawamura, T. & Larsen, J. T. (2003). Perceiving an object and its context in different cultures: A cultural look at new look. *Psychological Science, 14*(3), 201–206.

Kitayama, S. & Park, J. (2010). Cultural neuroscience of the self: Understanding the social grounding of the brain. *Social Cognitive and Affective Neuroscience, 5*(2–3), 111–129.

Kozhevnikov, M. (2007). Cognitive style in the context of modern psychology: Towards an integrated framework of cognitive style. *Psychological Bulletin, 133*(3), 464–481.

Lewis, B. N. (1976). Avoidance of aptitude-treatment trivialities. In Messick and Associates, *Individuality in learning* (pp. 301–308). San Francisco, CA: Jossey-Bass Publishers.

McKenna, F. P. (1984). Measures of field dependence: Cognitive style or cognitive ability. *Journal of Personality and Social Psychology, 47*(3), 593–603.

McKone, E., Davies, A. A., Fernando, D., Aalders, R., Leung, H., Wickramariyaratne, T. & Platow, M. J. (2010). Asia has the global advantage: Race and visual attention. *Vision Research, 50*(16), 1540–1549.

McLeod, S. A. (2007). *Simple psychology: Vygotsky.* Retrieved from www.simplypsychology.org/vygotsky.html.

Masuda, T. & Nisbett, R. E. (2001). Attending holistically versus analytically: Comparing the context sensitivity of Japanese and Americans. *Journal of Personality & Social Psychology, 81*(5), 922–934.

Miyamoto, Y., Nisbett, R. E. & Masuda, T. (2006). Culture and the physical environment: Holistic versus analytic perceptual affordances. *Psychological Science, 17*(2), 113–119.

Miyamoto, Y., Yoshikawa, S. & Kitayama, S. (2011). Feature and configuration in face processing: Japanese are more configural than Americans. *Cognitive Science, 35*(3), 563–574.

Moll, L. C. (1990). Introduction. In *Vygotsky and education: Instructional implications and applications of sociohistorical psychology* (pp. 1–30). Cambridge, UK: Cambridge University Press.

Moskvina, V. & Kozhevnikov, M. (2011). Determining cognitive style. In S. Rayner & E. Cools (Eds.), *Style differences in cognition learning and management: Theory, research and practice* (pp. 19–31). New York: Routledge.

Nicolaou, A. A. & Xistouri, X. (2011). Field dependence/independence cognitive style and problem posing: An investigation with sixth grade students. *Educational Psychology, 31*(5), 611–627.

Nisbett, R. E. & Miyamoto, Y. (2005). The influence of culture: Holistic versus analytic perception. *Trends in Cognitive Science, 9*(10), 467–473.

Norenzayan, A., Smith, E. E., Kim, B. J. & Nisbett, R. E. (2002). Cultural preferences for formal versus intuitive reasoning. *Cognitive Science, 26*, 633–684.

OECD. (2011). *Education at a glance.* Paris: OECD Publishing.

Paivio, A. (1971). *Imagery and verbal processes.* New York: Holt, Reinhart & Winston.

Park, D. C. & Huang, C. M. (2010). Culture wires the brain: A cognitive neuroscience perspective. *Perspectives on Psychological Science, 5*(4), 391–400.

Pashler, H., McDaniel, M., Rohrer, D. & Bjork, R. (2009). Learning styles: Concepts and evidence. *Psychological Science in the Public Interest, 9*(3), 105–119.

Pask, G. & Scott, B. C. E. (1972). Learning strategies and individual competence. *Journal of Man-Machine Studies, 4*, 217–253.

Peng, K. & Knowles, E. (2003). Culture, ethnicity and the attribution of physical causality. *Personality and Social Psychology Bulletin, 29*, 1272–1284.

Peterson, E. R., Carne, S. S. & Freear, S. J. (2011). Teaching secondary students about style: Should we do it? In S. Rayner & E. Cools (Eds.), *Style differences in cognition, learning and management* (pp. 160–172). New York: Routledge.

Peterson, E. R., Deary, I. J. & Austin, E. J. (2003). The reliability of Riding's cognitive style analysis test. *Personality and Individual Differences, 34*(5), 881–891.

Peterson, E. R., Deary, I. J. & Austin, E. J. (2005a). A new measure of verbal-imagery cognitive style: VICS. *Personality and Individual Differences, 38*(6), 1269–1281.

Peterson, E. R., Deary, I. J. & Austin, E. J. (2005b). Are intelligence and personality related to verbal-imagery and wholistic-analytic cognitive styles? *Personality and Individual Differences, 39*(1), 201–213.

Peterson, E. R., Rayner, S. G. & Armstrong, S. J. (2009). Researching the psychology of cognitive style and learning style: Is there really a future? *Learning and Individual Differences, 19*, 518–523.

Prashnig, B. (2000). Learning styles – Here to stay. *Education Today, 2*, 30–31. Retrieved from www.webbps.com/asktbs/sas/HereToStay.pdf.

Rayner, S. & Cools, E. (2011). *Style differences in cognition, learning and management.* New York: Routledge.

Rescher, N. (1997). *Predicting the future: An introduction to the theory of forecasting.* Albany, NY: State University of New York Press.

Rezaei, A. R. & Katz, L. (2004). Evaluation of the reliability and validity of the cognitive styles analysis. *Personality and Individual Differences, 36*(6), 1317–1327.

Richardson, A. (1977). Verbalizer–visualizer: A cognitive style dimension. *Journal of Mental Imagery, 1*, 109–125.

Riding, R. (1991). *Cognitive style analysis – CSA administration.* Birmingham: Learning & Training and Technology.

Riding, R. (1998). *Cognitive styles analysis – Research applications.* Birmingham: Learning & Training Technology.

Riding, R. (2002). The nature and effects of cognitive style. In R. J. Sternberg & L. F. Zhang (Eds.), *Perspectives on thinking, learning and cognitive styles* (pp. 47–72). New Jersey: Lawrence Erlbaum Associates.

Riding, R. & Agrell, T. (1997). The effect of cognitive style and cognitive skill on school subject performance. *Educational Studies, 23*(2), 311–323.

Riding, R. J. & Calvey, I. (1981). The assessment of verbal-imagery learning styles and their effect on the recall of concrete and abstract prose passages by 11-year-old children. *British Journal of Psychology, 72*, 59–64.

Riding, R. & Cheema, I. (1991). Cognitive styles – an overview and integration. *Educational Psychology, 11*(3&4), 193–215.

Riding, R. & Craig, O. (1999). Cognitive style and types of problem behaviour in boys in special schools. *British Journal of Educational Psychology, 69*(3), 307–322.

Riding, R. & Douglas, G. (1993). The effect of cognitive style and mode of presentation on learning performance. *British Journal of Educational Psychology, 63*(2), 297–307.

Riding, R. J. & Dyer, V. A. (1980). The relationship between extraversion and verbal-imagery learning style in twelve-year-old children. *Personality and Individual Differences, 1*, 273–279.

Riding, R. J. & Pearson, F. (1994). The relationship between cognitive style and intelligence. *Educational Psychology, 14*(4), 413–425.

Riding, R. & Rayner, S. (1998). *Cognitive styles and learning strategies.* London: David Fulton.

Riding, R. J. & Read, G. (1996). Cognitive style and pupil learning preferences. *Educational Psychology, 16*, 81–106.

Riding, R. J. & Sadler-Smith, E. (1992). Type of instructional material, cognitive style and learning performance. *Educational Studies, 18*, 323–340.

Riding, R. J. & Staley, A. (1998). Self-perception as learner, cognitive style and business studies students' course performance. *Assessment and Evaluation in Higher Education, 23*, 43–58.

Riding, R. J. & Wigley, S. (1997). The relationship between cognitive style and personality in further education students. *Personality and Individual Differences, 23*(3), 379–389.

Roberge, J. J. & Flexer, B. K. (1983). Cognitive style, operativity, and mathematics achievement. *Journal for Research in Mathematics Education, 14*(5), 344–353.

Slemmer, D. L. (2002). The effect of learning style on student achievement in various hypertext, hypermedia, and technology-enhanced learning environments: A meta-analysis. (Unpublished doctoral dissertation.) Idaho: Boise State University.

Tiedemann, J. (1989). Measures of cognitive style: A critical review. *Educational Psychologist, 24*(3), 261–275.

Tinajero, C. & Paramo, M. F. (1998). Field dependence-independence cognitive style and academic achievement: A review of research and theory. *European Journal of Psychology of Education, 13*(2), 227–251.

Vygotsky, L. S. (1978). *Mind in society.* Cambridge, MA: MIT Press.

Witkin, H. A. (1950). Perception of the upright when the direction of the force acting on the body is changed. *Journal of Experimental Psychology, 40*, 93–106.

Witkin, H. A. & Asch, S. E. (1948a). Studies in space orientation, III. Perception of the upright in the absence of a visual field. *Journal of Experimental Psychology, 38*, 603–614.

Witkin, H. A. & Asch, S. E. (1948b). Studies in space orientation, IV. Further experiments on perception of the upright with displaced visual field. *Journal of Experimental Psychology, 38*, 762–782.

Witkin, H. A. & Goodenough, D. R. (1981). *Cognitive styles: essence and origins.* New York: International Universities Press.

Witkin, H. A., Oltman, P. K., Raskin, E. & Kidd, A. H. (1971). *A manual for the embedded figures test.* Palo Alto, CA: Consulting Psychologists Press.

Yamazaki, Y. & Kayes, D. C. (2004). An experiential approach to cross-cultural learning: A review and integration of competencies for successful expatriate adaptation. *Academy of Management Learning and Education, 3*(4), 362–379.

Yamazaki, Y. & Kayes, D. C. (2010). Learning and work satisfaction in Asia: A comparative study of Japanese, Chinese and Malaysian managers. *International Journal of Human Resource Management, 21*(12), 2271–2289.

Yates, G. C. R. (2000). Applying learning style research in the classroom: Some cautions and the way ahead. In R. J. Riding & S. G. Rayner (Eds.), *International perspectives on individual differences* (pp. 347–365). Stamford, CT: Ablex Publishing Company.

Zhang, L. F., Sternberg. R. J. & Rayner, S. (Eds.). (2012). *Style differences in cognition, learning, and management: Theory, research and practice.* New York: Routledge.

17 The role of verbal reasoning in critical thinking

Kelly Y. L. Ku

Introduction

Teaching for critical thinking is a fundamental aim of modern education. In the past decade, it has been listed as a top priority in educational reports of countries of the West and the East, including the United States, United Kingdom, Australia, Hong Kong China, and Japan (see reports of Association of American Colleges and Universities, 2005; Australian Council for Educational Research, 2002; Higher Education Quality Council, 1996; Hong Kong Education Bureau, 2003; and discussion in Atkinson, 1997). The information society is characterized by abundant but fast-changing information. To assess information in a critical manner is a prerequisite to academic achievement in higher education, which has been emphasizing the application of critical thinking skills to connect knowledge of different disciplines for a multidisciplinary understanding of global issues (Chan, 2005).

In general, thinking concerns the method of generating and deciding among potential actions and beliefs (Baron, 2000), whereas critical thinking concerns the strategic use of cognitive skills to maximize favorable outcomes in the course of finding and choosing among possible actions (Halpern, 1998). This chapter makes use of Vygotsky's (1965) view on the relation between language and thought as a basis to explore the role of language-based reasoning, or verbal reasoning, in critical thinking. In Vygotsky's work, he mainly referred the term "verbal thinking" to thoughts presented through speech. This chapter adopts a broader definition that refers verbal reasoning ability to competence in language-based analysis and evaluation of written and spoken information. Overall, the term describes the ability to comprehend text in a precise manner, the sensitivity to subtext, embedded assumptions, ambiguous and loaded language, and the fluency in concept formation and expression (Halpern, 1998, 2003b). Mainly, I put forth the argument that how well a person thinks is either empowered or confined by his or her ability to use language to reason. Empirical findings on the relationships between students' verbal reasoning ability and critical thinking performance are presented. I make a particular reference to a recent investigation of Chinese secondary and undergraduate students that has revealed differentiated performance with critical thinking tasks that ask for self-constructed and forced-choice answers. The chapter closes with a highlight on the social dimension to critical thinking, in which culturally specific dispositions about the kinds of thinking that are encouraged or prohibited may be deep-rooted in social experiences. How culturally specific dispositions are likely to influence the way we approach thinking is discussed. The implication being that nurturing an inclination toward critical thinking which encourages making personal thought known to others in social contexts is a prerequisite for verbal reasoning to be valued and cultivated in Chinese students.

232 *Kelly Y. L. Ku*

The role of language in thinking

We reason with words. Language is the tool for constructing, shaping, and understanding ideas. In critical thinking, the relation between language and thought is reciprocal; we use language to articulate thoughts and the language we use in turn guides and shapes our thinking processes (Halpern, 2003b). This linkage precisely echoes Vygotsky's (1965) view on the development of language and thought, in which he termed the relation among the two "a living process":

> The relation of thought to word is not a thing but a process, a continual movement back and forth from thought to word and from word to thought. In that process the relation of thought to word undergoes changes which themselves may be regarded as development in the functional sense.
>
> (p. 125)

Every thought serves an intellectual function through word. Language does not only act to organize and integrate thoughts, but it *advances* one's cognition as more sophisticated use of language breeds the development of more sophisticated thinking. Vygotsky holds that the advancement of language and thought takes place both privately within an individual and publicly through verbal-based interactions between an individual and his environments. The social-based nature of cognition is much stressed by Vygotsky, in which social experiences have an impact on the way we approach thinking (Wertsch, 1985). In view of that, this chapter explores both the significance of language and the social–cultural dimension to critical thinking.

Vygotsky's view on the interlocking dynamic between language and thought is exemplified in critical thinking, a form of applied informal reasoning. Very often, critical thinking makes a false impression on people as being equivalent to formal logic, where in fact the two share more differences than similarities. In this chapter, I attempt to distinguish the nature of critical thinking from that of formal logic. The distinction between the two is a prerequisite to understanding the particular meaning of relying on language to reason in the process of critical thinking, and is further discussed in the following section.

Defining critical thinking

Characteristics of non-everyday reasoning – formal logic

I begin the orientation to the conception of critical thinking by drawing a line between critical thinking and formal logic. Traditionally, training for thinking has been emphasized on acquiring the skills of logic. Yet formal logic is a rather restrictive form of reasoning and in many cases does not describe how we commonly think in everyday living (Scriven, 2003; Baron, 2000). Formal logic concerns the absolute principles or rules of correct reasoning. Consider this argument:

> All As are Bs. (first premise)
> All Cs are As. (second premise)
> Therefore, All Cs are Bs. (conclusion)

In determining whether the conclusion necessarily follows from the two given premises, language is largely irrelevant. The line of reasoning can be represented by mere symbols and the conclusion would hold regardless of what A or B stands for. Formal logic does not illustrate how we normally think for two reasons. One is that in everyday life we rely on language to draw inference while language plays a relatively isolated role in formal logic. On the contrary, in everyday thinking, when we process information we first pay attention to the semantic meanings of a piece of information. The fact that the line of logic in an argument often comes after its semantic meaning is demonstrated in the following arguments where words are used instead of symbols.

> Some Women are Teachers.
> Some Teachers are Painters.
> Therefore, Some Women are Painters.

I anticipate many of us would evaluate the conclusion as valid. Now, let us look at another argument with the same structure:

> Some Women are Teachers.
> Some Teachers are Fathers.
> Therefore, Some Women are Fathers.

The two arguments share the exact same logical structure. Yet there is a tendency to judge the first argument as valid while the second as invalid. The reason why we would tend to judge the first argument as valid is because its conclusion resembles something that is compatible with our experience in the real world (Evans, Over, & Manktelow, 1993), in which some women are indeed painters. However, in the second argument, the conclusion that some women are fathers is obviously out of place because women cannot be fathers to our mind. What is just being demonstrated is that, in determining what constitutes logical and illogical, we apparently have relied on the semantic meanings of the argument, as opposed to focusing on its logical structure. This phenomenon describes a fallacy that is *natural* to human thinking, which highlighted the important role of language in everyday reasoning. The second reason why formal logic does not illustrate how we normally think is that information is often, if not always, incomplete and uncertain in real-life situations. Yet, for formal logic tasks, premises are always given and are certain (assumed to be true regardless of whether they are in fact true or false), hence an individual is given complete information for evaluation. With complete information, an absolute conclusion is possible in reasoning, in which it can be either valid or invalid; there is no room for multiple conclusions or for a conclusion to be probative.

In sum, features of formal logic are very much unlike the kind of thinking we undertake in daily life in two ways: (1) The line of reasoning in formal logic is detached from the language of the argument. It has its concern in the absolute principles of correct reasoning (Baron, 2000), while in everyday reasoning we use the semantic meaning to evaluate an argument. (2) Information given in a formal logic task is often complete and certain, whereas in day-to-day thinking we are to deal with tentative and incomplete information (this point will be further illustrated in the following section). Hence formal logic describes how we ought to think, instead of how we normally would think.

Characteristics of everyday reasoning – critical thinking

On the contrary, critical thinking describes the kind of informal reasoning in everyday contexts where we draw *probative* inferences (Scriven, 2003) from fuzzy information, and arrive at one or more conclusions with a high enough probability/desirability within a given

234   *Kelly Y. L. Ku*

context. Earlier definitions of critical thinking conceptualized it as a set of skills, a mental process, or simply as rationality (Baron, 1985; Ennis, 1962; McPeck, 1981). For instance, Ennis defines critical thinking as "correct assessing of statements" (Ennis, 1962, p. 81), in which the focus was on the thinking method and rules of formal logic instead of the implications of thoughts. Recent conceptions reflect a broader perspective that takes into account the goals and contexts of thoughts. For instance, Halpern provides a more elaborated definition as "the use of those cognitive skills or strategies that increase the probability of a desirable outcome. . . . [and] is purposeful, reasoned, and goal directed – the kind of thinking involved in solving problems, formulating inferences, calculating likelihoods, and making decisions" (2003a, p. 6). Likewise, Paul and Elder (2004) define critical thinking as the "mode of thinking about any subject, content or problem in which the thinker improves the quality of his or her thinking by skillfully taking charge of the structures inherent in thinking and imposing intellectual standards upon them" (p. 1).

Standards and principles of critical thinking are therefore informal, multifaceted in nature and highly context dependent (i.e., a conclusion may be true in one context but not in another) (Scriven, 2003). To say that critical thinking adopts informal standards is not to imply that it is peripheral or open to fallacious reasoning, but to acknowledge that in everyday reasoning we can at best arrive at possible, as opposed to absolute, conclusions because real-life issues do not present themselves in black-and-white terms; we are therefore always dealing with uncertain and ambiguous information. Unlike the domain of formal logic, critical thinking is, by definition, context-dependent. It denotes standards of good thinking given various limitations imposed by real-life situations where we cannot afford certainty and precision in information. Critical thinking concerns not just the conclusion but by what means the conclusion is derived, and in what manner the conclusion is meeting the needs and goals of a given context. These characteristics of critical thinking do not only require but demand complex use of verbal reasoning to support assessment of information, evaluation of claims and beliefs, as well as defending and persuading a point of view.

Skills in verbal reasoning and critical thinking performance

The role of verbal reasoning ability in critical thinking has not been clear. Skills in verbal reasoning are less associated with critical thinking in comparison to skills in analytical and scientific reasoning. Table 17.1 presents a summary of skills proposed by various scholars as essential to critical thinking.

Though skills in verbal reasoning are listed by a few scholars, they are not as frequently associated with critical thinking as skills in analytical and scientific reasoning; they are even more rarely taught explicitly and systematically in classrooms. For instance, there have not been any empirical studies that have examined the effect of training skills in verbal reasoning on students' critical thinking performance, or that have pointed to the importance of the linkage between language and critical thinking. Previous studies investigating the effectiveness of critical thinking training have mostly focused either on the teaching of a particular category of skill, such as inductive reasoning skill (Fong, Krantz, & Nisbett, 1986) and statistical reasoning (Kosonen & Winne, 1995; Neilens, Handley, & Newstead, 2009), or on a particular type of approach (i.e., direct instruction versus inquiry-based instruction) in enhancing general critical thinking competence (e.g., Semerci, 2006; Angeli & Valanides, 2009). These studies vary in terms of factors such as educational level of participants, length of intervention, content of training, and assessment of critical thinking; as a result, evidence has been mixed and difficult to translate into real-life classroom practices.

The role of verbal reasoning in critical thinking 235

Table 17.1 Summary of essential skills to critical thinking proposed by various scholars

Scholars	Cognitive skills essential to critical thinking
Watson & Glaser (1980)	1. Inferences – discriminating true and false inferences 2. Recognition – recognizing a stated or unstated assumption 3. Deduction – deciding whether certain conclusions can be made by following the given information 4. Interpretation – weighing the available evidence and deciding whether a generalization can be made 5. Evaluation of arguments – making judgments on the salience of inferences
Beyer (1984)	1. Distinguishing between verifiable facts and values claims 2. Determining the reliability of a source 3. Determining the factual accuracy of a statement 4. Distinguishing relevant from irrelevant information, claims, or reasons 5. Detecting bias 6. Identifying ambiguous or equivocal claims of arguments 7. Recognizing logical inconsistencies or fallacies 8. Distinguishing between warranted and unwarranted claims 9. Determining the strength of an argument
Facione (1990)	1. Interpretation – categorizing, decoding significance, and clarifying meaning 2. Analysis – examining ideas, identifying arguments, and analyzing arguments 3. Evaluation – assessing claims and arguments 4. Inference – querying evidence, conjecturing alternatives, and drawing conclusions 5. Explanation – stating results, justifying procedures, and presenting arguments 6. Self-regulation – engaging in self-examination and self-correction
Dick (1991)	1. Identifying arguments – identifying issues, reasons, and conclusions 2. Analyzing arguments – identifying assumptions and ambiguity, and seeking additional information 3. External sources – avoiding value postures and the use of emotional language 4. Scientific analytic reasoning – relating observations to determine cause and using proper statistical judgment 5. Reasoning and logic – providing analogy and deduction; applying general reasoning principles
Halpern (1998)	1. Verbal reasoning skills – comprehending and defending against persuasive techniques that are embedded in everyday language 2. Argument analysis skills – being aware of facts that run counter to the conclusion, stated and unstated assumptions, irrelevant information, and intermediate steps that lead to a conclusion 3. Skills in hypothesis testing – formulating beliefs or hypotheses and using the information collected to decide whether it confirms or disproves the hypotheses 4. Likelihood and uncertainty – using probabilities and likelihood correctly 5. Decision-making and problem-solving skills – generating, selecting, and judging alternatives

Empirical evidence: Predictors of critical thinking performance

In general, a number of factors have been proposed to be related to a student's critical thinking performance. Those that have been identified empirically as making such a contribution include school achievement (Marin & Halpern, 2011), thinking disposition of open-mindedness (Clifford, Boufal, & Kurtz, 2004), an inclination toward evidence-based thinking (Ku & Ho, 2010), beliefs about the nature of knowledge as tentative and non-absolute (Chan, Ho, & Ku, 2011), and verbal-based cognitive ability (Taube, 1997; Toplak & Stanovich, 2002). Among these factors, verbal-based cognitive ability is consistently shown to be the strongest predictor (further elaborated in the preceding paragraphs), while the contribution of school achievement is inconsistent. A moderate correlation has been reported in a sample of American undergraduates' grade point average and their critical thinking performance (Marin & Halpern, 2011). However, utilizing the same critical thinking assessment, grade point average was found to be unrelated to critical thinking performance in a sample of Chinese Hong Kong undergraduates (Ku & Ho, 2010). These findings suggested that high achievers in school might not naturally be better thinkers and pointed to the possibility that school assessment in the US might be able to better capture and reflect students' critical thinking compared to that of Hong Kong.

There is some initial evidence for the contribution made by verbal reasoning ability to critical thinking performance. For instance, Clifford, Boufal, and Kurtz (2004) looked at the relative contribution made by different cognitive abilities to undergraduates' performance on a critical thinking assessment. Three cognitive domains (i.e., Perceptual Organization, Verbal Comprehension, and Working Memory) of the Wechsler Adult Intelligence Scale, Third Edition (WAIS-III, 2002), a composite intelligence test commonly used as an estimate of individuals' cognitive strengths and weaknesses (Groth-Marnat, 2003), were examined. Scores from the WAIS-III are not interpreted as fixed, unchangeable, and innate (Groth-Marnat, 2003). The test measures individuals' cognitive abilities in four sub-domains or indexes: Working Memory, Perceptual Organization, Verbal Comprehension, and Processing Speed. The non-verbal domain of Perceptual Organization consists of subtests that assess perceptual cognitive abilities or non-verbal reasoning (Groth-Marnat, 2003). These include problem solving and matrix reasoning that relies on spatial and visual-motor skills, whereas the domain of Verbal Comprehension consists of subtests that are presented in the form of oral questions. The test materials tap into verbal knowledge, verbal concept formation, and ability to express ideas with words and to infer meanings from language-based social rules and conventions. Clifford and colleagues (2004) found that the verbal domain subtest score was the only unique predictor of critical thinking performance; cognitive abilities, including attention, concentration, and short-term memory skills, as well as non-verbal abstract reasoning skills, as examined by the Perceptual Organization and Working Memory subtests, made no contribution. Similarly, a more recent investigation (Ku & Ho, 2010) with Chinese university students found that verbal reasoning ability, as measured by the Verbal Comprehension subtests of the WAIS-III, accounted for 20% of the unique variance in critical thinking performance.

Assessment of critical thinking and verbal reasoning ability

The findings on the significant contribution made by verbal-based reasoning ability are interesting as they contradict the common perception that good thinking relies primarily on abstract reasoning. To further illustrate the importance of language-based assessment of information and articulation of one's thoughts in critical thinking, I present here preliminary findings from a recent investigation of Chinese high school and university undergraduates' critical thinking competence as measured by the Chinese version of the Halpern Critical Thinking Assessment (HCTA; Halpern, 2007). The HCTA is a critical thinking assessment that allows multi-response format. The HCTA was administered to 135 and 642 local students who were attending university and high school, respectively. The assessment consists of 25 scenario-based questions. The questions are set in authentic contexts, with each question asking for both open-ended responses and multiple-choice responses. That is, test-takers are required to answer the same question twice; first in their own words, and then by selecting appropriate option(s) from a given list of alternatives. I include here a hypothetical item that is similar in the form and nature to those of the HCTA:

The role of verbal reasoning in critical thinking   237

Scenario: A group of parents from the ABC Secondary School is circulating a petition that states "since teachers who are friends with students will lose respect from their students, the school should not allow teachers to engage in non-teaching-related activities with students after school hours."

Open-ended question: Would you sign this petition? State "yes" or "no" and explain your answer.

Forced-choice question: Based on this information, which of the following is the best answer? (Six choices provided; students may choose more than one choice.)

Sample choice: A friendly teacher–student relationship and respect from students are not mutually exclusive.

The question was a decision-making task that consisted of an argument set in a believable situation. The structure of the argument goes: since X (premise *"teachers who are friends with students will lose respect from their students"*), then Y (conclusion *"the school should not allow teachers to engage in non-teaching-related activities with students after school hours"*). The question requires the test-taker to state whether they would support the petition. To make the decision, test-takers must first evaluate the validity and soundness of the argument presented. Regardless of whether an individual agrees or disagrees with the petition, he or she will be given marks as long as the justifications are consistent with their points of view. A list of possible ways to go about answering this question is as follows:

Questions the truthfulness of the premise *"teachers who are friends with students will lose respect from their students."* Individual may choose not to support the petition by pointing out that the truthfulness of the premise is in question because there is no justification provided to support the premise. He or she may suggest that there is no known evidence for the imbedded assumption that a friendly teacher–student relationship will cause or result in disrespect. Whether the premise is true, false, or unknown affects the validity of the conclusion and the strength of the argument.

Questions the effectiveness of the conclusion (i.e., *"the school should not allow teachers to engage in non-teaching-related activities with students after school hours"*). Individual may provide justifications for the premise but argue that the conclusion is not an effective solution.

Points out ambiguity. Marks can also be earned if he or she questions the ambiguity that lies in the ideas/phrases, such as *"are friends with students"* and *"teaching-related activities."*

Exact marks to be given depend upon quality of reasons and evidence generated, as well as whether the answer was articulated precisely. High marks reflect a comprehensive approach in the test-taker's evaluation of the issue, combined with language facility. This example highlights the characteristics of critical thinking tasks that are putting students in a disadvantaged position if they are not sensitive to word meanings or do not possess the verbal skills that are needed to elaborate, defend, or persuade a point of view.

Our preliminary findings utilizing this test have provided us with a glimpse into how thoughts may be limited by a person's competence to use language to reason. In the investigation, 135 undergraduates answered all 25 questions, while the 642 secondary students answered 10 questions selected from the HCTA. Paired-sample t-tests using the nonparametric method revealed that performance on the multiple-choice questions is significantly better than the open-ended questions for the undergraduates and the secondary students ($p < 0.001$ in both samples). The implication is that, given the same questions, students were more able to recognize and select the correct answers from a given list, but they were less able to organize and express the right answers using their own words. The HCTA was selected as the instrument for assessing students' critical thinking competence because it effectively captured the multifaceted nature of critical thinking. It requires the test-taker to think from more than one perspective. The two-part response format of the HCTA tests somewhat different abilities and skills: The open-ended part tests an individual's ability to generate, construct, and articulate solutions on his or her own, whereas the multiple-choice part is a test of recognition – responses that are correct or are more appropriate are to be identified among a list of alternatives (Halpern, 2007).

Context that facilitates verbal reasoning ability: Nurturing a habit of mind that values open exchange of thoughts in students

To enhance verbal reasoning ability, a context that allows open and fair exchange of thoughts is vital. As Vygotsky (1978) put forth, full cognitive development of the mind requires a context that enables exchange of thoughts. For young children, learning about ideas of themselves and others first takes place in the circle of immediate family members. This circle later extends to peers and teachers, by the time children begin to grasp abstract propositions and prepositional logic, and eventually to the society. A person's social context communicates to this person not only the criteria and standards of good thinking, but also the dispositions of good thinking that are culturally specific: What approaches to thinking are encouraged or prohibited?

Thinking habits are grounded in the belief systems, values, and attitudes of a culture (Atkinson, 1997; Perkins, Jay, & Tishman, 1993). They are "tendencies toward patterns of intellectual activity that condition and guide cognitive behavior specifically" (Perkins et al., 1993, p. 6). The literature describes a critical thinker as "habitually inquisitive, well-informed, trustful of reason, open-minded, flexible, fair-minded in evaluation, honest in facing personal biases, prudent in making judgments, willing to reconsider" (Facione, 1990, p. 2).

Cross-cultural studies examining traits relating to critical thinking of Chinese and Western students revealed interesting patterns that bear resemblance as well as differences. Students of both cultures rated themselves alike in intellectual curiosity and willingness to appreciate new points of view. Compared to students in the United States and Australia, Chinese students perceived themselves as less inclined to search for evidence that runs counter to their ideas and beliefs and were reported to be less confident about their own ability to think critically (Ip et al., 2000; McBride, Xiang, Wittenburg, & Shen, 2002; Tiwari, Avery, & Lai, 2003). These findings describe not actual differences in ability but a relatively lower self-efficacy and a reluctance to commit to objective truth in reasoning of the Chinese students. Students of both cultures experience similar pleasure in thinking but differ in their approaches and regard toward what underlines good thinking.

Thinking dispositions of Chinese students

Chinese students' patterns of thinking habits, as revealed in the above findings, might to some extent be attributed to the Chinese culture. Though a part of the Chinese culture has been seen as integrating values of the global society well, the core part of it has its roots in the Confucian philosophy, which is generally viewed as valuing social harmony, compliance, and the experiences of the ancestors (Kim, 2003; Yang & Lin, 2004). The collectivist culture emphasizes social relationships in which the individual's behavior is often dependent on and determined by others (Atkinson, 1997). Knowledge is somewhat reliant on an expert's or authority's opinion when making decisions or solving problems, and this is viewed positively by the Chinese, as it is a way to show respect and maintain group unity (McBride et al., 2002). Thus, people are often reluctant to voice their thoughts, not due to incompetency, but "for fear of offending" (McBride et al., 2002), since "frankness, abruptness, or criticism that causes humiliation is avoided in public in order to maintain harmonious interpersonal relationships" (Yeh, 2002).

Verbal discussion and inclination to engage in critical thinking

In recent education reforms in Hong Kong, autonomous thinking has been stressed, yet teachers of conventional Chinese classrooms struggle to find their way to nurture critical thinking. The nurturance of a critical mind in students must not be oversimplified to a list of independent cognitive operations (Facione, 1990). In the training of critical thinking, controversial problems set in authentic contexts are frequently utilized, such as the Drug Patent issue of the World Trade Ordinance, genetic engineering, same-sex marriage, family planning policy in China, and global-warming and global-cooling theories, to name a few. These problems share several features: (1) They can be understood differently, from different perspectives, and frequently lead to polarized viewpoints; (2) They challenge the assumptions underlying our conventional beliefs in social, economic, scientific, and political domains; (3) It is likely that these issues may evoke a certain degree of emotional involvement in the process of reasoning and hence are more prone to biases; (4) There exists no single absolute conclusion. Together they pose a set of new challenges to teachers and students: Critical discourse in the classroom is essential in helping students to move beyond "either/or" reasoning as multiple conclusions can be derived through different means that may all seemingly be "correct." Yet our students are less familiar and at ease when sharing what they think with others. They are given less opportunity to practice independent thinking and are less inclined to express personal thoughts or to challenge others' ideas.

Facilitating critical thinking through reasoned discussion of ill-structured controversial issues is not an easy task. Dialogues between students in discussion-based learning activities can easily "deteriorate into unproductive free-for-alls on the one hand, or thinly veiled recitations with occasional student comments on the other—and neither is likely to lead to the benefits envisioned for open discussion" (Barton & McCully, 2007, p. 1). Thoughts are internal conversations that must be made external for a discussion to be effective and meaningful. For critical discourse to take place in classrooms, it requires language to be seen in relation to how a single thought is formed, reasonably connected to a chain of thoughts, precisely articulated into concepts, and fluently presented and defended. Teachers should encourage students to clarify their opinions, identify embedded assumptions and loaded language in dialogues, and have students comment on the impact of the different use of language on the presented ideas. These will nurture in students the essential skills of verbal reasoning, which will enable them to read beyond the literal or surface meaning of text and to identify how people seek to manipulate others through their choice of words. In addition, verbal reasoning skills are best cultivated in a community of inquiry, one that sets open, reflective, and intellectual discussion as ground rules (Tishman, Jay, & Perkins, 1993). In such context, students learn to expect and respect open sharing of diverse views, reflect on

240 *Kelly Y. L. Ku*

biases and unstated assumptions, and develop skills in defending and persuading a point of view in a reasoned manner. This practice gives emphasis to verbal-based exchange of thoughts and helps to nurture an inclination toward critical discourse in classrooms.

Concluding thoughts

Critical thinking is a form of reflective and self-regulatory thinking that helps a person to evaluate and decide what to believe and do (Ennis, 1987; Halpern, 1998). The urge for critical thinking education is in part a response made to the shift in higher education's purpose from teaching knowledge to teaching skills of knowledge construction (Kuhn, 2007). The new educational goal aims for students to engage in global, social, and political issues in a way that is justified and free of biases. Yet information in today's society, though abundant, often comes in forms that are hectic, ambiguous, manipulative, or deceptive. Words can be used deliberately to encourage or discriminate a particular belief or inclination and, in so doing, exert an influence on the way we think. Disruptive language and reasoning emerge in political speeches, advertisements, and various forms of texts that we encounter on a daily basis. The whirl of fast-changing and messy information increases the complexity of discerning facts from opinions and truthfulness from falsehood, placing an immense impact on our understanding of the world's issues.

Vygotsky's sociocultural theory points out that thinking cannot be done in a vacuum without language, nor can it be understood in isolation of the social context. This chapter has focused on the linkage between language and thought. Through examining the features of critical thinking, I have pinpointed the importance of language-based reasoning ability in engaging in informal reasoning. Thoughts may be empowered or limited by verbal reasoning ability. Initial empirical findings supporting a significant role of verbal reasoning ability in critical thinking performance are presented. However, cognitive skills that are commonly suggested for teaching in schools emphasize skills in logic, abstract reasoning, scientific thinking, and argument analysis (e.g., Beyer, 2001; Browne, Haas, & Keeley, 1978; Dick, 1991; Ennis, 1962; Facione, 1990). These skills are undoubtedly important to critical thinking, but they are better learned and applied with the support of a sophisticated verbal reasoning ability.

Lastly, an individual's critical thinking has a cultural dimension to it, as values and beliefs of the social context form the basis of disposition toward thinking. Verbal reasoning competence is of foremost importance to a modern education that aims for students "to use their minds well, in school and beyond" (Kuhn, 2007, p. 110). This chapter has emphasized the importance for teachers to create a culture of critical inquiry that encourages open-mindedness and fair sharing of views in order to foster a positive inclination toward critical thinking, as well as to provide students with the opportunities to practice verbal reasoning skills in constructive discussions about real-life issues.

References

Angeli, C., & Valanides, N. (2009). Instructional effects on critical thinking: Performance on ill-defined issues. *Learning and Instruction, 19*(4), 322–334. doi: 10.1016/j.learninstruc.2008.06.010

Association of American Colleges and Universities. (2005). *Liberal education outcomes: A preliminary report on student achievement in college*. Washington, DC: AAC&U. Retrieved from www.aacu.org/advocacy/pdfs/leap_report_final.pdf.

Atkinson, D. (1997) A critical approach to critical thinking in TESOL. *TESOL Quarterly, 31*(1), 71–94. *doi*:10.2307/3587975

Australian Council for Educational Research. (2002). *Graduate skills assessment*. Australia: Commonwealth of Australia. Retrieved from www.aair.org.au/app/webroot/media/pdf/AAIR%20Fora/Forum2002/Butler.pdf.

Baron, J. (1985). *Rationality and intelligence*. New York, NY: Cambridge University Press.

Baron, J. (2000). *Thinking and deciding* (3rd ed.). Cambridge, MA: Cambridge University Press.

Barton, K., & McCully, A. (2007). Teaching controversial issues where controversial issues really matter. *Teaching History, 127*, 13–19.

Beyer, B. K. (1984). Improving thinking skills: Practical approaches. *Phi Delta Kappan, 65*(8), 556–560.

Beyer, B. K. (2001). What research says about teaching thinking skills. In A. L. Costa (Ed.), *Developing minds: A resource book for teaching thinking* (pp. 275–282). Alexandria, VA: ASCD.

Browne, M. N., Haas, P. F., & Keeley, S. M. (1978). Measuring critical thinking skills in college. *The Educational Forum, 42*(2), 219–226.

Chan, D. W. (2005). Liberalizing liberal studies in pre-university education in Hong Kong: Leadership development and beyond. *Educational Research Journal, 20*(1), 1–14.

Chan, N. M., Ho, I. T., & Ku, K. Y. L. (2011). Epistemic beliefs and critical thinking of Chinese students. *Learning and Individual Differences, 21*, 67–77. doi: http://dx.doi.org/10.1016/j.lindif.2010.11.001

Clifford, J. S., Boufal, M. M., & Kurtz, J. E. (2004). Personality traits and critical thinking skills in college students: Empirical tests of a two-factor theory. *Assessment, 11*(2), 169–176. doi: 10.1177/1073191104263250

Dick, W. (1991). An instructional designer's view of constructivism. *Educational Technology, 31*(5), 41–44.

Ennis, R. H. (1962). A concept of critical thinking. *Harvard Educational Review, 32*, 81–111.

Ennis, R. H. (1987). A taxonomy of critical thinking dispositions and abilities. In J. B. Baron & R. J. Sternberg (Eds.), *Teaching thinking skills: Theory and practice* (pp. 9–26). New York, NY: W. H. Freeman.

Evans, J. St. B. T., Over, D. E., & Manktelow, K. I. (1993). Reasoning, decision making and rationality. *Cognition, 49*, 165–187. doi:10.1016/0010-0277(93)90039-X

Facione, P. A. (1990). *Critical thinking: A statement of expert consensus for purposes of educational assessment and instruction ("The Delphi Report")*. Retrieved from ERIC database (ED315423).

Fong, G., Krantz, D., & Nisbett, R. (1986). The effects of statistical training on thinking about everyday problems. *Cognitive Psychology, 18*(3), 253–292. doi: 10.1016/0010-0285(86)90001-0

Groth-Marnat, G. (2003). *Handbook of psychological assessment* (4th ed.). Hoboken, NJ: John Wiley & Sons, Inc.

Halpern, D. F. (1998). Teaching critical thinking for transfer across domains: Dispositions, skills, structure training, and metacognitive monitoring. *American Psychologist, 53*(4), 449–455. doi: 10.1037/0003-066X.53.4.449

Halpern, D. F. (2003a). The "how" and "why" of critical thinking assessment. In D. Fasko, Jr. (Ed.), *Critical thinking and reasoning: Current research, theory and practice* (pp. 355–366). Cresskill, NJ: Hampton Press.

Halpern, D. F. (2003b). *Thought and knowledge: An introduction to critical thinking* (4th ed.). Mahwah, NJ: Lawrence Erlbaum Associates.

Halpern, D. F. (2007). *Halpern Critical Thinking Assessment: Background and scoring standards*. Claremont, CA: Claremont McKenna College.

Higher Education Quality Council, Quality Enhancement Group. (1996). *What are graduates? Clarifying the attributes of "graduateness"*. London: HEQC.

Hong Kong Education Bureau. (2003). *Progress report on the Education Reform (3)*. Hong Kong: Education Bureau.

Ip, W. Y., Lee, D. T. F., Lee, R. F. K., Chau, J. P. C., Wooton, R. S. Y., & Chang, A. M. (2000). Disposition towards critical thinking: A study of Chinese undergraduate nursing students. *Journal of Advanced Nursing, 32*, 84–90. doi: 10.1046/j.1365-2648.2000.01417.x

Kim, H.-K. (2003). Critical thinking, learning and Confucius: A positive assessment. *Journal of Philosophy of Education, 37*, 71–87. doi: 10.1111/1467-9752.3701005

Kosonen, P., & Winne, P. (1995). Effects of teaching statistical laws on reasoning about everyday problems. *Journal of Educational Psychology, 87*, 33–46. doi: 10.1037/0022-0663.87.1.3

Ku, K. Y. L., & Ho, I. T. (2010). Dispositional factors predicting Chinese students' critical thinking performance. *Personality and Individual Differences, 48*(1), 54–58. doi: 10.1016/j.paid.2009.08.015.

Kuhn, D. (2007). Is direct instruction an answer to the right question? *Educational Psychologist, 42*, 109–113.

McBride, R. E., Xiang, P., Wittenburg, D., & Shen, J. (2002). An analysis of preservice teachers' dispositions toward critical thinking: A cross-cultural perspective. *Asia-Pacific Journal of Teacher Education, 30*, 131–140. doi:10.1080/13598660220135649

McPeck, J. E. (1981). *Critical thinking and education*. New York, NY: St. Martin's Press.

Marin, L.M., & Halpern, D.F. (2011). Pedagogy for developing critical thinking in adolescents: Explicit instruction produces greatest gains. *Thinking Skills and Creativity, 6*, 1–13. doi: 10.1016/j.tsc.2010.08.002

Neilens, H. L., Handley, S. J., & Newstead, S. E. (2009). Effects of training and instruction on analytic and belief-based reasoning processes. *Thinking & Reasoning, 15*(1), 37–68. doi: 10.1080/13546780802535865

Paul, R., & Elder, L. (2004). *The nature and functions of critical and creative thinking*. Dillon Beach, CA: Foundation for Critical Thinking.

Perkins, D. N., Jay, E., & Tishman, S. (1993). Beyond abilities: A dispositional theory of thinking. *Merrill-Palmer Quarterly, 39*(1), 1–21.

Scriven, M. (2003). The philosophy of critical thinking and informal logic. In D. Fasko, Jr. (Ed.), *Critical thinking and reasoning* (pp. 21–45). Cresskill, NJ: Hampton Press.

Semerci, N. (2006). The effect of problem-based learning on the critical thinking of students in the Intellectual and Ethical Development Unit. *Social Behavior and Personality: An International Journal, 34*(9), 1127–1136. doi: 10.2224/sbp.2006.34.1.41

Taube, K. T. (1997). Critical thinking ability and disposition as factors of performance on a written critical thinking test. *Journal of General Education, 46*, 129–164.

Tishman, S., Jay, E., & Perkins, D. (1993). Teaching thinking dispositions: From transmission to enculturation. *Theory into Practice, 32*(3), 147–153.

Tiwari, A., Avery, A., & Lai, P. (2003). Critical thinking disposition of Hong Kong Chinese and Australian nursing students. *Journal of Advanced Nursing, 44*, 298–307. doi: 10.1046/j.1365-2648.2003.02805.x

Toplak, M. E., & Stanovich, K. E. (2002). The domain specificity and generality of disjunctive reasoning: Searching for a generalizable critical thinking skill. *Journal of Educational Psychology, 94*(1), 197–209. doi: 10.1037//0022-0663.94.1.197

Vygotsky, L. S. (1965). *Thought and language* (E. Hanfmann & G. Vakar, Eds. & Trans.). Cambridge, MA: MIT Press, Massachusetts Institute of Technology.

Vygotsky, L. S. (1978). *Mind in society: The development of higher psychological processes*. Cambridge, MA: Harvard University Press.

Watson, G., & Glaser, E. M. (1980). *Watson-Glaser critical thinking appraisal*. Cleveland, OH: Psychological Corporation.

Wechsler Adult Intelligence Scale-Third Edition (Chinese Version) (2002). San Antonio, TX: The Psychological Corporation.

Wertsch, J. V. (1985). *Vygotsky and the social formation of mind*. Cambridge, MA: Harvard University Press.

Yang, S. C., & Lin, W. C. (2004). The relationship among creative, critical thinking and thinking styles in Taiwan high school students. *Journal of Instructional Psychology, 31*(1), 33–45.

Yeh, C. J. (2002). Taiwanese students' gender, age, interdependent and independent self-construal, and collective self-esteem as predictors of professional psychological help-seeking attitudes. *Cultural Diversity and Ethnic Minority Psychology, 8*, 19–29.

18 Cognitive perturbation with dynamic modelling

A reconceptualization of conceptual change in science education

Sandy C. Li and Jacky W. C. Pow

Introduction

In the past decades, the advancement of computer technologies has opened up a new horizon in scientific investigations and science education. Computer modelling technologies provide new opportunities for scientists to explore the domains of phenomena that are inaccessible via existing experimental techniques alone (Hilder, Gordon & Chung, 2010; Hilder, Yang et al., 2010; Kuyucak & Li, 1995a, 1995b; Li, Hoyles, Kuyucak & Chung, 1998; Li & Kuyucak, 1996). Likewise, computer modelling has been widely used in education to help students formulate hypotheses and articulate their own explanations for various natural phenomena (Tao & Gunstone, 1999; Wenning, 2008). Through these exploratory and expressive activities, students are then able to externalize thoughts as well as to interact with them (Bliss & Ogborn, 1989; Li, 2006, 2011; Wright, 2008). In this way, students are given the chance to learn scientific theories in a richly contextualized environment by theorizing and evaluating their own hypotheses (van Joolingen, de Jong & Dimitrakopoulou, 2007; Windschitl & Andre, 1998).

We believe that these computer-supported modelling activities are effective means to facilitate students' conceptual change through engaging them in the learning activity and enabling them to represent and explore their thoughts collaboratively, and that they provide conceptual anchors to help bridge students' zones of proximal development (Vygotsky, 1978). If conceptual change is a journey of advancing knowledge by building better theories in a contextualized environment, computer modelling is an appropriate and desirable tool for students to externalize their thoughts and to make conjecture and refutation of their own theories. While Vygotsky's notion of the zone of proximal development (ZPD) provides insights into understanding students' conceptual development, it gives no account for how students' conceptual understandings advance and develop in their ZPD. We argue that, coupled with appropriate instructional strategies, computer modelling tools help portray students' paths of conceptual understanding and at the same time provide individualized scaffolding to facilitate student learning.

Classical conceptual change models

Conceptual change models (CCM) were emerging in science education in the early 1980s and were first coined by Posner, Strike, Hewson and Gertzog (1982). The CCM views learning as conceptual change in two fundamental patterns of change – namely, assimilation and accommodation (Tao & Gunstone, 1999; Wenning, 2008). According to the CCM, assimilation happens when a learner uses the existing concepts to interpret new phenomena, while accommodation occurs when a learner replaces or reorganizes the central conceptions (Strike & Posner, 1982). Since then, research in the area of students' conceptual understanding in science has been flourishing. Over the past three decades, it is evident that students' pre-instructional conceptions have been identified in different areas in science education, such as ecology (Ergazaki & Zogza, 2008; Li, 2011; Wright, 2008), force and motion (Tao & Gunstone, 1999; Vosniadou, 1994), heat and temperature (Linn & Songer, 1991; Wiser & Carey, 1983), condensation, evaporation and boiling (Osborne & Cosgrove, 1983; Tytler, 2000; Tytler & Peterson, 2000) and particulate model of matter (Nussbaum & Novick, 1982). It is believed that the discernment of alternative conceptions has strong implications in learning of science, which is often seen as a process of conceptual change or development rather than a fragmentary acquisition of new information. As a result, the CCM has been used to explain the surprising prevalence of some alternative conceptions and has become very influential and widely accepted in science education communities.

However, the use of the CCM alone in the explanation of student learning in science seems to over-simplify the complexity in learners' conceptual change and there are a growing number of empirical studies (Tao & Gunstone, 1999; Wenning, 2008; Windschitl & Andre, 1998) that reveal the inadequacy of the CCM in explaining conceptual change in individuals. They assert that students' growing conceptual understanding would not be an orderly and predictable process, as suggested in the CCM, but rather would be a complex and contextually situated process. Hence, the use of a single coherent framework as in many CCM has been questionable in contributing to our understanding of students' conceptual progress in science (Tytler, 2000). That means we should incorporate a wider range of social, contextual and non-cognitive factors in framing our understanding of the process of conceptual change (Strike & Posner, 1992) because we believe that scientific concepts are socially constructed and publicly shared (Gilbert & Mulkay, 1993).

The role of computer-supported modelling technologies in conceptual change

Computer-supported dynamic modelling technologies are widely used in science teaching since they enable students to theorize, test, evaluate and reflect upon their own hypotheses in richly contextualized environments. These modelling technologies usually provide a customizable environment so that students can explore scientific theories and use them to account for various natural phenomena through articulating and formulating their own explanations. These modelling environments allow students not only to modify models but to build their own models with their own theoretical assumptions. Hence, in science education, modelling is more than a tool for exploration of physical phenomena; it is for more expressive activities that facilitate conceptual change to reconcile one's conceptual conflicts (Ogborn, 1998; Ogborn, Boohan, Mellar & Bliss, 1994; Wenning, 2008).

We argue that a dynamic modelling environment which provides appropriate conceptual anchors for the facilitation of conceptual change is a good vehicle for theory building, as it helps students to better articulate their thoughts in relation to some natural phenomena through discussion among their peers and/or with stimulation from a teacher. For instance, the dynamic modelling environment WorldMaker (Law, 1999; Law, Li, Li & Tang, 2000) is reported to be able to facilitate students' progressive refinement of their conceptions. Students can negotiate, refute or refine their thoughts in this modelling environment and then externalize their thoughts and build models and theories to explain the observed phenomena. When they are confronted and challenged by the dynamics and consequences of the models constructed based on their own conceptualizations, the process will continue until they finally reach a scientifically acceptable explanation of the observed phenomena. In other words, these intermediate models or theories serve as further conceptual anchors and are instrumental in the process of progressive refinement of conceptions.

Cognitive perturbation and sociocultural theory

The cognitive perturbation strategy (CPS), proposed by Li, Law and Lui (2006), is a student-oriented approach to promote conceptual change in a less intrusive way in comparison with the classical conceptual conflict strategy (CCS) (Nussbaum & Novick, 1982; Posner et al., 1982). In CCS, students are provoked by a discrepant event that aims to trigger conceptual change by assuming, although not explicitly stated, that learning is a linear, rational, deterministic, one-step and revolutionary process (Nussbaum & Novick, 1982; Tao & Gunstone, 1999). As such, the CCS treats students as either being naïve to science or having scientific conceptions without deliberating the possible "intermediate" conceptions developed during the change process, supposing that simply confronting students with discrepant events will result in conceptual change. However, chances are some students may not be able to figure out the discrepancy if they find that the evidences in the discrepant events are unconnected to the phenomenon concerned. In this case, students may refuse to make any conceptual change and stick to their alternate conceptions (Maloney & Siegler, 1993; Niaz, 1995; Scott, 1992; Trumper, 1997).

Instead of putting well-prescribed confrontation and denial of alternative conceptions in the CCS, CPS gears students' conceptual change towards a more scientifically inclined one, with appropriate dissonance as a starting point. In CPS, students are being challenged by the teacher at appropriate junctures of time along the processes in conceptual change. The notion of CPS rests on the consideration that paths of conceptual change for different students are idiosyncratic, diverse and context-laden (Li, 2006). That means the CCS is insensitive to the non-cognitive elements and social contexts that are essential for conceptual progression and fails to provide students with appropriate conceptual anchors to reconcile the incongruity between their alternative conceptions and the scientific conceptions.

Taking Vygotsky's (1978) sociocultural theory into consideration, CPS sees conceptual change as an incremental and evolutionary process or ZPD (Daniels, 2001; Wells, 1999), while seeing conceptual progression as a journey of advancing students' knowledge of the observed phenomena by constantly revising and building better theories through teachers' incremental prompts or scaffolding (Hammond, 2002; Rasmussen, 2001).

Studies and findings

Based on two studies published in three articles (Li, 2006, 2008, 2011), we use Vygotsky's sociocultural theory and cognitive perturbation as a lens to examine how computer modelling environments can be employed in facilitating learning of science.

Study one. The first study (Li, 2006, 2008) aims to illuminate, with the support of WorldMaker, the role of sociocultural theory and cognitive perturbation in facilitating students' conceptual changes during the process of building explanatory models, discussion and model refinement.

Participants. Forty Grade 6 students from a local, government-aided, co-educational school of ages around 12 participated in this study. The class was divided into two groups:

control and experimental, 20 in each. The two groups were selected on the basis that both of them exhibited similar profiles of academic ability.

Procedure. The entire study consisted of two phases extended over a two-week teaching period that included eight single periods of about 35 minutes each. The first phase was a set of teaching sessions aimed to teach students the essential skills for building dynamic models with WorldMaker. In the second phase of the study, CPS coupled with WorldMaker was applied to facilitate the experimental group to learn about the basic concepts of evaporation. At the beginning of the lesson, the teacher asked students to predict what would happen if alcohol were spilled on a table. He then performed a simple demonstration by dropping a few alcohol droplets onto the glass cover of a visualizer. The entire process was projected on a screen so that every student could see the disappearance of the alcohol droplets and smell the alcohol in the room. Right after the demonstration, the experimental group was further divided into four sub-groups of five students (i.e., Sub-group A to Sub-group D). Each sub-group was asked to construct a model to account for what they observed. They would present and discuss their model with the teacher and make subsequent rectification if necessary. The purpose of conducting discussion sessions with each sub-group was twofold. First, we would like to emphasize that conceptual change is an incremental process rather than a one-step change, as described in the classical CCM (Nussbaum & Novick, 1982; Posner et al., 1982). To help bridge students' ZPD, the teacher tried to establish students' confidence in model-building by appreciating the progress or achievement they had made. Second, students were challenged at appropriate intervals by comparing the tentative model they created with that of the real physical phenomenon they observed during the demonstration. During the discussion sessions, the teacher intentionally posed questions to help students identify the discrepancies between the theory they proposed and the observations. In this connection, the questions and challenges from the teacher served as a vehicle to provide students with cognitive perturbation or disturbance that might eventually help students refine their model. Upon identifying the discrepancies, each sub-group was encouraged to revise their existing model. Although the teacher provided social support and posed cognitive perturbations to students, he deliberately did not provide students with immediate solutions or direct them to follow a prescribed inquiry path during the model-building process. The teacher was to work with, rather than against, the students' naïve or alternative conceptions in the process of their model-building and refinement. This process of model-building–discussion–model refinement would continue till the end of the whole modelling session. To examine effect of CPS and the use of computer-supported modelling on student learning, a concluding session was held to let each group present their models and explain the theories they used in accounting for the observed phenomenon. For the control group, the teacher elicited the basic concepts of evaporation through direct exposition without any support of computer modelling. Pre-/post-tests were administered to both experimental and control groups to gauge their understanding of the basic concepts about evaporation.

Analysis. To facilitate the analysis and examination of the conceptual progression, the model-building process of each sub-group was divided into a number of stages corresponding to the number of discussion sessions conducted. The number of stages varied slightly from sub-group to sub-group as the modelling activity for each sub-group progressed at a different pace. The explanations manifested by each model were transcribed into statements for coding and analysis. Three levels of understanding were identified (Li, 2006): (1) surface understanding – students provided only phenomenological descriptions of their observations with no indication of any understanding of the particle nature of matter; (2) shallow understanding – students demonstrated some level of understanding of the particle nature of matter yet their explanations remained scientifically incorrect; and (3) deep understanding – students' explanations consisted of in-depth and scientifically acceptable interpretations of the underlying mechanisms and particulate dynamics of the observed phenomena. For the pre-/post-test scores, analysis of covariance (ANCOVA) was conducted with SPSS 16.0 (SPSS Inc., Chicago, IL, US) using the pre-test scores as the covariate.

Results. One of the purposes of our analysis was to depict the conceptual change in students' understanding of evaporation across different stages of their modelling process. To portray the path of conceptual development as reflected in the models they created at different stages, we counted the numbers of explanatory statements in each discussion session and mapped them to the three prescribed levels of explanation (Table 18.1). Although the composition of the explanatory statements at the three levels varied among the four groups across different stages, there was an increase in deep (scientifically acceptable) explanations and a drop in the surface and shallow (phenomenological and particulate mechanism) explanations as the modelling process progressed, indicating that students were developing a better model (or the scientific theory used) in explaining the observed phenomenon.

In general, students were able to transcend from their original naïve conceptions to a more scientifically sound model for the observed phenomenon. To compare the trajectories of conceptual change of the different groups, we assigned a score to each type of explanatory statements (5 for deep, –3 for shallow and –5 for the surface statements). The scores were put together in a diagram to provide a better visualization of the conceptual progressions of each group (Figure 18.1).

It seems clear that conceptual change does not always follow a rational sequence: from conceptual conflicts to assimilation and to accommodation, as suggested in the CCM. Rather, conceptual change is seen as an incremental conceptual path that progresses from shallow (phenomenological) explanations to deep (scientifically acceptable) explanations. More interestingly, the results indicated that the process of conceptual change might not progress in a stepwise manner. For instance, both models constructed by Sub-group A and Sub-group D at Stage 2 regressed to a less scientifically inclined one. The results of ANCOVA indicated that, after controlling the pre-test scores, the post-test scores of the experimental group were significantly higher than that of the control group, with $F_{(1,37)}$ 85.95, $p < 0.005$ and $\eta^2 = 0.69$.

Table 18.1 Number of explanatory statements at three different levels of explanation across the different stages of model-building for the four groups

| Sub-group | Level | Stage | | | | | |
		1	*2*	*3*	*4*	*5*	*6*
A	Surface	4	6	5	4	1	0
	Shallow	0	0	0	0	0	0
	Deep	0	0	2	3	4	5
B	Surface	2	2	2	1	1	0
	Shallow	0	0	1	1	1	1
	Deep	3	3	3	4	5	6
C	Surface	1	1	1	0	0	—
	Shallow	1	1	0	0	0	—
	Deep	2	3	4	5	6	—
D	Surface	1	1	1	1	0	—
	Shallow	0	2	2	0	0	—
	Deep	3	0	4	5	5	—

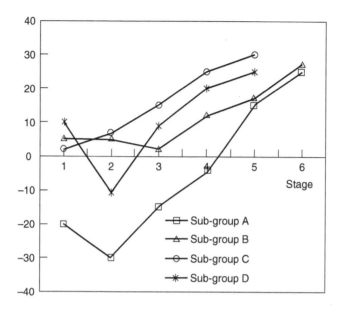

Figure 18.1 Graph showing the total scores associated with different sub-groups' models at the different stages of model-building

Study two. In study two (Li, 2011), marine ecology was chosen as the knowledge domain under scrutiny. As many concepts associated with ecology, such as population dynamics, carrying capacity, competition among species and energy flow, cannot be illustrated by performing either simple demonstrations or experiments, common misconceptions about ecology prevail among students. In this regard, computer modelling may play a pivotal role in facilitating students' conceptual change in learning ecology.

Participants. We invited 73 Secondary 2 (Grade 8) students and 103 Primary 6 (Grade 6) students from two different government-aided schools in Hong Kong Special Administration Region to participate in this study. The samples were selected on the basis that they represented students with average academic ability in the territory.

Procedure. The Secondary 2 students came from two classes, 2A (n = 35) and 2D (n = 38). Students in class 2A were assigned to work collaboratively. They were divided into groups of three and each group was asked to take up a series of modelling tasks. Students from 2D were required to work on the modelling tasks individually. For students in the Primary 6 classes (6C, n = 32; 6D, n = 31; and 6F, n = 40), all of them were instructed to work on the tasks on an individual basis. These students came from families of similar socio-economic background, but the students from the 6F class academically outperformed the students of the other two classes. All the participating students were working on the same set of modelling tasks and attending instructional programs with similar contents. However, in the instructional program designed for students working collaboratively, prompts were given to facilitate student discussion. Moreover, no student in the study had received any prior training regarding modelling a marine ecosystem so as to minimize the effect of prior experience on data collection.

CPS (Li, 2006) was incorporated in the design of the instructional programs to facilitate students to progress through their ZPD (Vygotsky, 1978). Students were exposed to their deeply rooted misconceptions and were confronted with scientific conceptions. We anticipated that this kind of cognitive perturbation can facilitate students in accommodating scientific concepts. The focus of the instructional program was on students' prevailing misconceptions about energy flow and population dynamics among different species of a marine ecosystem. This specially constructed marine ecosystem model consisted of phytoplankton, zooplankton such as shrimps, predators such as tunas and lancets, and the top predators such as sharks and human beings. In the process, the teacher provided some guidance to students so that they could explore a set of marine ecosystems with different degrees of complexity. To facilitate students' conceptual change, a *"predict–observe–explain"* strategy was used. This strategy helped students to externalize their conceptual change so that the teacher could monitor their progress. In the modelling process, students were given a particular ecosystem and prompted to make conjectures about certain phenomena before they embarked on any modelling activities. After they had made their conjectures, they were asked to play with the model parameters to see whether there was any discrepancy between their conjectures and observations. Students could choose to account for the observed discrepancies to the teacher or they could further explore the discrepant outcomes until they eventually formulated a reasonable explanation for what they observed.

This study employed a quasi-experimental (pre- and post-test multiple comparison) study to compare the impact of an instructional program on students' conception change with the modes of learning (collaborative versus individual) and the level of academic ability.

Analysis. Both the pre- and post-tests consisted of 12 multiple-choice questions and the questions in both tests were identical. Among the 12 questions, seven tested students' understanding of the population dynamics of different species found in a food chain. Three of them were employed to examine students' misconceptions about energy transfer and relative sizes of biomass at different layers of a food chain. The remaining two questions were devised to probe students' misconceptions about the relationship between two competitors of an ecosystem. A mixed between–within subjects analysis of variance (ANOVA) analysis in conjunction with an ANCOVA analysis were conducted to analyze the pre/post-test scores with SPSS 16.0.

Results. The mean post-test scores of the five classes, 2A, 2D, 6C, 6D and 6F, suggested that the post-test scores were higher than their corresponding pre-test scores (see Table 18.2). We also administered a mixed between–within subjects ANOVA to see the impact of the instructional programs. Results obtained from the tests of within-subjects effects showed that the difference between the pre- and post-test scores was statistically significant. The tests of between-subjects effects indicated that the difference in the pre- and post-test scores among the five classes was also statistically significant. The post-hoc comparisons show that the main differences in pre-test and post-test scores arose from the high scores obtained in Class 2A and Class 6F. A significant difference among the post-test scores of the five different classes was found when the pre-test score variable was controlled. Further, the

Table 18.2 The mean scores and standard deviations of the five classes

	Descriptive statistics				
Class	Mean		Standard deviation		n
	Pre-test	Post-test	Pre-test	Post-test	
2A	5.51	6.46	1.522	2.147	35
2D	4.66	4.95	1.849	1.845	38
6C	3.56	4.59	1.076	1.829	32
6D	3.94	4.48	1.340	1.842	31
6F	5.15	5.68	1.626	1.639	40

ANCOVA results of the two Secondary 2 classes indicated that there was a significant difference between their post-test scores.

Discussion and implications

In study one, it was obvious that students, working in a group setting, learned science through a variety of idiosyncratic conceptual paths. The results indicated that the students' explanations generated at the early stages of their model-building process varied from surface to deep understanding of the phenomenon. Interestingly, some students regressed to adopt a set of scientifically less favourable explanations as their modelling-building process progressed (see Figure 18.2). In other words, the contours of each group's or individual's ZPD is quite individual-dependent and context-laden. Thus, to facilitate learning, the pedagogical design must be flexible enough to cater for the idiosyncrasy in students' conceptual changes. We argue that the ZPD can be conceived metaphorically as an undulating terrain, as shown in Figure 18.3. The local minimum points and the global minimum point

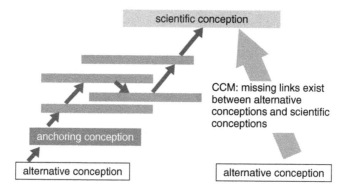

Figure 18.2 Conceptual change is a non-linear process and students may regress to a lower level of understanding as their learning progresses

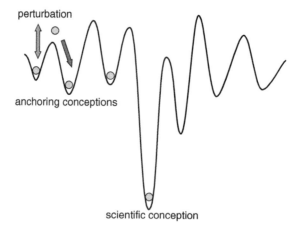

Figure 18.3 The zone of proximal development can be conceived metaphorically as an undulating terrain in which the local minimum points and the global minimum point represent, respectively, prevailing misconceptions and scientific conception

represent, respectively, the prevailing misconceptions and the scientific conception. To facilitate conceptual change, teachers have to provide appropriate cognitive perturbation to help students leap out of their conceptual troughs and migrate toward the global minimum position. The results presented in this chapter indicated that, with appropriate cognitive perturbation from the teacher, students were gradually migrating from their original naïve conceptions toward a more scientifically sound one. The teacher was there to provide social support and cognitive perturbation in a computer-supported modelling environment to facilitate students' conceptual change. With cognitive perturbation and social support from the teacher, students were able to look for evidence to refute or modify their models simply by their own reflection and observation. Hence, if the teacher could stimulate and facilitate students to look for possible discrepant events to refute or rectify their theories with the immediate visual simulation from the computer modelling tool, students would be able to advance their theories to build their scientifically inclined models. In short, the CCM failed to provide a satisfactory account on students' conceptual progression, while the instructional strategy adopted in this study provides appropriate conceptual "anchors" for students to gear their alternative conceptions toward a more scientific one.

In study two, the results of the mixed between–within subjects ANOVA indicated that the implementation of the instructional program supported by WorldMaker was effective in facilitating conceptual change in explaining the phenomena concerning marine ecosystems. Moreover, the ANCOVA results showed that students in class 2A, who were working in a collaborative setting, had gained a higher score in the conceptual test. Results obtained in study two also suggest that grounding the modelling activities on a social constructivist framework helps foster the construction of knowledge within a community of learners (Ergazaki & Zogza, 2008; Grotzer & Basca, 2003; Li et al., 2006; Papaevripidou, Constantinou & Zacharia, 2007; van Joolingen et al., 2007; Wright, 2008). Moreover, we found that, after controlling for the effect of the pre-test scores, students' attainment in the post-test was independent of academic abilities, meaning that students with different levels of academic ability could benefit from this instructional program.

The quantitative results presented in study two provide evidence that the computer-supported modelling environment WorldMaker, together with the instructional program, is an effective tool in promoting students' conceptual change in the population dynamics and the complex relationship among different entities of a marine ecosystem. We find that the computer modelling tool which provides a rich contextualized environment that allows students to articulate and manipulate their own thoughts and theories is essential in facilitating conceptual change in science education. This is because the computer modelling tool can let students regularly compare their own models with the observed phenomenon with instant feedback given to them. In this way, students are able to identify cognitive conflicts or discrepant events, which are developed from students' own models, and therefore they are more relevant to students' current understanding of the phenomenon. In other words, these tentative models provide conceptual anchors that facilitate students to progress in the journey of advancing their understanding of scientific concepts.

Conclusion

The use of computer modelling in fostering conceptual change in science education was put forth in this chapter. The results showed that students were having positive conceptual changes in a computer-supported modelling environment and these changes were not in a one-step style as described in the CCM. However, students' conceptual change should not be attributed to the computer modelling tool alone. Without CPS that encourages students to review their own theory and without the scaffolding that the teacher provided at appropriate intervals, we might not have been able to witness the paths of conceptual change that took place and understand the importance of Vygotsky's ZPD and social support in science learning. We hope we have succinctly illustrated that computer modelling is a necessary vehicle for theory building, but Vygotsky's scaffolding is a sufficient condition in fostering conceptual change in science education.

References

Bliss, J. & Ogborn, J. (1989). Tools for exploratory learning. *Journal of Computer Assisted Learning,* *5,* 37–50.

Daniels, H. (2001). *Vygotsky and pedagogy.* New York: Routledge/Falmer.

Ergazaki, M. & Zogza, V. (2008). Exploring lake ecology in a computer-supported learning environment. *Journal of Biological Education, 42*(2), 90–94.

Gilbert, G. N. & Mulkay, M. (1993). *Opening Pandora's box: A sociological analysis of scientists' discourse.* New York: Cambridge University Press.

Grotzer, T. A. & Basca, B. B. (2003). How does grasping the underlying causal structures of ecosystems impact students' understanding? *Journal of Biological Education, 38*(1), 16–29.

Hammond, J. (Ed.). (2002). *Scaffolding teaching and learning in language and literacy education.* Newtown, Australia: PETA.

Hilder, T. A., Gordon, D. & Chung, S.-H. (2010). Synthetic cation-selective nanotube: Permeant cations chaperoned by anion. *The Journal of Chemical Physics, 501,* 423–426.

Hilder, T. A., Yang, R., Ganesh, V., Gordon, D., Bliznyuk, A., Rendell, A. P. & Chung, S.-H. (2010). Validity of current force fields for simulations on boron nitride nanotubes. *Micro & Nano Letters,* *5,* 150–156.

Kuyucak, S. & Li, S. C. (1995a). 1/N expansion formalism for high-spin state. *Physics Letters B, 349,* 253–260.

Kuyucak, S. & Li, S. C. (1995b). High-spin states in boson models with applications to actinide nuclei. *Physics Letters B, 354,* 189–195.

Law, N. (1999). *Making physics concepts accessible and explorable using WorldMaker: An iconic modelling tool.* Paper presented at the International Conference on Physics Teaching, Guilin, PRC.

Law, N., Li, S. C., Li, R. & Tang, P. (2000). *WorldMaker: Making collaborative exploration of complex systems accessible to children.* Paper presented at the 4th Global Chinese Conference on Computers in Education, Singapore.

Li, S. C. (2006). A constructivist approach to designing computer supported concept mapping environment. *International Journal of Instructional Media, 33*(2), 153–164.

Li, S. C. (2008). Examining the use of dynamic modeling environment to support learning and teaching of science. *International Journal of Instructional Media, 35*(4), 443–454.

Li, S. C. (2011). Cognitive perturbation and conceptual change in learning ecology with dynamic modeling. *International Journal of Instructional Media, 38*(4), 359–367.

Li, S. C., Hoyles, M., Kuyucak, S. & Chung, S. H. (1998). Brownian dynamics study of ion transport in the vestibule of membrane channels. *Biophysical Journal, 74,* 37–47.

Li, S. C. & Kuyucak, S. (1996). Description of deformed nuclei in sdg-interacting boson model. *Nuclear Physics, 604,* 305–340.

Li, S. C., Law, N. & Lui, A. K. F. (2006). Cognitive perturbation through dynamic modelling: A pedagogical approach to conceptual change in science. *Journal of Computer Assisted Learning, 22*(6), 405–422.

Linn, M. & Songer, N. (1991). Teaching thermodynamics to middle school students: What are appropriate cognitive demands? *Journal of Research in Science Teaching, 28,* 885–918.

Maloney, D. P. & Siegler, R. S. (1993). Conceptual competition in physics learning. *International Journal of Science Education, 15,* 283–295.

Niaz, M. (1995). Cognitive conflict as a teaching strategy in solving chemistry problems: A dialectic-constructivist perspective. *Journal of Research in Science Teaching, 32*, 959–970.

Nussbaum, J. & Novick, S. (1982). Alternative frameworks, conceptual conflict and accommodation: Toward a principled teaching strategy. *Instructional Science, 11*, 183–200.

Ogborn, J. (1998). Cognitive development and qualitative modelling. *Journal of Computer Assisted Learning, 14*(4), 292–307.

Ogborn, J., Boohan, R., Mellar, H. & Bliss, J. (1994). *Learning with artificial worlds: Computer-based modelling in the curriculum*. London: Taylor and Francis.

Osborne, R. J. & Cosgrove, M. M. (1983). Children's conceptions of the changes of state of water. *Journal of Research in Science Teaching, 20*(9), 825–838.

Papaevripidou, M., Constantinou, C. P. & Zacharia, Z. C. (2007). Modeling complex marine ecosystems: An investigation of two teaching approaches with fifth graders. *Journal of Computer Assisted Learning, 23*, 145–157.

Posner, G. J., Strike, K. A., Hewson, P. W. & Gertzog, W. A. (1982). Accommodation of a scientific conception: Towards a theory of conceptual change. *Science Education, 66*(2), 211–217.

Rasmussen, J. (2001). The importance of communication in teaching: A systems-theory approach to the scaffolding metaphor. *Curriculum Studies, 33*(5), 569–582.

Scott, P. (1992). Pathways in learning science: A case study of one student's ideas relating to the structure of matter. In R. Duit, F. Goldberg & H. Neidderer (Eds.), *Research in physics learning: Theoretical issues and empirical studies* (pp. 203–224). Kiel, Germany: IPN – Leibniz Institute for Science Education.

Strike, K. A. & Posner, G. J. (1982). Conceptual change and science teaching. *European Journal of Science Education, 4*(3), 231–240.

Strike, K. A. & Posner, G. J. (1992). A revisionist theory of conceptual change. In R. A. Duschl & R. Hamiliton (Eds.), *Philosophy of science, cognitive psychology, and educational theory and practice* (pp. 147–176). Albany, NY: SUNY Press.

Tao, P. K. & Gunstone, R. F. (1999). The process of conceptual change in force and motion during computer-supported physics instruction. *Journal of Research in Science Teaching, 36*(7), 859–882.

Trumper, R. (1997). Applying conceptual conflict strategies in the learning of the energy concept. *Research in Science and Technology Education, 15*, 5–18.

Tytler, R. (2000). A comparison of year 1 and year 6 students' conceptions of evaporation and condensation: Dimension of conceptual progression. *International Journal of Science Education, 22*(5), 447–467.

Tytler, R. & Peterson, S. (2000). Deconstructing learning in science – young children's responses to a classroom sequence on evaporation. *Research in Science Education, 4*(30), 339–355.

van Joolingen, W. R., de Jong, T. & Dimitrakopoulou, A. (2007). Issues in computer supported inquiry learning in science. *Journal of Computer Assisted Learning, 23*, 111–119.

Vosniadou, S. (1994). Capturing and modelling the process of conceptual change. *Learning and Instruction, 4*, 45–69.

Vygotsky, L. S. (1978). *Mind in society: The development of higher psychological processes*. Cambridge, MA: Harvard University Press.

Wells, G. (1999). *Dialogic inquiry: Towards a sociocultural practice and theory of education*. New York: Cambridge University Press.

Wenning, C. J. (2008). Dealing more effectively with alternative conceptions in science. *Journal of Physics Teacher Education, 5*(1), 11–19.

Windschitl, M. & Andre, T. (1998). Using computer simulations to enhance conceptual change: The roles of constructivist instruction and student epistemological beliefs. *Journal of Research in Science Teaching, 35*(2), 145–160.

Wiser, M. & Carey, S. (1983). When heat and temperature were one. In D. Gentner & A. Stevens (Eds.), *Mental models* (pp. 99–129). Hillsdale, NJ: Erlbaum.

Wright, J. M. (2008). Web-based versus in-class: An exploration of how instructional methods influence postsecondary students' environmental literacy. *The Journal of Environmental Education, 39*(2), 33–45.

Part 7

Conclusion

19 The role of culture in constructing educational achievement

Sivanes Phillipson and Shane N. Phillipson

Introduction

The broad objective of this book is to explore the many contributing elements to educational achievement, including those elements that originate within an individual (personal plane and mental plane) and those elements that exist in the social plane (cultural–historical, institutional plane and social plane). Extending Vygotsky's (1978) two planes, the socio-cultural paradigm provides a rich opportunity to examine closely the many approaches to understanding the development of academic achievement. The book's contributors demonstrate that each plane provides a framework for researchers to develop a holistic understanding of the relationship between child development and academic achievement. The contributors also provide specific examples of these elements at work in a variety of cultural historical settings, including migrant children from China, Māori students in New Zealand, co-regulation amongst North American children and beginning teachers in Hong Kong, amongst many others.

As well as meeting the book's objectives, the authors in this volume have an important role in contributing to the debate of the role of culture in education, particularly in relation to the inability of educational reform to reduce the achievement gap based on socio-economic status and gender (Cole, 2010). The main aim of this concluding chapter is to test Cole's thesis that the success of educational reform to achieve this end depends on taking into account the role of culture.

We begin by briefly outlining Cole's (2010) argument that the failure of educational reforms around the world is due to our inability to move beyond architectural and instructional models that are rooted in antiquity. We then focus on the conditions that Cole considers are important for educational reform, before examining the evidence based on the examples from the contributions within this book. In agreement with Cole's view, we also consider that culture plays a central role in educational achievement. In contrast to Cole, we are optimistic that educational reform can be successful, and that there are many examples of its success.

Cole and the role of culture in educational reform

Educational achievement is a topic of enduring interest. Cole (2010) argued that the purpose of educational reform is to narrow the gap in educational achievement that is based on social class and/or ethnicity, and increase the number of students in economically important areas, such as science and technology. Governments around the world devote vast resources to developing educational systems that enhance the quality of life of their citizens and to maintain their economic viability. The role of educational reform is to ensure that educational systems evolve in order to meet these twin demands.

On the other hand, Cole (2010) views education as being "intimately linked to the human capacity and need to live in a cultural environment" (p. 461), and that its role is to ensure that people are provided with the knowledge and skills that enable them to live in social groups. As the demands of the social group increase with succeeding generations, the importance of education also increases. Cole views culture as an accumulated body of knowledge and skills that enables new members of the social group, usually children, to contribute to and ensure the growth of the social group.

Furthermore, Cole (2010) argues that much of the failure of educational reform around the world is due to a misunderstanding of the role of education in the formation of cultural groups. He also believes that reforms are doomed when policy makers do not comprehend the complex interplay between the process of education (how humans learn) and the specific historical, economic, social, political and cultural contexts.

As Cole (2010) pointed out, the needs of social groups are not static, and different social groups have different needs. Nevertheless, the increasing interconnectedness of people around the world tends to blur the boundaries between social groups, and individuals need to acquire knowledge and skills that enable them to contribute to multiple cultures. Indeed, people may be members of many, albeit ill-defined, cultural groups. Consider, for example, one boy in a classroom in Hong Kong. The boy has an Australian father and a Malaysian-born mother and his classmates are mostly Chinese Hong Kong students, speaking fluently both Cantonese and English. Moreover, the female teacher is from New Zealand. If the boundaries between the social groups are not already blurred, the Malaysian-born mother is a "Chindian", an informal term that refers to her Chinese and Indian ancestry. Furthermore, the school has adopted the International Baccalaureate (IB) as the curriculum.

The cultural forces at work in this classroom are giddying and, at first glance, the teacher faces a seemingly impossible task if there is a need to enhance the educational achievement of the students in the classroom by "leveraging family cultural resources" (Cole, 2010, p. 466). Luckily, the classroom culture is heavily geared toward educational excellence, reflecting the prevailing cultural view that education is highly valued and high academic expectation is expected. The teacher's role is also simplified because the students and their families agree, perhaps implicitly, that the knowledge and skills that are deemed important are those that are common to all cultures.

Recent attempts to characterize the Chinese classroom have identified a peculiarly Chinese approach to learning and teaching that, from a Western perspective, appears paradoxical (Chan & Rao, 2009; Phillipson, 2007; Phillipson & Lam, 2011; Watkins & Biggs, 1996, 2001). If Cole (2010) is to be believed, Chinese Hong Kong classrooms should not be successful because they are based on antiquated architectures and educational processes that are highly formalized. Nevertheless, they are successful for the vast majority of students. For these students, knowledge is imbued with special powers and high academic achievement takes precedence over self-esteem, and collaboration is the norm.

For East Asian students, the link between culture and education is very strong. The classroom is a natural extension of the broader culture and there is no need for the teacher in a Chinese classroom to leverage the family cultural resources. If anything, the real danger is to try and explain the successes of East Asian students without a clear understanding of the Chinese culture, including aspects of Chinese culture that work toward or inhibit academic success (Phillipson, 2013).

Culture and educational achievement 259

Educational reform in the US

Although Cole (2010) does not refer to it explicitly, the most significant educational reform in the US in recent years centers on the No Child Left Behind Act (NCLB) of 2002. The NCLB Act relies on the annual testing of students using standardized tests of achievement to help identify and support schools that do not report gains in student achievement. Critics of the Act point to the lack of a national achievement standard, allowing each US state to set its own standards. As a result of this and other problems in the implementation of the Act, researchers working in gifted education report that funding to support the development of exceptional students across many US states has all but disappeared (Golden, 2003). More importantly, there are concerns that educational standards are falling across the US (Neal & Schanzenbach, 2010; Reback, 2008).

Although Cole (2010) mentioned other educational systems and cultures, his focus concerns the failure of educational reforms in the US and using these as examples of educational reform around the world. However, there are many examples where educational reform has been successful, including Finland and the many East Asian societies, such as Japan, Hong Kong, Taiwan and Singapore. Indeed, much of the reform agendas in the West, including the US and Australia, are driven by concerns that the educational achievements of students from these societies are falling behind those students from East Asia.

The Programme for International Student Assessments (PISA) 2009, for example, measures the ability of 15-year-old students to apply knowledge and skills to real-life problems and situations in 34 OECD countries and 31 partner countries and/or economies, such as Hong Kong-China (Thomson, De Bortolli, Nicholas, Hillman & Buckley, 2011). The performance of students in reading literacy, mathematical literacy and scientific literacy are ranked by country. Importantly, trends in the performance of 15-year-old students can be compared over time, demonstrating the relative effectiveness of educational systems.

Interpreting the performance of Australian students, Thomson et al. (2011) raised concerns over the significant decline in reading literacy, mathematical literacy and scientific literacy since PISA 2000, as well as gaps in performance based on gender, geographic location and socio-economic background. Particularly disturbing were indications that the decline in reading literacy was highest amongst the high-achieving students. In terms of policy, Thomson et al. were concerned about maintaining Australia's international attractiveness and whether the future work force could contribute effectively to the development of Australia. Issues concerned with social justice, gender and educational equity were rated highly in Thomson et al.'s report.

Clearly, however, Cole's (2010) concerns regarding educational reform do not seem to be echoed amongst other educational jurisdictions. For example, countries and economies such as Shanghai-China, Korea, Finland, Hong Kong-China and Singapore consistently rate amongst the top echelon of student performance. Despite the research effort, policy and financial investment, the overall performance of 15-year-old students in the US continues to be of great concern. On the other hand, the cultural pressures to be found in the Hong Kong classroom described earlier do not seem to present a problem.

The conditions for educational reform

The focus on the sociocultural perspectives on academic achievement in this book provides an opportunity to test Cole's thesis about the link between culture and educational reform, particularly in relation to the educational reform that addresses achievement gaps based on social class, gender and ethnicity.

According to Cole (2010), the several conditions necessary for educational reform begin with a "sea-change" (p. 469) in the purpose of education, where the current focus on high achievement and the "conquering of nature" (p. 465) is replaced by the notion that people and nature are exquisitely interrelated. In addition, Cole suggests that curricula need to be personally and socially significant, and that "assembly line" schooling be replaced with instructional strategies that focus on the individual student. Next, there should be an alignment between the broader culture and the classroom culture, particularly when the broader culture insists on and celebrates high achievement.

Cole (2010) also suggests that research focuses on understanding the conditions and processes of learning in order to better measure gains in learning. In order to help reduce the power relationships within classrooms, to assist inquiry-based schooling, and to enhance collaborations within and across classrooms, Cole recommends that the new technologies have a key role to play. Last, Cole emphasizes the fundamental role of reading literacy in educational achievement. Hence, the enhancement of reading literacy plays a key role in any educational reform.

The purpose of education

Cole (2010) suggests that the long-term sustainability of human life depends on making fundamental changes to the way we view the purpose of education. Rather than educate human beings in order to conquer nature, we must educate them to understand that human beings are part of nature. Although this view of education is not addressed specifically by any author in this book, Vadeboncoeur (Chapter 2) argued that Vygotsky's approach to learning recognized the interrelationship between the cognitive and emotional self, and the social environment.

Clearly, changing the social environment or culture, including the purpose of education, has the potential to change the cognitive and emotional self. However, it is difficult to see how this transformation may occur, at least within the American public, given their reluctance for change (Cole, 2010). As Renshaw (Chapter 5) pointed out, classroom "chronotopes" are amenable to change. Currently, the classroom chronotopes around the world focus on testing. Renshaw advocates changing this classroom chronotope into "relationship learning" but recognizes the difficulty of effecting change given the worldwide preoccupation with testing.

One approach may be to relocate values from cultures that already view human beings as part of nature. Hence, an important research program may begin with identifying cultures that already emphasize this relationship. Alternatively, a greater emphasis on affective, moral and leadership training as outlined in Sivan and Chan (Chapter 10) and O'Brien, Plotnikova and Mills (Chapter 14) may trigger the realization of the importance of change.

Curricula that is personally and socially significant

Cole (2010) argued that education reform depends on developing a curriculum that is personally and socially significant for the student. Curriculum, of course, is the link between culture (usually initiated via educational policy) and the classroom, and the development of a curriculum with these traits is informed by research that focuses on both the classroom and the culture. As we have already discussed, Sivan and Chan (Chapter 10) and O'Brien et al. (Chapter 14) highlight the need for a greater emphasis on affective, moral and leadership training.

In the Hong Kong context, affective education focuses on the need of students to develop self-discipline and the capacity to deal with the expectations of their family and the demands of an examination-oriented curriculum. Moral education, as part of civic and national education, focuses on the education of the whole person, including the development of positive values and the ability to judge local, national and international issues (Education Bureau, 2007). Importantly, moral education builds on Hong Kong's Confucian and (more recent) Christian heritage, as well as the creation of agencies such as the Independent Commission Against Corruption (Cheng, 2004).

Other examples of educational reform in Hong Kong, for example, focus on the needs of students rather than schools and include a reduction in secondary education by one year and increasing tertiary education by one year. Other aspects of the reform include changes in school-based management, curriculum and learning, assessment and accountability and quality assurance (Tommis & Phillipson, 2013).

Although it is premature to judge the success of these reforms, they are underpinned by a cultural basis that has its origins in Confucianism and, to a lesser extent, Buddhism and Taoism (Sun, 2008), helping to ensure the success of any reforms. In the Chinese culture, for example, the Confucian traits and values, such as filial piety, benevolence, righteousness and propriety, play an important role within the Chinese classroom (Sun, 2008). Certainly, classrooms also encourage competition as a means to deeper understanding of, but not to the cost of, social harmony and collaboration (Tang, 1996). For these students, what is personally and socially significant is an extension of their culture.

It is tempting to suggest that educational reform in East Asian countries and economies is easier to implement because there is a cultural expectation to do so. This cultural expectation is a manifestation of the Confucian respect for authority and of maintaining social harmony. In other words, the default position is that education reform in countries and economies within East Asia become individually relevant. As Cole (2010) pointed out, it is much more difficult to develop curricula that are personally and socially relevant because every individual student has different needs.

Replacing assembly-line teaching with deliberate and child-centered instruction

According to Cole (2010), the modern model of instruction is best described as "assembly-line teaching" (p. 464). This model has its origins in ancient times and reflects the increasing demands of a technologically and economically advanced society, thereby helping to ensure the survival and growth of that society. Cole recognized that an enormous amount of time and deliberate practice is needed to ensure the "full range of socially inherited accomplishments" is acquired.

Cole (2010) suggested that the success of school reforms depends on abolishing such models of schooling since formalized education is not our preferred way of learning. Instead, Cole recommended a return to child-centered schooling where "deliberate instruction" (p. 465) is practiced, since it reflects our species-specific preferred mode of learning. Cole cited many examples of deliberate instruction, beginning with hunter–gatherer societies. According to Cole, the movement away from child-centered instruction to assembly-line schooling was made possible by economic surplus and society's need to maintain a division of labor. Cole argued that a focus on deliberate instruction requires a change in the way teachers are viewed by society and how they are educated.

The contrast between assembly-line teaching and deliberate instruction broadly reflects the distinction between teaching and learning. Many recent textbooks that support the education of teachers, including texts that focus on classrooms in the West and in East Asia (cf. Phillipson, 2007; Phillipson & Lam, 2011), focus on learner diversity. In addition, there is increasing awareness that the effectiveness of student learning depends on understanding the teachers' perceptions of their roles and competencies rather than class size per se (Loughran, 2010).

Research in Hong Kong suggests that it is possible to have child-centered learning in classes that appear to be based on assembly-line models (Cortazzi & Lixian, 2001; Mok et al., 2001), particularly when the teaching profession is highly valued and when the classroom culture is an extension of the wider culture (Salili, 2001). As Draper (Chapter 6) and Sivan and Chan (Chapter 10) point out, teacher effectiveness in large classes can be maintained in times of educational reform and when teacher–student relationships are strong.

In discussing classrooms in Hong Kong, Salili (2001) stressed the strong link between the Chinese culture and the high status of teachers. This link contributed to the academic achievement of students because it reinforced cultural expectations of respect, obedience and filial piety. In addition, Chinese teachers are more likely to emphasize the holistic development of students, including their values, morals and conduct (Gao & Watkins, 2001; Ho, 2001), thereby helping to reinforce the link between the broader culture and the classroom.

As Wu (Chapter 3) showed, migrant children in mainland China construct a view of their family's social capital and this view affects their academic achievement. This research suggests that there is a mediating link between parental social capital and school academic achievement. Simply put, it is not sufficient to have the necessary family support and financial means: The child's view of this social capital impacts their academic achievement. By extension, efforts to reduce the achievement gap through school reform need to take into account the variability in the child's construction of the reforms.

Developing Vygotsky's concept of the zone of proximal development, Baucal (Chapter 12) suggests an important distinction between knowledge that is individually constructed through self-negotiations and interactions with peers, and knowledge that is socially scaffolded when interacting with more competent others. The cognitive tension between these two constructions supports Cole's (2010) suggestion that both a child-centered and a collaborative approach work best in the classroom.

Aligning classroom culture with broader culture, focusing on real-world tasks, problem solving and collaboration

In aligning the classroom culture with the external culture, Cole (2010) believes that classrooms should focus on tasks that reflect what happens in the real world, including problem solving and collaboration. In distinguishing between what happens in the real world as compared to classrooms, many classrooms have little relationship to the real world, where problems are well defined and have one (correct) solution, and focus on individual effort. In contrast, the problems in the real world are ill-defined and have many possible solutions, and there is an emphasis on collaboration. When there is alignment, educational reform is likely to be more successful in reducing achievement gaps based on socio-economic status and gender.

Research within this book shows that it is possible to build collaborations within the classroom, as suggested in Cole (2010), by building on collaborations that begin in the child's first real world, their home. Fleer (Chapter 8) shows that motives for learning begin in the home through interactions between the child and their family. Significantly, this motive indicates that, at least for the child, play and learning are interrelated. Extending Cole's suggestion, perhaps the success of educational reform would be enhanced if classrooms were based on a pedagogy that was based on "play".

McCaslin and Vega (Chapter 9) broaden the notion of collaboration to include the co-regulation of peer interpersonal dynamics and its relationship with competence and well-being. A greater understanding of these nuances may enhance the success of collaboration within (and perhaps beyond) the classroom. For adult learners where English is the second language, Hay, Callingham and Wright (Chapter 11) demonstrated that meaningful, planned and encouraged dialogue between teachers and students enhanced the interactive links between language development, cognitive reasoning and educational success. This finding expands Cole's (2010) role of collaboration to include teachers and reinforces the link between collaboration and educational success.

Li and Pow (Chapter 18) focused on science education in Chinese Hong Kong class-rooms. They reported research that showed the need to extend the notion of collaboration between people to include technology. Using computer-supported modeling tools, learners are able to enhance their understanding of scientific concepts by allowing them new opportunities to articulate thoughts, formulate hypotheses and construct theories.

Creating a culture of excellence where high achievement is expected and celebrated

Of the means to enhance the success of educational reform, perhaps the most problematic for educational systems is the creation of a culture that expects and celebrates success. Although Cole (2010) was able to provide a number of examples, they are the exception rather than the rule. As he also pointed out, sustaining a classroom culture where success is expected and celebrated depends on similar expectations in the broader culture.

There are several instances in this book that demonstrate the link between parental expectations and their children's academic achievement. For example, Phillipson (Chapter 7) drew from a meta-analysis to explore the notion of parents as the "significant other". Of course, her research begs the question as to the origins of parental expectations. Although some parental expectations are in contrast with the prevailing cultural expectations, the link between parental expectations and cultural expectations of academic success and hard work is strongest amongst Confucian-heritage cultures in East Asia. As we have already discussed, this expectation and celebration of academic success is shared also between teachers and students.

A poignant example of Cole's (2010) argument is described in Pui Ling Wong's chapter (Chapter 15). Her study follows the development of a learning and achievement motive in three Hong Kong–Australian families and highlights the tendency of the parents in these families to retain their expectations in a new cultural context, but do so under increasingly difficult circumstances.

Developing tools that tap into and measure learning gains

Of course, being able to determine whether educational reform has an impact on student achievement depends on being able to measure academic success. As we have already discussed, the NCLB Act in the US depends on the availability of instruments that measure educational achievement. Keegan, Brown and Hattie (Chapter 4) provide a vivid example of the need to develop instruments that are sensitive to the sociocultural needs of all cultural groups. Using the indigenous people of New Zealand as the educational context, Keegan et al. describe an instrument that is psychometrically valid because it takes into account the

264 *Sivanes Phillipson and Shane N. Phillipson*

sociocultural nuances within this particular group. Their approach to instrument development is a model for other cultural groups.

New technologies that change classroom relationships

Cole (2010) is skeptical that new technologies can transform learning. Although there are some examples where technology can enhance learning (Li and Pow, Chapter 18), Cole is hopeful that these technologies may transform classrooms by redistributing the power relationships between teachers and students and by breaking down the barriers between the classroom and the wider community. However, we have already provided a number of examples where the existing power relationships in some cultures support student learning and to break this relationship in these cultures could risk reducing student achievement.

Furthermore, breaking down barriers between the classroom and the wider community assumes, of course, that the barrier is a hindrance to learning. Again, there are a number of examples where the barriers are very "porous", with classrooms being a natural extension of the wider community. Under such circumstances, the new technologies may bring into focus hitherto unknown barriers, such as the contrast between East Asian cultures and cultures from the West. The relative influences of different cultures upon each other, as facilitated by the new technologies, will be an increasingly important area of research.

Enhancement of reading literacy

Educational achievement depends increasingly on reading literacy (Cole, 2010). Hence, this skill should be part of educational reform. A number of authors in this book emphasize the link between reading and educational achievement. For example, Ku (Chapter 17) highlighted the importance of verbal reasoning that comes from wider reading and exposure to knowledge literature. She argued that, through exposure to wider knowledge acquired from reading, the skill of critical reasoning arises, which very much depends on the ability to reason verbally. Furthermore, there are culturally specific dispositions that influence the way verbal reasoning is understood by others.

Li and Pow (Chapter 18) used computer-supported modeling tools to develop students' understanding of scientific concepts. In addition, they showed that language, as shown by their ability to read and understand concepts, also plays an important role in the development of scientific concepts.

In considering the importance of literacy in educational reform, Simpson Wong's research (Chapter 13) asks whether variability in reading ability reflects nature or nurture. He points to research evidence to support the conclusion that there are strong genetic influences for reading skills, rapid naming ability and phonological awareness. In contrast, environmental influences are greatest on vocabulary knowledge. This work provides a focused rationale for enhancing reading literacy.

Culture, learning and educational achievement: A systems perspective

Extending Vygotsky's two planes into five provides a framework for making sense of the complexity behind academic achievement (Phillipson and Renshaw, Chapter 1). In providing a framework for this book, however, it was not always easy to decide where the contributions should be located. This, of course, is to be expected since the boundaries between the planes are not clearly defined, reflecting Vygotsky's view that the components within and between each plane are integrated and interrelated.

In scientific terms, the five planes can be considered a taxonomy, with each plane providing a different explanatory level. If we are to move forward in trying to integrate the various explanatory levels, then it is useful to consider academic achievement as an outcome of a system. Indeed systems approaches to understanding complex interactions have been applied to a number of phenomena. For example, the actiotope model of giftedness (Ziegler, 2005; Ziegler & Phillipson, 2012; Ziegler, Vialle & Wimmer, 2013) describes exceptional achievement as the outcome of a system, not the individual. However, exceptionality is one end of the continuum and, hence, the actiotope model is as much a model of achievement per se, not just "exceptional" achievement.

Systems approaches recognize the complex interactions between many variables. In the actiotope model, two broad categories of variables are understood, including those that arise within the individual and environmental components, such as family, culture and financial resources. The three components within the individual include the goals, action repertoire (skills and knowledge available to the individual) and subjective action space (the skills and knowledge considered by the individual to reach the goal) (Tommis & Phillipson, 2013; Ziegler, 2005; Ziegler, Vialle & Wimmer, 2013). Not included in the actiotope model are psychological traits such as intelligence and creativity.

At the broadest level, changes within self, such as the setting of a goal, can affect changes in the set of skills and knowledge as well as changes in the environment. In turn, changes in the environment will affect changes in self, such as setting new goals. The system is dynamic, although the system may appear to be static with small changes in one part of the system able to affect large changes in other components. However, it is only through the continuing adaptation of the system that exceptionality will be achieved.

For example, the setting of the goal of passing a forthcoming mathematics examination requires the student to understand the mathematical skills and knowledge that they already have. Furthermore, the environment must be conducive to achieving the goal (i.e., the teacher must be suitably skilled, time must be available and there should be no competing goals). On achieving the goal, the environment changes in that the student is now recognized as having achieved a certain level and new opportunities are now available to the student.

Applying the actiotope model

The actiotope model has been implemented to support the development of exceptionality in German students (Ziegler & Stoeger, 2007). Through a detailed counseling process involving the student and parents, the attainment of exceptionality required the identification of a possible pathway and an understanding of various levels of influences, including motivational state, self-regulation, the starting and end points required in term of skills and knowledge, the roles played by parents and other support persons, and the environmental factors. Although exceptionality cannot be guaranteed, the counseling process recognized that the attainments of exceptionality required careful planning and sought to take into account all of the possible influences on the pathway.

The five planes and the actiotope model

Since each seeks to understand the development of achievement, reconciling the five planes (Phillipson & Renshaw, Chapter 1) with the actiotope model is relatively straightforward. Of the five planes, the mental and personal planes refer to aspects of self, although the terminology, of course, differs. Within the actiotope model, the action repertoire, subjective action space and goals interact with each other and with the external environment, corresponding with the mental and personal planes. Within the environment, the actiotope model recognizes the distinction between sociotopes that enhance or inhibit the development of exceptionality, corresponding with the social, institutional and cultural–historical planes.

Importantly, both the actiotope model and the five planes refer to the need to consider the cultural (environmental) context and that this context can change. Hence, it is important to consider a developmental trajectory. Whereas the actiotope model contemplates a future trajectory to map a pathway for future achievement, Phillipson and Renshaw (Chapter 1) consider the sociocultural basis of current achievement.

Of course, both the actiotope model and sociocultural theory consider academic achievement to be dependent on the interactions of a number of components. Whereas the actiotope model refers to a system, sociocultural perspectives consider these components as layers integrated between the personal and the social. Recognizing that these components are part of a system opens up the distinct possibility of empirically testing Vygotsky's ideas. Modern data analytic techniques, such as multi-level structural equation modeling, can be used to model the complex interrelationships between the components. Other possibilities include the integration of cognitive architectures with the modeling of multi-agent interactions (Sun, 2006b). For example, work has begun in the cognitive modeling of social behaviors (Clancey, Sierhuis, Damer & Brodsky, 2006; Sun, 2006a).

Conclusion

This chapter began with a discussion of Cole's (2010) thesis that educational reform needs to take into account the important role played by culture. We provided evidence to support Cole's argument that educational reform requires several conditions, including a sea-change in the purpose of education, constructing a personally relevant and socially significant curriculum, reinstating a child-centered instruction, aligning classroom culture with the broader culture, creating a culture of excellence, developing tools that measure learning gains and utilizing new technologies to link the classroom with the community and to enhance reading literacy. Whereas Cole took a rather pessimistic view that these conditions were not forthcoming, at least in the West, there is ample evidence to suggest that these conditions are already in place in other parts of the world, particularly in East Asian communities such as Hong Kong. Finally, we proposed that it is possible to empirically test Vygotsky's sociocultural approach by recognizing the systems aspects of Vygotsky's ideas.

References

Chan, C. K. K. & Rao, N. (Eds.) (2009). *Revisiting the Chinese learner: Changing contexts, changing patterns*. Hong Kong and the Netherlands: Springer and Comparative Education Research Centre, The University of Hong Kong.

Cheng, R. H. M. (2004). Moral education in Hong Kong: Confucian parental, Christian religious and liberal civic influences. *Journal of Moral Education, 33*(4), 533–551.

Clancey, W. J., Sierhuis, M., Damer, B. & Brodsky, B. (2006). Cognitive modeling of social behaviors. In R. Sun (Ed.), *Cognition and multiagent interaction: From cognitive modeling to social simulation* (pp. 151–185). New York: Cambridge University Press.

Cole, M. (2010). What's culture got to do with it? Educational research as a necessarily interdisciplinary enterprise. *Educational Researcher, 39*(6), 461–470.

Cortazzi, M. & Lixian, J. (2001). Large classes in China: "Good" teachers and interaction. In D. A. Watkins & J. B. Biggs (Eds.), *Teaching the Chinese learner: Psychological and pedagogical perspectives* (pp. 115–134). Hong Kong and Australia: Comparative Education Research Centre, The University of Hong Kong and ACER.

Education Bureau (2007). *Moral, civic and national education*. The Government of the Hong Kong Special Administrative Region. Retrieved 29 August 2012 from www.edb.gov.hk/index. aspx?nodeID=2397&langno=1.

Gao, L. & Watkins, D. D. (2001). Towards a model of teaching conceptions of Chinese secondary teachers of physics. In D. A. Watkins & J. B. Biggs (Eds.), *Teaching the Chinese learner: Psychological and pedagogical perspectives* (pp. 27–46). Hong Kong and Australia: Comparative Education Research Centre, The University of Hong Kong and ACER.

Golden, D. (2003). Initiative to leave no child behind leaves out gifted. *The Wall Street Journal Online*, 29 December. Retrieved 29 August 2012 from http://online.wsj.com/public/resources/documents/Polk_Gifted.htm.

Ho, I. T. (2001). Are Chinese teachers authoritarian? In D. A. Watkins & J. B. Biggs (Eds.), *Teaching the Chinese learner: Psychological and pedagogical perspectives* (pp. 99–114). Hong Kong and Australia: Comparative Education Research Centre, The University of Hong Kong and ACER.

Loughran, J. J. (2010). *What expert teachers do: Enhancing professional knowledge for classroom practice*. Australia: Allen & Unwin.

Mok, I., Chik, P. M., Ko, P. Y., Kwan, T., Lo, M. L., Marton, F . . . Szeto, L. H. (2001). Solving the paradox of the Chinese teacher. In D. A. Watkins & J. B. Biggs (Eds.), *Teaching the Chinese learner: Psychological and pedagogical perspectives* (pp. 161–179). Hong Kong and Australia: Comparative Education Research Centre, The University of Hong Kong and ACER.

Neal, D. & Schanzenbach, D. W. (2010). Left behind by design: Proficiency counts and test-based accountability. *Review of Economics and Statistics, 92*(2), 263–283.

Phillipson, S. N. (Ed.) (2007). *Learning diversity in the Chinese classroom: Contexts and methods for children with special needs.* Hong Kong: Hong Kong University Press.

Phillipson, S. N. (2013). Confucianism, learning self-concept and the development of exceptionality. In S. N. Phillipson, H. Stoeger & A. Ziegler (Eds.), *Exceptionality in East-Asia: Explorations in the actiotope model of giftedness* (pp. 40–64). London: Routledge.

Phillipson, S. N. & Lam, B.-h. (2011). *Learning and teaching in the Chinese classroom: Responding to individual needs.* Hong Kong: Hong Kong University Press.

Reback, R. (2008). Teaching to the rating: School accountability and the distribution of student achievement. *Journal of Public Economics, 92*, 1394–1415.

Salili, F. (2001). Teacher–student interactions: Attributional implications and effectiveness of teachers' evaluative feedback. In D. A. Watkins & J. B. Biggs (Eds.), *The Chinese learner: Cultural, psychological and contextual influences* (pp. 77–98). Hong Kong: Comparative Education Research Centre; Australia Council for Educational Research.

Sun, C. T.-L. (2008). *Themes in Chinese psychology*. Singapore: Cengage.

Sun, R. (2006a). The CLARION cognitive architecture: Extending cognitive modeling to social simulation. In R. Sun (Ed.), *Cognition and multiagent interaction: From cognitive modeling to social simulation* (pp. 79–99). New York: Cambridge University Press.

Sun, R. (Ed.) (2006b). *Cognition and multiagent interaction: From cognitive modeling to social simulation.* New York: Cambridge University Press.

Tang, C. (1996). Collaborative learning: The latent dimension in Chinese students' learning. In D. A. Watkins & J. B. Biggs (Eds.), *The Chinese learner: Cultural, psychological, and contextual influences* (pp. 183–204). Hong Kong; Melbourne, Australia: Comparative Education Research Centre; Australia Council for Educational Research.

Thomson, S., De Bortolli, L., Nicholas, M., Hillman, K. & Buckley, S. (2011). *Challenges for Australian education: Results from PISA 2009.* Camberwell, Victoria: ACER.

Tommis, S. D. & Phillipson, S. N. (2013). Gifted education policy and the development of exceptionality: A Hong Kong perspective. In S. N. Phillipson, H. Stoeger & A. Ziegler (Eds.), *Exceptionality in East-Asia: Explorations in the actiotope model of giftedness* (pp. 232–254). London: Routledge.

Vygotsky, L. S. (1978). *Mind in society: The development of higher mental process.* Cambridge, MA: Harvard University Press.

Watkins, D. A. & Biggs, J. B. (Eds.) (1996). *The Chinese learner: Cultural, psychological and contextual influences.* Hong Kong: Comparative Education Research Centre, The University of Hong Kong.

Watkins, D. A. & Biggs, J. B. (Eds.) (2001). *Teaching the Chinese learner: Psychological and pedagogical perspectives.* Hong Kong and Australia: Comparative Education Research Centre, The University of Hong Kong and ACER.

Ziegler, A. (2005). The actiotope model of giftedness. In R. J. Sternberg & J. Davidson (Eds.), *Conceptions of giftedness* (2nd edn., pp. 411–436). New York: Cambridge University Press.

Ziegler, A. & Stoeger, H. (2007). The role of counseling in the development of gifted students' actiotopes: Theoretical background and exemplary application of the 11-SCC. In S. Mendaglio & J. S. Peterson (Eds.), *Models of counseling gifted children, adolescents, and young adults* (pp. 253–283). Austin, TX: Prufrock.

Ziegler, A. & Phillipson, S. N. (2012). Towards a systemic theory of gifted education. *High Ability Studies, 23*(1), 3–30.

Ziegler, A., Vialle, W. & Wimmer, B. (2013). The actiotope model of giftedness: A short introduction to some central theoretical assumptions. In S. N. Phillipson, H. Stoeger & A. Ziegler (Eds.), *Exceptionality in East-Asia: Explorations in the actiotope model of giftedness.* London: Routledge.

Index

Page numbers in **bold** refer to figures and tables.

ACB sequence of emotion episodes 118, 125
accommodation as a coping strategy 120, 121
accommodation in conceptual change 243, 244, 247
accommodations in educational assessment 48–9
action repertoire in the actiotope model of giftedness 265, 266
actiotope model of giftedness 265–6
activity theory 119
adult second-language learners 148–58, 263
affect and intellect 118–19, 122, 140
affective learning outcomes 139, 140–1, 143
aggression as a coping strategy 120, 121
Alexander, Robin 63
amalgamation (cultural) 42–3
Antecedent, Behavior, Consequence (ABC) 128–9
appropriation 144, 164, 169, 171; *see also* mediation and internalization process
aspirations of parents for children 90, 98, 101
assembly-line teaching 261–2
assessment of educational achievement 18, 19, 20, 42–52
Assessment Tools for Teaching and Learning (asTTle, New Zealand) 49–52
assimilation (cultural) 42, 43, 45
assimilation in conceptual change 243–4, 247
Australia: adult second-language learner intervention 151–8; critical thinking in education 231, 238; East Asian background students 3, 201–13; educational reform in 259; educational testing case study 62–7; teacher–student relationships 138, 139, 141; twin studies of reading ability 182
Australian Council of Deans of Education 61–2
authentic leadership 190
avoidance as a coping strategy 121
Awatere, Donna 44

Bakhtin, Mikhail 58, 59

Bandura, Albert 71, 80
Bauman, Zygmunt 60
behavioral genetics 178, 179
Berry, John 222
bias in educational assessment 46–7
"biological child" 57
biological factors and cognitive style 222
biological-evolutionary based mental functions 164
Blank's four levels of language complexity (questioning) 149–50, **149**, 151–8
Bligh, Anna 65
body adjustment task 219
brain functioning 150
Brazil 150
Bronfenbrenner, Urie 180
Brown, Ann 61
Brunei 138, 139, 141
Bruner, Jerome 60
Buddhism 260

Cambridge Primary Review 63
Canadian Council on Learning 114
Carlyle, Thomas 190
Center on Education Policy 63
child-centered instruction 261–2
children's perceptions of parental expectations 90, 98
Chinese concept of learning (*haoxuexin*) 203, 206, 209–10, 212, 213, 258
Chinese migrant children: education of 27, 262; study on the role of personal agency 26, 29–39
Chinese students' thinking dispositions 238–9; *see also* Hong Kong
Chinese Twin Study of Reading (CTSR) 182
Chinese-Australian students 201–13
Christian heritage 260
chronotope, definition 58
citizenship education in Scotland 188–98
classical conceptual conflict strategy (CCS) 245

270 *Index*

classroom chronotopes 58–62, 260
classroom management 72, 73, 78, 137, 179
co-regulation model of the learner 119; *see also* peer co-regulation in small-group learning
cognitive development and learning 163–5
cognitive development theory 163
cognitive learning outcomes 139, 140, 143
cognitive perturbation with dynamic modeling 243–52
cognitive style analysis (CSA) test 220–1, 222, 225
cognitive styles: cultural differences in 222–4; definition 218–19; and education and achievement 224–6; popular models 219–22; research on 217–18
cognitive support from more competent others 166–7, 169
Cole, Michael 257–60, 261, 262–3, 264, 266
Coleman, James 26, 27
collaborative learning 163–4, 165–72, 262–3
collaborative reading 179
collective motives 105
collective teacher efficacy 79–80
Colorado Longitudinal Twin Study of Reading Disability (LTSRD) 182
communities of learners 61, 62, 251
community plane 4
computer-supported modeling technologies in conceptual change 243–52, 263, 264
conceptual change models (CCM) 243–4, 246, 247, 251
conceptual conflict strategy (CCS) 245
Confucian heritage 239, 261, 263
content-based reading tasks 181
coping strategies 120–2; *see also* expressed coping strategies
correlation, invention of 178
critical thinking and verbal reasoning 150, 231–40
"cultural child" 57
cultural differences: in cognitive styles 222–4; in critical thinking 238; and educational achievement 44–5; in parental expectations 100–1, 263; in reading development 182
cultural test bias hypothesis 46
cultural tools: and cognitive styles 221; and the concept of unity 20, 21, 23; and reading development 177; and teacher–student relationships 136, 144; and the zone of proximal development 163–4, 165, 169, 171
cultural values 44
cultural–historical plane 4–5, 257, 266; *see also* Chinese migrant children; educational assessment in ethnic minority groups; unity and units of analysis
culture and educational reform 257–66
Curriculum for Excellence (Scotland) 189

deficit theories 45
deliberate instruction 261–2
dialectical logic 15
dialectical-interactive research methodology 205
differential validity in educational assessment 47
discovery learning 60
distraction as a coping strategy 120, 121
distributed leadership 190, 191, 198
"Dragon children" website 201
dynamic assessment 18, 19–20, 162–3
dyslexia 181

East Asian students: cognitive styles 222–3, 224; culture and educational achievement 3, 258, 259, 261, 262, 263, 264, 266; Hong Kong migrant children in Australia 201–13
ecological systems theory 180
Education for Citizenship in Scotland (review report) 189
educational assessment: Australian case study 62–7; and the concept of unity 18, 19, 20, 21–2; in ethnic minority groups 42–52
educational environments 19, 20, 21–2, 23
educational policy *see* policy reform in education
educational reform: Australia 259; and culture 257–66; Hong Kong 142, 239, 258, 259, 260, 261; and teacher efficacy 79–80; United States 259
elementary (lower) mental functions (LMF) 164, 165
Embedded Figures test 219, 220
emotion episodes 118–19, 119–20, 125
emotion regulation 119–20, 125, 133
emotional anticipation 210, 212
emotional experience (*perezhivanie*) 15, 16–18
emotional-motivational support from more competent others 166–7, 169–70
emotions and motivation 112–13
encouragement and learning motive 203–4, 210–12
endophenotypes of reading 181
England 80, 183, 189; *see also* United Kingdom
enhancement learning 205, 206, 208–9, 210, 212
environment: in the actiotope model of giftedness 265, 266; influence on reading development 177–85; role in child development 16, 17–18
escape as a coping strategy 120, 121
ethnic minority groups and educational assessment 42–52
everyday concepts 18, 20–1
exceptionality 265–6
expressed coping strategies 125, 127–33; *see also* coping strategies

factory time/spaces classroom chronotope 60
family and child development 27–9

family capital: study of Chinese migrant children 29–39; financial 27, 28, 38; human 27–8, 38; social 26, 27, 28, 29–30, **30**, 37–8, 39, 262
Field Dependence–Independence cognitive style 219–20, 221, 222, 225
Finland 259
Florida Twin Project in Reading (FTP-R) 182
formal logic 15, 232–3
fossilized behaviors 14, 19

Galton, Francis 177, 178, 184–5
game-playing strategies for improving test results 64
general genetic law of cultural development 17, 21, 165, 177–8
general intelligence (IQ) tests 22, 220
generalization 15, 16, 22
genes–brain–cognition–behavior framework 179
genetic influences on reading development 177–85
Germany 265
goals in the actiotope model of giftedness 265, 266
goals of teachers 72
grades and parental expectations 89–90, 98, 100
group affect 125
Group Behaviors Checklist (GBC) 123
Group Environment Summary (GES) 123

Halpern Critical Thinking Assessment (HCTA) 236–8
haoxuexin (Chinese concept of learning) 203, 206, 209–10, 212, 213, 258
Hattie, John 225
Hedegaard, Mariane 105–7
Hegel, G.W.F. 15
helplessness as a coping strategy 120
heritability 178
heritability in second-language acquisition 183
"hidden competencies" 170
hierarchy of motives 106–7, 113
higher mental functions (HMF) 164, 165, 166, 171, 221
home environment and reading 179, 180, 182
homework 88–9, 100, 107, 109–15
Hong Kong: accommodations in educational assessment 48–9; cognitive perturbation with dynamic modeling 248; critical thinking in education 231, 236, 238–9; educational reform in 142, 239, 258, 259, 260, 261; migrant children in Australia 201–13; teacher self-efficacy 76, 80; teacher–student relationships 138, 140, 141, 142, 143, 144; twin studies of reading ability 182
Hong Kong Curriculum Development Council 142

hukou (Chinese household registration system) 27
"human culture" 136

incentive systems 210, 211
independent achievement of children 162, 170
India 138, 150
individual construction of new competencies 169–72
individualistic, inventive time/spaces classroom chronotope 60
Indonesia 138
induction of beginning teachers 75, 76–7, 77, 78, 80, 81
Influence (Model for Interpersonal Teacher Behavior) 137, 139, 140, 141
inner speech 118, 150–1, 157, 177
institutional plane 4, 5, 257, 266; *see also* policy reform in education; teacher self-efficacy
intellect and affect 118–19, 122, 140
internalization *see* appropriation; mediation and internalization process
International English Language Testing System (IELTS) 151
International Longitudinal Twin Study (ILTS) 182
interpersonal plane 4
Inverclyde, Scotland 191
IQ (general intelligence) tests 22, 220

Japan 100, 223, 224, 231, 259
joint construction of new competencies 169–72

Korea 138, 139, 141, 259

language: and educational assessment in ethnic minority groups 43–4; multiple functions of 118; and reasoning 148–58, 231–40
leadership (pupil) 190–8
learning, defining 18–19, 22
learning and cognitive development 163–5
learning motive: developing 106, 107, 109–14, 115, 262; in Hong-Kong Australian children 201–13
learning outcomes 139–43
learning styles 217, 218–19, 224–6
learning/teaching relationships (*obuchenie*) 19, 20
literacy (reading) 259, 260, 264
literate thinking 43
lower (elementary) mental functions (LMF) 164, 165
Luria, Alexander 4, 15, 57

Macleod, Gale 188
Māori student assessment 42, 43, 44, 45–6, 47, 49–52

272   *Index*

Masters Report (Australia) 63, 65
Masters, Geoff 65
mastery experiences 71, 80
material rewards 210–11
mathematics: New Zealand 50–1
media cycle and educational policies 64–6
mediation and internalization process: and adult
  second-language learners 150; and cognitive
  styles 221; and parental expectations 87,
  88, 99, 101; and peer co-regulation in
  small-group learning 119; and the zone of
  proximal development 164, 165, 169; *see also*
  appropriation
memory 150, 164–5, 181, 183
mental functions 164, 165, 171, 221
mental plane 4, 7, 257, 266; *see also* cognitive
  perturbation with dynamic modeling;
  cognitive styles; verbal reasoning in critical
  thinking
metacognition 150, 170, 226
Model for Interpersonal Teacher Behavior
  (MITB) 137–9, **138**, 140
Moll, Luis 68
moral learning outcomes 142–3, 144, 260–1;
  see also values education
more competent others: and adult second-
  language learners 148, 153; and Chinese
  migrant children 28; and cognitive
  styles 221; and teacher self-efficacy 70; and
  the zone of proximal development 163, 164,
  165–6, 168, 169–72
motive hierarchy 106–7, 113
motives and motivation: cultural–historical
  perspective 105–7; developing a learning
  motive 106, 107, 109–114, 115, 262;
  developing a play motive 106, 107–9, 111,
  113, 114, 115
motives of parents 89, 100
Myslenie i rech (Vygotsky) 161, 162

National Assessment Program – Literacy and
  Numeracy (NAPLAN, Australia) 63–6
National Education Monitoring Project (NEMP,
  New Zealand) 50
negotiation as a coping strategy 120
Netherlands 138, 141
neurological markers of reading abilities 181
New Basics project (Queensland, Australia) 67
"new fast capitalism" 61
New Learning (Australian Council of Deans of
  Education) 61–2
new technologies for enhancing learning 264
New Zealand/Aotearoa 42–3, 44, 45, 49–52,
  263–4
No Child Left Behind Act (NCLB; US,
  2002) 63, 259, 263
Nuthall, Graham 157–8

O'Brien, Jim 188
obuchenie (learning/teaching relationships) 19,
  20
opposition and denial as a coping strategy 120
other-involved (OI) communication 125–6

parental expectations: and cultural
  background 100–1, 263; and parental
  involvement 88–9; meta-analysis of studies
  on in relation to school achievement 90–9,
  100; types of 89–90, 98–9; and Vygotsky's
  significant other 87–8, 100, 101, 263; for
  younger and older children 100
participatory action research 79
Pasifika people 42, 45
peer co-regulation in small-group learning:
  research on 122–33; sociocultural
  perspective 118–22, 263
perception 164, 181
perception and personal sense of learning and
  education in children 202–3, 204, 206–9,
  212, 213
perceptions of children about parental
  expectations 90, 98
Perceptual Organization (WAIS-III) 236
perezhivanie (emotional experience) 15, 16–18
personal agency 26; study of Chinese migrant
  children 29–39
Personal and Social Education (PSE) 188, 189,
  190
personal motives 105, 107, 115
personal plane 4, 6–7, 257, 266; *see also*
  citizenship education in Scotland; learning
  motive in Hong Kong-Australian children;
  reading development
phenotypes of reading 181, 183
physiological arousal 71, 80
Piaget, Jean 13, 57, 60, 163
play and learning 262–3
play motives 106, 107–9, 111, 113, 114, 115
pluralism 43, 48, 49, 50
policy reform in education: alternative
  narratives 66–8; analyzed through
  classroom chronotopes 58–62; effect of
  differing temporal cycles for policy, media
  and educational processes 64–6; increased
  importance of testing in 57; Queensland case
  study 62–4
policy/political cycle and educational
  policies 64–6
positive cognitive appraisal as a coping
  strategy 120
primary–secondary coping model 121
primary–secondary school transition 189–90,
  191, 192, 194, 197
problem solving and instrumental action as a
  coping strategy 120, 121

process-based reading tasks 181
Processing Speed (WAIS-III) 236
Programme for International Student
Assessment (PISA) 3, 50, 66, 67, 259
Progress in International Reading Literacy Study
(PIRLS) 3, 50
Project Zero 21
Proximity (Model for Interpersonal Teacher
Behavior) 137, 139, 140, 141
pseudoconcepts 171
Pupil Leadership Project 190–8

Queensland, Australia 62–7
Questionnaire on Teacher Interaction
(QTI) 138, 139, 140, 141, 142, 143, 145

racism concerns in education 45–6
Raven matrices 166, 169
reading comprehension skills 181
reading development 177–85
reading fluency skills 181
reading literacy 259, 260, 264
reasoning and language 148–58, 231–40
relational time/spaces classroom
chronotope 61–2
response-to-instruction (RTI) approach to
reading 184
rich accountabilities 67–8
Riding's cognitive style analysis (CSA) test 220–
1, 222, 225
ritualized activities in the classroom 157–8
Road and Frame test 219
Rogoff, Barbara 4
rural–urban migration in mainland China 27

scaffolded support: for beginning teachers 70,
72, 73, 74, 75, 78; for children 28, 38, 70,
74, 164, 165, 171, 245, 252
Scandinavia 182
school events attended by parents 89
school grades and parental expectations 89–90,
98, 100
science education and computer-supported
modeling technologies 243–52, 263, 264
scientific concepts: development of 244, 245,
248–9, 250, 251, 263, 264; and the concept
of unity 18, 20–1, 22
Scotland 73–4, 76, 188–98; *see also* United
Kingdom
second-language acquisition 148–58, 183, 263
self-direction 118
self-efficacy 71, 80, 151; *see also* teacher
self-efficacy
self-encouragement 210, 212
self-involved (SI) somatic complaints 126
self-perception in leadership 190, 191, 192–4,
197

self-regulated time/spaces classroom
chronotope 61
self-regulation 89, 118, 177, 198, 226, 240
self-reliance as a coping strategy 120
sensitivity in educational assessment 47–8, 51
Shanghai 27, 30, 259
significant others 21, 38, 71, 87–8, 99–100,
101, 263
Singapore 138, 139, 141, 259
skill of students 3
small-group learning *see* peer co-regulation in
small-group learning
Social Agenda of the School (O'Brien and
MacLeod) 188
social capital 26, 27, 28, 29, 38, 39
social capital theory 26, 27–8
social class and educational achievement 22
social isolation as a coping strategy 120
social learning and adult second-language
learners 148–58
social plane 4, 5–6, 257, 266; *see also* adult
second-language learners; motives and
motivation; parental expectations; peer
co-regulation in small-group learning;
teacher–student relationships; zone of
proximal development (ZPD)
social situation of development 15, 16, 21, 112,
202, 203–4, 205–6, **207**
social/instructional environments (SIEs) 125,
127–8, 133
sociocultural theory: and adult second-language
learners 148–9, 150, 151; and Chinese
migrant children 26, 28–9; and cognitive
perturbation with dynamic modeling 243,
245, 252; and cognitive styles 221–2, 224;
and ethnic minority groups and educational
assessment 43; and learning motive in Hong
Kong-Australian children 201–4, 212; and
motives and motivation 109, 112; and peer
co-regulation in small group learning 118–19;
and policy reform in education 57; and
reading development 177, 179, 184–5;
social and personal planes 4, 257; systems
aspects of 266; and teacher self-efficacy 70;
and teacher–student relationships 136, 140,
142, 144; and verbal reasoning in critical
thinking 231, 232, 238, 240
socioculturally mediated mental functions 164
South Africa 43
speech and thinking 14, 15–16, 22
"stereotype threat" 45
Student Attitudes toward Their Teachers
(SATT) 141
Subject Level Adjusted Variable (SLAV) 142–3
subject-specific attitudes of students 140–1, 143
subjective action space in the actiotope model of
giftedness 265, 266

274 *Index*

support for beginning teachers 70, 72, 73–5, 76–8, 79, 80, 81
support seeking as a coping strategy 120, 121
supportive action 210, 212
system (professional teacher) efficacy 80
systems approaches to achievement 265, 266

Taiwan 100, 259
Taoism 260
task organization responsibility in small groups 125
task-involved (TI) questions 125
Te Kotahitanga Project 45
teacher self-efficacy: contextual antecedents of 75–9; and education reform 79–80, 262; sociocultural perspective 70–5
teacher–student relationships 136–45, 264
Teaching for Understanding study 21
technologies for enhancing learning 264
Test of Science Related Attitudes (TOSRA) 141
test-taking strategies 64
testing times/spaces classroom chronotope 62–6
thinking 164–5, 177; and speech 14, 15–16, 22
Thought and Language (Vygotsky) 140
"tiger mother" parenting style 201
Tool and Sign (Vygotsky) 136
trading time/spaces classroom chronotope 62
trait theory approach to leadership 190–1
translation of assessment tests 49, 50
Trends in International Mathematics and Science Study (TIMSS) 3, 50, 115
twin studies 178, 179, 180–1; of reading ability 181–5
Twins Early Development Study (TEDS) 182

United Kingdom: Cambridge Primary Review 63; cognitive style testing 220; critical thinking in education 231, 236; East Asian background students 3; homework policy 114; research on primary–secondary school transition 189–90; Twins Early Development Study (TEDS) 182; *see also* England; Scotland; Wales
United States: critical thinking in education 150, 231, 238; cultural differences in cognitive style 222–3, 224; East Asian background students 3; educational reform in 259; homework policy 114; inequitable school and student funding 22; No Child Left Behind Act (2002) 63, 259, 263; parental expectations 100; reasoning and metacognition studies 150; teacher–student relationships 138; twin studies of reading ability 182
unity and units of analysis: concept of 13–18, 22; educational implications 18–23

values education 142, 143–4, 188, 189, 260–1
verbal (social) persuasion 71, 79, 80
Verbal Comprehension (WAIS-III) 236
verbal explanation 210, 211–12
verbal reasoning in critical thinking 231–40, 264
verbal recognition 210, 212
verbal-imagery dimension of the cognitive style analysis test 220, 221
"verbal thinking" 231
vicarious experiences 71, 80
Vygotsky, Lev *see* sociocultural theory

Wales 183; *see also* United Kingdom
ways of coping model 121
Wertsch, James 150
Wechsler Adult Intelligence Scale, Third Edition (WAIS-III) 236
Western Reserve Reading Project (WRRP) 182
wholistic–analytic dimension of the cognitive style analysis test 220, 221
will of students 3
Witkin's Field Dependence–Independence cognitive style 219–20, 222, 225
word decoding skills 181, 185
word meaning 15–16, 17–18, 20, 22, 118, 119
word recall 20, 21, 22
word recognition 20, 21, 22
words, functional use of 163–4, 171
Working Memory (WAIS-III) 236
WorldMaker 244–5, 246, 251
written language 164–5

zone of actual development (ZAD) 38, 162, 167, 168
zone of proximal development (ZPD): adult second-language learners 153, 156, 157; and cognitive perturbation 243, 245, 246, 248, 250, 252; concept of 19, 70, 149, 161–5; and educational assessment 18, 22; effect of family social capital on 38; extended conceptualization of 169–72; research study on 165–9